THE ART OF THE CABINET

THE ART OF THE CABINET

MONIQUE RICCARDI-CUBITT

INCLUDING A CHRONOLOGICAL GUIDE TO STYLES

With over 400 illustrations, 135 in color

THAMES AND HUDSON

To the memory of
Mutti, Elizabeth and my husband Michael,
and to all my friends and students,
with whom I have shared
so much beauty

Page 1
Design for a Florentine *stipo* of the seventeenth century,
showing the influence of Counter-Reformation church façades
and Roman Baroque architecture.

© 1992 Thames and Hudson Ltd, London

First published in the United States in 1992 by
Thames and Hudson, Inc., 500 Fifth Avenue,
New York, New York 10110

Library of Congress Catalog Card Number 92-80825

Printed and bound in Japan by Dai Nippon

CONTENTS

Gilles Corrozet: 'The Blazon of the Cabinet'   6

Preface and acknowledgments   7

INTRODUCTION   9

1 FROM ANTIQUITY TO THE RENAISSANCE   13

2 THE AGE OF MAGNIFICENCE   47

3 GRANDEUR AND DECLINE   97

4 REVIVALISM IN A NEW AGE   139

Notes on the text   171

Notes on the colour plates   172

Catalogue: a chronological guide to styles   185

Biographies of cabinetmakers, craftsmen and designers   210

Glossary   219

Bibliography   221

Index   223

'THE BLAZON OF THE CABINET'

From *Les Blasons Domestiques* (1539)
by Gilles Corrozet

In addition to its heraldic meaning, the word 'blazon' was also formerly used to signify a type of short eulogy in verse; in sixteenth-century France this form of praise was applied to specific topics which, in the case of Gilles Corrozet's collection of poems, included all manner of subjects associated with a house and its contents. In 1535 Clément Marot (1496–1544) had published a blazon entitled 'Le Beau Tétin' (The Beauteous Bosom) in a typical Renaissance conceit and celebration of feminine beauty. It started a fashion for verses in the same vein, and an anthology of erotic blazons was published in 1543 as *Blasons anatomiques du corps féminin*. Corrozet's *Blasons Domestiques* – applying the anatomical analogy to the home and its furnishings – were a direct riposte to the erotic genre, which he denounced in a shorter poem, 'Contre les blasonneurs des membres' (Against those who write in praise of the human body).

The complete set of twenty-three blazons by Corrozet was reprinted by the Société des Bibliophiles François (Paris, 1865) and in *Furniture History: Journal of the Furniture History Society*, vol. xxv (1989), pp. 5ff., with an introduction and translation by Simon Jervis.

Le Blason du Cabinet

Cabinet remply de richesses
Soit pour roynes ou pour duchesses,
Cabinet sur tous bié choisi
Paré de veloux cramoisi
De drap d'or & de taffetas,
Ou sont les ioyaulx à grandz tas
Et les bagues tresgracieuses
Pleines de pierres precieuses,
Qui illustrent ce Cabinet,
Premier le diament bien nect,
L'escharboucle tresreluysante,
Le rubis, la perle plaisante
Le saphir, la Iacinte fine,
L'esmeraulde, la Cornaline,
L'amatiste, la Crisolite,
Le Balay & la marguerite.
Cabinet de tout accomply
Cabinet de Tableaulx remply
Et de maintes belles ymages
De grandz & petis personnages,
Cabinet paré de medailles
Et curieuses antiquailles
De marbre, de Iaphé & Porphire
Tant qu'il doibt à chascun suffire,
Cabinet ou est le buffect
D'or & d'argent du tout parfaict,
Cabinet garny de ceinctures
De doreures, & de bordures
De fers d'or, d'estocz, de tableaulx,
De chaisnes, de boutós tresbeaulx,
De mancherons, de braceletz,
De gorgerins & de colletz,
De perles d'Orient semez:
De gantz lauez & parfumez,
De muscq plus cher qu'or de ducat
D'ambre fin & sauon muscat
De pouldre de Cipré & pommade
Pour restaurer la couleur fade:
D'eaux de Damas, d'oeilletz, de Roses
En fiolles de verré encloses.
Aultres cent compositions
De differentes mistions
Et parmy tant diuers ioyaulx,
Sont les riches & gros signeaulx,
Les patenostres cristallines.
Celles de strin & Coralines,
De perles & du fin Rubis,
Qui sont mises sur les habitz,
Puis les houppes, d'or & de soye,
Pour mieulx se monstrer par la voye,
Puis les mignons & bons cousteaulx,
Les forcettes, & les Ciseaulx,
Le Mirior, la genté escriptoire,
Le chappeau l'eschiquier D'yuoire.
Les heures pour seruir à Dieu,
Brief en ce beau & petit lieu,
Sont tant d'aultres choses ensemble
Qui'impossible le diré il semble.

The Blazon of the Cabinet

Cabinet filled with riches,
Whether for queens or duchesses,
Cabinet above all well chosen,
Bedecked with crimson velvet
And with cloth-of-gold and taffeta,
Where jewels lie in great piles
And most elegant rings
Filled with precious stones
Which are the pride of this Cabinet,
First the flawless diamond,
The brightly gleaming carbuncle,
The ruby, the attractive pearl,
The sapphire, the fine hyacinth,
The emerald, the cornelian,
The amethyst, the chrysolite,
The balas and the marguerite.
Cabinet of all perfection,
Cabinet filled with Paintings
And numerous beautiful images
Of individuals both great and small,
Cabinet adorned with medals
And curios from antiquity
And with marble, jasper and porphyry,
As much as anyone could wish for,
Cabinet in which the buffet
Consists of the best gold and silver plate,
Cabinet fitted with sashes,
With gilding and with borders
Tooled in gold, with swords, with paintings,
With chains, with beautiful buttons,
With cuffs, with bracelets,
With gorgets and with collars
Embroidered with Oriental pearls;
With gloves washed and perfumed,
With musk more costly than gold ducats,
With fine amber and musk-scented soap,
With powder from Cyprus and pomade
To enhance a pale complexion;
With rose- and carnation waters from Damascus
Enclosed in glass phials.
A hundred other compositions
Of many different mixtures,
And among such a variety of jewels
Are rich and imposing signet rings,
Crystal paternosters.
Those of coloured paste and coral,
Of pearls and fine rubies
Which are affixed to garments,
As well as tassels of gold and silk
To enhance one's appearance,
Then well-made pretty little knives,
Forks and scissors,
The mirror, the graceful scriptor.
The hat, the ivory chessboard,
The Book of Hours to praise God.
In short, in this small and beautiful place
So many other different things are assembled
That it is impossible to describe them all.

<table>
<tr><td>

PREFACE

</td><td>

THIS BOOK AIMS TO PROVIDE AN INTRODUCTORY SURVEY OF A complex and intriguing subject, presented in a way that has never previously been attempted. I have tried to draw together the various threads of an intricate historical web, summarizing the ethos, functions and technical virtuosity of craftsmanship associated with a furniture type which, given its often ornate form and lavish decoration, must be considered the ultimate *meuble parlant*. Obviously, some historical periods – notably the seventeenth century – stand out as being richer than others, in terms of both design and materials, but I have tried throughout to strike the right balance between the quantity and quality of pieces produced in different countries at different times, giving suitable emphasis wherever appropriate. This account is of necessity concise and selective. The cabinets illustrated in the colour plates and in the text have been chosen for their historical and representative importance, a wider cross-section of examples being provided in the catalogue of styles (pp. 185–209); an indication of size is given wherever possible. The availability of archival records and source material varies greatly, and in historical documents up to and including the eighteenth century spellings of names were often inconsistent (here the most usual or familiar form of proper names has been used, with an indication where necessary of other spellings sometimes encountered elsewhere).

</td></tr>
</table>

I am greatly indebted to the many friends and professional colleagues in the field of furniture history and art history who have been generous with their advice and support in the course of my research for this book. I wish to thank especially Michael Rogers, John Carswell, William Robinson and Bashir Mohammed for their help on aspects of Islamic art; Georgina Fantoni for her inspired comments on matters of Egyptology; and Brian Cook of the British Museum for his suggestions regarding Graeco-Roman antiquities. Particular thanks are also due to the staff of the Furniture Department at the Victoria and Albert Museum for their constant help and support, especially Bathsheba Abse, Frances Collard and James York.

Collectors and connoisseurs all over Europe have generously given of their time, sharing with me their own personal enthusiasms. I am particularly grateful to Paolo Canelli, Wilfried de Kesel, Alain Moatti and Edric van Vredenburgh. The realization of this project would not have been possible without the unfailing support of my friends and 'field researchers': Diane de Portalon de Rosis in Paris; Lorenza Bianda-Pasquinelli in Florence; Astrid Rückert in Amsterdam; Michael Sögner in Vienna; and Angela Hücke in Germany. My thanks also go to Julie Wood for drawing my attention to archaeological remains on Orkney, and to Alexandra Phillips for her timely help with the cataloguing of photographs; specific details of sources of illustrations are listed overleaf.

London, 1992   M.R.-C.

SOURCES OF ILLUSTRATIONS

The author and publisher are grateful to the following institutions and individuals for permission to reproduce photographs supplied by them:

L. P. M. van Aalst, Breda: pl. 52
Betty Aardewald, The Hague: page 83
Didier Aaron, London: plates 119, 121, 136
Ader Tajan, Paris: plate 95
Alinari, Florence: pages 40, 41 above, 42, 43, 95 above, 102 (Museo degli Argenti, Florence)
The American Museum in Britain, Bath: pages 131 below, 132, 133
Antonacci Collection, Rome: plate 84; page 87 below; cat. no. 120
Apter Fredericks Ltd, London: plates 59–61, 63, 78, 79, 86; page 129; cat. no. 114
Ashmolean Museum, Oxford: page 84; (Griffith Institute) page 15
Bayerisches Nationalmuseum, Munich: pages 53, 55 below left and right
Bibliothèque Nationale, Paris: pages 47, 135
Tony Bingham, London: cat. no. 62
Blairman & Sons, London: plate 128
J. Boccador, Paris: plate 8
Bonhams, London: plate 111; cat. nos. 41, 52, 97, 113, 118, 184, 192
Arthur Brett & Sons Ltd: cat. no. 142
Bridgeman Art Library: plates 3, 101, 102
Brighton Museum and Art Galleries, Sussex: pages 166 above and below, 170 above and below
Trustees of the British Museum, London: pages 17 below, 19, 21
The Burghley House Collection, Stamford, Lincs: cat. no. 76
Cameo Gallery, London: cat. no. 185
Paolo Canelli, Milan: plates 18, 30; cat. no. 78
Carlton Hobbs, London: plates 87–9, 98–100
Chaucer Fine Arts, London: plates 9, 31; page 82 below
Christie's, Amsterdam: cat. nos. 24, 39, 46, 48, 89, 90, 108–10, 125, 160–7
Christie's, London: plates 14, 15, 41–4, 47, 49, 50, 54, 64–9, 71, 77, 91, 92, 109, 112–14, 116, 124, 127; pages 93 above left, 96; cat.

nos. 10, 26, 27, 44, 49, 54, 63–6, 69, 71, 77, 79, 80, 83, 96, 101–4, 123, 124
Christie's, London (South Kensington): plate 37; page 139; cat. nos. 154, 178, 183
Christie's, Rome: pages 89 below, 163; cat. no. 32
Galerie Claes, Paris: cat. no. 50
Country Life, London: page 92 (Collection of the Duke of Northumberland); cat. no. 67 (Collection of the Duke of Buccleuch)
Arthur Davidson, London: cat. nos. 12, 13
Durini Collection, Argentina: plate 131
Anthony Embden, Paris (photos by Axel Winther): plates 21, 22
Fine Arts Society, London: cat. no. 186
Frémontier, Paris: page 130 right
Gasparini, Rome: cat. no. 53
Germanisches Nationalmuseum, Nuremberg: page 99
J. Paul Getty Museum, Malibu, Cal.: plate 45; cat. no. 36
Jonathan Harris, London: cat. no. 51
Peter Hempson Collection, London: plates 96, 97
Hispanic Society of America, New York: cat. no. 5
Hyde Park Antiques, New York: page 143 above
Israel Museum, Jerusalem: page 16
Istituto Centrale per il Catalogo e la Documentazione, Rome: (Palazzo Barberini, Rome) page 34 above and cat. no. 6; (Palazzo Doria Pamphili, Rome) page 75 above and cat. no. 20; pages 76–7
Michel d'Istria, Paris: cat. no. 7
J. Kugel, Paris: plate 58; cat. nos. 37, 95
Kunstgewerbemuseum, Berlin: pages 51, 52
Kunsthistorisches Institut, Florence: pages 1, 56; cat. nos. 2, 3 (Pepoli Collection, Bologna), 21 (Castello Sforzesco, Milan), 22 (Palazzo Davanzati, Florence)
Kunsthistorisches Museum, Vienna: pages 45, 46, 54, 55 above, 74 above; cat. nos. 61, 68
Gabrielle Laroche, Paris: page 74 below
Ronald A. Lee, London: plates 53, 80, 81; page 50 above; cat. no. 130
Leicestershire Museums Service: cat. no. 175
Mallett at Bourdon House Ltd, London: page 134 below; cat. no. 105
Metropolitan Museum of Art, New York: pages 17 above, 168 above (Gift of Charles Tisch, 1969), 168 below (Purchase, The J. Edgar Kauffman, Jr, Gift, 1968)
Alain Moatti, Paris: plates 20, 40; page 13; cat. no. 17
P. Moufflet, Cannes: cat. no. 70
Musée des Arts Décoratifs, Paris: cat. nos. 187, 191
Musée des Arts Décoratifs, Strasbourg: page 88
Trustees of the National Gallery, London: page 37 below

By courtesy of His Grace the Duke of Northumberland: plate 1; cat. nos. 74, 88, 93, 94
Oudenaarde Stadhuis, Oudenaarde, Belgium: plate 28
Pelham Galleries, London: plates 55, 76; pages 93 below, 131 above (Museum für Kunstgewerbe, Hamburg); cat. nos. 31, 33, 55, 84, 87, 91, 98–100, 135
Phillips Fine Art Auctioneers, London: plates 23, 26, 27, 90, 105; pages 37, 48 above, 104, 162; cat. nos. 29, 30, 42, 47, 72, 116, 126, 127, 129, 133, 134, 141, 150, 155, 158, 169, 170, 174, 188, 190
Prado Museum, Madrid: pages 38 left, 48 below
Private Collections: plates 38, 82; pages 11, 50 below, 89 above, 97; cat. nos. 23, 121, 131
Revillon d'Apreval, Paris: plate 48
Rijksmuseum, Amsterdam: cat. nos. 81, 132
Service Photographique de la Réunion des Musées Nationaux, Paris: plates 103 (Musée de Versailles), 104 (Musée du Louvre); page 90 (Musée de Versailles); cat. no. 25 (Musée de la Renaissance, Château d'Ecouen)
Sotheby's, London: plates 11–13, 29, 34, 38, 39, 46, 51, 56, 57, 62, 72, 75, 83, 85, 93, 94, 107, 108, 110, 111, 115, 117, 118, 120, 122, 123, 125, 129, 130, 133, 134; pages 134 above, 142; cat. nos. 1, 16, 18–20, 28, 35, 40, 56–9, 73, 75, 106, 107, 112, 115, 117, 122, 128, 136, 138, 139, 145, 147–9, 156
Sotheby's, New York: pages 35, 38 right; cat. no. 8
Sotheby's, Sussex: cat. nos. 11, 43, 85, 86, 92, 140, 144, 146, 151–3, 157, 159, 168, 172, 177, 179–82, 189
Spink & Sons, London: plates 35, 36
Jacob Stodel, London: plate 10
Uppsala University (photos Augusto Mendes): plate 19; page 9
Axel Verwoordt, Antwerp: plate 16; page 93 above right
Trustees of the Victoria and Albert Museum, London: plates 5–7, 17, 132, 135; pages 34 below, 75 below, 82 above, 85 above and below, 86, 87, 94, 95 below, 103, 130 left, 138, 165 left and right, 169 left and right; cat. nos. 4, 14, 82, 143, 171
Edric van Vredenburgh, London: plates 70, 126; pages 78, 143 below; cat. no. 15
Wallace Collection, London: page 101; cat. no. 137
Westfälisches Landesmuseum, Münster: page 44
Witney Antiques: plates 73, 74
Julie Wood: page 14
Harriet Wynter, London: plates 2, 4, 106; cat. no. 9
J. Zeberg, Antwerp: plates 24, 25, 32, 33; cat. nos. 45, 60, 119

INTRODUCTION

THE FIRST KNOWN USE OF THE TERM 'CABINET' TO DESCRIBE A PIECE OF furniture occurs in an inventory prepared for the French King Francis I in 1528. Whether serving personal, political, religious or ritualistic purposes, the chest with compartments and drawers – which we may take as the basic definition of the cabinet – was present in the most sophisticated and richest of interiors, and had its place on the most solemn of occasions. Throughout the history of mankind, besides essential household furniture – beds, tables, chairs and chests, however ornate these might have been – the cabinet has enjoyed a special place in domestic life.

Previous page
Marquetry panel depicting the interior of a seventeenth-century German cabinetmaker's workshop, in which a master craftsman is shown with a client examining a Schreibtisch. *The panel was included as part of the contents of the* Kunstschrank *(see colour pl. 19) made for Philipp Hainhofer and presented to King Gustavus Adolphus of Sweden in 1632 by the City of Augsburg (see pp. 51–2).*

When the tomb of Tutankhamun, built in the mid-fourteenth century BC, was opened in 1922, over thirty chests were revealed; these would have contained the valuables and personal possessions of the young pharaoh, together with objects endowed with important ritualistic meaning to accompany him on his journey to the afterlife. The Ark of the Covenant, described in the Bible and depicted on some early Jewish artifacts, was a special cabinet with gabled top and temple front, made to hold the most sacred pact between God and His chosen people. The basic form, inspired by the ancient Egyptian prototypes, was adopted in the classical world, first in Greece and later in Rome. The Latin word *arca* echoed the meaning with which the piece was endowed.

The form survived in small caskets dating from the early Christian and Byzantine period, and continued in the nest of drawers found in medieval times in the *armarium* and in bridal chests (the Italian *cassone* or the Catalan *hembra*). Muslim influence was of seminal importance in the dissemination and development of early European cabinets in the fifteenth century. The Portuguese and Spanish *escritorio* (later termed *vargueño*) and the Italian *scrittorio* were both related to the first function of the European cabinet, to serve as a portable writing desk and a case for carrying documents and valuables, a purpose which was echoed in the characteristic *Schreibtisch* associated with Nuremberg and Augsburg.

The decorative techniques used reflected Middle and Near Eastern influences: the geometric inlay of wood, bone and ivory of the *mudejar* style in Spain and the *alla certosina* or *embriachi* work in Italy; and the damascened metalwork produced first in Venice and later in Milan in the sixteenth century.

Cabinets were first recorded in England in the sixteenth century. A German traveller, Paul Hentzner, noted in 1578 at Whitehall Palace 'Two little cabinets of exquisite work, in which the Queen [Elizabeth I] keeps her papers and which she uses for writing boxes'; no doubt this was a Portuguese or Spanish *escritorio*, or a *Schreibtisch* from Augsburg or Nuremberg. 'Nests of drawers' had already been known in Tudor times and during Edward VI's reign in 1550 'three cabinets set in the wall covered with crimson velvet and garnished with gold and silver', in the 'secrete juelhouse', recalled French antecedents.

German cabinetmakers continued to use the term *Schreibtisch* for their ornate ebony cabinets – pieces decorated with gold, silver, semi-precious stones, ivory, coral and amber – well after they had refined the form into the *Kunstschrank*, in which the container itself – the cabinet – became as precious as the contents. In Italy the concept of the humanist *studiolo* in the fifteenth century reflected a desire to represent a microcosm of the known world; it was of profound importance in the

Detail of table-cabinet showing internal drawer-fronts surmounted by portraits of the Holy Roman Emperor Charles V and Philip II of Spain flanking the Royal arms of Spain. Naples, c. 1600; see p. 50.

development of the later Cabinets of Curiosities, or *Wunderkammer*, and of the cabinet as a piece of furniture. The *studiolo* (or *stipo*) grew in complexity and richness of decoration, reflecting the all-encompassing humanist approach to worldly knowledge and the resulting growth of intellectual curiosity and scientific discovery.

The cabinet was at the forefront of experimental innovations. Every possible technique was employed to further its embellishment, giving a new status and name to the furniture makers involved in its realization throughout Europe: cabinetmaker, *ébéniste*, *ebanista*, *Tischler*. Many different crafts were involved in its adornment: the gold- and silversmith; the lapidary cutter of cameos, intaglios, *pietra dura*, amber and coral; the engraver of ivory; the painter; the sculptor and bronzeworker; and the embroiderer. The interiors grew in richness and complexity, allying the use of the *camera obscura* and the creation of an imaginary world by means of a mirrored perspective to the contemporary fascination with the theatre and illusion. Interiors were often made to resemble miniature palaces and would conceal secret drawers and compartments, further enhancing the magical quality of the cabinet and the virtuosity of the cabinetmaker's art.

In the seventeenth century the cabinet became the most highly prized single piece of furniture, a work of art in its own right which would further the dynastic and political interests of the absolute monarchies of the time. Major examples were made to order as diplomatic presentation pieces or as gifts between kings and princes, and were thus endowed with individual emblematic significance. The status it enjoyed was never higher, and the new wealth generated from European trade with the East led to the use of oriental lacquer to impart an exotic gleaming richness to decorative finishes.

The Netherlands, France and England were now producing cabinets of larger size in the grand Baroque manner, each country contributing its own special style and technique which in turn influenced production in other European countries. Tortoiseshell, floral marquetry and metal inlays were among the materials and techniques used on cabinets of regal grandeur and magnificence. The stands too, often sculptural in form, reflected this ostentation and richness in their gilt or silvered finish. The cabinet had become essentially a showpiece; in France it was the *meuble de parade et d'apparat* essential to the ethos of the *Grand Siècle* and the royal court at Versailles.

The eighteenth century saw a reaction against the grand formality and strict etiquette associated with absolute rule, and a renewed sense of hedonism and informal intimacy encouraged the development of smaller pieces of furniture incorporating some of the attributes of the traditional cabinet, but with a different emphasis in terms of its use. Types such as the scriptor, *secrétaire*, *bonheur du jour* and *bureau* continued the format of the cabinet-on-stand with the emphasis on the writing function, while the *serre-bijoux*, or jewel cabinet, and the *médaillier*, or coin and medal cabinet, were used to hold precious personal possessions and collections.

The English form of the bureau-cabinet, with its accent on storage, writing function and practicality, was adopted throughout the world with the exception of France, a distinctive local style being developed in America. The Empire style in France influenced only the outer decoration of the *secrétaire* and *bonheur du jour* without altering the basic structure, while the display cabinet was an extension of the form of the bureau-cabinet.

The concept of the cabinet as a showpiece was revived in the nineteenth century, when it served as the vehicle for nationalistic displays of recently developed industrial techniques, notable pieces being shown in the numerous international exhibitions held in Paris, London, New York and Philadelphia. Eventually, advances in technology and modernism were to rob the cabinet of both its role and its artistic value. In the twentieth century, although the form may have survived in derivations or pastiches by a small number of makers who can still practise traditional cabinetmaking skills, the substance has long since disappeared.

1

FROM ANTIQUITY TO THE RENAISSANCE

T HE FIRST RECORDED USE OF THE WORD *CABINET* IN FRENCH OCCURS in the inventory of Anne of Brittany (1505), where it is used to describe a small storage room in which to preserve her gold plate, described as being 'now stored in the cabinet of the said Lord [Louis XII] at the Château de Blois'.[1] The term is a diminutive of *cabane* or *cabine*, and is ultimately derived from the Latin *cavea*, a stall, a spectator's seat in a theatre, an enclosure, which suggests the idea of a container, whether in the form of a room or a piece of furniture.

The small chambers mentioned in 'Building works undertaken at the Château de St Germain en Laye since the month of December 1548'[2] were built in the large bedchambers as private retiring rooms for the Queen (Catherine de Médicis), Mme Marguerite (sister of Henry II), and Diane de Poitiers, Duchesse de Valentinois. These cabinets became the object of much attention: a great deal of thought and care was lavished upon them. In 1663, the Duchesse of Montpensier (cousin of Louis XIV), known as 'la Grande Mademoiselle', wrote in her *Mémoires* from her place of exile at her country estate at St Fargeau: 'I decorated my cabinet with many pictures and mirrors. I was delighted and thought that I had achieved the most magnificent effect.'[3]

The earliest reference to a cabinet as a piece of furniture dates from 1528; it is found in an inventory of silver plate drawn up for Francis I, 'Comptes de l'Argenterie'; this includes a mention of 'a cabinet of gilt leather decorated in the Moorish style with three compartments, two drawers and a small oratory closed by four hinges, four locks and two bolts',[4] purchased from Pierre Robert, a bookseller in Paris, for the sum of 51 livres 4 sols. It was then praised by Gilles Corrozet in *Les Blasons Domestiques* in 1539 (see p. 172).

Previous page
A small wooden leather-covered table-cabinet with tooled gilt and painted decoration; the fall-front is shown open, revealing the internal arrangement of drawers and compartments. France, c. 1580–1600; width 32 cm (12¼ in.).

Ancient origins

The desire to store small, sometimes rare and precious items in a special confined space echoes not just a fundamental human desire for order, therefore classification, but also for safekeeping and secrecy. Examples are found in surviving remains from various early cultures. The remains of the houses at the prehistoric site of Skara Brae on the shores of the Bay of Skaill, Orkney, dating from *c.* 3100–2500 BC, display built-in compartmented stone cupboards likely to have contained some of the intricately decorated pottery found in fragments on the site. The concept of storage spaces was, however, first translated into special pieces of furniture in the Near East, Egypt in particular.

Thus, excavation of one of the tombs at Saqqara, dating from *c.* 3100 BC, revealed a small wooden box with inner partitions, made to hold gaming pieces. Wall-paintings in the tomb of Hesy-re, a scribe during the reign of Zoser during the IIIrd Dynasty (2730–2650 BC), provide a pictorial inventory of the luxurious furnishings of a wealthy contemporary household: four cabinets on legs are depicted, each opening from the top and with inner compartments to hold personal and precious possessions, such as jewelry or cosmetics.

The use of decorative inlay and veneering in Egypt dates back to *c.* 3000 BC. Pre-dynastic wooden fragments displaying delicate carvings have survived, together with ivory veneers and thin sheets of gold and silver finely embossed and chased, decorated with semi-precious stones

Stone compartments in the remains of a prehistoric dwelling at Skara Brae, Orkney.

or 'faience'. This coloured composition, made of powdered quartz and capable of being moulded and glazed, was widely used in inlay, mostly in the favoured blue, but also in black, white and red. The box from Giza, near the Great Pyramid of Cheops, built c. 2580, found in the tomb of his mother Hetepherses, is covered with silver and inlaid with faience.

Such rich and costly decorations were applied to the gabled chest (used for storing linen, clothing and other personal articles) depicted at Saqqara in wall-paintings in the tomb of Mereruka, Vizier under Teti I, of the VIth Dynasty, who reigned c. 2345–2333 BC. There the chests, of large dimensions, are shown being carried on poles by a procession of bearers, an occasion which might have been a ceremonial funerary one.

The sumptuousness of the art of cabinetmaking was also used by the pharaoh for his own self-glorification and in the pursuit of his diplomatic and political aims, as the kings, princes and popes of the Renaissance would do later. Cuneiform texts on tablets discovered in the archives at Tell el-Amarna, the city founded c. 1370 BC by Amenophis IV, husband of Nefertiti, in honour of his personal god Aton, record – under the pharaoh's new name, Akhenaton – a gift sent by him to Burna-Buriash, king of Babylon, consisting of 'five wooden arks overlaid with gold, one ark overlaid with silver'.[5]

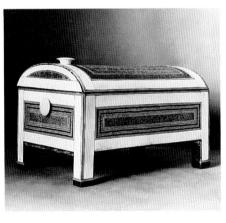

View of the southern end of the Antechamber of Tutankhamun's tomb (above), showing ritual couches, chariot parts and one of the marquetry caskets, as found in 1920; another similar casket (below) shows the use of ivory veneer and the knobs attached to the side and top around which a cord would be tied and the knot sealed to secure the contents.

Funerary rituals practised in ancient Egypt have allowed many pieces of furniture to survive. Convinced of the existence of an afterlife, the Egyptians buried deceased notables in elaborate tombs, in which the dead person's earthly environment was recreated, including familiar domestic and precious possessions. The tomb of Tutankhamun (reigned c. 1354–1345 BC), successor of Akhenaton, when discovered by Howard Carter in 1922, had lain undisturbed except for two break-ins by grave robbers soon after the young pharaoh's death. It yielded a treasure-trove including over thirty chests, cabinets and caskets for domestic, personal and ritual use, ranging in size from small jewelry caskets or toilet boxes to large coffers for bedding and linen. The very number is in itself impressive, considering the other pieces of furniture found in the tomb. The variety and richness of forms and techniques demonstrate not only the virtuosity of the ancient Egyptians in the art of cabinetmaking, but also the importance they attached to these pieces.

Forms vary from large gable-topped or shrine-shaped chests to graceful cabinets on slender legs and fretwork pattern and rectangular or bow-fronted caskets. As storage was the primary function, the larger pieces are either compartmented or divided internally to house smaller boxes, a design feature also seen in European chests of medieval times. Solid wood, mostly a redwood of the cedar family, or sometimes ebony, was used in panels joined by dovetailing or by a mortice-and-tenon arrangement secured by wooden dowels. Veneering involved the use of thin layers of redwood, ebony and ivory attached to a soft base with a black resinous glue as well as wooden dowels or metal rivets capped with ivory. The refinement, taste, elegance and sophistication of some of the cabinets are on a par with the best work of the Renaissance era. One rectangular cabinet on short square feet was veneered in ivory and ebony in an intricate marquetry of herringbone pattern; another, with vaulted lid, required, according to Howard Carter's records, no less than 45,000 separate glued pieces of veneer.[6] The legs and cross-rails, veneered with ivory, are decorated with small gold studs.

Polychromy was favoured in all decorative schemes. Domestic, hunting or war scenes were painted in bright, lively colours on a gesso ground. Various precious materials were combined in seemingly infinite variations for their intrinsic values as well as their visual appeal; ivory might be carved in low relief or stained in clear tones; faience, coloured glass and calcite evoke inlays of precious and semi-precious stones. Gold, silver and bronze provided hinges and foot-caps, while gold foil was applied on a gesso base to decorative hieroglyphs, fretwork and cartouches. All chests, cabinets and caskets had their lids secured not with a lock, but by looping and knotting a cord around two mushroom-shaped knobs, on the lid and the body of the piece respectively, which were painted, gilt or made of ivory. A seal would be applied to the knot.

At the time of the pharaohs knowledge and mystery were linked with religious beliefs and rituals. Funerary chests were made in the shape of a shrine or with a gabled top, like a temple. An outstanding example of the type depicted on the walls of Mereruka's tomb at Saqqara was preserved in the tomb of Tutankhamun; its form and use exactly fits the Old Testament description of the Ark of the Covenant (Exodus, ch. xxv). Moses, who led the Israelites out of Egypt through the desert, is instructed by God to build the Ark in which to keep the Tablets of the Law, the Pact of the Alliance:

. . . two cubits and a half *shall be* the length thereof, and a cubit and a half the breadth thereof, and a cubit and a half the height thereof. And thou shalt overlay it with pure gold, within and without shalt thou overlay it, and shalt make upon it a crown of gold round about. And thou shalt cast four rings of gold for it, and put them in the four corners thereof; and two rings shall be in the one side of it, and two rings in the other side of it. And thou shalt make staves of setim wood, and overlay them with gold. And thou shalt put the staves into the rings by the sides of the ark, that the ark may be borne with them. The staves shall be in the rings of the ark: they shall not be taken from it. And thou shalt put into the ark the testimony which I shall give thee.

The Tutankhamun chest consists of an ebony frame within recessed redwood panels. When not in use to carry the chest, the redwood poles could be slid back into the bronze rings attached to the bottom of the box and disappear from view, but were never removed. The panels of the gabled top, the borders of the side panels and the edge of the base were all finished with an ivory strip, the feet being capped with silver. The seal of Tutankhamun and the hieroglyph for gold (*nub*) are depicted on the knobs attached to the lid and side. At one end of the gabled lid are depicted the pharaoh and Osiris, the pharaoh presenting an offering with the accompanying inscription in hieroglyphs: 'Onnophris [another form for Osiris], who is at the head of the West, the great god, lord of the Necropolis'.[7] This incantation is reinforced by the band of funerary characters around the redwood panels, inlaid in ebony and ivory, assuring the pharaoh of a blissful afterlife in the company of all the gods in heaven, and Ra, the Father, the Sun, whose daily rebirth dictates life on earth and in heaven. The same concern for the pharaoh's well-being on his journeys to the other world is expressed in carved gilt hieroglyphs on one of the most elaborate cabinets in the tomb. The life-giving motifs of *ankh* (life), *was* (dominion) and *neb* (all) are used all over the surface in a repeating pattern of great richness and harmony.[8] The interior is divided into sixteen compartments, each finely edged with an ivory strip.

A fourth-century glass dish with gilt decoration discovered in the Jewish catacombs in Rome. The religious symbols include the menorah, shown as a pair below, and a representation of the Ark of the Covenant in the form of a gable-topped shrine.

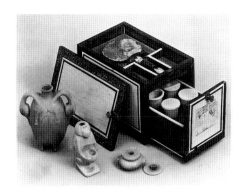

Toilet casket from the tomb of Kemu-ny at Thebes and a group of cosmetic jars from Girgeh; the casket, made of wood and ivory, is 20 cm (8 in.) high.

Time, thought and care were thus lavished on the cabinet, making it a highly valued piece of furniture, distinct from all others. Beyond its purely utilitarian purpose for storage, whether of domestic, mundane objects, or of prized personal possessions, the cabinet was also endowed with special meaning. The ritualistic, magical aspect of the cabinet was also linked with the idea of secrecy: to secure arcane knowledge from the eyes of the uninitiated. In both respects the humanist scholars and collectors of the Renaissance era would in their turn regard the cabinet in this light.

The lighter side of life was also represented in the craftsmanship of cabinets and caskets. Personal adornments, toilet accessories and also games were found. The gaming boxes display drawers to secure ivory sticks, knucklebones and other pieces. Drawers were also used with inner compartments to hold cosmetic jars and unguents, or assorted oddments: amulets, scarabs, beads, shells, pieces of aromatic woods, mostly in small boxes, as evidence of a basic human impulse to collect. One of the best-preserved toilet caskets belonged to Kemu-ny, Chamberlain and Butler to Ammenemes IV (1796–1790 BC). Made of cedar inlaid with ivory and ebony, its exquisite craftsmanship is visible in the construction of the drawer with sides shorter than the overlapping front, the silver knobs and the rare silver bolt, which slides into a tiny bar inside the drawer, providing a lock as well as the usual cord with seal. Similar types of toilet caskets have been discovered near Jericho in Palestine, displaying the same fastening method, but decorated with wood and bone inlay, and dating from the early Bronze Age.

No doubt such caskets and larger chests and cabinets of more practical use, such as the storage of tools, would have existed throughout ancient Western Asia. However, no complete example has survived and cylinder seals depict only a few items of domestic furniture: tables, stools and chairs. Royal tombs at Sumer in southern Mesopotamia, *c.* 2600 BC, have yielded fragments, a pale reflection of the splendour of ancient Near Eastern cabinetmaking techniques. The so-called Royal Standard of Ur, a lectern-shaped box now in the British Museum, is entirely covered with glowing mosaic tesserae made of shell, lapis lazuli and a red limestone. Similarly, the Goat and Tree group was one of a pair of stands for a small delicate table. Its outer decoration of carved stone, mother-of-pearl and gold sheets is glued to the wooden core with bitumen. Most of the materials used would have been imported, as some contemporary

The Royal Standard of Ur, side view showing mosaic decoration evoking 'Peace' (the opposite side is devoted to 'War').

inventories indicate. Ivory in particular came from Syria, where wild elephants lived until the eighth century BC. Thereafter merchants imported it from Africa and possibly India, archaeological excavations having revealed the existence of links between Mesopotamia and the Indus valley.

The records of the Assyrian king Assurnasirpal's spoils of war (883–859 BC) listed furniture made of ivory with embellishments of gold, silver and precious stones, as well as furniture inlaid with ivory made in Syria, schools of ivory craftsmen having been active in Damascus and Hama. Ivory techniques varied from lightly incised motifs, executed in Assyria itself, carved in low relief like stone sculpture from Urartu and Babylon, to the use of richly colourful stains and red and blue glass inlay, while the richer Phoenician examples featured gold foil, cornelian and lapis lazuli, as in the case of the Lioness fragment found at Nimrud, Iraq, where large numbers of fragments were uncovered in palace stores. Most of these would have been used as a veneer, some of them still showing the alphabetical mark on the back which enabled the cabinetmaker to fix each piece in its proper place. More rarely solid ivory would be used for small toilet caskets. Such pieces would be produced in quantity, and recurring decorative motifs include some Egyptian-inspired models, such as the sphinx, mostly found on Phoenician plaques. The griffin, the grazing deer, the cow licking her suckling calf and the 'Woman at the Window' (a fertility goddess) are motifs which were depicted in many variant forms.

The ancient Greeks also favoured ivory as a decorative material. Pausanias (v, 17.2) described the chest of Kypselos, dating from the seventh century BC, which he saw in the Temple of Hera at Olympia: 'the chest was made of cedar wood, and . . . on it were wrought figures, some of ivory, some of gold, and some of the cedar wood itself'.[9] Fragments from fifth-century BC ivory plaques a few millimetres thick and decorated with carved mythological scenes have been found in a tomb in Southern Russia at Ku Oba. The art of veneering was obviously practised in ancient Greece, for in the Odyssey (XIX, 56) Homer described an early example of veneering and inlay, even naming the cabinetmaker responsible for the chair of Penelope: 'It was overlaid with ivory and silver, and was the work of a craftsman called Icmalius.'[10] Similarly, the Parthenon in Athens featured furniture inlaid with silver and gold. Solid gold and silver furniture was used by the Persians – a particularly ostentatious custom commented upon by the historian Herodotus after the Persians' defeat at Marathon in 490 BC. Other decorative techniques employed included tortoiseshell inlay and brightly coloured painted motifs on wood, terracotta or gesso.

The forms of the Greek chests are also reminiscent of Egyptian prototypes: similarities include a gabled or flat lid, and the use of two knobs by which to secure the lid with a cord. Homer mentions that Odysseus 'straightaway fitted on the lid and quickly cast a cord upon it, a cunning knot which queenly Circe once had taught him' (Odyssey, VIII)[11] so securing the chest filled with gifts brought by Arete. This chest was doubtless very similar in appearance to the one carried by Danaë, seen pulling jewels from it, as depicted on a pyxis in the British Museum. Chests with gabled lids very close to the Egyptian Ark are found both in terracotta sarcophagi of the Aegean and in wooden coffins excavated in

Detail of decoration on the neck of a Greek red-figure vase, fifth century BC. Danaë (mother of Perseus by Zeus, who visited her as a shower of gold) is shown lifting a necklace from an open chest.

Egypt and Southern Russia, examples being preserved in the Cairo Museum and in St Petersburg. Such chests, known as *kibotoi*, would have been used for storage of personal and domestic items, while smaller articles such as toilet accessories and jewelry would be put in caskets, generally having a flat lid. Unfortunately, none has survived, though representations exist on vases, in reliefs or in small terracotta sculptural groups. Some miniature bronze chests now preserved in museums in Berlin and Athens display the usual panelled sides and short square feet, while the wooden coffins were built with the use of dovetailing and of wooden dowels, as in ancient Egypt.

The Greeks do not seem to have made use of separate drawers, although some of the *kibotoi* have two or four internal sections. Sets of shelves on a stand, the *kylikeon* (sometimes with a curtain to enclose it), were used to display everyday objects from the time of Aristophanes, in the late fifth century BC; examples are depicted in vase paintings and funerary reliefs. However, it was not until the Hellenistic period, when life became more complex and sophisticated and libraries were formed, that cupboards or wardrobes – the Roman *armarium* – were used and depicted in wall-paintings at Pompeii and Herculaneum, where actual examples were found preserved beneath a thick layer of volcanic ash and pumice.

The Roman *armarium* took over certain aspects of storage from the chest: one example discovered at Herculaneum contained glass, bronze and terracotta vases and some small statuettes.[12] However, several forms of chests existed in ancient Rome, each with a particular name describing its function. The *arca* was closer in function and meaning to the Egyptian Ark; the word 'arcane', meaning mysterious, secret, that which is hidden, is derived from this Latin root. The *capsa* and *cista* were small boxes or chests from which the word 'casket' (French, *cassette*; Italian *cassettone*) is derived. The *scrinium* was a case for documents, a reliquary, a compartment in a muniment chest, a sort of strongbox. A *loculus* was a small enclosed space, a coffin.

Representations in Roman painting and sculpture are not as numerous as Greek examples, but a wall-painting at Herculaneum depicts a servant bringing to her mistress a small jewel casket or toilet casket similar in form to that of the Greeks. At Pompeii a strongbox made of wood covered with iron and bronze plaques was found,[13] its style echoing earlier Etruscan bronze-plated chests based on the Greek prototypes with side panels, corner posts extended to form feet, and a flat or gabled lid. The Pompeian example, dating from the first century AD, has differently placed rectangular feet, but answers to Juvenal's contemporary description of an *arca ferrata*. Examples of a smaller type of strongbox without feet, but fitted with a lock and having handles for ease of transport, have been found in Egypt and Nubia; made of wood with bronze fittings, they also date from the first century AD, having been used during Roman military campaigns to hold documents and valuables.

Literary references to contemporary cabinetmaking abound, Pliny the Elder's *Natural History* being the most important source. The main woods are listed: beech, holly, willow, citron, oak, fir, juniper, lime, zygia. Of these citron, coming from Mauritania and North-West Africa, was the most highly prized; both Petronius and Pliny wrote that this species was more precious than gold. The art of cabinetmaking is described in detail, veneering being 'the luxury which displays itself in covering one tree with another, and in bestowing upon the more common woods a bark of higher price'.[14] Inlay of ivory, gold, silver and tortoiseshell are also mentioned. According to Pliny (IX, 39), one Carvillius Pollio, 'a man of prodigal habits and ingenious in inventing the refinements of luxury, was the first to cut the shell of the tortoise into laminae and to veneer beds and cabinets with it.'[15] Pliny (XVI, 232) further commented on certain wood-graining methods used to enhance the appearance and thus the price of furniture:

of late in the reign of Nero [54–68] there was a monstrous invention devised of destroying the natural appearance of tortoiseshell by paint and making it sell at a still higher price by a successful imitation of wood. It is in this way that the value of our couches is so greatly enhanced; it is this way too that they bid the rich lustre of terebinth [the turpentine tree] to be outdone and mock citrus to be made more valuable than the real one, and the grain of the maple to be feigned. At one time luxury was not content with wood, at the present day it sets us on buying tortoiseshell in the guise of wood.[16]

Not all furniture relied on decorative techniques to enhance its value, however, for solid gold, silver and ivory pieces are mentioned by several writers: Suetonius, Cicero and Pliny. Chests receive some special mentions: Pliny wrote that they were made of beech; Horace, in his *Art of Poetry*, spoke of stone, oak, fir, cedar and cypress; in the *Metamorphoses*, Ovid mentions ebony veneering, and apparently yew was used 'for the ornamental work attached to chests, footstools and the like'. (Theophrastos, *On the History of Plants*, V, vii, 6).[17] Recipes for the polishing of wooden furniture are mentioned by some writers: oil of skate and cedar by Pliny, oil of cedar and juniper by Vitruvius, and beeswax by Ovid.

The Decline of the Roman Empire

In 313 the Edict of Milan proclaimed Christianity as a state religion, in 330 the Imperial capital moved to Byzantium (Constantinople), and in 380 Christianity became the official religion of the Roman Empire. During the early centuries of the Christian era classical art forms continued to be adopted and adapted, and in the field of furniture-making traditional forms and techniques lingered on. The embossed silver Projecta casket depicting a bride at her toilet dates from the second half of the fourth century in Rome; it has a domed lid and two side handles, and is a smaller version of the sort of chest associating Graeco-Roman mythology with Christian symbolism which would have been used throughout the late Roman Empire and the Byzantine world. The latter carried on the legacy of the classical past after the final collapse of the Western half of the Roman Empire in 476. Byzantine ivory plaques, used as veneer on wooden cores, reflect the legacy of Greek and Roman ideals and were highly prized not only within the frontiers of the Empire, but have also been found in excavations in northern European lands then occupied by Germanic tribes. As early as the first century AD, however, trade routes had operated between China, India and the Mediterranean world. At Begram in Afghanistan, excavations carried out between 1937 and 1940 yielded Graeco-Roman artifacts, together with fragments of Indian ivory and Chinese lacquer furniture. In 26 BC Augustus was

Silver casket with embossed decoration, made for the bride on the occasion of the wedding of Secundus and Projecta, c. 380; although the bride and groom were Christians, the front panel of the lid depicts the birth of Venus – a subject harking back to classical antiquity. Width 55.5 cm (21 in.).

receiving an embassy from Ceylon and Roman envoys reached China in AD 166. It is a matter of speculation that precious commodities such as spices, incense, pigments and other substances may have been transported in chests or cabinets with drawers along the northern Silk Road, stretching from China to Western Europe via Persia. The Chinese poet Yu Xin (513–581) wrote in his 'Rhapsody on the Mirror': 'Set up the dressing case, pull out the mirror drawer.'[18]

However, by the seventh century a new power was rising as a threat to the might of the Byzantine Empire. In 630 the Prophet Muhammed began the process by which the future rival to Christianity – Islam – became established in the heartland of Arabia, from where the new religion spread rapidly eastwards and westwards. By 710 Muslim forces had occupied the whole of North Africa and advanced into Spain; their northward progress was finally halted in 732 by Charles Martel at Poitiers in France. The spread of Muslim power and influence, from China to Spain, ensured not only the rapid dissemination of the Islamic religion, but also – through politics and trade between East and West – of artistic traditions, forms and techniques, as had happened under the Roman Empire. In this way the portable *sundūq*, a type of chest which could be locked and used as a treasury or dowry chest, was not simply in the tradition of the Roman *arca ferrata*, but perhaps also had associations with a Far Eastern prototype. Because Islamic religion and civilization was based on the divine revelations to the Prophet Muhammed contained in the Qu'ran and on the 'Sayings' of the Prophet (*hadith*), particular attention was given to the art of the book and to the care of books and manuscripts. Libraries were created to house copies of the Qu'ran, as well as scientific books, based on the Greek tradition of astronomical, medical and botanical treatises. The shelves on which they were kept recall the Hellenistic libraries, and some miniatures depict scholars at work, with their books neatly arranged in a niche type of structure. However, underlying the form and function of the *hizana*, a cupboard for storage eventually having two doors, can be detected the Roman *armarium*. Paradoxically, Islamic civilization – while being diametrically opposed to the aims of the classical Graeco-Roman traditions – became the depository of the ancient cultural heritage of the Mediterranean world by uniting the whole of the Near East and retaining local traditions of each country following the conversion of its population to Islam. From the sixth century to the eighth the West reached its lowest ebb. Religion, as in the Near and Middle East, was the key civilizing element, with the Christian Church preserving in its rites and structure the continuation of cultural links with the classical Mediterranean past.

The monasteries became the repository not only of religious faith, but of secular history and scientific knowledge. Latin was the *lingua franca* of the Church and men of letters. The foundation of the Benedictine Order in 534 by St Benedict at Monte Cassino in Italy was to prove a determining factor in the establishment of Christianity in north-western Europe, together with the decree by Pope Gregory the Great that Europe should be christianized in the Roman fashion. In this way the survival of Graeco-Roman values was ensured in very dark and troubled times, during which the Roman Church was under threat from the barbarians in the north, Byzantium in the east, as well as from the spread of Islam in the eighth century.

Western Europe was eventually unified by Charlemagne in 800, when he was crowned Holy Roman Emperor by the Pope, brushing aside the claims of the nominal Emperor of Byzantium. The Western empire became a reality; founded in 887, it included by the beginning of the tenth century Allemania, Franconia, Saxony and Bavaria, and its frontiers stretched from the North Sea to the Adriatic and the Mediterranean. Charlemagne established his court at Aachen (Aix-la-Chapelle) and there East met West in splendour and learning. Byzantine ideals influenced the architecture and decoration, the Chapel being a copy of S. Vitale at Ravenna, and the establishment of the Palace School brought about the revival of ancient learning under the direction of the English scholar Alcuin, from the cathedral school of York. One can surmise that a *scriptorium*, such as the one that existed in the monastery founded at St Gallen in Switzerland in 850, would have been used at Aachen for the copying of manuscripts.

A surviving description of the palace of Charlemagne dating from 811 refers to a small room like a treasury (*thesaurus*) containing 'jewels of gold and silver adorned with great splendour'.[19] Indeed, if no furniture of the Carolingian period has survived, the splendour and richness of decoration can be imagined from ornate caskets and reliquaries covered with embossed gold sheets and decorated with cabochon-cut precious stones, or from the finesse of carved ivory plaques depicting classicizing figures allied to repetitive abstract motifs in the oriental manner. International politics and trade with the Orient were also important at court, for Charlemagne received the Emperor of Byzantium, and gifts were exchanged with the Muslim caliphs. This suggests that gifts, documents and valuables would have been carried in portable chests and caskets of the Roman and oriental type, while books, manuscripts and other treasures would have been housed in cupboards of the *armarium* type, whether in the *scriptorium*, the *thesaurus*, or the *Sancta Sanctorum* (the inner room in a chapel or church where precious relics were kept).

Mention of these special rooms set aside for a particular purpose appears in early inventories in the Middle Ages. In 1244–5 an inventory of the Papal Palace at Avignon records a *studium generale* and a *camera secreta*, i.e. a study and a private, hidden chamber. Petrarch, the humanist who died in 1374, was using a '*studio*' (a small study),[20] according to one of his visitors. From these various functions – administrative, scholarly and private – associated with the *vita contemplativa* would develop the use of the cabinet for various purposes.

In the thirteenth century a Chinese scholar, Li Rempu, had written that in order to aid his writing, he had made ten cabinets of wood, each with twenty drawers, and that whatever came to his attention was entered in these cabinets arranged in good order by date and sequence.

In medieval Europe the sorting out and storing of documents and records is described in the inventory of Jeanne de Valois, sister of King Philip of France, drawn up for her Château at Talent in 1354–5; this refers to 'three large *armoires* well made in oak, for storing the archives of the Trésor de Talent, the archives to be put in these *armoires* for greater security and so that they may be viewed and taken out more speedily whenever necessary'.[21] The scholastic tradition begun under Charlemagne at the Palace School in Aachen continued in the monasteries and nurtured the creation of the universities, Bologna and Paris in 1120, Oxford in 1167, Padua in 1222. With the introduction of paper, first produced in Europe by Muslims in Spain at the beginning of the twelfth century as a substitute for vellum, increased book production became possible. Libraries and archives must have contained pieces of furniture similar to that described in a French inventory – that of the Bastide St Antoine – in 1418, in which 'Ten large *armoires* marked A to K inclusive' are listed.[22] At first such pieces would have been built-in or fastened to the wall; thus in 1451 there was in the Castle of Peniscola, belonging to the Spanish Military Order of Montesa, a wooden cabinet called an *armario* fastened to the wall in the kitchens. Eventually this type of furniture became freestanding but without doors, the inclusion of drawers (*laiettes*) having been first recorded in 1430. Smaller pieces of more intricate designs existed to store precious possessions. At the Bastide St Antoine 'small *armoires* in three parts'[23] are mentioned in a *camera secreta* – a small turret room, study or treasury room. In an earlier inventory, that of the Bishop of Alet in 1354, reference had been made to both: 'in a small tower room . . . a wooden *armoire* containing two small leather boxes, one empty, the other containing various papers'.[24]

In due course doors with locks were added to provide further security. The *armoire*-cabinet of the Guild of Spanish Merchants in Bruges (now in the Gruuthusemuseum) is a fine example. Made of solid oak with four drawers marked A to D concealed behind two doors bearing the arms of Burgos, León and Castile, it was described in a document dated 23 April 1441 as an *arca*, its function being to hold the privileges and titles of the Guild. In 1441 six consuls of the Guild each held a key to its single lock. Made in Bruges, this piece is a characteristic product of north-western Europe – a simple box-like slab-ended chest.

The chest or trunk – French, *coffre*; Italian, *cassone*, Latin, *arca*; German, *Schrank* – remained the most versatile and ubiquitous piece of furniture in Europe until the Renaissance. It served as a storage piece and, according to contemporary records, as a seat, a table, or even as an occasional bed if large enough. It had the distinct advantage of being movable (hence the French term *mobilier*, furniture) in times when long journeys in the cause of war, crusades, pilgrimages, diplomacy and trade were necessary. However, a refining eastern influence was at work, transforming not only the execution and decoration of such chests, but giving these pieces a new status. The thirteenth-century Hispano-Moresque carved wooden chest in the Museo de la Fundacion Duque de Lerma in Toledo echoes the ark-shaped Egyptian and Hellenistic prototypes, featuring a domed lid and the side stiles extended as feet. Its concealed drawers behind a hinged fall-front secured by a lock make this a new form which, thanks to its small dimensions (64 × 49 × 35 cm; approx. 25 × 19 × 14 in.) served as an easily transportable cabinet in which to carry valuables and documents, while its hinged flap could be used as a writing support. Calligraphic decoration covers the whole piece, the Arabic characters in broad Kufic script being carved on the characteristic small panels and on the transverse bar joining them to the plain uprights.

The inventory of King Alfonso V of Aragon (reigned 1412–24) recorded four writing cabinets made by the king's carpenter Pascual Esteve. The *scritorio* or *escritorio* was differentiated both from the type of writing desk usually built into a wall and having a set of storage shelves above for books and manuscripts, and from a low free-standing piece of furniture with a shelf below. (The *scritorio* was first called a *vargueño*, the Spanish term by which it is now known, only in 1872 by Juan Facundo Riaño, in reference to Vargas, a small town near Toledo.)

Muslim rule endured in Andalusia until 1492, when Granada was recaptured. Throughout the twelfth and thirteenth centuries the Crusades renewed Western contacts with the Near and the Middle East. Religious fervour allied to political manoeuvring, diplomacy and trade ensured a continuity of cultural and artistic exchanges. Through coming into contact with Muslim scholars the Crusaders were introduced to the study of subjects such as astronomy, geography and medicine, all areas of knowledge inherited from the distant classical past, and enlarged upon in the Islamic world.

For centuries Genoa and Venice provided the trading link between the three most important political powers of the time: the Holy Roman Empire in central and western Europe, the Byzantine Empire and the Islamic sphere of influence stretching from Spain in the west to China in the east. In particular Venice – the Republic of St Mark – rose in glory and splendour in its dealings with the East. In 1000 Pope Basil II accorded it the title of 'favourite daughter of Byzantium' in thanks for the successful campaigns waged against the Saracens in the Adriatic. When, after the failure of the Second and Third Crusades, the Fourth was launched from Venice in 1202, the outcome in 1204 was the sack of Constantinople by the Venetian forces in a shrewd political and commercial manoeuvre. This victory marked the establishment of a virtual Venetian political and economic empire in the Levant. Trade was conducted with the Near and Middle East by sea, and with the Far East by land. Indeed, although several embassies had already been despatched to the Mongol court from Europe, it was two Venetians, Maffeo and Nicolò Polo, who were appointed ambassadors to the Pope by Kublai Khan in 1269.

Opposite
1 Detail of A Collector's Cabinet *by Frans Francken the Younger, oil on panel, 1617.*

CHRISTO · SACRVM
ILLE · DEI · VERBO · MAGNA · PIETATE · FAVEBAT·
PERPETVA · DIGNVS · POSTERITATE · COLI·
D · FRIDR · DVCI · SAXON · S · R · IMP·
ARCHIM · ELECTORI·
ALBERTVS · DVRER · NVR · FACIEBAT·
· B · M · F · V · V ·
· M · D · XXIIII ·

Hier begint onſ vroū gi
b̄ Aue maria gracia pleñ
dominus tecum; benedicta
tu in mulieribus: et benedi
fructus ventris tui Σ matͤ
Omine labia
mea apͤries
et os meū auͬ
ciabit laudͤ
tuam Deus in adiu
iuū intende: dn̄e ad
adiuuandum me feſt

3 Oak armoire *with carved decoration,
having two cupboards and two drawers;
Flanders, c. 1530–50. Each of the centre
panels has carved decoration of a head –
one male, one female – in profile within
a medallion, suggesting a specially
commissioned* meuble de mariage.

4 Walnut *cabinet en armoire, with
carved and moulded doors featuring
strapwork, shells and rosettes. France,
c. 1530; height 153 cm (5 ft 1 in.).*

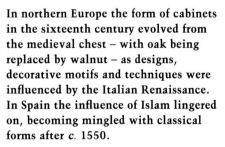

**In northern Europe the form of cabinets
in the sixteenth century evolved from
the medieval chest – with oak being
replaced by walnut – as designs,
decorative motifs and techniques were
influenced by the Italian Renaissance.
In Spain the influence of Islam lingered
on, becoming mingled with classical
forms after *c*. 1550.**

2 Walnut *dressoir with verde antico
marble inlay and carved allegorical
figures in the manner of Androuet du
Cerceau. France, c. 1580; height 173 cm
(5 ft 8 in.).*

Opposite
5 Walnut *vargueño with hinged top and
fall-front revealing two cupboards, each
door having a head carved in profile, and
drawers with openwork arabesque
carving applied over red cloth. Spain, c.
1550; height 137 cm (4 ft 6 in.).*

FROM ANTIQUITY TO THE RENAISSANCE

FROM ANTIQUITY TO THE RENAISSANCE

In the sixteenth century fall-front cabinets with drawers for storing personal valuables took on the additional function of a writing desk, and new decorative techniques (including pictorial marquetry and gilt and painted leather) were introduced. By the end of the century the use of ebony (imported from the East Indies) was combined in southern Germany with rare and costly decorative materials to produce the *Kunstschrank*, a lavish work of art in its own right, as precious as the objects it was intended to hold.

9 Cabinet in ebony, ivory, tortoiseshell and pietra dura, *in the form of a temple façade with columns and niches occupied by statuettes of the Virtues, and having drawers and secret compartments. Augsburg, c. 1580–1600; width 93 cm (3 ft).*

Opposite, above
6 Walnut fall-front studiolo *with inlaid decoration of biblical scenes and the arms of the Holy Roman Emperor Charles V in various coloured woods. Italy, c. 1532; width 134 cm (4 ft 5 in.).*

Opposite, bottom left
7 Oak and walnut fall-front writing casket. England, c. 1525. The later covering of painted and gilt leather includes the arms of Henry VIII flanked by figures of Mars and Venus after woodcuts by Hans Burgkmair. Width 40.5 cm (16 in.).

Opposite, below right
8 Walnut cassone with carved and gilt decoration and the arms of the Dal Pozzo family of Verona. North Italian, c. 1480–5; width 131 cm (4 ft 3½ in.).

10 Table-cabinet in ebony with gilt-bronze mounts including medallions depicting Mary Tudor and her husband, Philip II of Spain. Augsburg, c. 1575; width 71 cm (2 ft 4 in.).

11, 12 *Damascened brass casket (side and front views), showing inlaid silver decoration and Kufic script. Persia, fourteenth century; height 12.7 cm (5 in.).*

Small portable cabinets used for storing documents and valuables were made in the Far East as well as in Europe. The Islamic-inspired Spanish *escritorio* influenced the development in Germany of the *Schreibtisch* with its fall-front writing flap. Near Eastern decorative materials and techniques such as damascening were imported into Europe, as was the use of lacquer from the Far East.

13 *Wooden casket with inlaid decoration of Islamic geometric motifs in mother-of-pearl, tortoiseshell, ivory etc., the interior being lined with satin and having a mirror fitted inside the hinged cover. Ottoman, sixteenth century; width 66 cm (2 ft 2 in.).*

14, 15 *Table-cabinet (Schreibtisch; open and closed) with pictorial marquetry decoration. Augsburg, c. 1580–1600; width 91 cm (12 in.). The* trompe-l'oeil *architectural vista was inspired by Italian Renaissance models.*

16 *Schreibtisch with pictorial marquetry decoration in woods of various colours; two outer doors (not shown) open to reveal a façade resembling an Italianate Renaissance palazzo. Augsburg, c. 1570; width 98 cm (3ft 2½ in.).*

17 *Lacquered wooden cabinet (front removed) showing ten drawers and gilt-bronze handles. China, Ming Dynasty (c. 1410–35); width 56.5 cm (2 ft 10½ in.).*

Opposite
18 Table-cabinet with hinged top and fall-front, covered in leather with stamped, gilt and painted decoration. Veneto, northern Italy, c. 1590–1600; width 59 cm (1 ft 11in.).

Returning to Xanadu in 1275, the ambassadors brought with them Nicolò Polo's son, Marco, who would serve the Khan for seventeen years, and whose *Description of the World* was to be the leading contemporary account of the Orient. East met West in Spain and in Venice, the tie going even deeper as a result of Spanish Jews acting as Venice's emissaries to Egypt, as well as to Portugal and India.

In the realm of cabinetmaking a similarity of forms and techniques can therefore be detected. The type of small treasure-chest with drawers concealed behind a fall-front, already encountered in Toledo and in the inventory of the Bishop of Alet, was sometimes called a 'hutch chest',[25] no doubt due to the fact that most medieval cupboards were built into walls and the small portable casket was stored within a cavity. Larger chests and *armoires* incorporated them as well as easily removable treasury caskets. Examples of the north Italian *cassone* and the Catalan *hembra*, or bride's dowry-chest,[26] reveal *c.* 1480–1500 a set of small drawers behind a door on one side. In due course this type became fully independent in Spain as the *escritorio*, in Italy as the *cassetto* or *cassettone a ribalta da scrittorio*.

Medieval furniture decoration was entirely inspired by church architecture, whether in painted pieces such as the *armoire* of Isabel of Bavaria, recorded in Paris in 1397, with its images of the Crucifixion, the Virgin and the Apostles, or in carved and sometimes pierced tracery evoking rose-windows or tall lancet windows in Gothic cathedrals, a style which became truly international in Europe in the fifteenth century. Some early examples of the *scrittorio* and the *cassettone* (sometimes also called a *scrigno*, from the Latin *scrinium*, a compartment in a muniment chest), feature this late-Gothic style of carved gilt tracery combined with a coat-of-arms or other cipher or with heraldic devices. However, more sophisticated techniques were introduced by the Islamic craftsmen; leather, already mentioned in the 1354 inventory of the Bishop of Alet as a covering on two caskets, was now used on a wooden base, embossed with a relief pattern in gold and silver – a Moorish craft called *guadamecil*.[27] Venice also produced cabinets covered with painted or varnished leather decorated with tooled designs often featuring characteristic Muslim arabesques and the armorials of the patron who commissioned the piece.

The gilt-leather cabinet covered with Moorish arabesques mentioned in Francis I's inventory of 1528 could therefore have come either from Spain or from Venice, for although Moorish Spain seems to have gained the ascendant, most gilt leather was generically referred to as 'Spanish' leather, regardless of its origins. The tradition continued in Venice with the production of tooled and lacquered bookbindings 'in the Persian style' from the end of the fifteenth to the mid-sixteenth century.

The allusion to Persia can also be detected in another decorative technique, but of damascening. Introduced to Venice and Milan *c.* 1300, the first damascened wares came from Herat in eastern Persia, hence the Venetian metalworkers became known as *azziministi*, a term derived from the Arabic *'al agem'*, meaning 'the faraway country'.[28] The traditions of metalwork in the Near East go back to Byzantium and Persia, and indirectly once more to the classical Graeco-Roman culture. Presentation pieces were inscribed not only with the names of patrons but also with those of makers and decorators. The Crusaders brought

pieces back to the West, and some were specially commissioned: the Hugues de Lusignan basin in the Louvre bears a dedication to him in both Kufic and Latin script as King of Cyprus and Jerusalem (1324–59).

The art of damascening was practised in Venice, though whether by Saracenic craftsmen is a matter of debate, for the guild system precluded the employment of foreign craftsmen. However, a small colony of Persian metalworkers did come to the city during the alliance formed by the Republic with the Turkmen ruler Ūzūn Hasan in 1464 against their common enemy, the Ottoman Turks. In the sixteenth century the main centre for metalwork was Milan, caskets, cabinets, weapons and armour being produced and exported all over Europe, so disseminating the decorative Muslim arabesque. Strips of damascened ware were manufactured for use as decoration on furniture, e.g. on the 'Diane de Poitiers Cabinet' (now in the Victoria and Albert Museum), made *c.* 1550.

Islam was also the source of another form of decorative technique, inlay work, a technique called *embriachi* (from the name of the main

Spanish cabinet with four drawers and overall carved and gilt decoration of Gothic tracery, late fourteenth or early fifteenth century.

Ebony table-cabinet decorated with, on the drawer fronts, damascened plaques depicting allegorical and mythological subjects, and on the inside of the doors damascened inlay of grotesques and arabesques (including the cipher of Diane de Poitiers, a triple crescent moon). Milan, c. 1550; width 89 cm (2 ft 11 in.).

Small table-cabinet with eight drawers; the inlaid alla certosina *decoration consists of stylized Saracenic geometric floral designs and banding; northern Italy, c. 1450–60; width 50.5 cm (20 in.).*

family of Italian craftsmen) or *alla certosina* (from the manufacturing centre near the Certosa of Pavia). Originating from Mamluk countries where the combination of a shortage of wood and a hot climate encouraged the use of small panels to prevent warping, this inlay work employs small tesserae of various woods, bone, ivory, mother-of-pearl and metal. It became very popular in Lombardy and the Veneto in the fifteenth century, and is very close in materials, quality and technique to Ottoman pieces of the same period. Qu'ran boxes, chests and caskets were decorated with a rich inlay of wood, ivory (natural or green stained), silver and brass. Tortoiseshell was used after the middle of the sixteenth century and mother-of-pearl replaced ivory at the end of the century.

A maker of musket-stocks, Hasan-i Kālibi, is recorded in 1505–6 as making a walnut chest inlaid with boxwood, ivory and metal,[29] together with carved ivory panels, so illustrating the link between this type of inlay work on furniture and in the production of fine weapons – as was true of the damascening technique in the Middle East and in Europe. After the ending of Moorish rule in Spain in 1492, a similar technique, the *mudejar* style, was evolved by the remaining Muslim craftsmen in Granada, Toledo, Cordoba, Seville, Barcelona and the Balearic Islands. The complex repeating design that resulted was based on the star-and-flower motif, Muslim architecture and gardens, just as in *embriachi* work; characteristic of *mudejar* work is the *laceria*, a fine line of inlaid wood allied to arabesque scrolls.

At the Foundling Hospital of Tavera-Vega, founded in Toledo in 1541 by Cardinal Tavera and designed by the architect Bartolome de Bustamente in a classical style inspired by Bramante, the dispensary reveals a remarkable example of the alliance of Middle Eastern influences with a revived classical tradition. The storage of medicines, unguents and cosmetics had been associated with the chest or cabinet since antiquity, and medieval French inventories also include such references, e.g. that of the Comtesse d'Avelin at the Château des Beaux in 1426, according to which there was in her bedchamber: 'Item: a large *armoire* with many pigeon-holes, and in them various medicinal items'.[30] In the Toledo dispensary there is a large built-in *armario* with multiple drawers, the central part being occupied by a small removable cabinet with drawers concealed by doors, the so-called 'Apothecary's eye' containing the most precious and mysterious remedies handed down through centuries during the Moorish occupation.

New horizons in the fifteenth century

Voyages of discovery took the Portuguese sea-captains into new worlds and opened up new sources of wealth, which innovations such as printing, the compass and gunpowder made possible. The Moors had already been expelled from Portugal in the thirteenth century, and under Prince Henry the Navigator (1394–1460) the Portuguese began a series of explorations which by the beginning of the sixteenth century gave them control of the sea routes and trade ranging from Africa to India and China. In 1415 they established themselves on the East African coast, in 1488 Bartolomeo Diaz rounded the Cape of Good Hope and in 1498 Vasco da Gama reached India, so breaking the existing monopoly of the spice trade held by the Arabs and the Venetians.

However, it was a Spanish expedition in 1492, led by Christopher Columbus, which crossed the Atlantic and discovered the West Indies. Spain and Portugal signed a treaty in 1494, with the accord of a Papal bull, by which the trade routes to the East were given to the Portuguese, and those to the West to the Spaniards. In 1516 the Portuguese reached China and established a trade monopoly which was to last until 1602. Meanwhile, in 1580 Portugal and Spain had been united through the succession to the throne of Portugal of Philip II of Spain. In this way Spain controlled the largest trading empire, adding to its colonies in America the Portuguese trading posts on the coasts of India and Asia. The effects of this supremacy on the prosperity of the Iberian peninsula were reflected in its furniture.

The products of the fifteenth century were still dependent stylistically on the Gothic, but with increasing prosperity the basic portable chest developed into a more complex type, the *escritorio* or *vargueño*, which could be carried by means of two handles and rested on a trestle stand (*pie de puente*) or another chest of drawers (*taquillon*). All furniture makers belonged to the Carpenters' Guild, which included all wood craftsmen, although in Aragon a distinction was made between a furniture maker (*caixer*), a carpenter specializing in Moorish inlaid ceilings (*bosquer*), and a maker of plain boxes (*capser*). Corporation rules were very strict and competitive. In 1460 the guilds required an examination for admission, special privileges and protection being granted to native craftsmen and their relatives, as in other medieval European countries. In 1482 Valencia banned the import of chests from Barcelona.

The method of construction of the *vargueño* remained very basic and its decoration was at first very simple. The appeal of such pieces depended less on aesthetic values than on the austerity of their rigid rectangular lines, strength being emphasized in the thick slabs of oak used in the fifteenth century (subsequently replaced by chestnut, walnut and poplar), impressively bound with heavy iron locks and hinges. The fall-front was often embellished further with pierced iron plaques backed with red velvet, and when open it would rest on two pulls usually carved with the scallop shell associated with St James the Great – a distant reminder of the type of portable chest used by pilgrims on the routes leading to Santiago da Compostela. The inner drawers were faced with more ironwork laid on a colourful ground of red or yellow silk or velvet.

The first cabinets would have evolved from pieces used in church sacristies to store cult-objects, vestments, plate and holy books, but by the end of the sixteenth century most households of any standing would have owned at least one *vargueño*, judging by the large number still in existence. Indeed, with Spain at the height of its political and colonial powers in the sixteenth century, the portable *vargueño* would have been a most convenient piece to carry to the New World for administrative, diplomatic and personal use by Conquistadores and missionaries alike.

Decoration varied from a simple geometric wood inlay of contrasting colour, to the intricate ivory, bone and wood inlay of the *mudejar* style after 1492. By the mid-sixteenth century a new decorative motif inspired by Renaissance silverwork used light grotesques, urns, trophies, wreaths and profile heads, reflecting the Italianate carvings by Gregorio Pardo in Toledo Cathedral dating from *c*. 1549. A notable group of Catalan craftsmen produced a very high-quality type of *vargueño* in the

Walnut fall-front vargueño *with ivory inlay in the Plateresque style. Portugal, c. 1580–1600; width 107 cm (3 ft 6 in.).*

plateresque style, with delicate boxwood carvings backed by velvet on a walnut ground. The use of *plateresque* decoration continued until the end of the sixteenth century; thereafter, under the influence of the architect Juan de Herrera (who had travelled to Italy), a new Tuscan-inspired classical severity made its appearance, with architectural designs featuring arched pediments and temple fronts arranged symmetrically, executed in carved wood and sometimes gilded or adorned with ivory.

By then a smaller version of the *escritorio* had been developed, a form with no door or stand but having small feet: the *papelera*. As suggested by its name, this was used to hold documents, whereas the *vargueño*, though primarily a writing chest with a fall-front writing flap, was also used to store valuables, being referred to in contemporary writings as a treasure-chest, and might serve as a bookcase, one example being depicted in *The Calling of St Matthew* by Juan de Pareja. Following the Spanish conquest of the New World, a similar guild system was established there by craftsmen: the ordinance for the Carpenters', Joiners' and Furnituremakers' Guild in Mexico dated 30 August 1568 required its members, among other things, to execute a *vargueño* as a test of their skill. Subsequently, native craftsmen must have started to copy

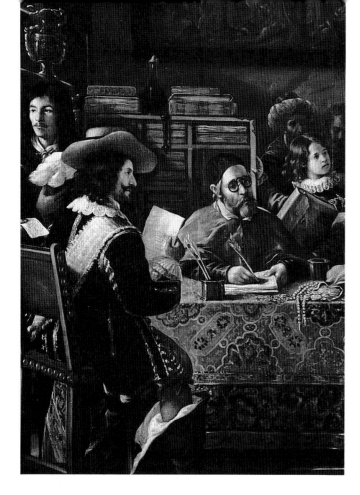

the European prototypes, for a further ordinance on 7 April 1589 decreed that the rule did not apply to the Indians and that Spaniards must not trade in furniture made by natives. Michoacán particularly was a centre of fine production, inspiration for its wares coming from the *plateresque* and *mudejar* styles of Andalusia, thanks to the direct links that existed between Seville and Cadiz and the New World.

The commercial rewards reaped from the New World were great, and ostentation grew in direct proportion. So extensive was the use of silver on furniture that sumptuary laws had to be passed in 1593, and again in 1600, restricting and prohibiting the practice. In Spain itself the *vargueño* was by then being rivalled in popularity on its home ground by the import of Nuremberg products, which it had inspired in the first place, so forcing Philip III to place a ban on such imports in 1603.

The rise of the House of Habsburg started in 1272 with the crowning of Rudolf of Habsburg as King of Austria. From 1438 onwards, following the election of Albert II as Emperor, the German crown was inherited by Habsburg princes until the nineteenth century. Thus, in 1477, when Mary of Burgundy, daughter of the great Duke Charles the Bold, married Maximilian I, head of the Habsburg dynasty, she not only enlisted the Habsburg might against Louis XI of France, but her dowry included most of the Netherlands and Flanders. In 1519, when Charles V of Habsburg was crowned Holy Roman Emperor, against the claim of Francis I of France, he became ruler not only of Germany, but of Spain, Naples (taken over in 1504), Sicily, Flanders and the Netherlands.

The administration needed to rule over such an empire required a vast amount of bureaucracy and diplomatic activity. The *escritorio* was invaluable for carrying documents and valuables, as well as serving as a portable desk. As a result, the Spanish prototype of a chest of small drawers enclosed by a fall-front door which would be used as a writing flap was superimposed on the native German cabinetmaking tradition. Medieval cabinets and chests with multiple drawers – a type called a *Kabinettschrank* – were already used in churches and universities for keeping records, as in the rest of Europe (one inventory of 1376 mentioned no less than eleven cabinets and nine chests). Likewise, smaller cabinets or caskets were used to secure valuables. This form was allied to the requirements of trade and legal matters within the empire and as the result of Spanish influence became the *Schreibtisch* (writing table), a literal translation of *escritorio*.

The German word for chest, *Schrein*, had given rise to the term *Schreiner*, meaning a carpenter, first recorded at Regensburg in 1244. In 1322 a distinction was made between carpenters and other craftsmen such as wood-turners and cabinetmakers, following the introduction of the sawmill (first mentioned at Augsburg). The term *Tischler* was now used to describe cabinetmakers, whose trade flourished in commercial centres such as Nuremberg and Augsburg. Indeed, such was the renown of the local craftsmen that in 1569 the Carpenters' Guild in Augsburg was able to boast to the town council that the fame of their 'craft of cabinetmaking has spread so far that apprentices come from abroad to study'.[31] Their fame reached the princely courts of Europe: Count Albrecht of Bavaria bought a piece from Augsburg, while the inventory of the French Queen Catherine de Médicis, drawn up after the death of her husband Henry II in 1589, listed several cabinets, seven of them in ebony and marquetry including 'a suite made in the German manner (*façon d'Allemagne*) with gadrooned silver pilasters at the corners of the drawers in marquetry, in the form of a theatre, or embellished with silver plaques on the front of the drawers.'[32] The whole range of the German *Tischler*'s art was here described.

The Renaissance had reached South Germany in the first quarter of the sixteenth century under the influence of designs by Peter Flötner, who had travelled to Italy and, although perhaps trained in Augsburg, was working in Nuremberg in 1522. His woodcuts of classical motifs with grotesques and arabesques echoed contemporary Italian decorative schemes. Italy had risen rapidly in prosperity during the Middle Ages with the growth and expansion of the banking system, the ramifications of which extended throughout Europe. (The first gold coinage was minted in Florence in 1252.) The Italian political and economic structure was unlike any other in contemporary Western Europe. Central and northern Italy was divided up into republics (in a manner reminiscent of the ancient Greek city-states). Patronage of the arts came from the dominant banking and trading classes and encouraged a rational, intellectual approach to all forms of artistic activity. Man and his position in life and nature became 'the measure of all things', as had been the case in the time of Pythagoras in the fifth century BC.

Italy naturally looked back to its classical past, the poetry of Petrarch being one of the first and finest expressions of this renewed humanism – a fact acknowledged by his being crowned with symbolic laurel wreaths on the Capitoline Hill in 1341 in the manner of the ancient Romans. At a time when in northern Europe the last of the great cathedrals inspired by religious faith and fervour were being built in the Gothic style, Italy was starting to apply the mathematical and geometric principles which culminated in the theoretical works of Alberti, *De Pictura* (On Painting) in 1435 and *De re aedificatoria* (On Architecture) in 1450. From the last quarter of the fourteenth century Florence, under the rule of the Medici, a banking family, became the most flourishing centre of the renaissance of the arts not of the infinite, but of the finite, in the words of Cosimo de' Medici, Florentine artists redefined the world in the terms of Euclidian geometry. Hence the craft of the *legnaiuolo* (woodworker) depended in matters of form and decoration upon architecture and painting. Woodworkers belonged to the same guild as that of the sculptors and stonemasons and, since no distinction was made between fine and decorative arts, cross-fertilization of ideas ensued. Furthermore, architects would prepare a wooden *modello* of a commissioned building for their patrons. So it is enlightening to read in Vasari's *Lives of the Artists* that Brunelleschi, the architect of the cathedral in Florence, taught perspective to the painter Masaccio, through the medium of *intarsia* (wooden inlay).

The art of inlay, which had been practised in the ancient world, reappeared in Italy in the late Middle Ages, as a result of Islamic influence, in the *alla certosina* technique, using bone, ivory and mother-of-pearl. It was particularly appropriate because of the chronic lack of wood in the Italian Peninsula since Roman times. Hence *intarsiatori* (inlay workers) are recorded as distinct from carpenters (*falegnami*) who would work on more ordinary undecorated pieces. Most of the early *intarsia* panels were used to decorate church stalls and the craftsmen responsible for their execution were not only woodworkers, but also sculptors and architects, such as Giuliano and Benedetto da Maiano, who executed *intarsia* panels for Florence Cathedral from designs by the painter Baldovinetti. At first linear patterns would be used, but after the middle of the fifteenth century, the Renaissance pictorial illusionism of 'a window opened on to the world' influenced the *trompe-l'œil* perspective views and landscapes then in favour. Doors would be represented half-open, revealing a humanist world in which the latest scientific discoveries such as the astrolabe and the compass were shown side by side with books and quills, musical instruments and armour, animals and perspective vistas, thus recreating a microcosm of the ideal world. Such was the humanist princely *studiolo*, examples of which existed at Urbino and Gubbio, for the study and delight of the Duke of Montefeltro, *c.* 1479–82, and in Florence at the Palazzo Vecchio for Francesco I de' Medici, *c.* 1570.

Even earlier, Petrarch had enjoyed the *vita contemplativa* from his studio, and many scholars' rooms must have looked like those depicted in paintings by Carpaccio or Antonella da Messina. However, the humanist princes did not merely study their libraries of rare manuscripts housed in a *studiolo* with *trompe-l'œil* cupboards, for they also concealed behind the pictorial doors their precious collections of bronze statuettes, antique objects and some contemporary pieces *all'antica* (in the antique manner), as well as coins and medals, plus objects of beauty, scientific interest or curiosity; such objects could be taken out and shown to a worthy visitor, so providing an opportunity for learned discourse about them. Thus, in content and decoration, the *studiolo* allied the revival of antique values to those of the contemporary world, linking the classical age to the Christian era. It also echoed the desire of man to reign over the

The interior of Federigo da Montefeltro's studiolo in Urbino (above) showing intarsia panels by Baccio Pontelli, c. 1479–82; the Duke is portrayed in another panel (opposite, above) and the double doors (opposite, below) show further trompe-l'oeil inlay suggesting cupboard doors opened to reveal the varied contents.

St Jerome in his Study, painted by Antonello da Messina in 1529, illustrates the kind of small room (studiolo) in which a humanist scholar would assemble objects of beauty, learning or curiosity for study and learned discussion.

whole known world, as Gianozzo Manetti expressed it in *On the Dignity and Excellence of Man* (1451–2). This renewed humanism built on the scholastic intellectual search of the Middle Ages. The description given in 1379–80 by Christine de Pisan of Charles V's study at the Château de Vincennes reads like an early inventory for a Cabinet of Curiosities: 'in the King's study in the tower room used for relaxation, there are many wondrous things such as terrestrial globes, a statue of a male nude, birds from Cyprus, scents and astrolabes'.[33]

'And so you may have in small compass a model of the universal, nature made private', wrote Francis Bacon in *Gesta Grayorum* in 1594. And in this *theatrum mundi* you must have 'a goodly, huge cabinet, wherein whatsoever the hand of man by exquisite art or engine had made rare in stuff, form or motion; whatsoever singularity, chance and the shuffle of things hath produced; whatsoever Nature has wrought in things that want life and may be kept, shall be sorted and included'.[34] Order must reign over such categories as *Naturalia*, *Artificialia*, *Exotica* and *Mirabilia*, in a god-like attempt to know the true meaning of the world and man's place in the world. This was achieved not through a scientific deductive intellectual process, but through association, using symbols to reveal hidden knowledge accessible only to the initiated. It is noteworthy that in the Medici *studiolo* there are depicted on its *intarsia* doors symbolic motifs related to its contents, and that Francesco de' Medici chose to have himself portrayed, not like the patrician figure of Federigo de Montefeltro, but (as the assistant in the panel by Stradano depicting the Alchemist at work) in search of arcane knowledge. Thus form, technique and meaning were transmitted from the *studiolo*, created as a small precious room in which to house securely even more precious objects which could be enjoyed behind closed doors, to the piece of furniture bearing the same name.

Already in the fifteenth century Florence was renowned for the excellence of its craft in the making of the *scrittorio* and portable writing desks. The former term would have referred to the larger type of cabinet with a writing flap, its *intarsia* panels of a cityscape in perspective echoing the theories of Alberti and Piero della Francesca. The latter phrase would describe the small, classical chest or cabinet with a fall-front brought to the West by the Arabs and introduced to Germany under Habsburg rule. A characteristic *studiolo* of the sixteenth century is the so-called Charles V Studiolo (named after the Habsburg Emperor), with its architectural forms, pilasters framing battle scenes at the back, while the fall-front reveals sets of drawers and illusionistic panels of *trompe-l'œil* writing implements and allegorical figures, all realized in an *intarsia* of various woods.

Italian influences was much to the fore in sixteenth-century Augsburg, as described in the eighteenth century by Paul von Stetten when referring to the marquetry techniques using variously coloured types of wood: 'The craftsmen would imitate paintings and the artists would give them instructions on how to do it.'[35] They produced mostly architectural and perspective views of the kind that Lorenz Stöer realized in woodcuts, but cityscapes, floral arrangements and historical scenes were also used as subject matter. In 1567 Lorenz Stöer had published a treatise of designs entitled *Geometria et Perspectiva* (Geometry and Perspective). His work inspired the type of marquetry portable writing cabinet – the

The Alchemist, *panel painting by Stradano from the* studiolo *of Francesco de' Medici, c. 1570; the Duke is depicted in the right foreground as the alchemist's assistant.*

Architectural perspective in intarsia, *detail of a panel from a* scrittorio *cabinet on a cupboard base in the Palazzo Davanzati, Florence, c. 1560–80.*

Schreibtisch – bearing scenes of fantastic ruined cities and strange abstract geometric designs for which Augsburg was famous. Augsburg became known for its production of writing desks, the most notable and elaborate example being produced for Charles V in 1554 by Lienhart Strohmeier: this piece had a façade in architectural form and was entirely carved with a complex allegorical theme allying literature, history and mythology (in a manner similar to that of the Galerie François I at Fontainebleau, executed in 1534–7).

After the Sack of Rome in 1527, a disastrous result of the recurring French campaigns in Italy, Francis I of France who, following his defeat at Pavia in 1525 and subsequent imprisonment in Madrid, had now been released, embarked upon his dream to recreate Rome on French soil. Work on the enlargement of Fontainebleau began in 1528 and Italian artists, lacking papal patronage, arrived there in 1530. Rosso and Primaticcio truly brought the Renaissance to the North and the decorative scheme of the Galerie was to provide new artistic inspiration for designers and craftsmen whose familiarity with it came about through engravings by Fantuzzi, Ruggieri, Limosin and others. The strapwork ornament used there became a standard Mannerist motif for all designers and *ornementistes* in northern Europe.

French designers published treatises on ornament: Androuet du Cerceau's *Les Petits Grotesques* (Small Grotesques) appeared in 1550 and Hugues Sambin's *Oeuvre de la Diversité des Termes dont on use en architecture'* (On the various Terms [Herms] used in architecture) in 1572. Cross-fertilization of ideas and motifs was taking place: Françis I had an Italian marquetry worker, Jehan Miquel Panthaleon, in his employ in 1532, while in 1576 a Saxon craftsman called Hans Kraus was recorded as '*Marqueteur du Roy*'. Until Fontainebleau French furniture had remained Gothic in style and form, with surface Renaissance decorative motifs making an appearance after the first Italian campaigns of Charles VIII in 1494.

The Burgundian tradition at the French court and in Flanders had always favoured a certain type of status-symbol furniture. Thus, the *dressoir* was used to show off the wealth of its owner with its display of silver and gold plate, but strict etiquette regulated the number of its

storeys at ceremonial functions: five for a reigning prince or the consort of a king: four for a younger prince; three for a Comte; two for a Chevalier; and none for an untitled host. They were always in evidence at official ceremonies, such as the reception of Isabel of Bavaria (wife of King Charles VI) in Paris in 1389, and also appeared in bedrooms, fulfilling the role of a cabinet. It 1380 the inventory of Charles V of France referred to 'Some of the smaller jewels to be found in the *dressoir* in the king's Bedchamber'.[36] In 1471 King René of Anjou had four such pieces in his study to hold his vases, lamps, silver and gold ewers, crystal cups and dishes, as well as curios and rarities.

The basis of the humanist idea of the private collection serving as a *theatrum mundi* was already apparent, and by 1539 in *Les Blasons Domestiques* the poet Gilles Corrozet was giving a description of the *dressoir* with two doors suitable for use as a cabinet.[37] Examples of collectors' cabinets of the time still exist all over Europe, being for the most part fairly plain, 'goodly' cabinets as described by Francis Bacon. Some, however became works of art in themselves, especially in Germany, and the *Wrangelschrank* of 1566 can be considered the first *Kunstschrank*, in which the idea of a writing desk has been abandoned and the many drawers are used to house works of art and curiosities, while the craftsmanship involved in the making of the piece itself makes it an object of wonder worthy of admiration. The *Wrangelschrank* was made in Augsburg by Lorenz Strohmeir and Bartlmä Weishaupt. Box-like in form, it has two doors decorated inside and out with pictorial marquetry of imaginary ruined cityscapes with birds and monkeys. Inside are two-storeyed alabaster double columns enclosing small doors decorated with historical scenes carved in boxwood, behind which are drawers and shelves. The marquetry of green-stained and burnt shaded wood is of outstanding brilliance and exuberance.

The sacrifice of convenience to art in the *Wrangelschrank*, remarked upon by Paul von Stetten in 1779,[38] increased in Augsburg as the dissemination of decorative motifs through engravings ensured a wealth of source material to be used in conjunction with new techniques and materials. Thus engravings by Virgil Solis of Nuremberg popularized the use of arabesques and classical allegorical figures. Vredeman de Vries made available the forms of classical architecture in 1560, in his *Variae*

The Wrangelschrank, *a table-cabinet with elaborate carved and marquetry decoration made in Augsburg and dated 1566, is considered the first example of the* Kunstschrank, *a piece with drawers and compartments to hold valuables which is also a work of art in its own right; width of cabinet 47 cm (18¼ in.).*

Opposite, above left
The central part of an ebony cabinet decorated with gilt-copper plaques depicting the Vices and Virtues by Wenzel Jamnitzer, Augsburg or Nuremberg, c. 1544–60; width 79.5 cm (18½ in.).

Opposite, above right
Table-cabinet damascened in gold and silver, with fall-front and representing an allegory of the rule of Emperor Maximilian II, shown as the central equestrian statuette in the guise of a Roman emperor. Made by Giovanni Battista Serabaglio, Milan, c. 1560; width 68.5 cm (2 ft 3 in.). See overleaf for an enlarged detail showing the elaborate decoration on the drawer-fronts.

Opposite, below
Ebony table-cabinet in the form of a temple, with embossed silver mounts depicting the Vices and Virtues, finials representing the Labours of Hercules, and a reclining statuette of Venus. Augsburg, c. 1580–90; width 62 cm (2 ft ½ in.).

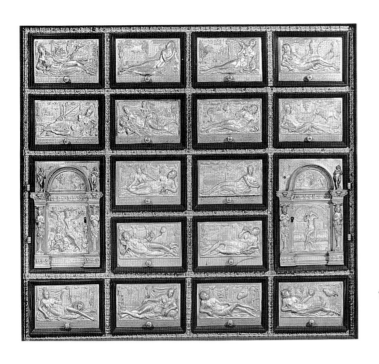

architecturae formae (Various architectural forms), so reinforcing the interest in classical Roman architecture already aroused by the drawings of Peter Vischer from Nuremberg following his visit to Italy in 1516.

Nuremberg was on a par with Augsburg for the production of fine-quality examples of the *Kunstschrank*. In 1483 a young Spanish knight returning from the crusades had described the free imperial city thus: 'Nuremberg is one of Germany's largest and richest cities . . . Many craftsmen live there, especially those who specialize in all kinds of bronzework, and it is there that Nuremberg coats-of-arms are made . . . The city is very rich, and because of its position in the middle of the continent its trade routes are many.'[39] Nuremberg became famous for its metalwork and produced the greatest Mannerist goldsmith in Germany, Wenzel Jamnitzer. As the demand for increasingly more costly *Kunstschränke* grew, he made plaques and statuettes to decorate them. An ebony-veneered cabinet now in Vienna shows his consummate skills in embossing and engraving the applied gilt-copper plates depicting Vices and Virtues, *c.* 1550–60. Also in Vienna is an ebony cabinet from Augsburg with silver mounts that evoke one of the favourite conceits of the late Renaissance, the idea that 'Love conquers all'.[40] This cabinet is built as a small ebony-veneered temple, with its uppermost storey occupied by an exquisite figure of a reclining Venus between representations of the Four Continents, while the finials of the second storey illustrate the Labours of Hercules, and the double doors of the cabinet proper open to reveal drawers with mounts in chased and embossed silver depicting the Vices and Virtues. The only hint of the distant antecedent of the *Schreibtisch* function of this *Kunstschrank* is provided by the inclusion of some writing implements in the upper drawer.

As a city, Milan was in a situation comparable to Nuremberg, both economically and artistically. In the sixteenth century it became the most important centre not only for the production of damascened steel used for arms and armour, but also for furniture-making. Its fame was widespread, and commissions were undertaken for foreign princes and aristocrats, hence the cabinet bearing the cipher of Diane de Poitiers. More important both historically and artistically is a cabinet in damascened work of iron, niello, gold and silver, in which the whole of past traditions was combined with a new symbolic message. Made in Milan *c.* 1560, it was conceived and realized as an allegory of the rule of the Emperor Maximilian II over Virtues, the Muses and classical deities. The Emperor, depicted on horseback wearing Roman armour – a treatment evoking the famous equestrian statue of Marcus Aurelius, thought then to represent the first Christian Emperor, Constantine – is represented as the embodiment of the notion of the 'Divine Right of Kings' on which the rule of all absolute monarchies in Europe was based in the seventeenth century. In form, decoration and meaning, the Maximilian Cabinet – with its classical figures, Mannerist vistas, Islamic arabesques – represents a seminal transitional piece heralding the late Mannerist *Kunstschränke* of the seventeenth century.

The whole ethos of the cabinet had changed irrevocably and while convenient pieces continued to be made for ordinary use, at the end of the sixteenth and the beginning of the seventeenth century major decorative pieces were closely linked with political power, the message being transmitted through the splendour of its art.

Detail showing decorated drawer-fronts on the Maximilian Cabinet (see previous page).

2
THE AGE OF MAGNIFICENCE

AT THE BEGINNING OF THE SEVENTEENTH CENTURY THE GERMAN cabinet trade was still very much in the ascendant in Europe. The power of Spain and Portugal was on the wane, and in 1597 Dutch traders had invaded the East Indies. According to a contemporary French chronicler, Pyrard de Laval, writing in 1610, cabinets 'à la mode de ceux d'Allemagne' (in the manner of those from Germany)[1] were being exported to Europe from the East Indies and from Japan. Examples of the *Schreibtisch* decorated with pictorial marquetry were still being produced, particularly in the Tyrol, which was the gateway to southern Germany for the introduction of the art of *intarsia* from Italy. Innsbruck, for example, had a long history of producing pictorial marquetry pieces, but the local production was more modest than that of Augsburg and Nuremberg, being aimed at a bourgeois clientele. Hence the subjects represented were of a more homely nature: hunting scenes, flowers and musical instruments adorned medium-sized cabinets having two doors and sometimes a hinged lid and side handles. Music was important to the Tyrolean clientele, and the Bayerisches Nationalmuseum in Munich owns an early example of a Mannerist *Schreibtisch* incorporating a small virginal in a plinth drawer. The upper part opens as a lid, while the inner door, decorated with the characteristic 'Hunter with a hare' motif in marquetry, reveals a central part in the form of an Italianate temple surrounded by small drawers.

The cabinet was no longer regarded simply as a convenient storage piece for valuables and documents, although this function remained, and its form was adapted as it came to be thought of primarily as a collector's cabinet, a *Kunstschrank*, to be used and displayed in the *Kunstkammer* or *Wunderkammer* – the cabinet of curiosities. The concept of the cabinet of curiosities had evolved from the medieval scholastic tradition via the humanist *studiolo* of the Renaissance. The Mannerist *studiolo* was still very much a private *camera secreta*, a secret chamber of small dimensions and without windows, which emphasized the arcane aspect of knowledge understandable only by the initiated.

At the end of the sixteenth century, however, new forces were at play. Political and religious instability associated with the Reformation movement in northern Europe no longer encouraged the pursuit of the *vita contemplativa*, even in the small city-states of Italy, whose rulers found themselves drawn into larger conflicts. Significantly, the Medici *studiolo* in Florence was transferred in 1584 from the Palazzo Vecchio to the Uffizi, where its whole ethos became transformed from a secret, private source of knowledge into a public statement intended to symbolize the legitimacy of the Medici dynasty.

This new public function of the *Kunstkammer*, originally a treasure chamber, became more intimately linked with the concept of the *Wunderkammer*, where not only wonders of art and nature could be admired, but through which a prince or king could be seen to encourage new scientific discoveries, hence bestowing on a particular dynasty the prestige of enlightened patronage. Prized objects once hidden behind doors decorated with learned metaphorical motifs were now displayed openly to give pleasure to the visitor and gratify the pride of the owner.

The art treasures of the Habsburg Empire were divided between the various princely residences: Vienna, Prague, Ambras each had a cabinet of curiosities. In Prague, wrote Thomas da Costa Kaufmann, 'Rudolf's

Table-cabinet with pictorial marquetry decoration, including (on the inside of the fall-front) a panel depicting musical trophies. Tyrol, c. 1600; width 52 cm (21 in.).

An Allegory of Sight *(detail) by Jan Brueghel the Elder, 1617; a cabinet with painted panels decorating the open doors is seen in the background.*

Kunstkammer had a role in diplomacy that was stressed by its stately setting'.[2] Cabinets would be used for display and storage, but often the cabinet itself became imbued with a distinct status and message.

Augsburg and Nuremberg retained their supremacy as centres for the production of fine princely pieces. As their proportions grew smaller, the materials used to decorate them became more precious, reflecting the exquisite aspect of the collections contained within. By then the wood most often used was ebony, an exotic and expensive hardwood. Its use prompted the Augsburg *Tischler* to identify their cabinets not only with their usual pine-cone mark, but from *c.* 1625 to add the word 'EBEN', to differentiate their work from the products of Munich, which were made mostly of ebonized pear-wood. The difference was an important one, and was reflected in a 1641 tax record of foreign goods entering France which pointedly mentioned 'Cabinets in ebony, embellished with gold, silver, gilt brass, painting, embroidery, large or small: the large ones 150 livres, the medium-sized ones 100 livres, the small ones 60 livres. Cabinets made of other painted woods coming from Germany or from other places 30 livres.'[3]

Ebony had been used for veneering and inlay in ancient Egypt. Now it was cut into plaques about 8 mm thick, which were glued to a plain carcase of cheaper wood. The extensive use of ebony veneers seems to have begun in Italy: a 1566 record described a room in the Ducal Palace of Mantua decorated by Francesco Capriani with panels of ebony and ivory. Ivory had never waned in popularity and, unlike the ebony trade which was renewed in the sixteenth century through Portuguese maritime expansion to the East Indies and along the African coast, it seems to have been readily available throughout the late Roman Empire and during the Middle Ages. The combination of ebony and ivory to produce an austere black-and-white colour contrast reflecting that of contemporary Spanish court dress, which had become fashionable throughout Europe, inspired the craft skills of a group of cabinetmakers in Spanish-ruled Naples at the turn of the century.

The art of ebony veneering and ivory engraving appears to have been brought to Italy by German and Netherlandish emigrant craftsmen. In 1568 the Electress Anna of Saxony was recorded in Dresden as possessing an ebony and ivory desk. In 1569 in Naples, a contract was signed on 31 July by Giovanni Battista de Curtis, described as an '*intarsiatore in avolio*' (ivory engraver), and Giacomo Fiammingo, a '*scrittorista*' (cabinetmaker), for the making of two cabinets in ivory, to be adorned with engraved designs based on Ovid's *Metamorphoses*. The Museum für Kunst und Gewerbe (Museum of Arts and Crafts) in Hamburg owns a *scrittorio* in ebony and ivory which bears the inscription '*Io Battista de Curtis faciebat*'.

Contemporary engravings inspired the designs of the ivory plaques: on the outside the depiction of the Four Ancient Monarchs (Alexander the Great; Nimrud of Assyria; Cyrus the Great of Persia; and Julius Caesar) are after Adriaen Collaerts, the scenes from the lives of the legendary founders of Rome, Romulus and Remus, were inspired by Giovanni Battista Fontana (who was commissioned by the Archduke of Tyrol to execute a series of scenes), and the world map on the writing flap is after the French cartographer Postel, *c.* 1581. The map bears a further signature '*iannuarius picicaro fecit anno 1597*'. The iconography of the cabinet as a whole illustrates a complex and elaborate dynastic history of the House of Habsburg.

Several other examples of Neapolitan production in ebony and ivory are known: two similar *scrittori* now in the Museo di San Martino in Naples are dated 1619 and 1623 respectively, and other pieces also display a definite political and diplomatic message. One such piece in London has been attributed to Theodore de Voghel, a Netherlandish craftsman employed at the Royal Armoury in Naples, so providing a link between this type of cabinetwork and the art of decorating weapons, as well as with the metalworkers' technique of damascening. Another cabinet, now in a private collection, bears the signature of the engraver – 'Antonio Espano' – and is dedicated to the greatness of the Kingdom of Spain and its dynastic rule over Naples. Above the central door of the temple front is a portrait of Fernando of Aragon (1452–1516), who had been instrumental in driving the French out of Naples in 1503. When the central door is opened, the internal drawers are revealed, surmounted by the Royal arms of Spain flanked by portraits of Charles V (1500–58), the Holy Roman Emperor, and Philip II of Spain (1527–98), respectively the grandson and great-grandson of Fernando. These cabinets seem to have been produced to order as presentation pieces and diplomatic gifts. Other cities followed the example of Naples, but without the strong political connotations. Milan, once more an important centre for making fine arms and armour, produced some ebony and ivory cabinets with engraved decoration of allegorical subjects and arabesques inspired by the work of Virgil Solis.

In Augsburg and Nuremberg cabinetmaking had become not only the art of veneering by woodworkers, but allied their skills to those of the gold- and silversmith, the ivory turner, the sculptor, the lapidary cutter. Many different precious and exotic materials glowed against the shiny dark surfaces of ebony: ivory, coral, amber, coloured shagreen, tortoiseshell, mother-of-pearl, brightly coloured enamelled panels, cameos and intaglios, coins and medals both antique and *all'antica*, as well as *pietra dura* panels from Italy and exquisite statuettes and reliefs by Matthäus Wallbaum, the eminent Augsburg goldsmith – all of these were used to create microcosms of artistic virtuosity and aesthetic wonderment.

In 1610 Philipp Hainhofer, a scholar, diplomat, connoisseur, collector and art dealer in Augsburg, wrote: 'Here very beautiful *Schreibtische* are made of ebony, ivory and other woods, with secrets or without, which are bought as far afield as Prague, France, Italy and Spain.'[4] Hainhofer was truly a man of the Renaissance. Having studied law in Padua and travelled extensively in Europe on diplomatic missions on behalf of several German princes and Henry IV of France, he was not only able to absorb the sum of knowledge available at the time by making personal visits to scholars and humanists, but was also keenly aware of beauty, beautiful objects and how to acquire them, for he brought back luxury items such as furs, elegant foreign garments and exquisite toilet objects, as well as acting as a dealer and banking broker for the princes and kings he served. He was a shrewd businessman who know how to promote his trade, as his extensive correspondence shows.

Hainhofer brought the concept and the form of the humanist cabinet to its greatest height. From a practical storage piece which had developed into a work of art in its own right, as the *Wrangelschrank*, he conceived

Table-cabinet in ebony with ivory plaques depicting scenes from Ovid's Metamorphoses, *made by Theodore de Voghel, Naples, c. 1600; width 62 cm (2 ft ¼ in.).*

Detail of table-cabinet in rosewood and ebony with ivory plaques depicting scenes associated with the history of Naples and Spanish rule over the city; the detail (from the front of the cabinet) includes a portrait of Fernando of Aragon. Naples, c. 1600; height 60 cm (23½ in.). See also p. 11.

The delivery of the Pommersche Kunstschrank *by Philipp Hainhofer to Duke Philipp II of Pomerania at Schloss Stettin in 1617; oil on copper by Anton Mozart.*

and had realized by the best craftsmen of Augsburg, not only works of art, but the ultimate miniature *Kunst- und Wunderkammer* – cabinets enclosing other works of art and curiosities, a microcosm of the whole known world in a princely precious setting. However, as Maurice Sceve wrote in 1562 in his *Microcosme*, these cabinets had to be 'as much for delight as for convenience' and the concept of the cabinet of curiosities as a *theatrum mundi* advocated that it should represent 'not only art but also the practical aspects of the world' (*Muséographie*, 1727). It also had to reflect the *argutezze della natura* – the wit of nature.[5] In the words of Oliver Impey, 'It would make little difference whether a beautiful vessel was turned in ivory by an artist, or was shaped in the form of a conch shell by God the Almighty, the greatest artist of them all.'[6]

This all-embracing cosmic awareness of the inherent link of all that exists within the hidden order of things came to fruition in 1610 with the commission from the Duke of Pomerania for a small *Schreibtisch*. There ensued a lengthy exchange of ideas and proposals leading to the execution of the so-called 'Pommersche Kunstschrank' and its delivery in 1617 at the castle of Stettin by Philipp Hainhofer himself. The occasion was recorded by Anton Mozart in a small oil painting on copper, depicting the moment of presentation and including the contents of the cabinet as a perpetual reminder. The presentation and the viewing of a cabinet was an important event in its own right. Hainhofer would deliver these exceptional pieces personally, accompanied by the craftsman (*Kunsttischler*) in charge – in the case of the Pommersche Kunstschrank this was Ulrich Baumgartner – who would explain the secret features of the piece and hand over the keys to the owner.

The cabinet, 130 cm in height, had an outer case made of walnut, ebony and ivory. Once it was removed, the full splendour of the cabinet itself would be revealed: at the top the silver group of Mount Parnassus with the nine Muses and the Liberal Arts; on the lower part the Four Continents, the Heavens with the Zodiac, the planets, stars, days of the year etc. were represented, Man, with his virtues and attributes, being the underlying theme throughout. The Cosmos was thus defined gradually as the cabinet doors and drawers revealed the fruits of the labours of members of thirty-one different corporations who contributed to the realization of the works of art, silver and gold objects of everyday use – a clock, a silver canteen, boxes and rings, a prayer-book, games – as well as tools of various trades which the humanist prince would have very likely used himself. Ivory turning, medal engraving and clockmaking were all pursuits favoured by royal princes and aristocrats from the sixteenth to the eighteenth century. All these objects would have been taken out carefully one by one to be viewed, discussed and meditated upon for several days. Indeed the Pommersche Kunstschrank was intended to be exhibited in Schloss Stettin's *Kunst- und Wunderkammer* as its main and central feature, a highly complex intellectual scheme linking its component parts with the exhibits from Art and Nature displayed all around on shelves. Reminiscences and associations governed the particular use of certain woods and other natural materials: leather, silk, tortoiseshell, mother-of-pearl, ivory, minerals and metals, linking the whole in an esoteric system of correspondences, depicted on the *scrittorio di pietre dure*, where a flat strapwork embraces symbols and devices representing Life and Death, Night and Day, together with the Liberal Arts and humanist activities.

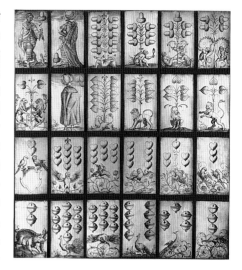

A humanist microcosm of contemporary universal knowledge conceived on such an ambitious scale would only be realized for very special scholarly clients at a very high cost. The total cost of the cabinet and its contents would have been about 1,000 Gulden, which Hainhofer would then sell for between 5,000 or 6,000 Gulden. Such cabinets were obviously aimed at a rarified élite, but Hainhofer had two others made and filled with items drawn from his own collection. One of these, now in Uppsala, was begun in 1625 for Hainhofer himself but was eventually sold to the City of Augsburg for presentation to King Gustavus Adolphus of Sweden in 1632. It is a work of art as well as wonderment, with its small proportions, its glowing inlay of semi-precious stones, and the astonishing top sculptural group made of shells and coral, with a coco de mer from which emerges a ravishing golden figure of Venus. Its many drawers and cupboards conceal rarities of art and nature and include a small spinet with French music sheets. Another cabinet is now in the Pitti Palace, Florence, having been given to Ferdinand II, Grand Duke of Tuscany, by Archduke Leopold of Austria in 1628: *Lo Stipo d'Alemagna*, made of ebony and decorated with semi-precious stones, is on a larger scale than the two previous ones, and has strongly architectural lines.

Hainhofer's cabinets were exceptional in their refinement of conception and execution, but were not the only such cabinets being produced in Augsburg: in Hamburg there is an ebony cabinet with ivory, stamped 'EBEN', *c.*1625; another in the Art Institute of Chicago displays a clock not as part of the content, but as a frontal ornamental feature, a development which was to become a standard design feature thereafter. Dated *c.*1630–40, the Chicago cabinet incorporates a complete set of apothecary's wares and instruments. The association of the cabinet with pharmacy was a longstanding one, going back to antiquity, but

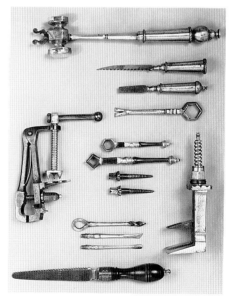

A selection of the varied content of the Pommersche Kunstschrank: *sets of silver-gilt German and Italian playing cards with engraved designs, and specimen tools.*

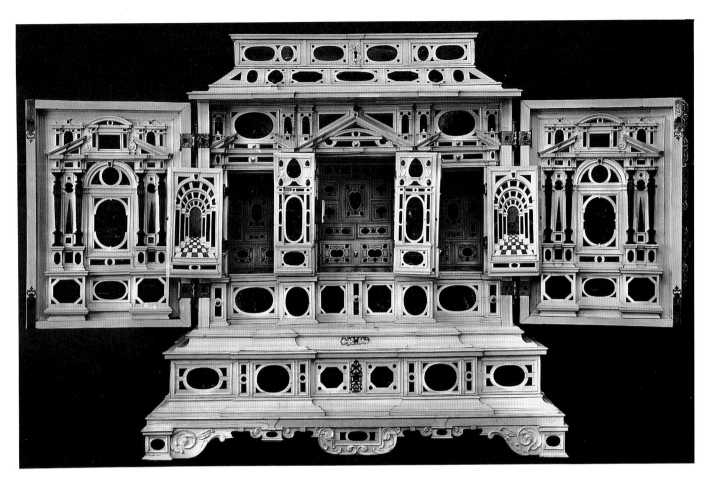

Table-cabinet with overall veneer of ivory combined with lapis lazuli, made by Melchior Baumgartner for the Bavarian court, c. 1646; width 100.5 cm (3 ft 3¼ in.).

Hainhofer's cabinets and related pieces include a pharmacy set as a demonstration of another aspect of humanist knowledge of the time. The tradition seems to have continued until the end of the century, and the standard fittings would include five or six parcel-gilt vessels each with a lid and a lion mask, some square bottles with screw-top stoppers, a mortar, silver sieves, a beaker and a large silver bowl, scales and weights, as well as assorted spoons, knives, scissors, spatulas and scrapers. The prevailing fascination with alchemy may have prompted the interest of humanists, such as Francesco I de' Medici, as much as any legitimate curiosity they may have had in the science of medicine.

Like ebony, ivory could be used as an overall veneer. In 1646 Melchior Baumgartner signed an ivory and lapis lazuli cabinet (now in the Bayerisches Nationalmuseum), as well as one combining ivory and enamelled silver plates. Both have a two-door façade, with doors on the sides, and must have been commissioned by the court in Munich to incorporate the blue-and-white national colours of Bavaria. The pieces display a strongly architectural form, with arches and perspectives and behind the façades a multitude of drawers and secret drawers. Secret drawers and compartments would be included so as to astonish the viewer on seeing the artist-craftsman's ingenuity and virtuosity, hence the need to have a 'demonstration' of the cabinet's particular features when it was acquired. The ivory and enamelled cabinet includes no less than 177 drawers and compartments, one of the latter being used specifically to house chess pieces. This cabinet was bought in 1655 by the Electress Maria-Anna of Bavaria, for the sum of 3,150 Gulden. The refinement and virtuosity apparent in these two cabinets are evidence of the tradition of cabinetmaking skills built up over a century in Augsburg.

The Bavarian court had become an important artistic centre under Maximilian I, whose reign brought stability and a unified legal system to the country, confirmed in 1616 by the *Codex Maximilianus*. He was an enlightened humanist who organized a workshop of craftsmen and artists to embellish and expand the Residenz in Munich under the supervision of Peter Candid. His art collection was renowned, and he also collected coins and medals, for which he commissioned Christoph Angermair to make him a cabinet *c.* 1618. Angermair, a well-known ivory turner, had carved the chess set included in the Pommersche Kunstschrank. In 1613 he was recorded as being active in Munich, where he became Ivory Turner to the Court.

The concept of a coin cabinet was not new. Italian princes and humanists had started collecting ancient coins and medals, especially after Pisanello revived the art of the medal in the fifteenth century. Later, royal collectors came to regard antique coinage as a direct dynastic link with the past and collecting as a way of acquiring power and political prestige. The Kunsthistorisches Museum in Vienna has two coin cabinets from former royal collections. The earlier of the two, dated 1590, was made in Innsbruck for Ferdinand II; it is a box-like construction with multiple drawers, function being all-important, and the piece has surface decoration of marquetry. Self-glorification was an important factor in the seventeenth century, and the 1638 Augsburg coin cabinet, made of ebony and stamped 'EBEN', produced for Ferdinand III is a complex structure; it has two doors concealing a combination of drawers and a central niche, the whole being decorated with silver, cameos and ivory, with a silver allegorical statuette of Germany depicted as a crowned female figure holding an eagle. The piece bears an inscription in Latin listing the various titles of its royal owner.

The Maximilian coin cabinet, made roughly twenty years earlier, is likewise a complex piece with a significant political message. Like the Pommersche Kunstschrank, it has an outer cover, made of walnut, ebony and ivory, to protect the cabinet proper. Opening this cover, which is notable for its startling abstract geometric design, would be part of the anticipated pleasure of viewing the collection within. The cabinet therefore fulfilled not just the function of a storage place for the precious and extensive collection, but it would also encourage meditation and contemplation by virtue of the classical allusions visible on its outside, dominated by an equestrian statuette in ivory depicting Marcus Aurelius (then thought to represent the first Christian Roman Emperor) on the Campidoglio in Rome. A highly allegorical theme based on the idea of monarchy runs through the whole decorative scheme, accompanied by a cryptic inscription – *Sedulo quaesita recondunt* (They are hiding what they have been seeking eagerly) – referring to the coins and perhaps also to past glory. The doors open to reveal a blue-and-white interior of ivory, enamel and lapis lazuli, a lighter note being provided by the interior decoration of the doors, on which the love of music shared by the Elector and his wife is depicted in Arcadian scenes. The cabinet thus served to combine pleasures of the mind and those of the senses.

In order to fulfil the increasing artistic needs of a powerful dynasty, Cosimo I de' Medici (1519–74) opened, on the first floor of the Uffizi, a workshop – the Galleria dei Lavori – with the renowned artist Vasari at its head. The Galleria employed native and foreign craftsmen whose

Coin cabinet in Brazilian rosewood with marquetry decoration of box, pearwood, walnut and maple, made for the Emperor Ferdinand II. Innsbruck, 1590; 77.5 cm (2 ft 6½ in.) square.

Opposite, above
Coin cabinet in ebony with applied silver and ivory cameos and surmounted by a silver statuette symbolizing Germany, made for the Emperor Ferdinand III. Augsburg, 1638; width 77.5 cm (2 ft 6½ in.).

Opposite, below
Coin cabinet in ivory and lapis lazuli (right) made for Maximilian I of Bavaria by Christoph Angermair, c. 1618–24, together with its outer cover in walnut, ebony and ivory (fitted with carrying handles); width of cabinet 44.5 cm (17¼ in.).

entire production for the benefit of the Medici court. During the last years of the sixteenth century, German *Kunsttischler* from Augsburg and Nuremberg had introduced the fashion for ebony furniture to Italy. In Florence they served the Medici court, working in the Galleria dei Lavori. Thus, in 1600, when the centre of the Galleria, the Tribuna, had to be decorated and furnished, the alcove was adorned with an ebony-veneered cabinet designed by Buontalenti for Ferdinand I; this cabinet was encrusted with jewels, in the German tradition, and built on strongly architectural lines, following the earlier Florentine tendency to use classical motifs. The *stipo* (now lost) was described by John Evelyn when he visited Florence in October 1644:

They then led us into a large Square roome, in the middle whereoff stood a Cabinet of an octangular forme, so adorn'd and furnish'd with Christals, Achat, Sculptures etc as certainly exceeds any description. . . . Likewise another, which had about it 8 oriental Columns of Alabaster, on each whereof was plac'd a head of a Caesar, cover'd with a Canopy so richly beset with precious Stones, that they resembled a firmament of Starrs! This Cabinet was valued at 2 hundred thousand crownes. Within it was our Saviour Passion & 12 Apostles of incomparable Amber.

In another, with Calcidon Pillars, was a Series of Golden Medaills. In this [the] Cabinet is called the 'Tribuna', in which is a pearle as big as a haizel nut. The Cabinet is of Ebonie, [Lapis] Lazuli and Jasper; over the doore a round of M: Angelo; on the Cabinet, Leo the Tenth, with other paintings of Raphaels, del Sartos, Perugino & Correggio viz a St. John, a Virgin, a boy, two Apostles and 2 heads of Durer rarely carved. Here is also another rich ebony Cabinet cupola'd with a tortois shell and containing a collection of gold Medaills esteem'd worth 50,000 crounes, a wreathed Pillar of Oriental Alabaster, divers paintings of Da Vinci, Pontormo, del Sarto, an Ecce Homo of Titian, a Boy of Bronzini [sc. Bronzino] etc. . . . .[7]

This meticulous description echoes the splendour of the Augsburg workshop and also highlights the very public function the Tribuna was now performing, as distinct from the private nocturnal world of the original *studiolo* in the fifteenth and early sixteenth centuries. It was now more of a treasure room and personal museum reflecting both the taste and wealth of the owner and the power of the dynasty, to be visited and viewed as a museum echoing its earlier forms, content and decoration, though without its original humanist scheme.

The system of organization in the Galleria dei Lavori was of seminal importance for the development of the decorative arts in the seventeenth and eighteenth centuries. Tapestry weavers, cabinetmakers, bronze casters and gilders, goldsmiths and silversmiths, were all rigidly organized as *cottimanti* (craftsmen) working under the supervision of a *capomaestro*, who ran the workshop. A famous artist was usually employed in this capacity, Vasari being succeeded by the architect and sculptor Buontalenti.

The circumventing of local guild regulations by having a princely workshop employing 'free' craftsmen from all over Europe spread fashion and techniques far and wide. The idea was adopted at the court of Rudolf II in Prague, where Italian workers were employed; at the Louvre in Paris by Henry IV, eventually leading to the creation of the Manufacture des Gobelins under Louis XIV; and in the workshops of Buen Retiro in Madrid under Charles III of Spain, who, as Don Carlos, King of Naples, took into his service the Florentine craftsmen left without patronage following the death of the last of the Medici Grand Dukes, Gian Gastone, in 1737.

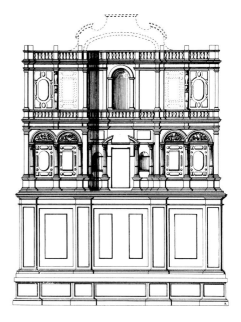

Reconstruction of the Tribuna in the Galleria dei Lavori of the Uffizi, Florence, made for Ferdinand de' Medici c. 1600.

Opposite
19 Kunstschrank *in ebony with* pietra dura *and* pietra paesina *inlay, made for Philipp Hainhofer and presented by the City of Augsburg to King Gustavus Adolphus of Sweden in 1632. The top decoration includes rock crystal, coral and coco de mer; height 184.5 cm (6 ft ¾ in.).*

20 Table-cabinet in ebony with pietra dura panels depicting scenes from Aesop's Fables. Florence, c. 1615–23; width 96.8 cm (3 ft 2 in.).

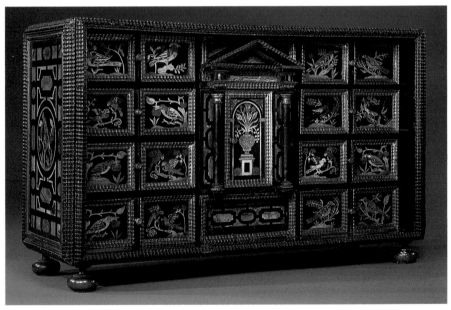

21, 22 Table-cabinet in ebony and ivory shown closed and with hinged flap open revealing drawers around a central cupboard, executed in the manner of Jacopo Fiammengo, Naples c. 1600–20; width 84 cm (2 ft 9 in.).

23 Table-cabinet in ebonized parcel-gilt pearwood with scagliola panels featuring geometric patterns and motifs based on the pietra dura 'Chaffinch' design. Florence, c. 1640; width 110 cm (3 ft 7 in.).

In Naples, which was under Spanish rule at the beginning of the seventeenth century, the *escritorio*-type cabinet with a fall-front opening to reveal drawers continued to be made; such pieces feature a characteristic black-and-white colour contrast resulting from the use of ebony and ivory. The *papelera* – a small table-cabinet with feet but no door – was also imitated in Italy. The generally horizontal emphasis of its form was combined with decoration in imitation of classical architecture and the use of techniques from ancient Rome.

24, 25 Interior façade and general view of table-cabinet in ebony with scagliola panels imitating pietra dura inlay (lapis lazuli, cornelian, jasper) and rock-crystal columns, the upper part enclosing secret compartments. Florence, c. 1650–60.

Above and right
26, 27 Architectural table-cabinet in ebony with tortoiseshell decoration and gilt plaques, surmounted by statuettes of figures from classical antiquity; when opened, the side doors reveal intricate internal perspectives. Naples or Rome. c. 1650, width 129 cm (4 ft 2¾ in.).

Left
28 Ebony cabinet (on later stand) with cupboard doors and drawer fronts veneered with tortoiseshell and decorated with lacquer. Flanders, c. 1650–70; width 89.5 cm (2 ft 11¼ in.).

In the seventeenth century the proportions of the cabinet grew larger under the influence of the Baroque, resulting in a grand furniture type – the *meuble de parade et d'apparat* – largely based on architectural lines and using a variety of rare and precious materials. From *c.* 1640 tortoiseshell was employed as a veneer, with a backing of red pigment or gold foil to simulate the rich, warm tones of amber.

29 Ebony and tortoiseshell cabinet-on-stand (one of a pair) with scenes painted in the manner of Luca Giordano under glass; the stand features carved figures of blackamoors. Naples, c. 1650–70; width 2.49 m (8 ft 2 in.).

30 Cabinet-on-stand in ebony and ebonized wood with inlaid tortoiseshell, the central cupboard door and flanking niches containing mythological figures in gilt bronze. Naples, c. 1630–40; width 174 cm (5 ft 8 in.).

After the separation of the Northern Provinces of the Netherlands in 1579, Flanders remained under Spanish rule and continued to be exposed to strong Italianate influences which affected both techniques and styles of decoration. Antwerp, where Rubens settled in 1608, became an important cabinetmaking centre from which luxury furniture in the grand Baroque style was exported all over Europe.

Above
31 Ebony table-cabinet with painted panels of biblical subjects after works by Paolo Veronese and Domenico Fetti. Antwerp, c. 1650–70; width 107 cm (3 ft 7 in.).

Left
32, 33 Cabinet-on-stand in ebony with tortoiseshell and ivory veneer and panels with scenes painted on copper depicting the 'Loves of the Gods' and the Trojan War in the manner of Rubens (detail below). Antwerp, c. 1650–70; width 109 cm (3 ft 7 in.).

Opposite
34 Ebony cabinet with painted alabaster panels depicting Italianate landscapes; the gilt stand incorporates sculptures of the Four Seasons. Antwerp, c. 1670; width 141 cm (4 ft 7½ in.).

Woven fabrics were used in England and Flanders as a base for pictorial decoration. The techniques employed included embroidery in *gros* and *petit point*, stumpwork and cut paperwork, all on a silk background. In addition to historical and biblical events, subjects ranged from floral still-lifes to animals (derived from bestiaries) and motifs from pattern books.

Above
37 *Small needlework casket covered with decoration depicting the life of Joseph in silk embroidery on an ivory-coloured ground. England, c. 1660; width 35 cm (14 in.).*

38 *Table-cabinet in ebonized wood with panels of silk embroidery in gros and* petit point *depicting flowers. Antwerp, c. 1670–80; width 86 cm (2 ft 10 in.).*

Left
35, 36 *Silk-covered casket with paperwork decoration made to celebrate the marriage in 1661 of Charles II and Catherine of Braganza. England, c. 1661, width 28 cm (11in.).*

39 Table-cabinet in ebony with hinged
mirrored lid and decorative panels of
stumpwork and embroidery on silk.
Antwerp, c. 1660–80; width 52.5 cm
(20½ in.).

40 Ebony table-cabinet with fall-front
showing drawers with gold and silver
embroidery depicting whales and
cachalots. Antwerp, c. 1650–70.

After the middle of the seventeenth century veneers began to be used throughout Europe. Variegated wood burrs forming striking patterns were favoured in England and Holland, while Germany maintained its traditional use of pictorial marquetry. In Holland a distinctive floral version was developed, and in France tortoiseshell and metal were combined to form the stylized *rinceaux* of Boulle work.

41 Cabinet-on-stand with laburnum oystershell veneer. England, c. 1690–1700; width 94 cm (3 ft 1 in.).

42 Cabinet-on-stand with kingwood veneer, England, c. 1685–95; width 112 cm (3 ft 8 in.).

Above
44 Cabinet-on-stand with floral marquetry by Jan van Mekeren. Amsterdam, c. 1690–95; height 2.05 m (6 ft 9 in.).

Left
43 Cabinet-on-stand in walnut and ebonized wood with pictorial marquetry and three Salomonic columns. South Germany, c. 1680–90; width 152.5 cm (5 ft).

Opposite
45 Cabinet with ebony, pewter and tortoiseshell inlay and floral marquetry, mounted on a painted and gilt stand. André Charles Boulle, France, c. 1675–80; width 134 cm (4 ft 5 in.).

Increased European trade with the Orient following the formation of the Dutch and English East India Companies in the early seventeenth century encouraged the importation of lacquered cabinets from China and Japan. The original lacquer wares made for export were imitated in Europe using shellac or gumlac varnishes. The rich colours of oriental lacquer and japanned decoration were set off by combining the cabinets with carved stands, either gilt or silvered, in an exuberant Baroque style.

46, 47   White-japanned cabinet (closed and open), Anglo-Dutch, c. 1690–1700; width 111 cm (3 ft 8 in.). The locks and gilt stand are of continental origin.

48 Chinese Coromandel lacquer cabinet on a gilt stand, Anglo-Dutch, c. 1690–1700; width 114 cm (3 ft 9 in.).

Below, left
49 Japanned cabinet on a silvered stand; the floral painting is in the Dutch manner. England, c. 1680; width 108 cm (3 ft 6½ in.).

Below
50 Cabinet with Japanese lacquer decoration of the Momoyama period (1573–1615), reconstructed in Goa, c. 1640–50; width 94 cm (3 ft 1 in.).

The development of floral marquetry and the contemporary 'tulipomania' in Holland led to the fashion for floral decoration being disseminated throughout Europe, notably by the Dutch cabinetmakers Leonardo van der Vinne (active in Florence) and Pierre Gole (working in Paris); through them the technique was endowed with local characteristics and further refinements.

51 Cabinet-on-stand in ebony, rosewood and tortoiseshell, with floral marquetry of stained bone and mother-of-pearl, in the manner of Leonardo van der Vinne. Florence, c. 1680; width 126 cm (4 ft 1½ in.).

52 Small table-cabinet in ebonized wood with floral painting in the Dutch manner; the interior has eleven drawers plus one secret drawer. Holland, c. 1660–70; width 42 cm (16½ in.).

Opposite
53 Cabinet-on-stand in ebony with tortoiseshell and floral marquetry, attributed to Pierre Gole. France, c. 1660; width 142 cm (4 ft 8 in.).

54 *Walnut cabinet-on-stand with oystershell and floral marquetry, England, c. 1690–1700; width 130 cm (4 ft 8 in.).*

Pietra dura

Unlike the art of mosaic using tesserae (small cubes of stone) set in mortar, the ancient Roman technique of inlaying semi-precious stones and marble – *pietra dura* or *commesso di pietre dure*, reintroduced in the mid-sixteenth century – is more like *intarsia*, each piece being cut to fit tightly on a prepared ground, the intention being to achieve a homogeneous whole. No doubt the rediscovery of nature and the classical tradition during the Renaissance prompted a renewed interest in the technique, together with its obvious pictorial quality.

In 1580 Duke Francesco I de' Medici attracted some Milanese *pietra dura* workers to his palace in Florence, the Casino di S. Marco, and in 1599 Ferdinand I opened the Opificio delle Pietre Dure as a specialist workshop for the *intagliatori* in the Galleria dei Lavori. The distinctive inlay of hard and semi-precious stones (agate, chalcedony, lapis lazuli, malachite etc.) was used for *objets d'art* and decorative panels featuring birds, flowers, grotesques and landscapes, for which the Opificio became famous. Ferdinand I wrote that the *commesso di pietre dure* was a Florentine and Medici invention – a '*più ingegnoso artificio*' (a more ingenious technique) than mosaic, utilizing the natural colouring of the stones in order to achieve a greater range of nuances.

The technique of *commesso di pietre dure* was described in 1597 in a treatise on the history of glyptics by the Dominican monk Agostino de Riccio. The art carried much prestige and presentation pieces were often made as gifts for foreign sovereigns. In the late sixteenth century, Queen Elizabeth I of England was given a table with a *pietra dura* top by the Grand Duke. In 1604 the Opificio was given a major commission: the decoration of the entire wall space in the Medici Mausoleum. This extensive project was never completed, but it brought the exquisite quality of works executed in *pietra dura* to the attention of travellers making the Grand Tour. The Uffizi Galleria was used to exhibit some of the most ravishing pieces realized for the altar of the mausoleum and visitors were encouraged to commission similar panels to take home as souvenirs.

Thus John Evelyn, who visited the Galleria in 1644, recorded that the *pietra dura* tabernacle exhibited there was 'estemed one of the most curious pieces of art in the World' and that it had already 'ben 40 yeares in finishing'.[8] In fact it was never finished, but it certainly helped spread the fame of the Florentine craft far and wide. Evelyn himself bought from Domenico Benotti, whom he called 'a celebrated master . . . for Pietro Commesso, 19 panels of the same work for a cabinet'.[9] The resulting piece (now in the Victoria and Albert Museum) would have been executed in Florence during Evelyn's stay in Rome. The Evelyn Cabinet is just one example of a number of such works to be found in European collections. Italian craftsmen were also called to foreign courts, the most notable being Cosimo Castrucci, a Florentine, who was employed at the court of Rudolf II in Prague, where a distinctive style of pictorial landscape evolved, featuring a carefully composed recession in space, with rocks, villages, rivers and paths, punctuated by trees and shrubs in the foreground and middle distance. Members of the Miseroni family from Milan were also active as *intagliatori di pietre dure* in the service of Rudolf II. Other leading centres of *pietra dura* production included

Table-cabinet in ebony with inlaid pietra dura *panels, one of which is shown enlarged. Florence, c. 1620–30; width 96.8 cm (3ft 2 in.).*

Rome, where the art of mosaics had been practised almost without interruption since antiquity. It was revived in 1516 when the banker Agostino Chigi commissioned some mosaic work, based on cartoons by Raphael, for his funerary chapel in Sta Maria del Popolo.

In the early seventeenth century the virtuosity of the so-called 'Florentine work' was unsurpassed. The highly skilled craftsmen involved in the various stages of the process included: the prospectors (*scarpellini*), who assessed the quality of the stone; the stone cutters (*segatori*), who revealed the veining effect or translucency of the material to its greatest advantage; the carvers (*intagliatori*), who bevelled the cut stones very precisely before fitting them to the prepared ground, on which a mixture of resin, wax, gypsum and turpentine would be used. The final stages would be undertaken by the *commettitori*, who would fix the whole composition onto a ground, often of white or black marble, before the polishers (*lustratori*) applied the finishing touches. It is therefore nearly impossible to attribute a finished piece to a particular artist or studio with any accuracy, such was the division of labour and the complexity of the process.

The favoured themes were *vedute*, landscapes, mythological and literary scenes, still-lifes, birds and flowers. From the beginning the art of *commesso di pietre dure* was intimately linked with that of lapidary craftsmen and of jewellers, who were the first *intagliatori*. However, as the craft developed, its own painterly characteristics took over and presented different aspects from the art of glyptics. In the early sixteenth and seventeenth centuries *pietra dura* work had a translucent background of white marble or other light-reflecting stone, often backed with gold or silver foil to emphasize this quality further. Bands or sheets of precious metals were also used, the technique and resulting effect being close to the art of the jeweller. Favourite materials were agate, amethyst, rock crystal, chalcedony, jasper and lapis lazuli. The *commesso* used the natural quality of each stone to depict the scene in a realistic manner:

Ebonized table-cabinet with scagliola *panels in imitation of red marble from Verona. Florence, c. 1630–50; width 53.5 cm (21 in.).*

Architectural table-cabinet in ebony with columns and decorative panels of pietra dura. Rome, c. 1600–20.

Table-cabinet in oak and ebony incorporating pietra dura *panels, made in Florence c. 1644–5 for John Evelyn (the gilt-bronze plaques by Francesco Fanelli date from c. 1646–52 and the ogee top and gallery were added in the nineteenth century); width 123 cm (4 ft ½ in.).*

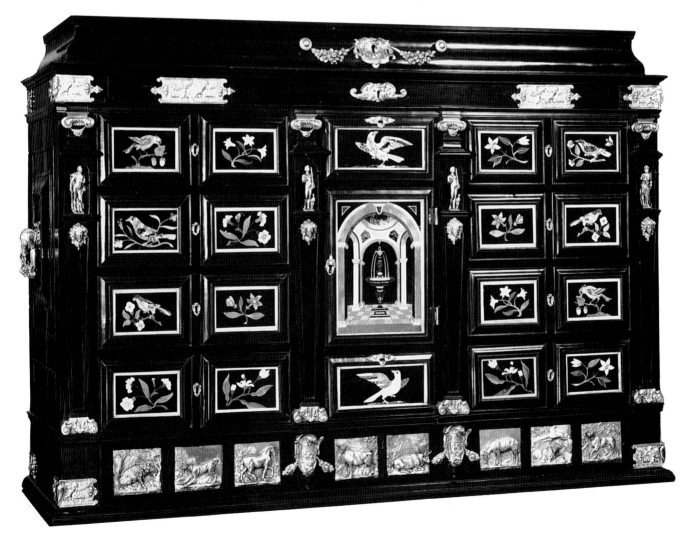

thus lapis lazuli would recreate the sky and water while rocks and mountains would be evoked with the brown-green-yellow veining of jasper, which was highly regarded for its versatility and praised in 1587 by the physician and philosopher Andrea Bacci.

From 1612 onwards the background was often of black marble, later replaced by a blue-black, white-veined flint known as *paonazetto di Fiandra*. The pieces used became smaller and more numerous; the sky was now rendered in chalcedony or a speckled stone, instead of lapis lazuli, no longer in common use, while the richly-veined Sicilian jasper was replaced by a Bohemian variety. In the 1620s taste and fashion veered towards the use of a particular type of stone with characteristic and evocative veining: this was the *pietra paesina* (literally, 'landscape stone'), an Albarese limestone which, after being polished, reveals a natural pattern resembling rocky mountainous outlines, and *Arno lineato*, a different variety of the Albarese limestone featuring wavy patterns suggestive of seas and rivers. Both stones provided a perfect background for painted landscapes, which became very fashionable at that time. This latter technique would have had a special appeal to the humanist's view of the world, bringing together as it did the wonders of the natural world and the refining influence of man's artistic and scientific achievements.

As well as reviving the ancient art of *pietra dura* inlay, the Opificio resumed the use of an imitation version, *scagliola*, formerly employed as a cheaper substitute in classical times. Finely powdered coloured marble and selenite were mixed with plaster and glue to form a reconstituted marble, which was then applied to a wet plaster ground and finally polished to bring out colour and sheen. Not only was *scagliola* a cheaper technique, but it also enabled artists to achieve a finer, more painterly quality in the depiction of subject-matter adopted from *pietra dura* models. *Scagliola* was highly prized in its own right and was used by Philipp Hainhofer in the decoration of the Pommersche Kunstschrank, completed in 1617.

By the middle of the seventeenth century the characteristic Florentine cabinet, combining *pietra dura* panels and gilt-bronze mounts glowing against the dark surface of the ebony, had evolved from past architectural forms and a new sense of the Baroque inspired by Rome. The present cabinet displayed in the Medici Tribuna has all the attributes of a dynastic showpiece made to glorify the Medici and Ferdinand II, whose emblems it bears. Designed by Matteo Nigetti, the gilt-bronze mounts were executed by Carlo Balatri and Francesco Mocchi. This cabinet is altogether a departure from the earlier one made for the Tribuna; its sculptural quality and architectural form inspired by Baroque façades show the influence of Bernini, who had executed a display cabinet for the Medici court, a *scarabattolo* for the Duke's amber collection.

Smaller Florentine table-cabinets continued to be made in the *scrittorio* tradition, but, like their Augsburg counterparts, became works of art in their own right. An example made for Maffeo Barberini, dating from *c.* 1615–23 and now in the Metropolitan Museum, New York, displays all the refinement of the technique and the high degree of virtuosity achieved by the craftsmen of the Opificio. The carefully chosen and graded stones evoke the art of miniature painting, while the humanist theme is reflected in the depiction of stories from Aesop's

The Teatro Olimpico, Vicenza, designed by Palladio and completed by Vincenzo Scamozzi in 1585 – a clear source of inspiration for artists of the Baroque era in the seventeenth century.

Fables and the evocation of Arcadia with, in the centre panel, Orpheus charming animals with his music.

These table-cabinets became increasingly complex and took on the form of miniature palaces, reproducing on a smaller scale the sumptuousness of the larger pieces. Whereas the earlier examples offered decorated drawers, with or without doors, now the cabinet opens to reveal a microcosm – a *theatrum mundi* – of its own. Rock-crystal columns were often used to punctuate the architectural façade where the central niche includes a complex arrangement of mirrors which reflect a geometric perspective (made of ebony or ivory) enclosing a sculptural group or some pilasters in *pietra dura* or gilt-bronze.

The play of optics and the art of perspective had already been explored in the first century AD by Hero of Alexandria. In 1589 G. B. della Porta took the exploration of theatrical space further, at a time when interest in theatre was very much to the fore in Italy, Palladio having recently built the Teatro Olimpico at Vicenza (completed in 1585 by Scamozzi). Theatricality, the play of light and shade and illusion, lies at the root of Baroque art, and throughout the seventeenth century theorists took up those optical studies again, in parallel with contemporary experiments by artists with the 'camera obscura' and the laws of visual perspective. Among those who explored the subject were J. F. Niceron in 1638, Athanasius Kircher in 1646 and G. Shot in 1650.

The design of cabinets was therefore allying the latest scientific theories with aesthetic enjoyment of artistic virtuosity and precious materials, carrying on the early humanist tradition which had contributed to the development of the cabinet as a work of art and a treasured piece of furniture. The storage element of these cabinets is hardly relevant any longer, but they were destined for private use, chiefly as a safe place for valuables and jewels; the top lid often opened to reveal a small mirror at the back, and the set of drawers would conceal secret drawers and compartments, provided for added security, as in the German pieces.

The international character of the cabinet

Beginning in the sixteenth century during the heyday of the Habsburg Empire, small cabinets were used as travelling strongboxes and document cases, as well as having a writing function in the form of the *Schreibtisch* or *escritorio*. In the seventeenth century cabinets were produced as princely offerings and status symbols, with foreign craftsmen being employed for their technical skills at various courts. This development, as well as the idea of the Grand Tour becoming a standard feature of a young aristocratic gentleman's life, meant that form, materials and techniques became truly international, throughout Europe and in colonial territories. However, the Thirty Years' War, from 1618 to 1648, depleted the power of the German states and generally caused upheaval with trade. One of the German centres of cabinetmaking which suffered was Eger in Bohemia, a 'free' city since 1322. Its geographical position, as a gateway to Bohemia, caused Eger to become an arsenal during the war, 20,000 soldiers being garrisoned in the city. The tradition of cabinetmaking built up over nearly a hundred years was disrupted but not obliterated, and the craftsmen of Eger continued to

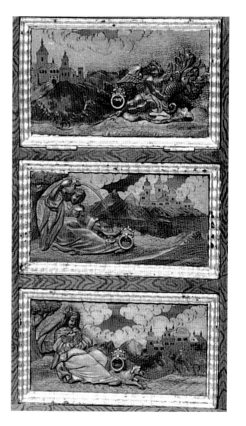

Table-cabinet in ebonized wood, beech, birch and walnut, decorated with relief intarsia *panels in the manner of Adam Eck. Eger, c. 1640–50; width 62 cm (2 ft ½ in.).*

produce *Schreibtische* in the old-fashioned style, regardless of fashion and politics, until the eighteenth century.

The Eck family seems to have been the first to introduce the technique of relief *intarsia* which became the trademark of the city. Peter Eck, whose birthplace was Nuremberg, arrived in Eger *c.* 1588 and became a *Bürger*. He was a carpenter and sculptor who worked in *intarsia* relief only for a short while. His successors are better known and documented, notably Adam Eck who was mentioned in the Eger *Book of Deliveries* as having received on 18 May 1644 the sum of '612 florins for the production of *Schreibtische* and board games made between 1640 and 1644 for Courts and Lords, to whom they were presented by the city for its greater glory'.[10]

Just like Augsburg, Eger sought patronage by presenting samples of its craft to the great and mighty: Generals Piccolomini, Wrangel and Colloredo, as well as Archduke William of Austria, all received gifts of Eger cabinets. Their more subdued appearance and conservative style, as compared with cabinets produced elsewhere in Europe, were the principal attraction. The form relied on the basic box-like construction of the early *Schreibtisch*, in ebony or ebonized pearwood, combined with an *intarsia* of paler wood – beech, birch, box or walnut – contrasting with the dark background. Cabinetmaking skills were handed down in families who included – beside the celebrated Eck family – numerous important makers: Fischer, Bauer, Haberstumpf, Haberlits and Bernhard Dreschler. This explains the large number of pieces from Eger found throughout Europe between 1640 and 1730, the products being a cheaper alternative to the more ornate Augsburg output featuring rare and precious materials and humanist undertones. However, secret drawers and compartments were also found in the Eger cabinets, on which narrative scenes after allegorical and mythological engravings and designs appeared as carved decoration. One such example in the Bayerisches Nationalmuseum has reliefs depicting the 'Wonders of the World' and the Liberal Arts after engravings by Maarten van Heemskerk (1498–1574), and works by François Briot (c. 1550–1615) inspired the reliefs of the Arts and Elements. The cabinet appears to have been the work of Johann Georg Fischer (1587–1669), the most celebrated of the Eger craftsmen, who had some of his work displayed during his lifetime in the *Kunstkammer* of the Elector of Saxony. However, for all its restrained charm and the great carving skills employed in presenting these scenes, the treatment remains endearingly naive, betraying a provincial carpenter at work rather than a court sculptor.

Indeed, the courtly Mannerist tradition of Nuremberg and Augsburg was giving way to new needs and demands, and new centres of production were becoming established in northern Europe. Flanders had come under the dominion of the Dukes of Burgundy during the fifteenth century, and the brilliance of the court was sustained by the wealth derived from the prosperous wool trade. Textile production encouraged the growth of cities, Antwerp among them, where medieval tradition and the Gothic style lingered on. Even after the fall of the House of Burgundy at the beginning of the sixteenth century, little classical influence had filtered through to Flanders. Indeed, it was the painter Mabuse, who, on his return from Italy in 1508, first introduced classical architectural elements and new perspective vistas to north European painting. It was not, however, until the rise of the School of Fontainebleau in the mid-sixteenth century and the dissemination of decorative motifs, such as grotesques and strapwork, through engravings that Netherlandish artists started using Renaissance ornaments.

Designers such as Cornelis van Bos (1506–70) and Cornelius Floris, who published a treatise on grotesques in 1560, helped to disseminate the new forms which were often superimposed on existing native structures. In the field of furniture the *buffet* and *dressoir* were gothic types which continued to be made in Flanders and France well into the seventeenth century, for they had been associated with the elaborate court etiquette favoured by the Dukes of Burgundy. Classical motifs began to appear on such pieces after the publication in 1539 of the *Fourth Book of Architecture* by Serlio, followed in 1565 by Hans Vredeman de Vries's volume of furniture designs published in Antwerp under the title *Differens pourtraicts à savoir portaux, bancs, escabelles, tables, buffets, licts de camp propres aux menuiziers de l'invention de Jehan Vredeman dict de Vriese, mis en lumière par Philippe Gallé* (Various designs for doors, benches, stools, tables, *buffets*, folding beds to be used by carpenters . . .).

From 1596 onwards, records of *ébénistes* (cabinetmakers working in the art of ebony veneering and other woods) can be traced in Antwerp. The city remained an important centre for the arts throughout the seventeenth century, producing and dealing in paintings, prints, books, furniture, musical instruments, tapestries etc.

In 1608, following the death of his mother, Peter Paul Rubens, the famous artist, scholar and diplomat, returned to settle in the city in which his family originated. He brought with him sketches and designs executed during his Italian travels and built an Italianate *palazzo* for himself and his wife. He truly brought the forms and ideas of the Baroque to the north, and thus had an indirect influence on the scale of the cabinet, which became larger in overall proportions, bolder in decoration and more homogeneous in execution. Whereas south German Mannerist examples had relied on an accumulation of virtuoso details of exquisite craftsmanship, and had been realized mostly as table-cabinets, i.e. without a stand, a new type of cabinet now evolved in Flanders and eventually in France. The Baroque sense of theatrical grandeur was combined with the native traditional form, the tall Burgundian *buffet* or *dressoir*, which was always on a stand and intended to be placed against the wall. The frontal emphasis was maintained in the Flemish cabinets, hence the *dressoir* became a true cabinet when its traditional shelves and compartments were replaced by the characteristic sets of drawers. From the beginning therefore the Flemish cabinet was a familiar piece of furniture, with its function and status hardly changed but with decoration that relied on more exotic sources than previously.

Burghers and aristocrats alike were using cabinets and, as demand for them increased, they were produced in quantity for the home market and for export. In May 1656 the inventory of Queen Christina of Sweden mentioned '*Ung cabinet d'Ebenne et d'Yvoir guarny avec des agats*' (An ivory and ebony cabinet adorned with agates)[11] from Antwerp. One of the city's most successful firms of cabinetmakers was that of the Forchondt family. Melchior Forchondt, a craftsman of Silesian origin, had settled in Antwerp *c.* 1603. In 1632 he was registered with the Guild of St Luke and from 1636 his two sons managed the firm, exporting cabinets, via a complex network of commercial contacts, throughout northern Europe. A letter from a certain Ralph Hamson in London dated 12 April 1652 gives an indication of the volume of the cabinet trade: 'To send me 4 or 5 cabbenets, 3 with pictures and a perspective and 2 with tortoiseshell on the inside and some on the outside doors all with risingh heads and 2 with fframes. A gentile man which I mentioned in Mr. Thompson's letter brought over 10 about 12 months a goe.'[12]

The Antwerp pieces were, however, a far cry from the individual cabinets produced by Philipp Hainhofer and presented with great ceremony to the owners. Indeed, even if the Flemish *scriban* corresponded in size and echoed in its very name the Spanish *escritorio* and the German *Schreibtisch*, its concept was one of convenience and practicality. Ebony had been imported into Europe from the East Indies and Africa since the sixteenth century, mostly through Spain and Portugal. The latter's trade monopoly in the East Indies, China and Japan endured until the Dutch trade expansion at the beginning of the seventeenth century, followed by the Dutch East India Company's domination of the entire trade with the Far East from 1650.

However, lacquered objects had been imported into Antwerp from China and Japan, and the small, portable Japanese lacquered chest used as a writing box and for the safekeeping of documents and valuables by merchants would have been known there. This *Ko-Dansu*, in which to keep abacus, seals, money and certificates, was translated into its direct European counterpart, known in French as a *comptoir* and in Flemish as a *cantoor*. Commerce was firmly at the root of the Antwerp production and firms' ledgers recorded the prices of lacquered cabinets produced in imitation of oriental prototypes. At the firm of Forchondt prices varied between 150 and 380 florins, depending on the size and on the type of decoration. A small *cantoor* or table-cabinet would be priced at 22 to 40 florins, while an *escritorio* would fetch from 20 to 60 florins. Antwerp, being a port, became the centre of trade in lacquered furniture. Several mentions of transactions can be found in the archives of the Musson and Forchondt firms: Jaspar Van Den Berch delivered a 'lak' cabinet to Forchondt, as did Jaspar van de Brijs, Nicolaes Van Beclelaer and other *ébénistes*.[13]

Sometimes lacquer would be associated with *écaille* (tortoiseshell), mother-of-pearl or *scagliola*, achieving a rich combination of colours and materials. Indeed, the whole range of precious materials, whether organic or man-made, already encountered in German or Italian cabinet production, was used at Antwerp but on a larger, more commercial scale, to fulfil the demands of a different type of clientele. Tortoiseshell, first used as veneer in Roman times, became widely appreciated for its lustrous appeal when backed by a metallic foil, such as gold leaf, or more commonly with red pigment. The fashion seemed to have lasted from 1640 to 1680, one of the first mentions occurring in the 1638 inventory of Anne, Viscountess of Dorchester, which lists a small table-cabinet in 'tortas shell'; in 1653 the inventory of Cardinal Mazarin in Paris mentions, among others, 'a tortoiseshell cabinet with ormolu mounts on its sides'.[14] A letter dated 1652 written by a Mr Robert Spencer, recommending a friend to buy a tortoiseshell cabinet instead of an ebony one while in Antwerp, provides the first mention of the trade in such cabinets in the Forchondt records, and reflects the high regard in which the Antwerp production in tortoiseshell veneering was held.

The cabinets on which this exotic and costly material was used were often very grand and sumptuous, with gilt-bronze and silver adornments offsetting the rich red colour, and thus totally suited to the High Baroque desire for showy ostentation which had originated in Rome. Catholic Flanders was making use of southern architectural forms in these pieces, the grandest of which were designed as miniature Baroque churches and *palazzi*, with a strongly sculptural feel in decoration. An ebony and tortoiseshell cabinet now in the Rijksmuseum, Amsterdam, is an outstanding example of the sumptuous results achieved by contemporary *ébénistes*. Dated 1650, it is conceived as a spectacular showpiece for a set of marble panels painted with biblical scenes, mounted in ormulu on a rich red tortoiseshell ground contrasting with the dark ebony. The sculptural aedicule, surmounted by a bronze statuette and supported by two gilt-bronze dolphins, and the carved stand with its parcel-gilt blackamoors, are entirely in keeping with the Italian Baroque tradition.

Italian paintings were also strongly influential – works by Veronese, Titian and Domenico Feti were adapted for panels adorning ebony cabinets, often by reducing a large composition to the dimensions required by the cabinetmaker. Rubens himself, who had been inspired by the art of Venice as much as by the Florentine and Roman painters during his stay in Italy, had some panels for cabinets painted after his own work; two exceptional examples are now in the Rijksmuseum, Amsterdam, and the Rubenshuis in Antwerp. Both explore the theme of Ovid's *Metamorphoses*, a favourite subject in seventeenth-century art, which Rubens used for large compositions executed between 1636 and 1638, most of them for Torre de la Parada, the royal hunting lodge of King Philip IV of Spain. Some artists specialized in producing small panel

Table-cabinet in ebony with tortoiseshell inlay and embossed silver plaques illustrating scenes from Ovid's Metamorphoses, *also including one inspired by Titian's* Venus and Adonis *(now in the Prado, Madrid), width 126 cm (4 ft 2 in.).*

paintings for cabinetmakers: they included Otto van Veen, Jan Snellinx, Maarten de Vos and the Francken family, working mostly from engravings of original works. Scenes from the Old and New Testaments, as well as mythological and allegorical subjects, were favoured, particularly scenes from the Loves of the Gods from Ovid's *Metamorphoses*; the latter were appropriate as subject-matter, for in many instances such a piece would have been used as a dowry cabinet by a bride to store her most precious possessions and hence would have had pride of place in her bedroom.

The pictorial effect favoured on Antwerp cabinets at the time provided an echo of princely collections in humanist Italy and Germany. Indeed, it is as if the cabinet was now being used as vehicle for the paintings themselves rather than as a place in which to house paintings which could be shown and contemplated at some specially appointed time, in the company of like-minded connoisseurs. This new outlook was much in keeping with the Baroque attitude to social status and the making of overtly public statements, whether in the house of a prince or of a burgher.

Drawer-front with painted decoration after Veronese's Christ and the Woman of Samaria *(in the Kunsthistorisches Museum, Vienna), detail of the ebony cabinet, c. 1650–70, illustrated in plate 31.*

Needlework casket with embroidered designs (some in stumpwork) in coloured silks on an ivory-coloured silk ground. England, c. 1660.

This taste for descriptive narrative was also fulfilled through the use of other techniques. As in Italy, ivory was finely etched with black ink, the scenes reflecting not the dynastic ambitions of a princely house but the more familiar and homely subjects of hunting and fishing, so illustrating the contemporary interest in treatises on the subject such as G. Phebus's *Livre de Chasse* (Paris, 1563) and P. de Crescenzi's *Librum Ruralium Commodorum* (Milan, 1541). Engravings by Hans Bol (1534–93) and Antonio Tempesta (1555–1630) showing familiar country scenes also served as models for panels, often used on ebony table-cabinets.

Finely embroidered panels of silk in brilliant colours – sometimes picked out in gold or silver threads in *gros* or *petit point*, sometimes in relief (stumpwork) – were also used; the subjects were floral arrangements in the manner of contemporary Dutch paintings, domestic or exotic animals or, once again, episodes from Ovid's *Metamorphoses* or scenes from the Bible. Often these pieces would be of small proportions, table-cabinets for personal use, most likely for keeping jewels and toilet objects, since the lid would open to reveal a mirror mounted on the inside. Instead of embroidery panels, the inner drawers might be faced with plaques of *verre églomisé* (glass decorated on the reverse) using the same motifs.

Variety in shapes, forms and materials was a characteristic feature of these pieces. At one end of the range was the grand Baroque ebony cabinet-on-stand, of architectural design and frontal emphasis, embellished with red tortoiseshell, silver or gilt-bronze mounts, and incorporating panels with scenes painted on wood or marble, executed in *pietra dura* or *pietra paesina*, and sometimes in embossed silver. In the case of smaller cabinets the exterior might be quite understated, in plain ebony or ebonized wood, and would open to reveal antique cameos and intaglios, semi-precious stones, painted panels or embroideries. Whatever the size of the cabinet, the central cupboard would most often be executed as a tabernacle with a temple front. Once open, it would reveal a perspective of precious marquetry paving in ebony and ivory, enclosed by gilt pilasters, sometimes with a small statuette in the centre, or a painted scene reflected in the mirrored sides, echoing the interest shown by northern artists in exploring the effects of perspective with the aid of the *camera obscura* and studying the laws of optics, as had been done earlier in Italy.

This play on theatrical illusionism, a characteristically Baroque feature, was combined with the devising of secret drawers and compartments; these might be hidden behind side panels, or in the shape of a T at the back of a drawer, or concealed behind pilasters or an empty compartment which, once removed, would reveal yet another tier of drawers. The ingeniousness with which these drawers and compartments were concealed continued the earlier Mannerist tradition exemplified in Italian and German cabinets, albeit without the specialized content which formed part of a humanist microcosm of the intellectually perceived greater whole. These ingenious contrivances would, however, have been a source of great delight to the owner, marvelling at the virtuosity of the *ébéniste*. By contrast, on a mercenary level, such cabinets could also serve a useful purpose in the smuggling of contraband while in transit. For example, in 1685 a consignment of diamonds was sent by the firm of Forchondt to Vienna, hidden in the double bottom of a cabinet. Lace, silver plaques and tulips were other luxury goods transported illicitly in the inner recesses of cabinets, with or without the consent or knowledge of their owners. In such cases secret compartments would be locked, the key having yet another hiding place in the same cabinet.

In France the Wars of Religion at the beginning of the century had left the national economy and the fortunes of the furniture trade at a very low ebb. The accession of Henry IV in 1589 restored some prosperity and industry began to flourish again. The king, if not a great patron of the arts, was a gifted administrator and economist. He encouraged trade by controlling imports and created an institutional system to promote and develop artistic production. The guild system had a long tradition in France and rigidly divided and defined craftsmen according to their training. Thus, as early as 1254 Etienne Boileau, Provost of Paris, had issued a decree separating carpenters from furniture makers. In 1453 the Corporation Rules were revised when trade was resumed at the end of the Hundred Years' War with England. By the early sixteenth century, furniture-making revolved around the royal and princely courts, whether at Fontainebleau (started in 1528), the Louvre, or in Dijon, seat of the Dukes of Burgundy. In 1596 Henry IV asked Laffemas, his Minister, to 'introduce a general Rule to register the workshops in this realm, admit foreign craftsmen to France'[15] and make compulsory the Guilds and Corporations system.

Design for a cabinet for Marie de Médicis; drawing in pen and ink, bistre and grey wash by Jean Cotelle, c. 1620–30.

The admission of foreign craftsmen to France was essential for the growth and development of the trade. No French craftsmen at this date would have been capable of producing the cabinet recorded in 1601 in the inventory of Louise de Vaudemont, widow of Henry III; most likely of Italian or German origin, the piece was made of 'Lapis and Agate covered with scarlet velvet with the cipher of the said Lady-Queen'.[16] The same was true of the magnificent cabinet in the king's possession, described by Ludovic Lalanne in a 1603 Inventory of the Pictures and other Curiosities in the Louvre. It was 'made of cedarwood, with eight Corinthian columns in the same wood, the base and capitals being gilt, and in the central niche an equestrian statue of the King, above it all four elegant figures, two trophies and two angels bearing the arms of the Béarnais [the King], the whole being 6 ft 8 in. high and 4 ft $\frac{1}{2}$ in. wide'.[17]

It was certainly to prevent such costly imports that Henry IV established, by Letters Patent dated 22 February 1608, a network of craft workshops in the Grande Galerie du Louvre, following the precedent set by the Medici with the Galleria dei Lavori at the Uffizi. In 1608 the first *Menuisier en Ebeyne*, Laurent Stabre, was registered in the Grande Galerie, where he occupied his workshop until 1624, according to Abbé de Marolles in his *Revue Versifiée des Artistes Français*.

Following the assassination of Henry IV, Marie de Médicis became Regent from 1610 until 1617, when she retired to Blois until, owing to strained relations with her son Louis XIII, she was exiled in 1630. It was probably during this twenty-year period that the Marie de Médicis Cabinet (now in the Victoria and Albert Museum) was produced by the Royal Workshop. A drawing by Jean Cotelle (Ashmolean Museum, Oxford) illustrates the characteristically French manner of matching the design of the base with the upper part of the cabinet, the Queen's cipher, a double M surmounted by a crown, being repeated several times.

Ebony cabinet-on-stand with gilt-bronze mounts, made in France for Marie de Médicis, c. 1630; the relief plaques depicting Rinaldo and Armida (based on Torquato Tasso's Gerusalemme Liberata) are set between niches enclosing statuettes of Jupiter flanked by Juno and Minerva.

French craftsmen were also trained abroad. On 16 May 1644, Jean Macé, from Blois, was granted a royal warrant as Menuisier Ebéniste and, on 25 October, the lease of the accommodation in the Grande Galerie du Louvre still occupied by the widow of Laurent Stabre, 'because of the long practise he has acquired in this art [cabinetmaking] in the Low Countries, and the proof of excellence he provided in the various pieces veneered in ebony and other coloured woods he presented to the Queen Regent.'[18] Given the high regard he enjoyed in royal circles, Jean Macé has been credited with many important cabinets with royal associations. The Endymion Cabinet (Victoria and Albert Museum) and the Wolsey Cabinet (Royal Collection, Windsor Castle) are both veneered with finely carved ebony panels depicting scenes from *L'Endymion*, a novel published in 1624 by Jean Ogier Gonbauld. Another cabinet (Rijksmuseum, Amsterdam) is decorated with Old Testament scenes, the inner left door representing *Jephtha's Daughter*, a subject inspired by a tapestry designed by Simon Vouet and woven in Paris – evidence of the close connection which existed between craftsmen and designers at the Louvre workshop. In these examples the use of shiny dark wood emphasizes the severity of the rigid architectural forms, while the interiors are marvels of richness and virtuosity in the Flemish manner, revealing secret drawers and perspectives. The Endymion Cabinet has a concealed miniature palace, while the Wolsey Cabinet contains marquetry boards for playing chess, tric-trac and backgammon. All the interiors, lined with tortoiseshell, ivory, gilt bronze and mirrors, have a jewel-like appearance.

Aristocratic and bourgeois clients sought to emulate the royal patronage. When the famous author and playwright Molière died in 1673, the inventory of his effects included 'An ebony cabinet with two doors with a key, inside twelve drawers with eight turned columns'.[19] The largest French collection was that of the Ministre d'Etat, Cardinal Mazarin (or Mazarini, as he was of Italian origin). On his return to Paris in 1653, his inventory listed twenty-one cabinets: seventeen in ebony, four with tortoiseshell adorned with lapis lazuli, jasper, amethyst, cameos, paintings of Apollo and the Muses, gilt plaques of Ovid's *Metamorphoses*, figurines etc., all produced in the main European centres.[20] The

The Endymion Cabinet, a French carved ebony cabinet-on-stand made by Jean Macé, c. 1650–60; the inner doors open to reveal a central recessed mirrored theatre flanked by a marquetry façade on the inside of the doors. Width 175 cm (5 ft 9 in.).

second inventory drawn up after his death in 1661 showed that he continued to add to his collection, acquiring Italian cabinets and some French examples, in particular a pair of cabinets he specially commissioned, for the young King Louis XIV, from the *ébéniste* Pierre Gole, a Dutch cabinetmaker whose presence in Paris was first recorded in 1646; Gole was appointed *Menuisier en Ebeyne* to the king in 1651. For Mazarin he made the two cabinets decorated with tortoiseshell and marquetry depicting birds, flowers and insects, as listed in the 1661 inventory under his name.

In the same year Louis XIV's only brother, Philippe d'Orléans, had married Henrietta Anna of England. The inventory of their Paris residence, the Palais-Royal, at the time of her death in 1670 described 'Another cabinet of ivory with marquetry flowers . . .'.[21] This piece (now in the Victoria and Albert Museum) features the characteristic tripartite front associated with Gole and the harmonious unity of design between the upper and the lower parts, a French tradition brought here to peak of refinement and sophistication in a truly aristocratic piece specially commissioned for Le Cabinet Blanc, a small room lined with 'white moiré silk with embroidery picked out in gold and silver'.[22] Gole's ivory cabinet is just one example of the fashion for all-over marquetry decoration, mostly of a floral kind, which grew up in France under Dutch influence during the latter part of the seventeenth century.

After the separation of the Protestant Northern Provinces from Catholic Flanders in 1609, the Republic of Holland became a worldwide maritime power, and Amsterdam the richest city in Europe. The foundation of the Dutch East India Company in 1602 brought new wealth to the country as the Dutch traders who had invaded the East Indies in 1597 relentlessly took over Portuguese outposts; at the end of the seventeenth century Portugal retained only Goa on the west coast of India and Macao in China, the last remnants of a once powerful eastern trading empire. As prosperity in this Golden Age in Holland increased, so did the production of all forms of art, including cabinetmaking. However, in Protestant Holland the demands of the Baroque style were not met in the same sumptuous manner as in the Catholic Provinces of Flanders, where the influence of Rubens and Italy was important. Although the sculptural quality of the Roman Baroque was echoed in the heavily carved and gilt stands in the sinuous auricular style, inspired by the work of the van Vianen family of goldsmiths in Utrecht, on the whole materials and theatrical impact were more subdued than on the colourful Antwerp cabinets. Cabinetmakers in the north paid a more discreet homage to the Baroque by eschewing obviously ornate elements such as columns and pilasters, temple fronts and pediments, relying rather on a barely noticeable cornice and plane surfaces of architectural grandeur, covered with carefully selected veneers of native and exotic woods. Walnut, acacia and lignum vitae burrs provided the variegated decorative patterns used in oystershell, star, and various other forms of marquetry.

Flower paintings depicting blooms out of season, as well as the contemporary tulipomania, encouraged the development of floral marquetry in imitation of painting. Thus, towards the middle of the century, an Amsterdam craftsman, Dirk van Rijswick, was renowned for his floral mother-of-pearl inlay on black marble. Later, Phillipus van

Cabinet-on-stand with all-over floral marquetry in ivory, ebony, shell and exotic woods, made by Pierre Gole for the Cabinet Blanc in the Palais-Royal, Paris, c. 1662; width 84 cm (2 ft 9 in.).

Oak cabinet-on-stand with floral marquetry by Jan van Mekeren, Amsterdam, c. 1690; width 170 cm (5 ft 7 in.).

Display cabinet in ebonized wood on a carved and gilded base. Rome, c. 1680–90; width 2.47 m (8 ft).

Stantwijk in The Hague and from 1687 Jan van Mekeren in Amsterdam were producing outstanding examples of luscious floral panels as decoration for a simple rectangular furniture form, and these could also be allied to the burrs of walnut, acacia and laburnum in geometric patterns. Jan van Mekeren was the most famous of these cabinetmakers, the broad painterly quality of his floral marquetry – very close in design to contemporary still-life paintings – being enhanced by a dark ground of rosewood or mahogany. Floral marquetry became a Dutch speciality and was rare in other countries before 1650.

In Italy, Leonardo van der Vinne, who was of Flemish or Dutch origin, introduced in Florence a painterly style of floral marquetry, in which birds and insects are rendered very naturalistically. Thanks to his consummate skills in the technique, he was nicknamed 'Il Tarsia'; he was recorded in 1678 as *ebanista e inventore di tarsia* (cabinetmaker and inventor of marquetry) at the Galleria dei Lavori in the Uffizi, where he was *capomaestro* from 1677. His ebony *stipo* with floral marquetry decoration in the Palazzo Pitti is a grand Baroque version of the cabinet with a rhythmically constructed façade, while its exotic stand incorporates carved figures of blackamoors. The piece thus allies southern bravura and theatricality with northern technical skills.

The term *ebanista*, first recorded in 1659, was now used in Italy instead of *stipettaio* (cabinetmaker), emphasizing as in France the art of veneering as distinct from the previously used cabinetmaking techniques of inlay and carving. Traditional decorative methods continued to be used in more remote provincial centres: the art of the wood- and ivory-carver of Lombardy can be seen in a walnut cabinet on a cupboard base made for Canon Lucini Passalacqua (Castello Sforzesco, Milan). Around the Ligurian port of Genoa were made examples of a particularly exuberantly carved type of *studiolo* or *cassettone a bambocci*, so-called for their multiple small figures of musicians, jousters and entertainers, sometimes mixed with grotesques.

The various independent states within the Italian peninsula each had distinct regional characteristics, mostly defined by their political bonds and allegiances. However, by the middle of the century, the unifying influence of the Baroque, a style closely associated with Rome and the Roman Catholic Church's power and dominion, introduced common features to all the main cabinetmaking centres. Indeed, particular techniques were no longer associated with given centres, as foreign craftsmen were employed by Popes and princes, resulting in a truly international exchange of ideas. The native architectural sense of classical forms remained. In Rome leading architects such as Bernini and Borromini influenced the designs of furniture, which became grander, more opulent and dramatic, with contrasting rhythms and a strongly sculptural feel. Display cabinets with glazed fronts were now used to show off precious collections previously concealed behind solid doors. Bernini for example, designed the showcase (*scarabattolo*) for the amber collection of Cosimo III de' Medici. Another architect, Carlo Fontana (1634–1714), designed an ebony cabinet (Galleria Colonna, Rome) as an impressive *palazzo* structure complete with columns, pediment and sculptural finials, to set off the ivory plaques carved by the German-born brothers Francesco and Domenico Steinhardt, who also executed the kneeling figures of blackamoors of the base between 1678 and 1680.

Cabinet in ebony with pietra dura *panels, on a stand incorporating carved gilt figures, made at the Gobelins (possibly by Domenico Cucci), Paris, c. 1670–80.*

Another group of ebony cabinets built on strongly architectural lines and depicting views of Rome each surmounted by a central aedicule containing a clock and with an equestrian statue of Marcus Aurelius, has been tentatively attributed to Giacomo Herman, a German cabinet-maker. Examples are now in the Kunsthistorisches Museum, Vienna, in Rosenborg Castle, Copenhagen, and in a private collection in London; the last of these has an unusual feature in the form of a small octavina harpsichord, signed 'Roma 1676', which has been added to a plinth drawer under the central part. These cabinets, with their obvious papal allusions, may have been made as presentation pieces or diplomatic gifts.

In Naples (still under Spanish rule until the middle of the century) the use of tortoiseshell was allied with painted glass panels on ebony cabinets of large size, often on a carved base or stand. The tortoiseshell would be backed by red or gold foil, so producing a sumptuous setting within which lusciously painted mythological, allegorical or religious scenes, often after Luca Giordano, would gleam in a jewel-like manner. An example of this type of cabinet is in the Victoria and Albert Museum;

Table-cabinet veneered in ebony and rosewood and decorated with gouache views of Rome behind glass, jasper and lapis lazuli, and having a small octavina harpsichord in a plinth drawer. Rome, c. 1676; width 153.5 cm (5 ft ½ in.).

such pieces are listed in inventories, such as those of Cardinal Carafa and the Prince of Avellino. The availability of tortoiseshell from Spanish colonial sources encouraged the execution of large architectural pieces covered in red-backed tortoiseshell glowing against the dark ebony and gleaming gilt-bronze mounts and finials.

It was an Italian craftsman, Domenico Cucci, trained in Rome as a sculptor and *ebanista*, who brought the technique of *pietra dura* to France. He was strongly influenced by the Roman fashion for *palazzo* furniture richly decorated with relief work, sculpture and *pietra dura*. Cucci arrived in Paris in 1660, where his talent was immediately recognized. He was registered at the Gobelins in 1664, and in 1667 he is recorded in the official Comptes des Bâtiments as having been paid 30,500 livres for the two cabinets, known as the *Temples de la Gloire et de la Vertu*, commissioned for the Galerie d'Apollon in the Louvre and showing respectively Louis XIV as Apollo on his chariot, and Queen Maria-Theresa as Diana on hers, each as a sculptural group placed above the central aedicule of the cabinet; the pair were adorned with gouaches by Joseph Werner on the same theme, the bases each being composed of six terms of gilt wood.

The Manufacture Royale des Meubles de la Couronne, usually known as the Manufacture des Gobelins, was created in 1663 under the directorship of Charles Lebrun, on the same lines as the Galleria dei Lavori in Florence, by Jean-Baptiste Colbert, Minister to Louis XIV. After the fall of Nicolas Fouquet, Surintendant des Finances, in 1661, and his imprisonment, the tapestry workshops at Maincy used by Fouquet for furnishing his château, Vaux-le-Vicomte, were moved to Paris; the Flemish tapestry-weavers from Maincy, some 150 in number, now formed the core of the Gobelins workforce. In 1667 the Manufacture employed some 250 craftsmen, producing silver plate as well as furniture

Cabinet-on-stand in ebonized wood decorated with a central temple front in tortoiseshell and allegorical and mythological scenes painted in the manner of Luca Giordano. Naples, c. 1670–80; width 190 cm (6 ft 2¾ in.).

Gobelins tapestry 'La Visite de Louis XIV aux Gobelins', in which the king is being shown a large cabinet featuring Salomonic columns, c. 1671–6 (Museé de Versailles).

and tapestries for the royal palaces, all inspired by Lebrun's designs. In one of the set of tapestries entitled *L'Histoire du Roy* woven at the factory, Louis XIV is seen visiting the workshop. On the right a man is shown pointing at a large cabinet. This could well be Domenico Cucci, for the piece answers the description of one of the two 'large ebony cabinets inlaid with pewter, with four large twisted columns in imitation of lapis and vine scroll of gilt copper supported by ten lions' paws' made by him for the king.[24]

The 'Louis XIV style' allied a flamboyance and sense of political grandeur to the sculptural Italian Baroque forms and the craftsmanship from both northern and southern Europe. Two *pietra dura* cabinets (now at Alnwick Castle) made for the Palais de Versailles in 1681–3 were unprecedented in their opulence and sumptuous richness. Cucci had a profound influence on the development of the Louis XIV style and on his contemporaries, Pierre Gole and André-Charles Boulle. In fact Boulle was the first French *ébéniste* to enjoy the degree of success and fame achieved by Gole and Cucci. Born in Paris, he trained as a painter and was appointed *Ebéniste du Roy* in 1672 when, described as 'the most skilful in Paris',[25] he was granted the former lodging in the Louvre of Jean Macé – in preference to the latter's son's claim.

Boulle's talents as a *marqueteur*, together with his painter's training, lent a particular distinction to his floral marquetry, more controlled and finer in details than the Dutch counterpart. Stylistically, it would seem that the former pair of cabinets of tortoiseshell floral marquetry and gilt bronze, now at Drumlanrig Castle and in the Getty Museum respectively, must be attributed to Boulle on account of their originality of design and exquisite craftsmanship, although they have sometimes been attributed to Gole. Boulle's original contribution to the art is the refinement of an older form of Italian and Flemish tortoiseshell marquetry and its use on cabinets and other pieces with true Baroque richness, gusto and flair. The so-called Boulle work (see glossary), consisting of a marquetry of brass and tortoiseshell applied on a background of ebony, was particularly well-suited to the idea of symmetry inherent in the Louis XIV style using the *Première partie* and *Contrepartie* to this effect. It was also cheaper than other forms of decorative techniques, a particularly relevant fact as, since the death of Colbert in 1683, the national deficit brought about by the Thirty Years' War had increased. The situation became so bad that the Manufacture des Gobelins closed in 1694 and did not reopen until 1699.

Under the Sumptuary Edict of 14 December 1689, all precious metal was stripped from furniture and melted down.[26] It was the death-knell of the grand opulent cabinets of the kind that had been the *meuble d'apparat et de parade* during the reign of the Sun King. Yet Louis XIV still commissioned presentation pieces, with a strong political motivation and message, just as his German and Italian predecessors had done. In 1700 Boulle completed a pair of cabinets (both now in private collections) in *Première partie* and *Contrepartie* in a marquetry of pewter, brass and mother-of-pearl on a red tortoiseshell ground, illustrating Louis XIV's victories – with scenes based on engravings after Wouwermans, Parrocel and Van der Meulen – for the king's grandson, Philip V of Spain, whose portrait figures in the central theatre.

As the religious conflict between Catholics and Protestants flared up again, Huguenot craftsmen left France after the revocation of the Edict of Nantes in 1685, taking with them the forms and techniques prevalent at Versailles. Many fled to the Low Countries, including a nephew of Pierre Gole, Daniel Marot, who went to Holland where he was active in the service of William of Orange and his English wife Mary before their accession to the British throne in 1690. Daniel Marot brought a more southern flair for sculptural form in furniture, also involving the interplay of forms and mass and introducing pediments and arches on cabinets, above which fine Chinese porcelain or blue-and-white Delftware would be displayed.

The creation of East India Companies in England (1600), in Holland (1602) and in France (1664), had not only brought about increased prosperity but also, through trading links with the Orient, led to the importation of rare and precious artifacts, among them porcelain and lacquer. Lacquer cabinets had been exported from Japan to Europe since the late sixteenth century, the forms being mostly based on contemporary Portuguese prototypes. In 1569 Father Luis Frois, a missionary, noted that one of the Japanese Shoguns, Oda Nobunaga, had in his possession 'twelve or fifteen chests, like those of Portugal'. All the European colonies in China, India and Mexico produced examples of the *escritorio* or the *vargueño* to Spanish and Portuguese order. The trade intensified under Dutch rule. In 1617 Will Adams wrote to the British agent at Hirado in Japan: 'I have sent by this bearer 17 sundry parcels of contores [French *comptoirs*; cabinets-on-stand] and scrittores [scriptors] marked RW'.[28]

The earliest type of lacquer-decorated furniture to be imported seems to have been inspired by Near Eastern or Indian pieces with inlaid mother-of-pearl on a dark ground and with gold overpainting. Later, *c.* 1620, pictorial lacquer with raised relief and embellished with gold foil or gold dust became very fashionable and remained so until 1630–40, continuing into the eighteenth century. Throughout Europe, cabinets of this type were placed on carved gilt stands; in Holland and England such stands could be very elaborate, the cabinet itself being surmounted by a matching cresting. Coromandel lacquer, featuring bright colours with incised decoration on a dark ground, was also imported from China. All

Cabinet-on-stand (one of a pair) in ebony and pietra dura *made for Louis XIV at the Gobelins by Domenico Cucci, c. 1681–3; formerly in the Palais de Versailles, the two cabinets are now in the collection of the Duke of Northumberland.*

Opposite, above left
Cabinet covered with shagreen and decorated with lacquer, Japan, Momoyama period (1573–1615); the inclusion of a central rounded arch and pilasters betrays the influence of European Renaissance design on oriental wares imported through the Portuguese trade. Width 89 cm (2 ft 11 in.).

Opposite, above right
Silver writing casket with chased decoration of arabesque and allegorical figures by P. Flament, Paris, c. 1600–10; width 22.5 cm (9 in.).

these objects were, however, very costly and in the absence of natural lacquer obtained from *Rhus vernicifera*, which only grows in Asia, European countries developed an imitation of lacquer using shellac-based varnishes.

In the Middle Ages trade with the Far East had been carried out mostly through the Italian ports of Venice and Genoa and lacquer objects had also been transported via the Silk Road. In a damp climate such as that of Venice, protective varnishes were essential for the preservation of painted surfaces, and the first records come from a decree issued in 1285 by the Giustichieri Vecchi, the office in control of the guilds, mentioning a form of varnish to be used on leather and painted wood, and setting out rules for the guild of varnishers (*depentores*).

As early as 1560 an inventory of Francis I of France mentioned 'Une petite boîte façon des Indes'.[29] European terminology for lacquer and imitations of it varied from the Dutch *lac-werk*, to the German *Indianischwerk* (also encountered in Holland), the English *Japan work* or *Japanning*, the Italian *lacca* and the French *façon des Indes, façon de la*

Opposite, below
Cabinet-on-stand with japanned decoration in imitation of Japanese Talio-makie *lacquer, metal mounts in the manner of Chinese pierced work, and elaborately carved silvered stand and cresting. England, c. 1680.*

Chine or lachinage. A book by Leonardo Fioravanti giving recipes for
lacquer was published in Venice in 1562 under the title Compendio di
Secreti rationali and subsequently in Paris in 1582 as Le Livre des Secrets
(The Book of Secrets). In 1609 William Kick was producing lac-werk in
Holland. Nuremberg, Augsburg and Hamburg followed. In the Gustavus
Adolphus Cabinet (now in Uppsala), conceived by Philipp Hainhofer, a
small box with black-and-gold lacquer decoration and a red interior has
survived. In Nuremberg in the 1630s Paul Kick, related to the Dutch
craftsman, was producing lacquerware 'at the sign of East India'.

In 1601 in Paris, Etienne Sager (working in the Grande Galerie du
Louvre) was commissioned to decorate cabinets with 'lacquer gum and
gold'; this work was paid for by the Queen (Marie de Médicis), who
owned a genuine Chinese lacquer escritorio presented to her by the
Father-General of the Jesuits. In 1616 William Smith, an English lacquer
artist, was active in Rome, having spent seven years travelling in France,
Germany and Italy for the 'bettering' of his knowledge.

Between 1630 and 1660 European lacquerwork remained experimental. Records of exports of lacquer from Venice begin in the 1660s. On 12
February 1666 'Un cabinet noir façon de la Chine' (a black-japanned
cabinet)[30] was delivered at the Royal Garde-Meuble for Versailles, and in
1667 Pierre Gole made for Louis XIV 'a cabinet consisting of nine layers
of drawers in the form of a pyramid, covered with the finest work in the
Chinese manner'.[31] The Gobelins were producing 'Ouvrages de la Chine'
(japanned wares) in 1672, and in 1680 Charles II of England ordered a
'cabinet, frame, table-stands and glass all of Japan work' from the
Flemish-born Gerrit Jensen, for presentation to the Emperor of Morocco.
Japanned wares became very popular in England after the publication in
1688 of Stalker and Parker's Treatise of Japanning and Varnishing,

giving designs of *chinoiserie* and hints on techniques. Red, green, cream and, more rarely, imitation tortoiseshell were used, together with black. Lacquered cabinets would be placed on highly carved gilt or silvered stands of Baroque inspiration, at first in the Dutch-inspired auricular style, later in the French manner under the influence of Daniel Marot.

The earliest English cabinets were small-size table-cabinets intended for personal use. The earliest record is found in the Howard Household Books,[32] in 1620, accounting for the purchase of a London-made 'cabinnit', and later six cabinets for 'my Ladie', with 26 boxes in each of them for the sum of £2 8 shillings. They would have looked very similar to the cabinet with painted *chinoiserie* decoration in gold and silver and mother-of-pearl inlay on a black ground; the earliest English cabinet in the Victoria and Albert Museum, this piece is 60 cm (2 ft) high with a triangular stepped top containing a drawer, over two doors concealing a set of drawers.

Beginning *c.* 1650, elaborately made Flemish, Italian and French cabinets were imported into England, as well as examples made in Spain and German, introducing the technique of rich veneers in ebony, tortoiseshell, ivory and *pietra dura* with silver and bronze adornments. In the reign of Charles I (1625–49) the position of 'Cabinet-maker to the King' was created for Adrian Bolte, who in 1660, after the Restoration, applied to have his previous appointment confirmed. It was then that the furniture-making trade was reorganized, cabinetmakers being differentiated from the old-established guilds of joiners and carpenters to which they had previously belonged; in this development emphasis was once again placed on the art of veneering, as in the case of the Italian *ebanista* and the French *ébéniste*.

English cabinets of the Stuart period are very similar in form to the French and Dutch type. Indeed, the most famous cabinetmaker of the time in England was the Flemish craftsman Gerrit Jensen, who served under four English sovereigns and was responsible for creating the so-called Anglo-Dutch style during the latter part of the century. As in Holland, the taste for plain surfaces encouraged the use of burr veneers with striking variegated markings: walnut, laburnum, acacia and lignum vitae were all used in oystershell, geometric or seaweed patterns.

The grandest examples of this type were made *c.* 1665 for Queen Henrietta Maria: a pair of cabinets veneered in lignum vitae with embossed silver mounts (both now in the Royal Collection at Windsor Castle). As cabinets became more numerous, other techniques were used, inspired by continental practices. As early as 1614 an inventory at Northampton House listed: 'two Cabinettes whereof one is of ebony inlaied with white bone, the other of crimson velvet laid with silver and gold lace'.[33] Needlework decoration was also mentioned in referring to coverings 'richly embroidered in colours'. A burr walnut cabinet in a private collection in England commemorates the marriage in 1661 of Charles II and Catherine of Braganza in stumpwork embroidery adorned with silver decorations, seed-pearls and coral on a silk ground. The theme was a favourite one and also appears on smaller table-cabinets featuring embroidery, or in the fragile decoration made by young girls working with cut and moulded paper applied to a silk-covered ground. The latter technique seems to have been indigenous to England, whereas embroidered coverings were fashionable in Flanders too.

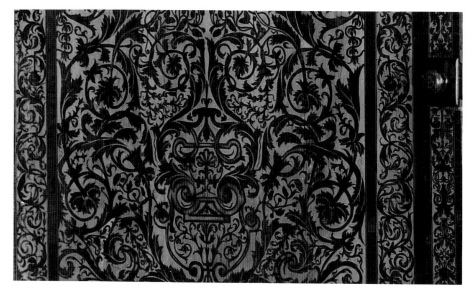

Walnut and satinwood cabinet-on-stand with enlarged detail showing seaweed marquetry. England, c. 1695; width 174 cm (5 ft 8½ in.).

During the last quarter of the century floral marquetry of the Dutch and French type became very fashionable on a certain form of cabinet which included a frieze drawer under the cornice and a pair of doors that open to reveal sets of drawers arranged around a central cupboard, as found in cabinets made in Flanders. The stand sometimes had a further set of drawers and the turned legs were joined by a flat curved stretcher. Ovals of floral marquetry included birds and a spray of jasmine in bloom made of white horn, the foliage being made of green stained horn, and the flowers depicted in bright, realistic colours. Among the contemporary furniture still at Ham House, near Richmond in Surrey, are many examples of the variety and quality of cabinets made in England during the latter part of the seventeenth century; they include the Duchess of Lauderdale's exquisite Scriptor still in her White Closet, a piece described in the 1683 inventory as 'One Scriptore of Prince['s] wood garnished with Silver'.[34] The house also contains a remarkable Dutch or Flemish ivory cabinet-on-stand, mentioned in 1679 as being in the Queen's Chamber.

Forms were becoming more varied and, in accordance with the spirit of the time, collections of rare objects were being displayed. Choice examples of Chinese blue-and-white porcelain were massed on the top of cabinets, and glazed cabinets were specifically designed to show off precious objects. Thus, Gerrit Jensen provided Queen Mary with a 'glass case of fine markatree upon a cabinet with doors' in 1693. This piece, in the Royal Collection at Windsor Castle, is entirely covered with a fine arabesque type of walnut and sycamore inlay inspired by Boulle work in metal and tortoiseshell. This inlay technique was used only by Gerrit Jensen in England; one example of his work in the Royal Collection, executed c. 1691–5, bears the royal monogram 'WM'.

As the century drew to a close under William and Mary, the writing function of the cabinet, already present in the small scriptor, gained in importance. This type of writing cabinet with a fall-front was now combined with a new type, no longer on a stand, but on a chest of drawers, so increasing the storage capacity. This pragmatic attitude is a far cry from the ornate *meuble d'apparat* of the High Baroque period and represents a tendency towards a more informal lifestyle and a desire for greater comfort, which was to characterize the eighteenth century.

3

GRANDEUR
AND DECLINE

IN THE EARLY YEARS OF THE EIGHTEENTH CENTURY THE GRAND BAROQUE style lingered on throughout Europe. In France, at the court of Louis XIV, the brilliance of Versailles and its dazzling opulence provided a model for royal courts in other European capitals. Its High Baroque style, characterized by great ostentation, served to assert a powerful political message, expressed just as much in its buildings and their decoration and furnishings as in the elaborate court etiquette, and was well suited to the needs of the absolute monarchies of the time. Lavishly decorated cabinets symbolized the king's glory, his magnanimity and generosity, and were used for political ends, as indeed was every aspect of life and art at court. Louis XIV himself expounded these kingly duties and necessities in his 'Instructions to the Dauphin' (*Instructions destinées au Dauphin*), in which he noted that 'A Prince and a King of France must look upon these diversions as something more than mere self-indulgence ... Regarding the cost of these pleasurable activities, which might appear to be frivolous, it provides an advantageous means of creating an impression of wealth, power, grandeur and magnificence.'[1]

In this spirit the Ambassadors from Siam had been suitably impressed in 1684 by the gift of 'Three cabinets of rock crystal carved with facets, slightly larger than normal caskets, but a lot taller, surrounded by silver-gilt columns of various architectural orders and other ornaments. They were also given several cabinets made of amber, with very delicately worked bas-reliefs and figures of the same material. For their king they received a large cabinet in rock crystal with decorations of silver-gilt flowers.'[2] In 1689, Louis XIV sent as a gift to the Queen of England (Catherine of Braganza) 'A cabinet that when open becomes a *Prie-Dieu*, and can then be transformed into an altar containing everything that is required in a chapel.'[3] Both descriptions were published in the *Mercure Galant*, a weekly journal founded in Paris in 1672 by Donneau de Vizé.

Cabinets were very valuable objects and as such were recorded in their own right, as part of the royal treasury, in the *Inventaire de la Couronne* of 1679: 'Eight cabinets with silver filigree, one with oval mirrors and sixteen columns of various forms, one in gilt brass adorned with chased silver bas-reliefs, one in ebony with a large silver niche within which is a statue of Neptune surrounded by several other figures, amongst them Louis XIII on horseback.'[4] Similarly, a special steel cabinet from Italy, very likely a damascened cabinet made in Milan, was treated with great care. The apparently large number of these cabinets was commonplace at the time. In 1679, during the official visit of the Queen of Spain to Paris, her quarters in the Palais-Royal were furnished with 'seven cabinets adorned with gilt silver, and miniature paintings set in silver',[5] while in the two galleries of the palace 'there were fifteen or sixteen cabinets of great richness and beauty, all containing miniatures', the *Mercure Galant* reported.[6] The taste for cabinets was also typical in humbler surroundings, examples being recorded in contemporary inventories; a *Traité de Police* even included the advice that 'in case of epidemics, cabinets had to be disinfected',[7] together with other everyday items of domestic furniture.

It was in the late seventeenth century too that the earlier *studio* and *Wunderkammer* (or cabinet of curiosities) took on a more academic aspect, with greater emphasis on order and clarity than previously, for didactic and professional purposes. Thus, all over Europe collections of

Table-cabinet with overall veneer of red and yellow amber, having sixteen drawers arranged around a central theatre. Germany, c. 1700–20; width 74 cm (2 ft 5 in.).

natural and man-made rarities were assembled either in specially designed cabinets with doors, or in display cabinets with open shelves in an early attempt at museology evoking the whole of art and nature; in 1688 the Monastère Ste Geneviève in Paris had such a *Cabinet de Curiosités*, which stood at the end of its library. This piece housed twelve smaller walnut cabinets on columnar stands; these provided storage space for medals depicting the gods and emperors of antiquity, popes and European monarchs, in an attempt to create an encyclopaedic historical survey. The principal towns and abbeys of France were also represented, together with views of cities in the Far East and Middle East. The content included scientific and mathematical instruments, clocks, etc., as well as modern and antique cameos and intaglios and natural and man-made curios.[8]

Cabinets were so much part of everyday life that they would lend themselves to flirtatious games, as well as being given as tokens of love or friendship, or to commemorate a marriage. In royal circles Louis XIV would invite thirty-one ladies of the court to the Château de Marly, where a lottery was held around a cabinet with only thirty drawers, each containing a jewel; this galant parlour game apparently cost the king the princely sum of 3,000 pistoles.[9] Indeed, it seems that Louis XIV was not alone in his liking for cabinets; for example the royal castle of Rosenborg in Denmark (rebuilt in 1613–15) still contains over twenty cabinets, some in pairs, of varying sizes and in different techniques, made in countries throughout Europe.

In France the Inventory of Crown Furniture drawn up in 1700 recorded 500 pieces, including 76 cabinets, of which 24 were japanned and some were in Florentine *pietra dura*, some decorated with painted floral miniatures *façon de porcelaine* (in the manner of Chinese porcelain decoration), and others recording the king's victories, one in steel (said to be from Florence but more likely from Milan), another in ivory carved in the Flemish manner; other pieces included the Henry IV cedarwood cabinet (recorded in 1603), the Louis XII cabinet in brazilwood, as well as some from the collections of Cardinal Mazarin, Anne of Austria and Mademoiselle de Fontanges, one bought from Abbé Strozzi and two given by the Papal Nuncio Pignatelli.[10] Fashion was changing, however, and in the same year the architect Jacques-François Blondel (1705–74) reported that 'These cabinets were much in use in the last century, but as they were occupying a considerable amount of space in the apartments, they were removed.'[11]

Although the actual disposal of the Royal cabinets did not take place until after the young Louis XV (still a minor) succeeded Louis XIV in 1715, the latter had, since marrying the pious and increasingly austere Madame de Maintenon in 1684, grown weary of the grand public style he had created to reflect his own image as the Sun King. He had come to favour privacy, and built Marly and the Grand Trianon at Versailles with this in mind, seeing intimacy and a fresher, lighter touch which he summarized in his instructions to Claude Audran, his designer for the Château de la Ménagerie at Versailles; in a note dated 10 September 1699 concerning the decorative scheme proposed two days earlier by Jules Hardouin-Mansart, he stated that 'We need the lightheartedness of youth in everything we shall do.'[12] Building on a large extravagant scale was a thing of the past. In contrast to the formal suite of rooms – *Les Grands Appartements* – suitable for the rigid etiquette of public life, it was now the comfortable cosiness of the *Petits Appartements* which concerned king and court. Versailles, although still important until the king's death in 1715, declined during the Régence proper (1715–23), when the Regent, the Duc d'Orléans, returned to Paris and members of the aristocracy started building themselves new *hôtels* (town-houses) in order to enjoy a more relaxed, elegant social life in the capital.

A new, more feminine, frivolous note was introduced by designers such as Jean Bérain, with his use of light arabesques and *singerie*, and Audran influencing a younger generation of artists and decorators, including the painter Watteau (1684–1721), whose *fêtes galantes* were a perfect evocation of a new society in which pleasure and comfort mattered most. In this new situation rooms were of smaller proportions, and there was a tendency to curvilinear detailings. More practical types of furniture were required, since grand, imposing, frontally designed cabinets did not fit within these airy rooms with their white and gold decorative schemes, in which mirrors included in the *boiseries* helped to create an even lighter effect. Boulle himself had sensed the change of fashion in 1708–9, when producing a new type of grand display furniture, but on a reduced scale, in the pair of commodes he made for the king's bedchamber at the Grand Trianon. The *commode en tombeau*, with its curvaceous lines and low profile, was perfectly attuned to the spirit of the time. Cabinets were rethought along similar lines; smaller overall but still magnificent in their decoration, the new pieces retained the storage function of the cabinet while continuing to be virtuoso showpieces. The term 'cabinet' was now applied in France to a low cupboard, sometimes called *bas d'armoire* or *corps de bibliothèque*, made in Boulle work and mostly used for storing medals and coins. It is very likely that pieces of this type would have been specially commissioned for the Cabinet des Médailles et Raretés (Cabinet of medals and curiosities) at Versailles; of the twelve marquetry cabinets recorded in the *Journal du Garde Meuble de la Couronne* as having been made to house the king's collection of medals, some are still at Versailles.

Boulle's designs were greatly influenced by Bérain's airy grotesques and arabesques, and so great was the prestige of the French court and French fashion generally that his technique spread quickly to the rest of northern Europe. Gerrit Jensen used it in England, and it was adopted in both Flanders and Austria, but most significantly the German courts vied with each other to achieve impressive grandeur and gain artistic patronage. Among the outstanding exponents of Boulle work were: Johann Daniel Sommer, who worked in Künzelsau am Kocher, Württemberg, where he specialized in tortoiseshell, mother-of-pearl and pewter veneering, 1643–c. 1685; Ferdinand Plitzner (1678–1724), who was employed at Schloss Pommersfelden in the service of Lothar Franz von Schönborn; and Joseph Effner (1687–1768), who worked at Schloss Schleissheim from 1701 to 1719.

Cabinet with Boulle-work veneer on front and sides, and a marble top. Probably by André Charles Boulle, c. 1710–15.

Although design books were published in Augsburg and Nuremberg, they were often nothing more than re-issues of French, Italian or English ornamental engravings. As a result, the German production represented a diverse cross-section of the various trends of the eighteenth century, and the anonymity demanded by the guilds' regulations further discouraged attribution of specific pieces to particular craftsmen. However, a large number of these Boulle-work cabinets still exist, sometimes in pairs and always displaying features of the High Baroque Louis XIV style; sometimes the grand political statement of earlier cabinets (such as the pair from the Saxe-Coburg-Gotha Collection) is combined with the bureau-cabinet, the new form inspired by English designs. Thus in 1732 a Thuringian craftsmen, Dietrich Schäffer, as official cabinetmaker to the King of Denmark, made for Christian VI a remarkable bureau-cabinet resting on four gilt-bronze dolphins, reminiscent of Bernini's designs for the fountains in Rome, the marquetry cabinet being surmounted by a gilt-bronze sculptural group representing the apotheosis of the King. This bureau-cabinet in the Danish Royal Collection at Rosenborg Castle can be associated with a group of late Baroque cabinets produced in the eighteenth century, representing the swansong of the cabinet as a symbol of dynastic pride and royal power.

This group also includes the late production of the Medici Galleria dei Lavori in Florence. The influence of Giovanni Battista Foggini, architect and *capomaestro* of the Galleria, was all-pervading. The proportions became monumental; the ebony and ivory cabinet made between 1704 and 1716 by the *ebanista* Suster with inlay by the Dutch craftsman Vittorio Crosten (now in the Pitti Palace) was already of impressive size, being 2.12 m (7 ft) high. The Elector Palatine cabinet in ebony, gilt bronze and *pietra dura*, also designed by Foggini, was 2.80 m (over 9 ft) high; executed as a gift to Cosimo III's daughter, the Electress Palatine Anna Maria Luisa, it bears the combined Medici-Palatinate armorials, flanked by dancing cupids and reclining allegorical figures.

Although this cabinet can be seen as representing the peak of the production of the Medici Galleria – for the workshop was disbanded when the last Grand Duke, Gian Gastone, died in 1737, with most of the craftsmen finding new patronage under King Charles III of Spain at Buen Retiro, Madrid – the last and largest of all the Galleria cabinets was made between 1726 and 1732 for an English aristocrat, the 3rd Duke of Beaufort, for the family seat, Badminton House. The so-called Badminton Cabinet was the last in a long and distinguished line of grand dynastic cabinets made in Italy, Germany and France. As such, it took on all the attributes of the French concept of a *meuble d'apparat et de parade*, at a time when the taste and the fashion for such ornate pieces had died out. The largest cabinet made in the Galleria – 3.86 m (12 ft 8 in.) in height – it features all the previously favoured components of the style: armorials surmounting the clock, classical bronze figures as finials. Yet if the detailing of the decoration in the *pietra dura* and gilt bronze remained exquisite, the general design was top-heavy and lacked the imposing Baroque plasticity and movement of the Foggini design for the Elector Palatine's cabinet.

The new spirit of the time was manifested in a move away from monumental pieces in glowing ebony, to the curvaceous, smaller pieces with serpentine lines of the Rococo style (known in France as *style*

The Elector Palatine cabinet, in ebony, gilt bronze and pietra dura, *designed by Giovanni Battista Foggini, c. 1707–9, and made in the Galleria dei Lavori, Florence; height 2.80 m (9 ft 2¼ in.).*

rocaille or Louis XV style) and featuring a lighter marquetry of exotic woods. Louis XV intensely disliked the grand cabinets of the preceding century which furnished the royal palaces. He started selling them at public auctions, the first one being held in the Tuileries in 1741, though the *Journal du Garde Meuble* gave no numbers or details. On 25 April 1748, by order of the king, twelve *pietra dura* cabinets and a table were delivered by the Garde Meuble to M. Buffon, Keeper of the Royal Garden 'to enrich the Cabinet of Natural History'.[13] Among them was the *Cabinet de la Paix* by Cucci, a marvel of art and nature originally made to serve the dynastic ambitions of Louis XIV and now relegated to a museum as a repository for its collection of semi-precious stones.[14] On 15 February 1751, a sale held in the Louvre disposed of a further twenty-two cabinets, including the cedarwood cabinet made for Henry IV which was bought by the dealer (*marchand-mercier*) Lazare Duvaux on behalf of Mme de Pompadour, who had it made into scented caskets, according to Duvaux's *Livre Journal* of the years 1748–58.

In France, a long period of political stability, interrupted only by the Seven Years' War (1756–63), brought a new prosperity to all levels of society, the resulting comfort and luxury being enjoyed by a larger proportion of the population than ever before. And although life at court still harked back to the formality and nobility of the *Grand Siècle* of Louis XIV, the 'Petits Appartements' encouraged a more relaxed private lifestyle. Among changes in the style and size of furniture the commode now took over the role of showpiece. Like the cabinet, it too was a storage piece, and the emphasis on practicality and comfort served to encourage the development of various types of writing desk, reviving a purpose – long-forgotten in France – formerly associated with the cabinet. The original Portuguese *escritorio* was recalled in the new French term *secrétaire à abattant* (sometimes *secrétaire en armoire*), a description reflecting the storage aspect of the early cabinet and of the Roman *armarium*. Another smaller type used by ladies was the *bonheur du jour*, which consisted of a writing table with a set of drawers on the top, combining two functions in an elegant, refined solution, completely French in character. As Nicolas Cochin (1713–90) wrote in his *Mémoires*, 'In this country the taste of pretty women rules.'[15]

The production of furniture in France increased considerably in response to demand from all classes of society. As a result the guild system was reorganized yet again. On 28 December 1743 the statutes of the *Menuisier-Ebénistes* were further codified by Letters Patent requiring inspection by an official panel, the *Jurande Menuisier Ebéniste*, whose mark 'JME' would be branded on every piece approved. Standards of excellence were further endorsed by the compulsory stamping of a maker's mark (*estampille*) on furniture made by every *maître ébéniste* from 1751 until the guild system was abolished in 1791.

Precious woods such as purplewood and rosewood were being used, followed later by elaborate pictorial marquetry inspired by Jean-François Oeben's work. A new type of commercial patronage now emerged: the Parisian *marchand-merciers*, who, as dealers and interior decorators were forbidden to open their own workshops, commissioned individual *ébénistes*. Poirier, Daguerre and Lazare Duvaux (regular purveyor to Madame de Pompadour) were the best-known dealers. In response to contemporary taste, which favoured gay, bright polychromy, they

Bonheur du jour decorated with Sèvres porcelain plaques and gilt-bronze mounts and gallery. France c. 1770; width 69.5 cm (2 ft 3¾ in.).

fostered a fashion for the use of porcelain plaques on furniture. Some *ébénistes*, such as Carlin and Weisweiler, worked exclusively for Poirier and Daguerre, producing the type of *mobilier de confort et d'agrément* (furniture for pleasure and comfort) which was in demand at the time.

The only type of cabinets which found continuing favour in the eighteenth century, being still recorded as treasured possessions in contemporary inventories, were those with lacquer decoration. In 1740 the inventory of Mademoiselle Desmares listed 'A Chinese lacquer cabinet with nine drawers with its supporting table made of japanning with gilt feet',[16] and in 1777 in the Randon de Boisset collection 'A superb cabinet with a black lacquer ground' was recorded.[17] In the 1720s and 1730s *chinoiserie* came to the fore in France, the word being used in conjunction with the work of Bérain, Audran and Watteau. Whole rooms were decorated in this lighthearted, fanciful manner, in keeping with the more relaxed lifestyle of the period and fostered by renewed imports following the reorganization of the French East India Company.

Cabinet containing ten drawers, with overall lacquer decoration in black and gold, made for export to Europe. Japan, c. 1720–30; width 96 cm (3 ft 1¼ in.).

Chinoiserie became assimilated to the Rococo style, which was spreading throughout Europe. Oriental lacquer panels, instead of being an integral part of a piece of furniture and so dictating its shape, were now applied as veneers. Old or new pieces were thus bent to conform with the new *bombé* shapes. The areas surrounding the lacquer panels were varnished in France – *vernis des Gobelins* being used by Jacques Dagly or *vernis Martin* in Paris – and japanned in England, Germany, Italy and the Netherlands. The love and mania for decorated porcelain was encouraging the taste for lacquer and japanned wares, and whole rooms would be designed in this *chinoiserie* taste.

One of the earliest examples of a decorative scheme in this style was the Porcelain Room created for the future Queen Mary in Holland by Daniel Marot and later rebuilt at Hampton Court Palace. At about the same time Gerhard Dagly decorated the *Porzellanzimmer* for Augustus the Strong, Elector of Saxony, at Schloss Oranienburg, outside Berlin. The architect Christoph Pitzler reported in 1694: 'It is beautifully furnished and is equipped with cabinets and chairs made in Japan, and also there are some made in Berlin by Dagly, one in the manner of porcelain in blue and white.'[18]

The taste for all things oriental encouraged the development of a large number of lacquer artists throughout Europe. England, however, seems to have led the way thanks to the East India Company's long-established trading links with the Orient. Such was the demand for japanned wares that as early as 1672–3 the Company's records mentioned that 'Several artificers were sent over to the east to teach the Indians how to manufacture goods to make them vendible in England and the rest of the European markets.'[19] A memorandum expressing the concern felt by the London craftsmen was presented to Parliament in 1700. It stated:[20]

Artificers, Members [of the Joyners' Company], have been bred up in the said Art or Mystery of making Cabinets, Scrutoirs [writing cabinets], tables, chests and all other sorts of Cabinet work. They have arrived to so great a perfection as exceeds all Europe. But merchants trading to the East Indies have procured and sent over to the East Indies, Patterns and Models of all sorts of Cabinet goods; and have returned from there such Quantities of Cabinet Wares, manufactured there after the English fashion by our models, that the said trade in England is in great danger of being utterly ruined. They also spoil the Exportation of the said Joyners and Cabinetmakers.

Opposite
55 Bureau-cabinet or trumeau *with* lacca contrafatta *decoration of landscapes and figures on a cream-coloured ground within crimson reserves. The cabinet is surmounted by the papal arms and figures of the Four Seasons as finials. Rome, c. 1740; height 2.77 m (9 ft 1 in.).*

The Boulle technique using
tortoiseshell veneers in combination
with brass and pewter continued to be
practised in France during the Régence
period (1715–23), after which it went
out of fashion until the 1780s. In
Germany Boulle work assumed an
impressive richness and grandeur, being
used on cabinets and bureau-cabinets to
express the pride of ruling princes.

56 *Cabinet-on-stand with domed top
and brass, pewter and tortoiseshell
Boulle-work decoration; the central
cupboard door matches the drawer
fronts on either side. Germany/Austria,
c. 1700; width 160 cm (5 ft 3 in.).*

57 *Medal cabinet (one of a pair) with
Boulle-work decoration, similar to
médailliers made for Louis XIV's Cabinet
des Médailles at Versailles. France, c.
1690–1700; width 122 cm (4 ft).*

Opposite
58 *Cabinet-on-stand (one of a pair) with
copper, pewter and tortoiseshell Boulle-
work decoration; the central cupboard is
surrounded by drawers on all sides.
South Germany, c. 1700; width 131 cm
(4 ft 3½in.).*

At the end of the seventeenth century the scriptor was succeeded in England by the bureau or *secrétaire* as a piece of furniture with a specific writing function, characterized by a sloping front and the provision of internal drawers and pigeon-holes. Simultaneously, the bureau-cabinet made its appearance. With its emphasis on convenience, this type combined storage, display and writing functions, and its greater height reflected the more generous proportions of contemporary interiors. Such pieces were, like cabinets of the period, generally finished in plain wood veneers or japanning.

Opposite, above
59, 60 Burr walnut bureau-cabinet with double mirrored doors and attached candelabra; the double-domed top is decorated with gilt finials. England, c. 1705.

Opposite, below left
61 Mulberry bureau-cabinet with double-domed top and double doors shown open to reveal a symmetrical arrangement of drawers, shelves and pigeon-holes. England, c. 1695; width 99 cm (3 ft 3 in.).

Opposite, below right
62 Walnut bureau-cabinet with domed top and a later glazed door; the interior features two fluted pilasters. England, c. 1715–20; width 54.5 cm (21½ in.).

63 Burr walnut bureau-cabinet with double doors below a single-arched cornice embellished with vase-shaped finials. England, c. 1710.

The Badminton Cabinet

64–69 This very large piece (opposite), made 1726–32 for the 3rd Duke of Beaufort, was the last of the grand dynastic cabinets produced by the Opificio delle Pietre Dure in the Galleria dei Lavori on the first floor of the Uffizi in Florence; height 3.86 m (12 ft 8 in.). A preliminary design is shown (right), together with details of the decoration on the front and (below, left) one of the pietra dura floral panels decorating the sides of the cabinet.

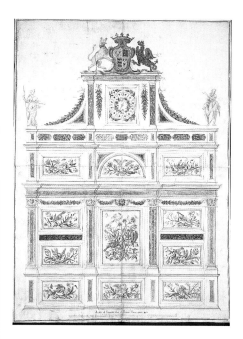

During the eighteenth century rare and exotic materials, such as *pietra paesina* and ivory, were used either alone or in combination with lacquer to decorate a wider variety of cabinet types. The diversity of their forms and finishes reflected a less formal approach, and a more intimate and relaxed lifestyle encouraged the development of pieces on a much smaller scale with more graceful 'feminine' lines.

70 Casket japanned in black and gold in the Japanese style; the drawers and the inside of the two doors are veneered in matching ivory and ebony. Dresden, c. 1740; width 29 cm (14 in.).

71 Small table-cabinet japanned in black and gold, with ten drawers faced with pietra paesina. *Germany, c. 1700; width 46 cm (18 in.).*

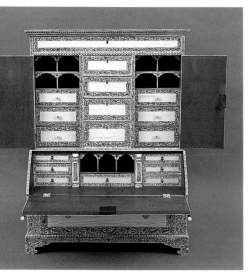

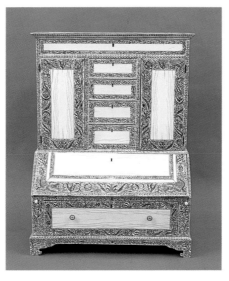

72 Cabinet-on-stand with lacquer decoration of turqueries on a black ground (the interior lacquered in cream, red and blue), signed 'Man. de la Zerda'. Spain or Portugal, c. 1730; width 102 cm (3 ft 4 in.).

73, 74 Miniature bureau-cabinet with ivory-veneered exterior and internal drawers, all with contrasting incised scroll decoration in black. Vizigatapam, India, c. 1760; width 61 cm (2 ft).

GRANDEUR AND DECLINE

The cabinet-on-stand form continued to be made in England during the eighteenth century. Such pieces were decorated with either oriental lacquer or japanning to create exotic exteriors that would blend with early Georgian decorative schemes. The stands were made in classical Palladian forms, and were assimilated to the 'Chinese Chippendale' style in mid-century.

75 *Black-japanned cabinet on a carved and gilded stand with paw-feet. England, c. 1720–25; width 107 cm (3 ft 6 in.).*

76 *Japanned cabinet-on-stand in the 'Chinese Chippendale' style, which is more akin to original Chinese decoration than most European* chinoiserie. *England, c. 1765; width 126 cm (4 ft 1½ in.).*

77 *Rosewood cabinet-on-stand with doors shown open to reveal drawers faced with Chinese lacquer panels. England, c. 1760–70; width 94 cm (3 ft 1 in.).*

The English form of the large bureau-cabinet became fashionable throughout Europe, except for France, where the smaller proportions of the Rococo (*style rocaille*) were preferred. The grand bureau-cabinet was often japanned in a wide range of colours, and decorated in keeping with the prevailing fashion for *chinoiserie* and the general fascination with all things oriental, especially porcelain.

Left
78, 79 *Bureau-cabinet with double doors (shown closed and open) and double-domed top, japanned in green and gold. England, c. 1705; width 104 cm (3 ft 5 in.).*

80, 81 *White-japanned cabinet (upper part and detail of side panel) with painted decoration and Chinese porcelain plaques. Probably Germany, c. 1700–20; width 109 cm (3 ft 7 in.).*

82 *Red-japanned bureau-cabinet with*
chinoiserie *decoration, attributed to*
Giles Grendey. England, c. 1720–30
(formerly in the collection of the Duke
of Infantado); width 104 cm (3 ft 5 in.).

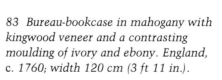

83 Bureau-bookcase in mahogany with kingwood veneer and a contrasting moulding of ivory and ebony. England, c. 1760; width 120 cm (3 ft 11 in.).

The European taste for oriental porcelain in the eighteenth century encouraged the development of the bureau-bookcase featuring a glazed upper part (as illustrated by Chippendale in his *Director* in 1754) for use in displaying personal collections. The straight classical lines of furniture made in the French Louis XVI and Directoire styles influenced Sheraton's and Hepplewhite's designs, in terms of both forms and techniques, towards the end of the century.

84 Bureau-cabinet in Brazilian rosewood with gilt-bronze mounts and having two glazed doors behind which a central cupboard is flanked by tiers of drawers. Dresden, c. 1750; width 108 cm (3 ft 6½ in.).

85 *Satinwood and marquetry cabinet (one of a pair) with rosewood cross-banding. England, c. 1780; width 70 cm (2 ft 3½ in.).*

86 *Satinwood display cabinet with double doors above a* secrétaire *drawer in the Sheraton style. England, c. 1790.*

In eighteenth-century Germany the form of the bureau-cabinet became the equivalent of a commemorative piece. The marquetry bureau-cabinet – a wedding commission – combined the earlier use of perspective design with contemporary Rococo scrolls.

87–89 Bureau-cabinet with overall veneered decoration of yew, poplar and boxwood and with ebonized banding and feet. The double doors of the upper part conceal a central cupboard surrounded by drawers; the inner cupboard door in turn opens to reveal a further set of smaller drawers (right). Germany, c. 1740; width 70 cm (2 ft 3¼ in.).

The *secrétaire à abattant* (or *en armoire*) was the most usual French furniture type used for storage and writing in the eighteenth century; it echoed the function and the lines of earlier cabinets-on-stand or cupboards. Oriental lacquer, *vernis Martin*, pictorial marquetry or rich veneers were used to decorate a form which was to be found all over Europe at the end of the century.

90 Secrétaire à abattant *with tulipwood marquetry and a marble top, stamped* 'BOUDIN' (as dealer) *and* 'MOREAU' (as maker). *France, c. 1770–80, width 79 cm (2 ft 7 in.).*

Right, above
91 Secrétaire à abattant *in rosewood with marquetry in the manner of Giuseppe Maggiolini. Northern Italy, c. 1780–90; width 89 cm (2 ft 11 in.).*

Opposite, below
92 Mahogany *secrétaire à abattant* with
a grey marble top and gilt-bronze
mounts. France, c. 1800; width 98 cm
(3 ft 2½ in.).

93 Secrétaire à abattant *with internal
shelves and drawers japanned and with
gilt-bronze mounts, the matching stand
having five drawers. Made by Adam
Weisweiler and supplied to Louis XVI for
the Cabinet du Roi at Versailles,
c. 1780–85; width 134 cm (4 ft 4½ in.).*

The taste for luxury and rich polychromy in the eighteenth century led to innovations in decorative techniques. In addition to the use of lacquer, japanning and painted panels, new methods and materials included penwork and rolled paper work in England, inset Sèvres porcelain plaques in France, and coloured engravings laid on a silk ground under glass in Italy.

94 Secrétaire à abattant *with geometric marquetry and inset Sèvres plaques. France (maker's stamp* 'A WEISWEILER'*), c. 1784; width 102.5 cm (3 ft 4¼ in.).*

95 Serre-bijoux *in tulipwood with inset Sèvres plaques and gilt-bronze mounts. Made for Marie-Antoinette as Dauphine of France, c. 1770 (maker's stamp* 'M. CARLIN'*); width 56 cm (22 in.).*

98–100 Walnut-veneered scrivania with gilt-bronze mounts and decorative panels with 42 coloured engravings on a silk ground under glass (two details shown enlarged). Rome or Venice, c. 1735; width 157 cm (5 ft 2 in.).

Opposite, right
96, 97 Red-japanned bureau-cabinet with a total of 66 painted panels; the piece has secret drawers concealed in its narrow sides. A detail of the upper part with open door shows a further set of small drawers. Attributed to Franz de Paula Ferg, Vienna, c. 1735; width 116 cm (3 ft 9½ in.).

In America the impact of English furniture design resulted largely from the publication of the 3rd edtion of Chippendale's *Director* in 1762. In the post-revolutionary Federal period determining factors included the publication of Hepplewhite's designs (1788) and Sheraton's *Cabinet-Maker & Upholsterer's Drawing-Book* (1791–4).

101 Bureau-cabinet with chamfered corners of cherry wood and veneered with mahogany and other woods. Connecticut or Rhode Island, c. 1790–1810; width 105 cm (3 ft 5¼ in.).

102 Lady's bureau-cabinet in mahogany inlaid with satinwood, and inset with scenes painted on glass, after a design from Sheraton's Cabinet-Maker & Upholsterer's Drawing-Book. *Baltimore, c. 1795–1810; width 78 cm (2 ft 7 in.).*

103 Serre-bijoux in mahogany decorated with Sèvres plaques, painted panels and gilt-bronze mounts; made by J. J. Schwerdfeger and presented by the City of Paris to Marie-Antoinette as Queen of France. Paris, 1787; width 2.10 m (6 ft 10½ in.).

At the beginning of the eighteenth century japanned cabinets, *escrutores* (scriptors), were being exported from England to Spain and Portugal; the leading London cabinetmaker and exporter was Giles Grendey, who supplied a whole suite of furniture with red, gold and silver decoration to the Duke of Infantado for his castle of Lazcano in Spain, and who deplored the loss of furniture worth £1,000, destroyed in a fire in 1731 at his Clerkenwell workshop. The volume of trade must have been very large; among other noted craftsmen recorded was Daniel Mills, active 1768–77. Indeed, such was the renown of the English wares that the Guild of Cabinetmakers in The Hague required every apprentice to produce a cabinet 'in the English style' as his masterpiece.

This type of cabinet in the English style would most probably have been a bureau-cabinet. The writing function of the cabinet had been apparent in the scriptor recorded in the 1679 inventory of the Duke and Duchess of Lauderdale, which was no doubt a direct descendant of the Portuguese *escritorio* and the German *Schreibtisch*. The first known mention of a bureau-cabinet occurs in a bill submitted by Gerrit Jensen to the Crown in 1693 for 'a large Bouro of fine markatrie with drawers to stand upon the topp carv'd and gilt pillars'.[21] The development of the bureau-cabinet in England ran parallel to a similar evolution on the Continent during the early years of the eighteenth century; there the *secrétaire, bonheur du jour* and *bureau* were produced in considerable numbers and in various techniques. Boulle himself saw the obvious appeal of the form as a showpiece also having a practical use, and produced a bureau for Maximilian Emanuel, Elector of Bavaria, who visited his workshop in 1723. Its upper part, a cabinet adorned with a clock and surmounted by a statue of Victory and finials bearing the armorials of the ruling House of Bavaria, was designed to rest on a writing table (the original is now in the Louvre and a copy exists in the Wallace Collection).

In England, patronage in the early part of the eighteenth century came not from the Church and the royal court, but increasingly from the aristocracy and the gentry. Just as in France, the furniture of the period reflected the needs of this new clientele, the emphasis being on practicality and convenience, although some older forms did survive, but with adaptations to suit current trends. Thus the cabinet-on-stand, whether with Japanese or Chinese lacquer or English japanned decoration, continued during the Georgian period, but the shape of the stand now echoed the classical architectural forms of William Kent and Lord Burlington's Palladianism.

The cabinet-on-chest had already appeared in the last decade of the seventeenth century during the reign of William and Mary, and both the sloping front and the earliest records of the bureau-cabinet are associated with the same period. The early examples of pieces in the William and Mary and the Queen Anne styles often have a top with double dome (still used to display porcelain) or with finials. They followed the customary decorative patterns of cabinets, and were either in burr walnut or japanned, often red, sometimes green; although John Stalker and George Parker, in *A Treatise of Japanning and Varnishing*, also refer to white and yellow, few examples have survived. Their forms would be very similar, usually with moulded panels on the upper doors and, on the finer examples, mirrors with bevelled edges. The interior revealed the

Bureau-cabinet in mulberry wood with double-domed top. England, c. 1695; width 99 cm (3 ft 3 in.).

standard disposition of a cabinet, with sets of drawers around a central cupboard, but also included shelves for display, as well as pigeon-holes. Pilasters and columns would adorn the compartments which sometimes contained secret drawers, harking back to an earlier tradition. The influence of Palladianism introduced a more classical approach to ornament, which now featured broken pediments enclosing an urn, armorials, or gilt finials. Pilasters, columns and niches, and occasionally a statuette, were used as decorative elements on these bureau-cabinets, in which the use of mahogany imported from Jamaica (replacing walnut) occurred after 1730.

In Germany, where French Rococo features were being allied to a late Baroque style, the design of the bureau-cabinet achieved a grandeur, variety and virtuosity unsurpassed in other European countries. The later, more fanciful *genre pittoresque* developed in France by Meissonnier and Pineau was translated by designers such as Cuvilliés into a sculptural use of curves and countercurves executed by master *Tischler* in fine Boulle work, pictorial marquetry, or sometimes japanned decoration. The new palace (Residenz) of Würzburg (1720) and Ansbach, where Martin Schumacher worked in the service of the Margrave, were centres of cabinetmaking. Gerhard Dagly worked in Berlin for the Elector Frederick William II of Brandenburg, and his assistant Martin Schnell

Below, left
Bureau-cabinet (Schreibschrank) with marquetry decoration, inlaid mother-of-pearl and ormolu mounts, surmounted by an asymmetrical cornice. Made for Augustus III, Elector of Saxony, by Christian Friedrich Lehmann, c. 1750; width 127 cm (4 ft 2 in.).

Below, right
Bureau-cabinet (Schreibschrank) japanned in blue and gold. Würzburg (maker's stamp 'KW'), c. 1730; width 120 cm (3 ft 7 in.).

Cabinet-on-stand with japanned decoration and carved polychrome flowers set in recesses in the Chinese manner. Attributed to Martin Schnell, Dresden, c. 1720–30.

Ebony cabinet with tortoiseshell veneer and ivory plaques engraved with hunting scenes. Probably Flemish, seventeenth century (from the collection of William Penn); the outer case and stand are of later date.

went to Dresden and realized the most English-looking japanned bureau-cabinets with *chinoiserie* motifs, sometimes painted on raised copper, and with a characteristic use of mirrored doors. Various colours were used – red, green, white and blue – sometimes with painted floral decoration reminiscent of porcelain taking the place of the usual *chinoiserie* designs.

The Rococo style lingered on in the German states, using the native talent for fine marquetry, whether pictorial or in a rich fanciful style all of its own, as seen on the Augustus III of Saxony bureau-cabinet now in the Victoria and Albert Museum. Based on the English prototype, the piece features a broken pediment, the use of movement in forms, volumes and curves, and displays outstanding craftsmanship in the inlay and ormolu; it is thus as much a *meuble d'apparat* as the grandest Florentine or Louis XIV cabinets.

In Italy, where the bureau-cabinet form became known as *bureau trumeau*, the *meuble d'apparat* function remained much in evidence. It could be achieved either by the use of plain walnut veneer, as in the Veneto, together with a mirrored door, much on the English style, and a moulded cornice, or it could take on a brilliant polychromy when decorated with *lacca* or *lacca povera*. This technique was a cheaper version of the process of japanning and became a pastime for society ladies. It was first described in France, where it was called *découpures* (literally, cut-outs) by the Sieur Crépy in 1727 when referring to the engravings after Watteau – these *compositions très galantes* – 'used by ladies to decorate furniture very prettily'.[22] In Venice, commercially produced prints sold by firms such as the Remondini from Bassano were cut out and stuck onto a painted ground. The whole would then be varnished to give it durability. Arcadian and *chinoiserie* scenes, *capricci*, animals and flowers were favoured, but because most of the bureau-cabinets thus decorated were made of soft woods, few examples have survived.

None of the bureau-cabinets made in America were treated to the type of rich and colourful japanned decoration found in England and Germany, or the Italian *lacca povera*. In the seventeenth century many of the first permanent settlers were fairly well-off and had brought their own furniture from Europe.[23] William Penn, founder of the city of Philadelphia in 1682, brought along an ebony, tortoiseshell and ivory cabinet, a piece most likely purchased in Antwerp in the course of his Grand Tour before setting out for the New World. This cabinet, subsequently mounted in a Palladian-style mahogany case and stand, is now in the American Museum in Britain, in Bath. The first recorded piece of native American furniture is an oak chest made at Hartford, Conn., *c.* 1680, and inscribed 'Mary Allyns Chisst Cutte and Joyned by Nich: Disbrowe'. One can reasonably assume that practicality and storage capacity were the early settlers' priorities and that in general the luxury function of the cabinet mattered little to them. Indeed, no cabinets were produced in America, the original humanist concept of the piece having already been supplanted by the practical convenience associated with the writing desk: the bureau-cabinet.

Japanning had been introduced around the turn of the century in the main cabinetmaking centres in New England, such as Newport, Rhode Island, and Boston, Massachusetts, *lacca povera* also being produced in these centres. However, it was the importation of mahogany from the West Indies, beginning soon after 1700, which was to determine the later forms of American furniture and the techniques employed. The grand decorative treatment was reserved for the highboy, or chest-on-chest. The most notable example of this type is the japanned highboy made by John Pimm of Boston for Commodore Joshua Loring, *c.* 1740–50, a masterpiece of the American Queen Anne style. It presents the same distinctive decorative features as the English bureau-cabinet, i.e. a broken pediment and gilt finials, yet its function is purely for storage.

English furniture styles were copied by American makers from existing pieces or from design books, the third edition of Chippendale's *Gentleman & Cabinet Maker's Director*, published in 1762, being particularly influential. Soon afterwards cabinetmaking workshops began to emerge in the larger centres of population. German colonists from the Rhineland area who had settled around Philadelphia brought their own native craft skills. By the middle of the eighteenth century Philadelphia had become the second largest city of the English-speaking world and trade grew accordingly, as it did in New England around the ports of Newport and Boston. All three remained the leading cabinet-making centres up to the Revolution in 1776.

During the Federal period, from *c.* 1790 to *c.* 1830, centres such as Boston grew in importance, together with Williamsburg and Charleston in Virginia. As prosperity grew, the number of cabinetmakers increased to meet the new demand for furniture. Although guilds did exist in some cities, itinerant 'joiners' were working their way across the country, while in the South some slaves were trained in cabinetmaking techniques, working in the plantations or in the workshops. Thus Peter Scott, when selling his property prior to his departure for England in 1755, could put up a notice in Williamsburg, Virginia, advertising 'Two negroes bred to the business of a cabinetmaker'.[24]

Some centres achieved particular distinction thanks to the talents of individual craftsmen. One such was Philadelphia, where Thomas Affleck, who arrived from Scotland in 1763, reportedly 'brought an unparalleled urbanity of Chinese Chippendale to Philadelphia work', some of it made for Governor John Penn. The mahogany butler's secretary of *c.* 1770 (now in the Metropolitan Museum, New York) is more like a cabinet-on-chest, its upper part with multiple-drawers being topped by a Palladian-inspired cornice and broken pediment. By the 1760s, in Newport, Job Townsend and John Goddard had brought innovations and variations on the theme of the bureau-cabinet, introducing the Rococo-inspired serpentine 'block front' allied to sinuous, carved shell motifs and a curved broken pediment.

After the Revolution the ornate carving associated with the Chippendale style gave way to lighter, plainer, simpler forms under the influence of Hepplewhite, whose designs were published posthumously by his widow in 1788 in *The Cabinetmaker and Upholsterer's Guide*. A new influx of craftsmen arriving from England, France and Holland participated in the expanding trade. Whereas mahogany, and sometimes walnut, had been used previously, now woods of lighter colours – holly, satinwood, tulipwood – were incorporated in contrasting inlay on a darker mahogany ground, depicting classical motifs which were also sometimes painted on.

Bureau-cabinet in cherrywood with broken pediment top, flame-like finials and a central carved shell. Suffield, Conn., c. 1750; width 89 cm (3 ft).

Mahogany slope-front desk with pigeon-holes and drawers, and full-height block-front. Boston, Mass., c. 1770; width 107 cm (3 ft 6 in.).

To the Hepplewhite influence was added that of Sheraton, with its undertones of the French Louis XVI and Directoire styles. Furniture types such as the *secrétaire, bonheur du jour* and even the bureau-cabinet were made, though with smaller proportions and with a more feminine gracefulness, by John Seymour of Boston and Duncan Phyfe of New York, among others.

North America was not the only distant part of the world where European techniques flourished and developed a style of their own. As early as 1669–79, Thomas Bowry, resident in India, was reporting 'Screetores finely wrought inlaid with turtle Shell or ivory, for which a very great trafficke is driven into most parts of India, Persia, Arabia, China and the South Seas, as well as into England and Holland.'[25] At the beginning of the seventeenth century the Dutch and the English East India Companies had carved out for themselves an eastern trading empire following the demise of Spain and Portugal as major powers. Prior to the opening up of sea-trade with Europe, no furniture-making tradition had existed in India and the Far East. Cabinets were therefore closely copied from European models in both India and Indonesia, where the first mention of the use of carved ebony in Batavia occurs in 1646; it was to dominate the decoration of cabinets until 1680. Ivory was also used in the form of finely carved plaques with tendril motifs, fixed by ivory pins onto a teak ground. After 1680 the floral decorations became larger and more luscious, influenced by the colourful chintzes exported to Europe in large quantities on account of the appeal of the luminosity of their highly resistant colours, painted or dyed, and their cheapness compared to their European counterparts. The size and style of these cabinets followed the European fashion: small table-cabinets and large cabinets-on-stand in the seventeenth century, sometimes with decoration inspired by European engravings; for example, the ivory cabinet in the Victoria and Albert Museum depicts the Garden of Eden, copied from a Dutch print of c. 1700 after Dürer.

In the eighteenth century the English style became all-important and miniature versions of the bureau-cabinet, mostly made in the second half of the century, featured ivory veneer decorated with incised black scroll and floral work, sometimes with scenes taken from the engravings in the Scottish architect Colen Campbell's *Vitruvius Britannicus*, published in several volumes (1715–25). This miniature bureau-cabinet form was adopted by the Royal Norwegian Silversmith J. Müller, of Bergen, for a presentation piece executed in silver filigree with a statuette of Fame above the Danish Royal armorials; the piece, commissioned for the occasion of the King and Queen of Denmark's official visit in 1733, is now in Rosenborg Castle.

In England, however, fashion had changed. The japanned cabinets of the first part of the century and the classically inspired architectural Palladian cabinets and bureau-cabinets were replaced following the appearance in 1754 of Chippendale's *Gentleman and Cabinetmaker's Director*, which introduced a lighter, more fanciful French Rococo touch; this in turn was fused with the Gothick style, promoted at Strawberry Hill by Horace Walpole, and with the popular *chinoiserie* style. In Chippendale's book 'Desks and Bookcases' (bureau-cabinets), 'Lady's secretary' (a variant of the French *bonheur du jour*) and cabinets were all illustrated, the designs ranging from traditional forms with Rococo detailings to Gothick examples and those in the Chinese manner. In the third edition, Chippendale wrote of one example featuring a pagoda: 'It is not only the richest and most magnificent in the whole, but perhaps in all Europe.' Bureau-cabinets or bureau-bookcases became very close in form and function to the display cabinet, a type which was already in use at the end of the seventeenth century.

The fashion for collecting coins and medals encouraged the development of collector's cabinets, in the tradition of such pieces made in Italy, Germany and France since the late-sixteenth and the seventeenth century. These cabinets were usually of small size, due not only to the nature of their content, but also in keeping with contemporary French Rococo fashion. Horace Walpole had several examples: one wall-mounted cabinet in rosewood with ivory plaques is now in the Victoria and Albert Museum. He wrote to Sir Horace Mann in July 1743 saying: 'I have a new cabinet for my enamels and miniatures just come home,

Miniature cabinet in ebony and satinwood on a carved stand. Batavia, Indonesia, c. 1680; width 48 cm (19 in.).

Miniature bureau-cabinet in ivory with floral penwork decoration. Vizigatapam, India, c. 1760; width 61 cm (2 ft).

which I am sure you would like; it is of rosewood, the doors inlaid with ivory'. Many different types of exotic woods were now used, together with mahogany and japanned ware, giving a rich variety of form and decorative techniques.

French influence is also much in evidence in the jewel cabinet made by William Vile for Queen Charlotte in 1761 to hold the diamonds given her by George III to be worn at the Coronation in September of that year and estimated to have cost £50,000. The mahogany frame is richly carved in the Rococo style and the veneers of padouk, amboyna, tulipwood, olivewood and rosewood are inlaid with ivory, as is the top showing the Royal coat-of-arms.

However, in France – as indeed in the whole of Europe – the impact of the discovery of Herculaneum (the official records of which were published in 1752) was creating a new taste for classical antiquity and ancient Rome. The Comte de Caylus published a *Recueil d'Antiquités*, a series beginning in 1752; Piranesi's *Le Antichità Romane* appeared in 1756; and Johann Joachim Winckelmann had his essay entitled *Gedanken über die Nachahmung der griechischen Werke in der Malerei und der Bildhauerkunst* (On the imitation of Greek works in painting and sculpture) published in Dresden in 1755, shortly before the author moved to Rome. In the early part of the century England had been alone among European countries in having a classical phase in design under the influence of Lord Burlington and William Kent, as well as the publication of Palladio's *Quattro Libri dell'Architettura* in translation and of *Vitruvius Britannicus* by Colen Campbell.

Although the pleasure-seeking Parisian society appreciated and enjoyed the forms of the Rococo, it is significant that the brother of Madame de Pompadour, the Marquis de Marigny, visited Rome from 1749 to 1751 in the company of the architect Soufflot, the Abbé de Blanc and the engraver Cochin, in order to prepare himself for his duties as Directeur Général des Bâtiments (Surveyor of the Royal Buildings). The visit prompted Cochin in 1754 to write in the French journal *Mercure Galant* an 'Appeal to the Gold- and Silversmiths and Woodcarvers'[26] to react against the excesses of the Rococo and to return to the restraint and good taste of antiquity. His message must have been heard, since Baron Grimm, visiting the capital in 1763, declared 'Tout Paris est à la Grecque' (In Paris everything is in the Greek style).

Whereas Louis XVI was only interested in furniture from a technical point of view, the *ébéniste* Jean-François Oeben introduced in the 1750s intricate mechanical pieces which created a new demand; the Queen and the King's brothers commissioned many items in the new Neo-classical style, and Parisian society followed suit. As a result French cabinet-makers enjoyed an unprecedented prosperity, with demand increasing at home and abroad. The Tsar of Russia and the Kings of Spain and Portugal, as well as German, Scandinavian and Polish princes, all made purchases in Paris, so helping to make the Louis XVI style truly international.

Various types of furniture such as the *secrétaire à abattant, bonheur du jour* and *médaillier* (medal cabinet) were still being produced with marquetry decoration, or adorned with Sèvres porcelain plaques, Japanese lacquer or *vernis Martin* by leading makers, including Riesener in his capacity as *Ebéniste du Roy*, Carlin, Leleu and Weisweiler; during

Secrétaire à abattant *incorporating Japanese lacquer panels of the late seventeenth or early eighteenth century, and with* vernis Martin *decoration and gilt-bronze mounts. Made by Philippe-Claude Montigny, France, c. 1785–90; width 94 cm (3 ft 1 in.).*

the late 1780s plain veneers of mahogany or thuyawood in the English manner were used in France. The taste for ostentatious richness encouraged a revival of the Boulle technique, which had been completely abandoned under Louis XV, and some older cabinets in *pietra dura* by Cucci were dismantled and their panels incorporated into Neo-classical pieces, particularly by Weisweiler.

Such was the sumptuousness of court life at the time that the old form of the cabinet was revived as a *meuble d'apparat*. The first recorded example was made for the Archduchess Marie-Antoinette as a presentation piece on the occasion of her wedding in 1770 to the Dauphin (later Louis XVI). The *serre-bijoux* or jewel cabinet, which no longer exists (though the design for it is preserved in the Bibliothèque Nationale, Paris), was made by Ewald. Another *serre-bijoux* made by Riesener for the King's brother, the Comte de Provence, is now in the British Royal Collection. This cabinet relates very closely to the lost piece and, although it must have been made to commemorate his wedding to the daughter of the King of Sardinia in 1771, it is closer stylistically to the 1780s and 1790s, when the use of mahogany became prevalent. A third *serre-bijoux* represents a poignant farewell not only to a particular type of grand presentation piece, but to the *Ancien Régime* altogether. It was commissioned by the City of Paris from Schwerdfeger in 1787 for presentation to Marie-Antoinette; this piece is now in Versailles. Its decoration unites mahogany, gilt-bronze caryatids, *verre églomisé*, antique cameos and intaglios, and its base features the use of the ancient Roman *fasces*.

In England the same nostalgic tribute to a past form was paid by Robert Adam in the Kimbolton Cabinet, made in 1771 for the Duchess of Manchester. Its satinwood frame, inlaid with the fine classical *rinceaux* of the late Adam style, provides a setting for *pietra dura* panels brought back from the Grand Tour. The front is only a façade, for the pilasters punctuating the composition are purely decorative and there are neither doors or drawers. As a furniture type the cabinet had become a display piece, and indeed it is as such that it survived until the end of the century with glazed doors (to permit the display of fine china) and retaining the elegant line of Adam's designs as popularized by Hepplewhite and Sheraton. Bureau-cabinets and *secrétaires* often included a glazed upper part similar in form to bookcases or display cabinets.

The English taste spread far and wide in Europe and was much admired; when the great German furniture-maker David Roentgen opened his workshops in Neuwied in the 1760s, he advertised as an 'English Cabinetmaker'. Roentgen was the first German maker to adopt the Neo-classical style, while others working in Berlin and Potsdam continued in the Rococo spirit well into the 1770s. However, in 1780 a book of designs in Neo-classical style was published by Franz Heissig in Augsburg, and the *Journal des Luxus und der Moden*, founded in 1787, helped spread the fashion.

Design for the serre-bijoux *made for the Archduchess Marie-Antoinette on the occasion of her marriage to the Dauphin of France in 1770.*

In Italy even the English-inspired bureau-cabinet, or *trumeau*, took on the rich *bombé* surfaces of the Rococo style and its asymmetrical rhythm with great gusto, retaining it well into the latter part of the century. Most Italian craftsmen were therefore in the categories of *falegname* (joiner) or *intagliatore* (carver), rather than *ebanista* (cabinetmaker). Exceptions were Piffetti, working in Turin in the Rococo manner, and Maggiolini, working in Milan (at first in the service of the Austrian Governor-General of Lombardy and eventually for Eugène Beauharnais, the Viceroy imposed by Napoleon) in a Neo-classical style of stricter archaeological discipline – an approach which the Directoire and Empire styles were to impress upon the whole of Europe at the beginning of the nineteenth century.

The Kimbolton Cabinet, satinwood inlaid with darker woods and decorated with pietra dura *panels set in gilt brass. Robert Adam, 1771; width 178 cm (5 ft 10 in.).*

4

REVIVALISM IN A NEW AGE

THE LAST YEARS OF THE EIGHTEENTH CENTURY AND THE FIRST TWO decades of the nineteenth were dominated by a man whose career was to change the face of Europe, Napoleon Bonaparte. Born in Corsica on 15 August 1769, shortly after the island was formally ceded to France, he became a lieutenant in the artillery in 1791, two years after the French Revolution, though earlier he had nurtured the Romantic dream of a free Corsica, and for a while supported the independence movement of Paoli. However, he clashed with his former ally in 1792, and fled to settle in France with his family in 1793.

He gained swift promotion in the army, saving the revolutionary regime, the Convention, from a royalist conspiracy in October 1795, a feat for which he was rewarded with command of the home army. The following year, a week before his marriage to Joséphine de Beauharnais, on 7 March 1796, he became Commander-in-Chief of the army in Italy. On the Italian campaigns, he gathered glory as he proceeded to win one victory after another. His rapid rise to fame made him unpopular with the Directoire, the new revolutionary regime established in October 1795 in France, whose members looked with suspicion and understandable fear upon the success of this ambitious young general.

Bonaparte was in no doubt about the feelings he inspired among his political and military peers, and in 1798 suggested the campaign in Egypt. This military operation was a shrewd political move in placating the Directoire, and it gave Bonaparte a golden opportunity to achieve greater glory for himself. It was to have far-reaching consequences, for in the political sphere Bonaparte's rise to power was enhanced. The campaign of 1798–9 had captured the public imagination in France, and helped to bring about a lively interest in all things Egyptian; Bonaparte exploited the resulting sense of elation to plan and execute the *coup d'état* of 18 Brumaire (9 November) 1799, in which he was supported by two members of the Directoire. After being appointed First Consul in 1800, he was eventually proclaimed Emperor in 1804, as Napoleon I.

During the ten years of his reign, Napoleon endeavoured to re-establish peace and order in France. He created a new administrative and legal structure, the *Code Civil*, which ensured greater stability and renewed economic prosperity. France's economy had been bled dry by the Revolution of 1789, and very few skilled craftsmen, such as *menuisiers* and *ébénistes*, had survived the days of the Terror. Under the interim government, the guilds and corporations were abolished in 1791, resulting in greater freedom for craftsmen by effectively removing the ban preventing *menuisiers* working in solid wood from practising the art of veneering, formerly the preserve of *ébénistes*; the cessation of controls regulating standards would, in due course, have far-reaching effects on production, owing to the breakdown of long-established traditions of craftsmanship. Lower standards also resulted in part from a change of clientele, to patrons whose demands were less exacting than had been usual during the Ancien Régime, and from a new unabashed commercialism which amounted to a total break with the previous system under which small workshops worked for wealthy patrons on commission. In 1797, the first industrial exhibition was held in the courtyard of the Louvre – a novel development anticipating modern marketing methods.

Stylistically, the Directoire period (which also included the years of the Consulate) saw the continuation of the Louis XVI style, with a

Previous page
Breakfront side cabinet in ebonized wood with marquetry panels in classical revival style. England, c. 1880–90; width 188 cm (6 ft 2 in.).

marked tendency towards greater austerity, influenced by classical antiquity and the English taste for plain veneers of exotic woods such as mahogany and thuya. However, previously used forms were modified, the proportions becoming thinner, more spindly, closer to characteristic features of the late Adam style in England. Examples of the *secrétaire à abattant* were still produced, mostly in plain mahogany, sometimes inlaid with contrasting woods, such as ebony or lime, depicting palmettes, foliage scrolls (*rinceaux*) or anthemion, instead of more costly pictorial marquetry. The use of gilt bronze was replaced by the incorporation of cheaper thin gilt-brass fillets. Furthermore, inspiration was no longer derived exclusively from classical antiquity, but ideas were stimulated by the contemporary Egyptomania. In 1802, Vivant Denon, a French archaeologist and engraver who had been a member of the team of scholars, artists and historians accompanying Bonaparte on his campaign in 1798–9, published his *Voyage dans la Basse et la Haute Egypte* in Paris and London, so providing a first-hand source of decorative reference for designers and craftsmen. Sphinxes and lotus-flowers mingled with classical nymphs and foliage scrolls, urns and trophies.

The true creators of the Empire style were two architects, Charles Percier and Pierre-François-Léonard Fontaine, who both trained in Rome; the latter had also spent some time in London. In 1798, they produced furniture designs for the *Conseil des Cinq Cents* (Council of the Five Hundred, part of the Directoire), for the *menuisier* Georges Jacob. In 1799, the painter Jacques-Louis David introduced them to Joséphine Bonaparte, who commissioned them to decorate and furnish Malmaison, her country house near Paris. Napoleon's patronage was by then assured, and in 1802 Percier and Fontaine published a *Recueil de Décorations Intérieures* (Collection of Interior Decorations; second edition 1812).

In becoming Emperor, Napoleon not only wanted absolute power for himself but also aimed to create a new ruling dynasty. In order to fulfil this ambition he looked back to the *Grand Siècle* of Louis XIV in search of a *gravitas* and nobility appropriate to the new regime. The charm, elegance and *joie de vivre* of the Ancien Régime typified by the Louis XV and Louis XVI styles were not emulated. Instead, the pomp, grandeur and magnificence of the reign of the Sun King, together with the strict court etiquette of the period, were to mark Napoleon's personal style. He took over the former royal palaces and superimposed upon them his own militaristic symbols, reminiscent of the Roman Empire: the laurel wreath of the conquering hero, the 'N' for Napoleon, the Imperial eagles, the bee with classical trophies, winged lions with Egyptian head-dress, and sphinxes. The designs by Percier and Fontaine illustrated this grand, decorous, masculine style, which tended towards a certain uniformity and repetitiveness, allied to an archaeological precision in matters of detail only, as Egyptian motifs mingled with those of Greece, Rome and Etruria. The wood used – flame or bird's-eye mahogany – encouraged this impression of masculine austerity and decorum in the large areas of plain surfaces, whether of solid wood or veneers. Forms were massive, with an emphasis on the angularity of designs, which suited the *secrétaire à abattant*, the effect being made even heavier through the addition of a raised plinth.

The accent on massive frontal rigidity even affected the frivolous, elegant, feminine *bonheur du jour*, a type created in the Rococo era. If such pieces still retained smaller proportions than those of the *secrétaire*, they took on similar angular lines and solid forms. The only elements relieving the severity of these pieces are gilt-bronze mounts and adornments, once more fashioned by a great artist, Pierre Philippe Thomire, who had survived the Revolution and restored to the Empire the lustre previously associated with the art of the Ancien Régime. Indeed, the leading *ébéniste* of the Empire style, François-Honoré-Georges Jacob-Desmalter, was the son of Georges Jacob, the leading *menuisier* of the Ancien Régime, who had become an *ébéniste* after the Revolution, taking advantage of the abolition of the rules governing guilds. Jacob-Desmalter went into partnership with his father in 1803, under the name 'Jacob-Desmalter & Cie', and produced the best-quality Empire-style furniture on an industrial scale. Special commissions were still undertaken, however: in 1809, Napoleon ordered a *serre-bijoux* for the Empress Joséphine, reviving a French royal tradition. This piece, of burr yew and mahogany with gilt-bronze mounts, featured the characteristic massive angularity of the Empire style, with little feminine accent apart from the gilt-bronze dancing nymphs made by Thomire, but even so it retained a harmony of concept, design and execution in which all details are subservient and merely part of a greater whole. This quality had been a feature of the best cabinetmaking work of the preceding centuries. As such, the *serre-bijoux* paid a fitting tribute to the art of the cabinet as practised in the *Grand Siècle*, commissioned by a man who sought to emulate the dazzling power of the Valois and Bourbon courts, and realized by a descendant of the best *menuisier* of the Ancien Régime, maintaining traditions and standards of craftsmanship which were never to be equalled again.

Although the Napoleonic Wars brought devastation to continental Europe, the Empire style became, paradoxically, the prevalent fashion in every country. In Italy, where the Rococo had lingered on – particularly in Venice – well after the change of fashion in France and England, the last years of the eighteenth century saw the use of Neo-classical and Egyptian motifs before members of Napoleon's family brought the French Empire fashion and craftsmen in their wake. Napoleon's brothers and sisters – Joseph, King of Naples; Lucien, Prince de Canino; Pauline Borghese in Rome; Caroline Murat in Naples; and Elisa Baciocchi as Grand Duchess of Tuscany – all attracted French *ébénistes*. One such, Jean-Baptiste-Gilles Youf, worked for the Grand Duchess from 1805, providing most of the furniture in the Pitti Palace in Florence and the Ducal Palace in Lucca, and contributed greatly to the dissemination of the Empire style in Italy. This style continued well into the 1820s after the fall of Napoleon, and remained the grand palatial style favoured by the restored monarchs in Naples, Genoa and Turin.

During the last years of the eighteenth century, French influence had been much in evidence in England, with Parisian *marchand-merciers*, such as Daguerre, providing furniture for the Prince of Wales's London home, Carlton House, as well as fulfilling orders from other English aristocrats, among them the Duke of Bedford. Thomas Sheraton, who had published *The Cabinet-Maker and Upholsterer's Drawing-Book*, a book of designs issued in parts from 1791 to 1794, published a second book of designs entitled *The Cabinet Dictionary* in 1803 and *The Cabinet-Maker, Upholsterer and General Artist's Encyclopaedia* in

Mahogany writing cabinet in the Empire style with brass inlay. England, c. 1815; width 108 cm (3 ft 6¼ in.).

Cabinet decorated throughout in penwork with classical scenes. England, c. 1815; width 91.5 cm (3 ft).

Collector's cabinet with eight drawers for specimens, with overall painted decoration of seashells on a light-blue ground. England, c. 1800–20; width 63.5 cm (2 ft 1 in.).

1806, bringing together all the decorative elements of the 'Regency' style. A new precision in reproducing archaeological details of classical and Egyptian origin in pieces of furniture which 'follow the antique taste and introduce into their arms and legs various heads of animals' echoed the current Napoleonic designs and motifs. Sheraton's *Encyclopaedia* was the first English treatise to depict ancient Egyptian motifs, albeit in a much more fantastic vein than Percier and Fontaine. A reaction to this trend was felt necessary and a return to 'the pure spirit of Antiquity' was advocated by Thomas Hope, a banker, connoisseur and archaeological dilettante, who in 1807 published his *Household Furniture and Interior Decoration*, illustrating the designs he had used for furniture in his own house in Duchess Street, London. His ideas were popularized by George Smith, a London cabinetmaker, who, in 1808, published *A Collection of Designs for Household Furniture and Interior Decoration*, which had considerable influence in promoting the so-called 'Antique' or 'Modern Greek' style fashionable during the Regency and the early Victorian period. Around the 1820s, however, there was a revival of the Rococo (then called the 'Louis XIV style') for furnishing drawing rooms and boudoirs, where more 'feminine' forms were felt to be appropriate, the 'Modern Greek' style being deemed suitable for 'masculine' surroundings, such as dining rooms and libraries. Earlier types of cabinet were still made but with new forms and decorations, whereas in the late eighteenth century English style had been emulating the lighter, smaller, elegant French *serre-bijoux* and *bonheur du jour*, of which Sheraton wrote in his *Dictionary*: 'the use of this piece is to accommodate a lady with convenience for writing, reading, holding her trinkets and other articles of this kind. The style of finishing them is elegant, being often richly japanned, and veneered with the finest satinwood.'

At the beginning of the nineteenth century, England was the only country in Europe to use japanning, though painted furniture was produced later. The interest in lacquer was most certainly influenced by the Prince Regent, later George IV, whose taste for and enjoyment of the frivolous, lighthearted and decorative quality of *chinoiserie* – a style already used at Carlton House and recorded by Sheraton in his first treatise in 1794 – culminated in the decoration and furnishing of the Royal Pavilion, Brighton (rebuilt in oriental style, 1815–17). *Chinoiserie* decoration was now used in conjunction with a drawing technique known as penwork, giving a delicate, sensitive line on a coloured or black lacquer ground. This essentially English technique was also used with the 'Modern Greek' style; decoration in both styles occurs on cabinets of fairly massive rectilinear forms, sometimes low like French eighteenth-century medal cabinets, sometimes raised like the older form of cabinet on a cupboard base. Decoration consisting of Neo-classical motifs after Flaxman would be delicately etched in black and white. Such cabinets would have served as collector's cabinets, the displaying of china having gone out of fashion as renewed interest in antiquity introduced a taste for collecting coins, medals and cameos, together with organic curios, at a time when Jane Austen's *Sense and Sensibility* encouraged an awareness of nature and its wonders. In this way, the sea-shells, butterflies or mineral specimens assembled by a Regency gentleman or a lady of leisure provided a link with the historical precedents of the early *studiolo* and the cabinet of curiosities in the fifteenth and sixteenth centuries.

The humanist spirit of the past was, however, far removed from this cosseted world of the early nineteenth century, in which the sense of relief felt after the devastation and horrors of the Napoleonic Wars encouraged a switch from the ideals of the Romantic hero, with all the disturbing and unstable elements inherent in such a figure, to a desire for a bourgeois existence characterized by comfort, respectability and stability. In 1814–15, the Congress of Vienna restored peace to Austria, and the re-establishment of the Habsburg dynasty created a new feeling of security. This sense of *Gemütlichkeit,* or homely cosiness, nurtured the development of a common decorative style in Germany, Austria and Scandinavia from the 1820s to the 1840s. In 1855 it was designated the Biedermeier style, after a fictional bourgeois character, symbolizing the spirit of simplicity and unpretentious elegance prevalent in the preceding decades in German-speaking countries.

Now middle-class values endowed pieces of furniture with a sentimental value, instead of status, while sober concepts aimed 'To uphold the old traditions within the bound of reason and keep the river of time flowing along a well-defined bed', according to the principles of Friedrich von Gentz, a close confidant of Metternich.[1] Practicality and comfort were the principal aims of the cabinetmakers of the time, the most important one being Joseph Danhauser in Vienna, one of the pioneers of the Biedermeier style.

The Biedermeier forms evolved from those of the Empire style and, although pieces remained solid and massive, in the early years some light and elegant ladies' *secrétaires* were produced. The simplicity of the lines and the clarity of design were enhanced by the use of light-coloured maple, cherry and other fruitwoods, close to the French Restauration style with its use of *bois clairs* – birch, maple, lime – employed for the simplified, more elegant furniture forms typical of the Empire style. There is, in fact, much similarity between the Biedermeier style and the French Restauration style, which is associated with the period between the restoration of the Bourbon monarchy under Louis XVIII in 1815 and the death of Charles X in 1830. The same sense of elegant bourgeois comfort pervaded the latest forms and designs in interior decoration and furniture published between 1802 and 1831 in the aptly named *Journal des Dames et des Modes* by Pierre de la Mésangère. The types of furniture remained the same, the severely rectangular *secrétaire à abattant* and the lighter *bonheur du jour* being realized in *bois clairs,* with a discreet brass fillet or mount.

The change of spirit in the art of cabinetmaking was due not only to new social attitudes and needs, but also to the inexorable advances in industrial techniques and the increasing number of major exhibitions. The first Exposition Industrielle had been held in France in 1797; in 1819 a crucial change was observed in the exhibition held in the Louvre. The use of steam power meant cheaper labour costs, which in turn brought about a lowering of artistic standards as furniture was now mass-produced for a mainly bourgeois clientele living predominantly in rented apartments. And although a marked improvement in the thinner slicing of veneers could be achieved by the use of machines, conversely the designs of contemporary *ornementistes,* such as Michel Jamsen, showed that furniture manufacturers were seeking to cut time and cost with a consequent reduction in quality.

Opposite
104 Serre-bijoux *veneered with burr yew and amaranth, with gilt-bronze mounts, commissioned from Jacob-Desmalter & Cie for the Empress Joséphine. Paris, 1809; height 2.70 m (8 ft 10 in.).*

REVIVALISM IN A NEW AGE

The Empire style spread from France to all parts of Europe. The austere lines of writing cabinets designed in an essentially masculine style were relieved by decorative elements inspired by motifs from ancient Egypt and classical antiquity.

Opposite
105 Secrétaire à abattant in mahogany with white marble pilasters and classical figures and a marquetry interior. Austria or Germany, c. 1820–40; width 114 cm (3 ft 9 in.).

106 Writing cabinet in Karelian birch wood decorated with two ebonized caryatids. Russia, c. 1820; width 95 cm (3 ft 1½ in.).

107, 108 Rosewood and gilt-brass musical secrétaire *in the French Empire style with a fitted mirrored interior (top) in the 'Gothick' manner. S. Jamar, England, c. 1820; width 114 cm (3 ft 9 in.).*

Revivalism in the nineteenth century encouraged the emulation of earlier forms and techniques. Furniture was sometimes painted to simulate the effect of inset Sèvres porcelain plaques. The dark surface of polished ebony was enlivened by intricate Boulle work and glowing panels of *pietra dura*, in some cases elements dating from the seventeenth century.

Opposite
112 Ebony cabinet-on-stand (one of a pair) incorporating pietra dura *panels dating from the seventeenth century as decoration on the central cupboard door and on the two full-height flanking doors. Italy, c. 1820; width 109 cm (5 ft 4½ in.).*

109 Serre-bijoux (one of a pair) in contrepartie *Boulle work and with a floral panel in* pietra dura. *France, stamped 'Mombro 18 Mars 1851'; width 85 cm (2 ft 9½ in.).*

110 Cabinet-on-stand (one of a pair) with painted decoration and penwork. England, c. 1805; width 82 cm (2 ft 8 in.).

111 Boulle-work cabinet (one of a pair identical to those made by John Webb for the 4th Marquess of Hertford in 1855). England, c. 1850–60; width 135 cm (4 ft 5 in.).

REVIVALISM IN A NEW AGE

113 *Walnut cabinet with marquetry decoration and with panels dating from the sixteenth century. South Germany, c. 1850–70; width 106 cm (4 ft 9½ in.).*

During the nineteenth century older pieces of furniture were frequently dismantled to permit the re-use of various elements in keeping with current needs. A romantic approach to historical styles led to direct imitations now capable of being achieved by industrial methods.

115 Bonheur du jour in tulipwood and kingwood with inset porcelain plaques in the French eighteenth-century manner. England, c. 1840; width 102 cm (3 ft 4 in.).

116 Table-cabinet in ebony and rosewood incorporating seventeenth-century elements. South Germany, c. 1850; width 77.5 cm (2 ft 6½ in.).

114 Cabinet-on-stand (one of a pair) with seventeenth-century elements and ormolu mounts. England, c. 1850–70; width 93 cm (3 ft ½ in.).

Technical advances brought about by the Industrial Revolution and the staging of major exhibitions, notably after 1851, fostered the wide use of precious materials. Ostentatious display reflected both pride in industrial achievement and aesthetic insecurity in a changing society.

117 Ebony cabinet inlaid with ivory decoration of grotesques and figures enclosed within lambrequins. Milan, c. 1875; width 110 cm (3 ft 7¼ in.).

Right, above
118 Walnut fall-front bureau-cabinet with ivory inlay in the alla certosina *manner. Northern Italy, c. 1870; width 109 cm (3 ft 10½ in.).*

119 Fall-front cabinet in ebony, rosewood and palmwood, with seventeenth-century ivory lion's-head supports. Germany, c. 1870–80; width 146 cm (4 ft 9½ in.).

Opposite
120 Ebony cabinet with inlaid ivory and pietra dura *and gilt-bronze armorials in the Renaissance manner. Milan, c. 1870; width 173 cm (5 ft 8 in.).*

REVIVALISM IN A NEW AGE

121 Tortoiseshell and marquetry cabinet-on-stand with silver mounts and allegorical figures of Faith, Hope and Charity. Flanders, c. 1860–70; width 200 cm (6 ft 6 in.).

Opposite
124 Architectural cabinet-on-stand in ebony with ivory inlay, made in the Baroque manner with a base featuring two kneeling figures of blackamoors. Northern Italy, c. 1880–90; width 148 cm (4 ft 10¼ in.).

122 Ebony cabinet-on-stand with pietra dura and lapis lazuli inlay in the manner of the early seventeenth century. Florence, c. 1870; width 129 cm (4 ft 3 in.).

123 Cabinet-on-stand in ebonized wood and rosewood with tortoiseshell veneer in the seventeenth-century manner. Portugal, c. 1870–80; width 122 cm (4 ft).

REVIVALISM IN A NEW AGE

REVIVALISM IN A NEW AGE

European design continued to be subject to oriental influence during the nineteenth century. In England the use of *chinoiserie* was still prevalent in the Regency period, a fashion fostered by the Prince of Wales at his London home, Carlton House, and in the décor of the rebuilt Royal Pavilion, Brighton. After 1854 the opening-up of trade with Japan introduced new aesthetic values and influenced designers throughout Europe.

Opposite
125 Japanned and silvered cabinet-on-stand with chinoiserie *decoration, one of a pair made in the Anglo-Dutch manner, c. 1870–80; width 71 cm (2 ft 4 in.).*

126 Japanned cabinet with penwork and chinoiserie *decoration in the manner of designs by John Claudius Loudon. England, c. 1820; width 82 cm (2 ft 7½ in.).*

Below
127 Cabinet lacquered in black and gold with shell inlay in the Shibayama style. Japan, c. 1880–90; width 135 cm (4 ft 5¼ in.).

Below, right
128 Ebonized, gesso-painted cabinet in the Japanese manner. England, c. 1880–90; width 114 cm (3 ft 9 in.).

REVIVALISM IN A NEW AGE

129, 130 Side cabinet with marquetry
decorations and gilt-bronze mounts
including two cupids (see detail), and
with a breche violette top. Made by
Zwiener or Linke, Paris, c. 1885; width
156 cm (5 ft 1½ in.).

Below
131 Cabinet-on-stand in burr walnut
and beech made in the Rococo manner.
Italy, c. 1890–1900; width 105 cm
(3 ft 5½ in.).

Below, right
132 Cabinet 'Les Baigneuses' in
mahogany and oak with marquetry
panels and carved corner features.
Shown by Majorelle at the Exposition
Universelle, Paris, 1900; width 89 cm
(2 ft 11 in.).

REVIVALISM IN A NEW AGE

In France the emphasis on organic forms, naturalistic modelling and fine craftsmanship evident in Art Nouveau design was heavily dependent on eighteenth-century cabinetmaking traditions, the typical flowing lines being inspired by Rococo art. At the Exposition Universelle held in Paris in 1900, François Linke was awarded a gold medal for his Rococo revival bureau. The Exposition was also a triumph for Emile Gallé and Louis Majorelle with their Art Nouveau showpieces.

133 Tulipwood bureau with gilt-bronze mounts; designed by Léon Message and made by François Linke c. *1890, the piece was displayed at the Exposition Universelle in Paris in 1900. Width 2.15 m (7 ft).*

134 Kingwood display cabinet enclosing a stainless steel safe concealed behind the central doors. François Linke, Paris, c. *1885; width 4.53 m (16 ft 10 in.).*

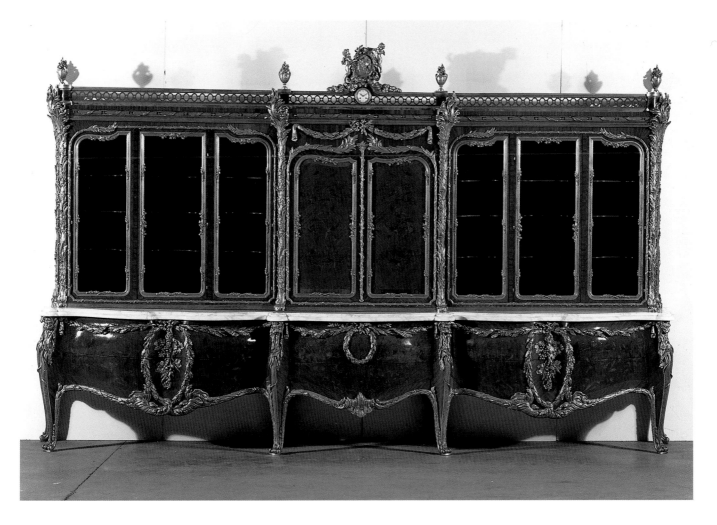

If technical precision was gained, it was at the expense of artistic creativity and originality. By the end of the 1820s, under the influence of a nostalgic romanticism, various revivals were taking place all over Europe, often simultaneously. In 1833, John Claudius Loudon's *Encyclopaedia* of *Cottage, Farm and Villa Architecture and Furniture* described the current fashions thus: 'The Grecian or Modern style, which is by far the most prevalent; the Gothic or perpendicular style, the Elizabethan, and the style of the age of Louis XIV, which is characterised by curved lines and an excess of curvilinear ornaments.' By 1849, the English *Journal of Design* remarked forlornly: 'Every one elects his own style of art, and the choice rests usually on the shallowest individualism. Some few take refuge in a liking for "Pure Greek" and are rigidly "classical", others find safety in the "antique", others believe only in Pugin, and some extol the Renaissance. We all agree only on being wretched imitators.' If the names used to describe a given style varied from country to country, the substance remained the same: the Gothic revival was called *style troubadour*, or *style à la cathédrale* in France; similarly, the Renaissance revival was known as *style Henri II*, and the Rococo revival as *style Pompadour*, which in America became known as 'French Modern' since it represented the latest fashion, or, paradoxically, as 'French Antique', due to its historicizing aspect.

The various industrial exhibitions held during the first part of the century now multiplied and became truly international, spreading fads and fashions, as well as becoming a stage upon which different manufacturers vied with each other to impress the public with the elaborate technical virtuosity of their showpieces. Sir Henry Cole, editor of the *Journal of Design* in London, wrote that 'One great advantage of exhibitions is that it teaches the public and people who are not otherwise taught at all.' Exhibitions demonstrated a range of current trends in design, and although the furniture exhibited did not include everyday household items available commercially, it reflected contemporary taste. In 1851 the Great Exhibition was held in London; England was the world's leading industrial nation and the exhibits shown at the Crystal Palace in Hyde Park reflected this wealth, as well as the poverty of artistic imagination.

Contemporary reviews outlined the shortcomings: a general lack of educated taste due to the change of patronage, now largely provided by an aesthetically uneducated middle class whose wealth was only recently acquired; and the demise of the cabinetmaker as a craftsman, now replaced by the furniture manufacturer, lacking in artistic inspiration, and whose products revealed a loss of attention to detail in realization. Such characteristics were internationally prevalent. The New York Crystal Palace exhibition of 1853, followed by the Paris Exposition of 1855, illustrated the growing tendency to attract attention by the use of overcrowded and over-elaborate decorative schemes used on large pieces, the scale of which became truly monumental. Showing such furniture served merely to advertise the skills of the cabinetmaker in creating a virtuoso *tour de force*. Time and money were no longer lavished on specially commissioned cabinets made for enlightened patrons by craftsmen using traditional skills; instead grand showpieces were designed and built to enhance the nationalistic pride of the country of origin.

At the Crystal Palace in 1851, French furniture exhibits had been awarded most of the Gold Medals, but in Paris in 1855 a monumental carved and gilt cabinet topped by a mirror, made by the English firm of Jackson and Graham, provided the direct answer to the French challenge. Cabinets, if no longer involved in the complex political interplay between courts and monarchs, as during the Renaissance and in the seventeenth century, now came to be used as the means of establishing national status and power of a different kind. Countries sought to outdo each other in ingenuity and in making grand public statements. A long-established furniture type such as the cabinet provided the ideal form of expression. Some materials were being used on an unprecedented scale. An outstanding example was the *Cabinet Chinois*, with decoration consisting entirely of enamelled porcelain plaques made by the Manufacture de Sèvres between 1834 and 1844; presented to the King of Sweden by Napoleon III, this cabinet was the largest piece of furniture ever produced by the Manufacture, showing evidence of a renewed interest in exoticism.

Japan had been cut off from Western trade since the eighteenth century, but on 31 March 1854 the American Commodore Matthew C. Perry re-opened trade with Japanese ports, and formal agreements between Japan and the Western world were signed in 1855. The discovery of a seemingly still medieval country and society whose art forms had not been contaminated by the industrial age captured the imagination of Western artists and craftsmen.

In 1862 Japanese textiles were exhibited at the London International Exhibition and the firm of Farmer and Rogers of Regent Street sent over to the Orient one of their assistants, Arthur Lasenby Liberty; a friend of the artists Whistler and Rossetti, he later opened his own shop (at first known as 'East India House') in Regent Street in 1875. This fortuitous incursion into a new artistic tradition corresponded to a great unease felt by certain leading designers and cabinetmakers concerning the general development of furniture and the deterioration of standards. The architect A.W.N. Pugin, for example, who died in 1852, had believed in a more honest and natural approach to the design and execution of furniture; he deplored the 'sprawling Rococo', and advocated that each component should have meaning and purpose, adding that the real source of art was nature and that 'to copy a thing merely because it is old is just as absurd as the imitation of the modern pagan.'[2] These theories were reflected in Japanese art, with its strong sense of design based on natural forms. Pugin had expounded his ideas in several publications: *Gothic Furniture in the Style of the 15th Century* (1835), *Designs for Iron and Brass Work* (1836), and more theoretically in *The True Principles of Pointed or Christian Architecture* (1841). At the Great Exhibition in 1851, his Mediaeval Court attracted much attention. The simplicity of his lines and his honest use of materials and forms were in stark contrast with the confused mixture of styles and techniques evident in the generally overblown and overcrowded pieces that were exhibited in the Furniture Court.

Yet not all of Pugin's theories were put into practice by his admirers, let alone by himself. In his own phrase, some of the 'Gothick enormities' which he produced for Windsor Castle were just as unashamedly romantically nostalgic in their revivalism as the work of his French

Walnut cabinet-on-stand in the style Henri II, *incorporating sixteenth-century panels carved in relief. France, c. 1850–70; width 78 cm (2 ft 7 in.).*

Small table-cabinet in ebonized wood having inset enamel plaques depicting scenes from classical mythology and gilt-bronze mounts. Vienna, c. 1850–60; width 25 cm (9¾ in.).

counterpart, Viollet-le-Duc, who in his *Dictionnaire raisonné du mobilier Français de l'époque carolingienne à la Renaissance* (1858) likewise advocated a return to honest solidity in forms and techniques, yet did not practise what he preached in his own work. It seemed as if the nineteenth century was unable to extricate itself from an emotional entanglement with the past, fostered by the literature of the time, including Sir Walter Scott's novels and Ruskin's *The Stones of Venice* (1851–3), and by a romantic appreciation of classic works, Shakespeare in particular. The American writer Nathaniel Hawthorne even deplored the fact that in his native country, there was 'no shadow, no antiquity, no mystery, no picturesque and gloomy wrong'.[3]

For the newly moneyed class, who lacked the taste, knowledge and confidence to make a definite original statement, taking refuge in artifacts of the past provided a safe option. Thus, remnants from the past – 'ancient material' – were salvaged and re-used; for example, at Snelston Hall in Derbyshire between 1828 and 1838 carved and painted furniture in Gothic style was made out of wood taken from old buildings and genuine Gothic furniture. This practice was common all over Europe, even in Italy; there, although the Gothic originally had little impact, a Gothic revival style began to emerge soon after the 1820s, to be replaced by a Renaissance revival, the Dantesque style, after the unification of Italy by the Risorgimento in 1861. The New World was likewise affected; in *The Cabinetmaker's Assistant*, published in New York in 1842, Robert Corner included Gothic designs to enable American craftsmen 'to unite the European style with the American'. Gothic- and Renaissance-style cabinets were being made from old boards cut from original pieces, reconstructed to suit contemporary taste.

England was leading the way in fashion and techniques. Prince Albert, Consort of Queen Victoria, took a keen interest in contemporary art and design, becoming President of the Society of Arts in 1843, and in 1848 his friend Sir Henry Cole founded 'Summerly's Art Manufactures', commissioning well-known artists to produce designs for manufacturers; this attempt to improve standards and promote public taste was a worthy cause, even if it had little effect on the exhibits displayed in 1851, on which occasion the innovations presented to the public were more of a decorative nature than of substance. This was reflected in the new techniques worthy of the leading industrial nation used and promoted at the Great Exhibition: cast iron, papier-mâché, inlaid slate imitating *pietra dura*, stamping and burning of designs in wood by mechanical means were among the novelties.

In direct reaction a group of young designers in the late 1850s and 1860s followed the precepts of Pugin, taking them even further. Thus William Burges's Bayeux Cabinet, shown at the 1862 exhibition, is a Gothic architectural structure, with painted scenes from classical antiquity and the Renaissance, yet a writing desk nonetheless; this piece put into practice the ideas of Pugin's 'revealed construction' more forcefully than he had done himself. At this exhibition the interest shown in the Japanese exhibits combined with the progressive ideas of the 'reformed' designs of Burges, William Morris (who in 1861 had founded the firm Morris, Marshall, Faulkner & Co.) and Bruce Talbert, who later published the influential design books *Gothic Forms applied to Furniture* (1867) and *Examples of Ancient and Modern Furniture* (1876). The so-called Anglo-Japanese style corresponded to the simplicity and feel for plain surfaces associated with the Queen Anne style revival. E. W. Godwin was one of the earliest advocates and practitioners of the style; described by Oscar Wilde as 'the greatest aesthete of them all', he started in his own house in Bristol *c*. 1862 by combining genuine Queen Anne furniture with Japanese prints and having floors left bare except for a few rugs. He was fascinated by the effects achieved by the clarity, boldness and asymmetry of Japanese prints. He wrote that his furniture was 'more or less founded on Japanese principles', illustrating the statement published in the trade journal *The Cabinet Maker and Art Furnisher* that 'Japanese art has taught the advantages of asymmetrical arrangements so that one need not always have pairs.'[4] However, unlike William Morris and the Arts and Crafts Movement, Godwin did not shun the machine but used mechanical methods to produce well-designed, simple furniture, mostly in ebonized wood; he used the interplay of solid and void to great effect, and this was much imitated.

The Japanese mania reached a highpoint in the Peacock Room (now preserved in the Freer Gallery, Washington, DC), originally designed in 1876–7 by Whistler for the London home of a shipping owner in Prince's Gate, Kensington, and the fashion reached its peak in the 1880s. This taste was an important element in the Aestheticism of the late nineteenth century, giving rise to an 'artistic' exoticism in which, as Oscar Wilde put it, 'Art does not imitate life, life imitates art.'[5] Liberty's in Regent Street promoted the style, as did new groups of like-minded

craftsmen who formed themselves into guilds with a structure similar to those of medieval times in order to produce furniture and other objects with a high standard of design and craftsmanship. The Arts and Crafts Movement led to the formation in 1888 of an Arts and Crafts Exhibition Society which brought the work of its members to the attention of the public. Thus, M. H. Baillie Scott, Lethaby, E. W. Gimson and C. F. A. Voysey practised William Morris's belief expressed in the first of his series of lectures on 'The Lesser Arts', given in London in December 1877: 'I do not want art for a few, any more than education for a few, or freedom for a few.'[6] This thoroughly modern idea was conveyed through a clarity and simplicity of design, suitability of function and sound craftsmanship, combined with the use of plain indigenous woods. The resulting pieces were sent to the Continent and had an influence on the development of Art Nouveau.

However, not all designers were so wedded to the ideals of high standards. In Scotland, Charles Rennie Mackintosh, working in Glasgow, was creating decorative schemes using Japanese-inspired simple lines for plain white-painted pieces of furniture to be put together by local joiners. His designs, allying the asymmetrical play of solid and void and featuring flat floral patterns inspired as much by Japan as by the Celtic tradition, did not become popular in England, but influenced continental furniture design, examples being exhibited in Venice in 1899, and most importantly in Vienna in 1900. 'There is a Christlike mood in this interior: this chair might have belonged to a Francis of Assisi. The decorative element is not proscribed, but it is worked out with a spiritual appeal,'[7] wrote the art editor of the *Wiener Rundschau* about Mackintosh's room in the Secession exhibition.

The Vienna Secession (*Wiener Sezession*) was founded in 1897 by a group of artists, among whom the designer Josef Hoffmann played a leading role. He greatly admired the work of English designers, who were breaking new ground and leading the avant-garde at the end of the century. Hoffmann's admiration for C. R. Ashbee's Guild and School of Handicraft led him, together with Koloman Moser, to found a craft studio, the *Wiener Werkstätte*, in 1903. Its aims were similar to that of their English counterparts, i.e. to offer the public furniture, metalwork, etc. of good quality, well designed and well crafted; its members disdained machine production and superfluous decoration, declaring 'Ornament is a crime'.

Cabinet with veneered decoration in thuya and satinwood, having glazed doors and a frieze drawer with writing slide. Designed by Koloman Moser, Vienna, 1903; width 100 cm (3 ft 3½ in.).

This sense of austere simplicity in design, echoing Mackintosh's work, was stylistically at odds with the development of Art Nouveau in France, even if sharing the same ideals. In 1895 the art dealer Samuel Bing opened a shop in the Rue de Provence, Paris, and called it 'L'Art Nouveau'; here he sold the works of contemporary French painters such as Vuillard, Toulouse-Lautrec, Bonnard and others. Bing, who moved to Paris in 1871, had been at the forefront of fashion since 1888, when he created the journal *Le Japon artistique* (with editions in French, German and English), thus disseminating contemporary designs all over Europe.

Art Nouveau was a truly international movement, of which the Arts and Crafts guilds can be said to be the earliest manifestation; the Vienna Secession was influenced by them, while the French development represented a more decadent version, seemingly reacting against the past yet relying heavily for its forms and style on the Rococo period. In Italy the inspiration provided by the English pioneers was reflected in the phrase *Stile Liberty*, an alternative term being *Stile Floreale*. Magazines were important in Art Nouveau's inception and development. These included: in Paris, *La Revue Blanche* of Thadée Natanson (founded in 1891); in London, Aubrey Beardsley's *The Studio* (1893); and in Munich, *Jugend* (Youth; 1896), from which comes the German term *Jugendstil*.

In France Japonisme became mixed with Rococo in the flowing tendrils of Art Nouveau cabinetwork by Emile Gallé and Louis Majorelle. Floral motifs and landscapes, the latter often inspired by the works of contemporary poets, are depicted in inlay of native woods on a mahogany ground in asymmetrical designs. 'All art is at once surface and symbol', wrote Oscar Wilde in *The Portrait of Dorian Gray*, and Art Nouveau in France was a manifestation of symbolism in the decorative arts. Thus, on a lady's writing desk of small Louis XV proportions with graceful cabriole legs Gallé inlaid the sloping front with a dreamy landscape called 'La Forêt Lorraine' (Forest in Lorraine), in which carved tendrils of plants echo the evocation of nature in the painterly depiction in inlaid native woods. The evocative quality of the whole piece is further enhanced by words from Charles Baudelaire's poem 'L'Invitation au Voyage', published in 1855, incorporated in decorative inlay work on the top. This example of the so-called *meuble parlant*, a concept echoing

Oak bureau with fruitwood marquetry and carved decoration of arum lilies, the top having an inlaid inscription from Baudelaire's poem 'L' Invitation au Voyage'. Emile Gallé, Nancy, 1900; width 79 cm (2 ft 7 in.).

the symbolist aspect of Gallé's creations in glass (*verreries parlantes*), was intended to appeal to the viewer's poetic imagination and aesthetic sensibility. Majorelle, working in Nancy, also had this painterly and symbolist approach to his marquetry and inlay, allying it to a sound knowledge of eighteenth-century cabinetmaking techniques learned from his father. He achieved a new sense of asymmetry and made playful use of solid and voids, giving his work a sense of graceful elegance that was entirely French.

The 1900 Exposition Universelle in Paris saw the climax of the style, with a whole room dedicated to works by members of the Ecole de Nancy (School of Nancy), in which Majorelle and Gallé were the leading figures. Cabinets were produced in asymmetrical forms with open or glazed shelves for the display of Gallé glass or other items such as pottery. Decoration is always vegetal or floral; Gallé kept a special garden for raising plants specially chosen for their curvilinear qualities – the vine, convolvulus and irises are frequently recurring motifs. Rococo revival was still important at the 1900 exhibition, as represented by the works shown by the Austrian-born François Linke.

If the style never became fashionable in England, it did have some following in America; French craftsmen had started opening workshops there in the 1840s, the firm of Ringuet Le Prince and Marcotte (with branches in Paris and New York) being influential in the 1860s for the introduction of a Louis XVI Neo-classical style. And although German craftsmen competed for trade with those from France, with the smaller workshops being overwhelmed in the 1870s by large furniture manufacturers working mostly in revival styles, the International Centennial Exhibition of 1876 held in Philadelphia was criticized on account of its 'vulgar rendition of the French Renaissance', evidence of that country's continuing pre-eminence in matters of style. At the same time the renewal of 'medieval principles of construction', as advocated by Morris and the Arts and Crafts Movement, was making an impact and was seen in some of the exhibits such as those submitted by the New York firm of Kimbel and Cabus, whose work was praised for being 'among the very best of the American exhibits in household art'.

Exoticism, which was influencing forms and decorations, was not confined to the current fashion for *Japonisme*, as the Moorish style adopted in the Rockefeller Smoking Room of 1884 (now in the Brooklyn Museum) makes clear. Exotic woods and bamboo lent a suitable texture and appeal to the style, and some display cabinets were realized in ornate forms of pseudo-orientalism using asymmetry and fretwork. The cabinet by Charles Tisch of New York (now in the Metropolitan Museum) closely emulated the work of his counterparts with a deliberate use of asymmetry in the Japanese manner as promoted in England by Godwin, but in combination with elaborate marquetry.

This piece, with its mirrored surface, would have been used both for storing and displaying the kind of curios and exotica which were then avidly collected. Charles Lock Eastlake, an English architect and writer, gave advice in his *Hints on Household Taste in Furniture, Upholstery and other Details* (1868); following the publication of this work in America in 1872, his name became a household word there. Eastlake wrote: 'The smallest example of rare old porcelain, of ivory carving, of ancient metalwork, of enamels, of Venetian glass, of anything which

Rosewood cabinet in the Queen Anne revival and Anglo-Japanese style with painted decoration and turned columns by Charles Tisch, New York, c. 1885; height 2.10 m (6 ft 10¾ in.).

Mahogany display cabinet with carved decoration in Art Nouveau style. George Flint, New York, c. 1909–13; height 149 cm (4 ft 10¾ in.).

illustrates good design and skilful workmanship, should be acquired whenever possible, and treasured with the greatest care. An Indian ginger jar, a Flemish beer jug, a Japanese fan, may each become in turn a valuable lesson in the decorative form and colour.' He was thereby reviving the humanist taste for collecting which had started in the Renaissance, a taste which gave the cabinet its characteristic quality as a prized piece of furniture; now, however, the emphasis was on educating the owner in artistic forms, which had not been the case with the Italian, German and French princes of the fifteenth and sixteenth centuries. By extension, the idea of education gave rise to the creation of public museums as a means of bringing culture to the masses; thus, after the Great Exhibition, the Museum of Manufactures (forerunner of the Victoria and Albert Museum) was founded in 1852, under the aegis of Prince Albert and Sir Henry Cole, for this very purpose.

Louis Comfort Tiffany brought the forms of Art Nouveau to America and some examples of furniture were produced by local firms in emulation of French craftsmen. The cabinet by George Flint in the Metropolitan Museum is very close in design to the style of Majorelle;

Trumeau *(designed by Gio Ponti)*
decorated with designs inspired by
seventeenth- and eighteenth-century
prints. Piero Fornasetti, Milan, c. 1950.
Width 79.5 cm (2 ft 7¼ in.).

Mahogany cabinet designed by Walter
Gropius. Germany, 1913; width 159 cm
(3 ft 7 in.).

this piece would have been made between 1909 and 1913, by which time the Art Nouveau style had lost its impetus in France.

The French were becoming concerned that their lead in contemporary design was under threat from foreign competitors. In 1909, however, a new source of inspiration materialized. The Ballets Russes, a company formed by Serge Diaghilev, brought to Paris a brilliant sense of colour, texture and exoticism which fired the craftsmen's creative imagination in a dramatic manner. Furthermore, the creation of the Compagnie des Arts Français by Louis Süe in 1910 brought back the Neo-classical forms, as illustrated in the works of Follot, Ruhlmann and others. The Russian sense of heightened colourful drama, the simplified forms inherent in primitive art, particularly Negro art, and in Cubism, as well as strong colour contrasts typical of Fauvism, influenced the development of the style called Art Deco (the phrase being derived from the Exposition Internationale des Arts Décoratifs et Industriels, held in Paris in 1925). It illustrated a very modern move away from literal depiction of natural forms identified with Art Nouveau to a greater simplification, stylization and eventual abstraction.

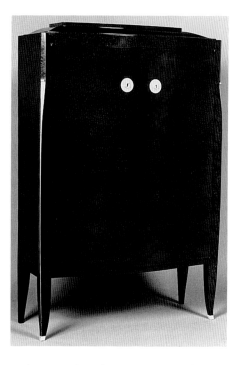

Cabinet with amboyna veneer and ivory bands and escutcheons. Emile-Jacques Ruhlmann, France, c. 1924; width 90 cm (2 ft 11½ in.).

Precious materials came back into use and earlier techniques were revived: veneering in exotic woods such as calamander, zebrawood and mottled maple; shagreen; wrought-iron mounts combined with the use of marble. All these brought a note of luxury to furniture. This richness was further enhanced by a renewed interest in lacquer. Both Jean Dunand in France and Eileen Gray in England had learned the secrets of lacquerwork as practised in Japan. This technique was exploited commercially, but in France particularly a new clientele influenced the development of furniture design; the wealthy Parisian couturiers – Schiaparelli, Lanvin, Doucet, Vionnet – all commissioned special pieces, in the making of which the utmost care would be taken, so re-introducing the idea of a piece of furniture as a unique work realized as the result of close collaboration between patron and cabinetmaker. The cabinet took on new forms: as a storage piece having its surface covered with precious materials and displaying simple, elegant lines; or as a cocktail cabinet, introducing a frivolous note in tune with contemporary taste, while occasionally retaining its former writing function.

If the spirit of Art Deco seemed very remote from the ideals of the German Bauhaus (founded in 1919), its aims were very similar, although directed to a different philosophy in its use of the machine as the extension of the craftsman's hand, with 'no barriers existing between the structural and decorative art'. Walter Gropius's designs for cabinets reconciled the necessity of the machine with the demands of the modern world, in which a piece of furniture endowed with special meaning, as the cabinet had been since the Renaissance, had little place and appeal, except as a piece simply for storage purposes and one that could be easily replaced by industrially produced units. Only the form and terminology associated with the cabinet now remained. One might look upon the bureau-cabinet by the Surrealist Milanese designer Pietro Fornasetti as simply a jokey pastiche of a furniture type with a long history, evoked both in its forms and by the architectural prints used to adorn it, but having no real place in the modern era of technology and efficiency, where the concepts of leisure and connoisseurship have lost their original meaning.

Cocktail cabinet veneered with bird's-eye maple, having fitted shelves and bottle holders. England, c. 1930–5; width 95 cm (3 ft 1¼ in.).

NOTES ON THE TEXT

Chapter 1

1 See 'Inventaire de la Vaisselle d'Or d'Anne de Bretagne' (1505) in H. Havard, *Dictionnaire de l'Ameublement et de la Décoration* (Paris, 1885), vol. I, p. 491.

2 See 'Ouvraiges de maçonnerye faicts au chasteau de Saint-Germain-en-Laye depuis le mois de décembre 1548'; Havard, loc. cit.

3 See *Mémoires de Mlle de Montpensier*, vol. II, p. 284; Havard, op. cit., p. 493.

4 Havard, op. cit., p. 482.

5 H. S. Baker, *Furniture in the Ancient World. Origins and Evolution, 3100–475 BC* (London, 1966), pp. 60f., quoted from Petrie.

6 H. Carter, *The Tomb of Tutankhamun* (London, 1922–3), vol. III, p. 66.

7 *Treasures of Tutankhamun* (British Museum exhibition catalogue, London, 1972), p. 15.

8 Carter, op. cit., p. 67.

9 G. M. A. Richter, *The Furniture of the Greeks, Etruscans and Romans* (London, 1966), p. 73.

10 Homer, *The Odyssey* (trans. E. V. Rieu), Penguin Classics, XIX (1946), p. 289.

11 Richter, loc. cit.

12 A. Maiuri, *Ercolano, i Nuovi Scavi* (Rome, 1958), p. 255.

13 E. Pernice, *Hellenistische Kunst in Pompei*, vol. V (Berlin, 1932), pls. 1, 2.

14 Richter, op. cit., p. 126.

15 Ibid.

16 Ibid.

17 Op. cit., p. 127.

18 C. Clunas, *Chinese Furniture* (London, 1988), p. 80.

19 'Auro et argento gemmisque et ornatu regio'; see W. Liebenwein, *Studiolo: die Entstehung eines Raumtyps und seine Entwicklung bis um 1600* (Berlin, 1977), p. 22.

20 'E stando uno dî con lui nel suo studio'; Liebenwein, op. cit., p. 49

21 P. Eames, 'Medieval Furniture in England, France and the Netherlands from the 12th to the 15th century', in *Furniture History*, vol. XIII (London, 1977), p. 5.

22 Havard, op. cit., p. 151.

23 Ibid.

24 '. . . parva camera di turri . . . unum armarium fusteum in quo erant duo coffreti parvi de corrio aperti; in uno nihil erat, in alio vero diverse littere'; see 'Inventaires Narbonnais du XIVe siècle', in *Bulletin de la Commission Archéologique de Narbonne*, vol. VIII (1904–5), pp. 207, 231. Cited in Eames, op. cit., p. 3.

25 G. H. Burr, *Hispanic Furniture* (New York, 1964), p. 37.

26 Ibid., p. 32.

27 Ibid., p. 28.

28 H. Huth, *Lacquer of the West. The History of a Craft and an Industry, 1550–1950* (London, 1971), p. 3.

29 J. M. Rogers and R. Ward (eds.), *Süleyman the Magnificent* (British Museum exhibition catalogue, London, 1988), p. 156.

30 Eames, op. cit., p. 4.

31 See Fritz Hellweg, *Die Geschichte des deutschen Tischlerhandwerks* (Berlin, 1924), p. 49; and G. Himmelheber, *Kabinettschränke* (illustrated guide no. 4, Bayerisches Nationalmuseum, Munich, 1977), p. 10.

32 'Inventaire de la Reine Catherine de Médicis' (Paris, 1882), quoted in Alfred de Champeaux, *Le Meuble*, vol. II (Paris, 1885), p. 36.

33 'Inventaire du Mobilier de Charles V Roi de France' (Paris, 1879); see W. Liebenwein, op. cit., pp. 38–45.

34 O. Impey and A. Macgregor (eds.), *The Origins of Museums. The Cabinet of Curiosities in sixteenth and seventeenth century Europe* (Oxford, 1985), p. 1.

35 Paul von Stetten, *Kunst-, Gewerb- und Handwerksgeschichte der Reichs-Stadt Augsburg* (1779); see Himmelheber, op. cit., p. 10.

36 Havard, op. cit., p. 204.

37 Gilles Corrozet, 'Le Blason du Dressover' in *Les Blasons Domestiques* (Paris, 1539); cf. note on p. 172.

38 Paul von Stetten, op. cit.

39 Otto Anders, 'Nürnberg um die Mitte des 15. Jahrhunderts im Spiegel ausländischer Betrachtung', in *Mitteilungen des Vereins für Geschichte der Stadt Nürnberg*, vol. 50 (1960), pp. 100–12; quoted in *Gothic and Renaissance Art in Nuremberg 1300–1550* (Metropolitan Museum of Art exhibition catalogue, New York, 1986), p. 51.

40 'Omnia vincit amor, nos et cedamus amori' (Love conquers all things, let us also yield to love); Virgil, *Eclogues* 10, 69.

Chapter 2

1 *Voyage de Pyrard de Laval*, vol. I (Paris, 1619), p. 186; quoted in John Irwin, 'A Jacobean Vogue for Oriental Lacquer-Ware', *Burlington Magazine*, vol. XCV (1953), p. 194.

2 Thomas da Costa Kaufmann, 'Remarks on the collections of Rudolf II: the Kunstkammer as a form of representation', *Art Journal*, vol. 38 (1978), pp. 22–28; see Impey and Macgregor, op. cit., ch. I, note 30.

3 See Havard, op. cit., p. 483.

4 See Himmelheber, op. cit., p. 35.

5 'Argutezze della natura', a chapter in Emanuele Tesauro's *Cannochiale aristotelico* (1675), pp. 49–53; see Giuseppe Olmi, 'Italian Cabinets of the sixteenth and seventeenth centuries' in Impey and Macgregor, op. cit., p. 3.

6 Oliver Impey quoted by David Carrier in 'The Display of Art – An Historical Perspective', *Leonardo. International Journal of the Contemporary Arts* (1987), pp. 83f.

7 E. S. de Beer (ed.), *The Diary of John Evelyn*, vol. II (*Kalendarium 1620–1649*; Oxford, 1955), pp. 190f.

8 *The Diary of John Evelyn* (*De vita propria*, 1644); see de Beer, op. cit., p. 119.

9 John Evelyn, *Kalendarium 1620–1649*; see de Beer, op. cit., p. 191.

10 Himmelheber, op. cit., p. 51.

11 'Inventaire de la Reine de Suède Mai 1656', quoted in J. Denucé, *Art Export in the 17th century in Antwerp* (Antwerp, 1931).

12 Denucé, op. cit. note 11; quoted by S. Jervis in 'A Tortoiseshell Cabinet and its precursors', *V&A Bulletin*, vol. IV, no. 4 (October 1968).

13 W. de Kesel, 'Laques Flamandes du XVIIe siècle', *Estampille – L'Objet d'Art*, March 1989, p. 32.

14 'Inventaire de tous les Meubles du Cardinal Mazarin d'après l'original dressé en 1653', in *Les Archives de Condé, par Henri d'Orléans* (London, 1861), pp. 250–63.

15 M. Burckhardt, *Mobilier Louis XIII, Louis XIV* (Paris, 1978), p. 46.

16 Havard, op. cit., p. 484.

17 'Inventaire des Tableaux & autres Curiosités qui se trouvaient au Louvre en 1603'; see Havard, loc. cit.

18 *Archives de l'Art Français 1872*, 1ère série, vol. II; quoted in A. de Champeaux, op. cit. (see chapter 1, note 31), p. 37.

19 Havard, op. cit., p. 485.

20 'Inventaire de tous les Meubles . . .' op. cit. (see note 14 above).

21 Archives Nationales, Paris: K 542, No. 5, fol. 6. Quoted in T. H. Lunsingh Scheurleer, 'The Philippe d'Orléans ivory cabinet by Pierre Gole', *Burlington Magazine*, June 1984, p. 334.

22 Arch. Nat., Paris: K 542, No. 5, fol. 13–16; see Lunsingh Scheurleer, op. cit., note 11.

23 A. de Champeaux, op. cit., p. 46.

24 Pierre Verlet, *French Royal Furniture* (London, 1963), p. 5.

25 Verlet, op. cit., p. 8.

26 Described in 'Le Luxe Détruit', *Mercure Galant*, February 1690; see Havard, op. cit., p. 490.

27 O. Impey, *Chinoiserie. The Impact of Oriental Styles on Western Art and Decoration* (London, 1977), p. 111.

28 Ibid., p. 112.

29 Hans Huth, op. cit. (see chapter 1, note 27), p. 13.

30 Impey, op. cit., p. 115.

31 T. H. Lunsingh Scheurleer, 'Pierre Gole, Ebéniste du roi Louis XIV', *Burlington Magazine*, June 1980, p. 389.

32 Thomas Howard, 2nd Earl of Arundel (1586–1646), was one of the most important English collectors of his time.

33 R. Edwards, *The Shorter Dictionary of English Furniture* (London, 1964), p. 91.

34 P. Thornton and M. Tomlin, *The Furnishing and Decoration of Ham House* [Furniture History Society], London, 1980, p. 79.

Chapter 3

1 See *Louis XIV, Faste et Décors* (exhibition catalogue, Musée des Arts Décoratifs, Paris, 1960), p. xv.

2 *Mercure Galant*, April-May 1687; quoted in Havard, op. cit., p. 488.

3 Loc. cit.

4 Loc. cit.

5 Loc. cit.

6 Loc. cit.

7 Havard. op. cit., p. 489, quoting Delamare.

8 See Du Molinet, *Le Cabinet de la Bibliothèque Sainte-Geneviève* (Paris, 1692).

9 A contemporary description of the lottery (ed. Dangeau) is quoted in Havard, op. cit., p. 488.

10 P. Verlet, op. cit., p. 3.

11 Havard, op. cit., p. 490.

12 F. Kimball, *The Creation of the Rococo* (Philadelphia, 1943), p. 117.

13 Verlet, op. cit., p. 47.

14 For a description of the 'Cabinet de la Paix' see Havard, op. cit., vol. I, p. 487.

15 F. Watson, *Louis XVI Furniture* (London, 1973), p. 24.

16 Havard, op. cit., p. 491.

17 Loc. cit.

18 Huth, op. cit. (see chapter 1, note 27), p. 70.

19 R. W. Symmonds, 'Furniture from the Indies', *Connoisseur*, no. 93 (May 1934), pp. 283–9.

20 Huth, op. cit., p. 38.

21 Edwards, op. cit. (see chapter 2, note 33), p. 72.

22 Huth, op. cit., p. 31.

23 The earliest recorded reference to a writing cabinet in America may be the 'scutore' (sc. scriptor) mentioned in the inventory of James Claypoole of Philadelphia in 1688; see E. McElroy, 'Furniture in Philadelphia. The First Fifty Years', in *American Furniture and its Makers* (Winterthur Portfolio 13, 1979), p. 75. See also B. Garuan, *Philadelphia: Three Centuries of American Art*, Philadelphia, 1976, pp. 14f., for a comparison

between a Philadelphia walnut writing cabinet by Edward Evans (signed and dated 1707) now in the Colonial Williamsburg Foundation, Virginia, and a nearly identical piece of English origin, made by John Guilboud, *c.* 1695.

24 Wallace B. Gusler, *Furniture of Williamsburg and Eastern Virginia 1710–90* (Richmond, Va, 1979), p. 26.

25 J. Veenendal, *Furniture from Indonesia, Shri Lanka and India during the Dutch period* (Delft, 1985), p. 27.

26 *Mercure Galant*, 1754: see S. Eriksen, *Early Neo-Classicism in France . . .* (London, 1974), pp. 26ff.

Chapter 4

1 Hellmut Andics, in *Das österreichische Jahrhundert. Die Donau-Monarchie, 1804–1918* (Wiener Kongress exhibition catalogue, Vienna, 1964), pp. 46ff.; quoted in *Vienna in the Age of Schubert. Biedermeier Interiors 1815–48* (Victoria and Albert Museum exhibition catalogue, 1979).

2 Pugin's *An Apology for the Revival of Christian Architecture in England* (London, 1843), p. 38; quoted in M. Trappes-Lomax, *Pugin, A Medieval Victorian* (London, 1932), p. 328.

3 *Nineteenth Century American Furniture and other Decorative Art* (Metropolitan Museum exhibition catalogue, New York, 1970), p. xvii.

4 E. Aslin, *The Aesthetic Movement. Prelude to Art Nouveau* (London, 1969), p. 84.

5 Aslin, op. cit., p. 79.

6 P. Thompson, *The Work of William Morris* (London, 1967), p. 153.

7 T. Howarth, *Charles Rennie Mackintosh and the Modern Movement* (Glasgow, 1952), p. 153.

NOTES ON THE COLOUR PLATES

1 Frans Francken the Younger, *A Collector's Cabinet* (detail), oil on panel, 1617. Collection of the Duke of Northumberland.

In his 'Blazon of the Cabinet' (see page 6), published in 1539, Gilles Corrozet had associated the idea of the cabinet as a repository for valuables of all kinds with 'queens and duchesses'. By the early seventeenth century, however, wealthy merchants – like those active in the Francken family's native city, Antwerp – were also among the privileged minority who could afford such luxuries. The trade with the East Indies – the major source of the collector's wealth – is hinted at in the seascapes in the foreground, the world globe and exotic curios such as shells, a sea-horse and a butterfly, which are shown mingling with precious jewels, antiquities and works of art, just as Gilles Corrozet described them.

What could be a portrait of the owner appears on the upper left-hand side of the detail, with a nautical symbol above his head, thus reinforcing the emphasis on overseas trade. The cabinet illustrated does not display the kind of objects for personal use and adornment mentioned by Corrozet, but such items could have been concealed within the closed drawers, the panels of which are painted with scenes often inspired by the works of Titian, Veronese, Rubens, Brueghel, or even Francken himself. Although the painting can be said to depict a *Kunst-* or *Wunderkammer* (a subject repeatedly painted by Francken), the religious symbolism and message is also very powerfully conveyed. The cult of the Virgin Mary was a highly contentious issue during the Reformation period, and here a Book of Hours, also mentioned in Corrozet's poem, is prominently displayed with a scene depicting the Annunciation (a similar painting by Francken in Frankfurt repeats the theme of the Virgin and Child, once as a sculpture and once in a painting). The strongly Roman Catholic symbolism and the link between Flanders and Rome (which persisted after the separation of the Protestant Northern Provinces in 1579) is further emphasized by the presence of classical sculptures depicted in the background.

2 French walnut *dressoir, c.* 1580; having an upper cabinet with two doors and two drawers decorated with carved allegorical classical figures; the base has double Doric columns and round arches inspired by designs for a classical triumphal arch published by Jacques Androuet du Cerceau in *Les Petits Grotesques* (1550).

The *dressoir*, a furniture type which began as a Gothic *meuble d'apparat* of Burgundian origin, is here realized in a French Renaissance style, with the inclusion of Italianate architectural elements and inlay techniques dating from antiquity which were reintroduced and became fashionable during the early Renaissance. However, the vertical emphasis of its forms and the restrained elegance of its classical allegorical figures are characteristic of the courtly Mannerist style of the School of Fontainebleau. The doubling of the columns was also used later as a design feature, particularly on French cabinets-on-stand of the seventeenth century.

3 Flemish *armoire* in oak, *c.* 1530–50, consisting of two cupboards of box-like shape, separated by two drawers. The construction is still medieval in character, panels being fitting into the rectangular framework of stiles by the tongue-and-groove method. The feet are formed by the extended corner posts and the side panels are decorated in the Gothic linenfold pattern. The cupboard fronts are decorated with carvings reflecting Italian Renaissance influence: the centre panel on each door is adorned with a profile portrait head, one male, one female; the important iron locks still belong to the Gothic tradition.

A *meuble de mariage* of this type would have been commissioned to commemorate a wedding; it represents a variation on the Burgundian *dressoir*, being intended to store and display personal valuables, a function fulfilled later by the cabinet-on-stand.

4 French walnut *cabinet en armoire, c,* 1530, the upper part consisting of twelve drawers, the base having two shelves. The front doors are decorated with carved and moulded strapwork, shells and rosettes, repeated on the sides. The high quality of the restrained decorative scheme and of the fittings (hinges, drawer-handles, locks, keys and bolts) denote the use of the piece as a collector's cabinet. The Renaissance interest in classical antiquity as well as in the natural world and faraway countries was represented in the collection of objects which aimed to recreate a microcosm of the known world.

5 Spanish walnut *escritorio* or *vargueño, c.* 1550, with a hinged top and fall-front shown open, revealing drawers and cupboards; the *pie de puente* stand has spirally fluted columns and round arches. The box-like form of the portable chest with a fall-front and drawers was inspired by Islamic prototypes, a tradition still apparent here in the inlaid geometric pattern of the sides and the carved boxwood arabesques. However, the profile heads within medallions and the carved and applied grotesques within a framework of arabesques reveal the influence of the Italian Renaissance, while the high quality of the craftsmanship marks this piece as Catalan in origin.

By the mid-sixteenth century the *escritorio* had become a very popular furniture type; it was used as a portable writing desk and also served as a display piece in well-to-do households. Ornate examples would have been specially commissioned, perhaps as commemorative wedding pieces.

6 Italian *studiolo* made of walnut inlaid with various natural and coloured woods, *c.* 1532. The surfaces of the fall-front cabinet are entirely covered with pictorial *intarsia* decoration of a narrative and emblematic nature. On the outside of the fall-front (not shown) is depicted the biblical account of Gideon's victories over the Midianites (Judges, 36–40, vv. 1–7 and 19–21) in three scenes within a framework of arabesques punctuated by profile busts of Roman emperors (each identified by his name: JULIUS CAESAR, AUGUSTUS, CALIGULA, TIBERIUS, CLAUDIUS, NERO, TITUS, DOMITIAN) above a balustrade revealing a landscape in the background. On the sides are allegorical figures of Justice and Temperance, respectively. When open, the inside of the fall-front reveals an inlaid stylized ribbon with the motto of Charles V 'PLUS ULTRA' and the heraldic device of a crowned eagle for the Holy Roman Empire, between the Pillars of Hercules representing Spain.

The drawer-fronts are adorned with inlaid classical motifs of dolphins, *amorini* and *rinceaux*, while the cupboard doors feature *trompe-l'œil* still-lifes inspired by fifteenth-century examples of the *studiolo*, such as those at Gubbio or Urbino (see p. 41), which were emulated by Isabella d'Este after her arrival in Mantua as a bride in 1490.

The emblematic aspects of the cabinet are: the fleece of Gideon, alluding to the Order of the Golden Fleece founded in 1429 by Philip III, Duke of Burgundy; the complex heraldic device designed by the Bishop of Tuy for Charles V as King of Spain from 1516 and Holy Roman Emperor from 1519; and the initials 'DM' (Domus Mantovana, i.e. House of Mantua). The military and imperial authority of Charles V is thus made clear, as well as the identity of the patron who commissioned it as a gift for the Holy Roman Emperor. Ferrante Gonzaga (1507–57) was the youngest son of Francesco, 4th Marchese di Mantua, and Isabella d'Este; his eldest brother Federigo inherited the Marquessate and was created on 8 April

1530 1st Duke of Mantua by Charles V during a state visit. Charles V visited Mantua again in November 1532, at the suggestion of and escorted by Ferrante, who had served in the Imperial army and had been present at the imperial Coronation in Bologna in February 1530; the following year he had been received at Tournai as a Knight of the Order of the Golden Fleece. The *studiolo*, with its complex symbolism linking Imperial Rome to biblical heroic deeds, heraldry to an order of chivalry, combined humanist knowledge with the art of the *intarsiatori* who would have worked in the celebrated *Grotta* or *Studiolo* of Isabella d'Este at Mantua; it was thus an appropriate piece for presentation to the Holy Roman Emperor and might have been part of the furnishings of the Imperial apartments during his stay in the city in 1532.

7 English writing casket in oak and walnut, *c.* 1525, covered with painted and gilt-leather depicting the royal arms of Henry VIII (reigned 1509–47).

The casket is covered on the exterior with shagreen dyed black and has gilt-brass fittings dating from *c.* 1700. The interior consists of leather-covered drawers and compartments with gilt and painted decoration; the symbolic narrative scheme alludes to Henry VIII as a Tudor King and Defender of the Faith, a title accorded him by Pope Leo X for his book on the Sacraments published in 1521 in reply to Martin Luther. The inner surface of the lid is adorned with the arms of Henry VIII encircled by the Garter ribbon bearing the motto 'Honi soit qui mal y pense', with two supporting putti sounding trumpets and on the left a standing figure of Mars, god of war, and on the right Venus, goddess of love, with her son Cupid, blindfolded; both figures are shown within Renaissance-style architectural niches.

The allusion to love and dynastic claims is carried further on the inside of the fall-front which, once opened, reveals an intricate pattern of strapwork enclosing the heraldic badges of Henry VIII and his first wife, Catherine of Aragon (widow of his brother), whom he had married in 1509 on his accession to the throne: the Portcullis, the Tudor Rose, the Fleur de Lis, the Castle (with the cipher 'HR') and the Sheaf of Arrows. The inner rim below the outer lid is lined with parchment bearing the inscription: 'Henrico Octavo regi anglie de . . . religiones christianae maxime tribue servo'. The Christian connotation continues on the inner compartments with images of Christ and St George and the Dragon, while the front reverts to figures from classical antiquity showing Paris and Helen in profile, inscribed 'Paris de Troy' and 'Helen de Greci' within arabesques and grotesques.

The decorative scheme combining classical and mythological figures (Mars and Venus, Paris and Helen), together with a clear Christian message and the heraldic devices of royalty is characteristic of the sixteenth-century humanist allegorical and emblematic conceit favoured by princes and monarchs. The design was inspired by woodcuts by the famous German engraver Hans Burgkmair, *c.* 1510, and demonstrates the international aspect of luxury objects of this kind, several examples of which are mentioned in Henry VIII's inventory of 1547, being covered with leather or velvet 'garnyshed with gilt nails', and containing among other things, 'a paiexe of sycssores, a payer of compass & a penne knyfe cased with metal'.

8 Italian *cassone*, *c.* 1480–5, in gilt and painted walnut with a set of five drawers decorated with carved gilt Gothic tracery behind the door on the left-hand side. Examples of the *cassone* or chest were usually produced in pairs and often incorporated, when forming part of a bride's dowry in Italy

and Catalonia (there called a *hembra*), a small set of drawers to contain the bride's valuables and prized personal possessions. Sometimes the small nest of drawers was made as an independent casket which could be removed in case of emergency.

Here the painted geometric *trompe-l'œil* decoration on the inner surface of the lid and the heraldic armorials, together with the carved gilt tracery, are characteristic of the late Gothic style to be found all over Europe in the fifteenth century. The armorials depicted in the three coats of arms are those of the Dal Pozzo family from Verona.

9 German ebony-veneered architectural cabinet in the form of a temple, *c.* 1580–1600; a Mannerist two-storeyed façade is surmounted by triangular pediment and flanked by volutes. The four fluted Corinthian columns enclose niches with gilt-bronze statuettes of the Theological Virtues (Faith, Hope and Charity) and the four Cardinal Virtues (Prudence, Fortitude and Temperance, with Justice in the centre). The feet are in the form of gilt recumbent lions. The entire surface of the piece is richly adorned with tortoiseshell and ivory veneers and with *pietra dura* inlay of jasper, lapis lazuli and agate, suggesting a foreign influence, which is further reinforced by the Venetian origins of the gilt-bronze statuettes and mounts and by the general form of the cabinet. Augsburg had become famous as a cabinetmaking centre in the Renaissance era, with the result that foreign apprentices went there to study, no doubt introducing their own Italianate forms and techniques to Germany.

The iconographic theme of this cabinet appears to be an allegory of the Church Triumphant, from its general form, reminiscent of the façade of Il Gesù (Della Porta, 1573–84), in Rome, to its decorative elements in keeping with the theological preoccupations of the Counter-Reformation at the end of the sixteenth century. Here the storage function is secondary to the religious message, all drawers being concealed behind the architectonic structure, the two sides of which can be removed to reveal drawers and secret compartments, while the central panel opens to reveal a theatre with ivory caryatids and nineteen drawers, the handles of which are made of red and blue coloured glass in imitation of jasper and lapis lazuli.

10 German ebony-veneered table-cabinet with gilt-bronze mounts, *c.* 1575. The rectangular box-like form is similar to that of the early *Schreibtisch*, but the fall-front has disappeared and with it the writing function of the cabinet, which has itself become a precious *objet d'art*, in terms of both materials and craftsmanship. The sides are decorated with a geometric marquetry of walnut and fruitwood, while the front consists of twelve drawers separated by agate columns, around a central theatre. The theatre is recessed behind a geometric paving of ebony and ivory; the rear panel opens to reveal eleven secret drawers. The gilt-bronze medallions adorning the cabinet illustrate a political theme linked to the Habsburg dynasty: the central panel has a portrait of Mary Tudor, Queen of England (reigned 1553–8), on a bronze medal based on a design by Jacopo Nizzola da Trezzo. Other portraits are: Philip II of Spain (reigned 1556–98), son of Charles V of Habsburg, Holy Roman Emperor (1519–56); and (top right) Giambattista Castalchi, Count of Piadena, one of Philip II's generals.

The cabinet is traditionally thought to have belonged to the Fugger family, a wealthy and powerful banking dynasty in Augsburg from 1367 to 1668; members of this family wielded power and influence throughout the Holy Roman Empire, Spain and England, having been instrumental in securing the throne for Charles V in

1519 and acting as bankers to his son Philip II and daughter-in-law Mary Tudor. The cabinet would therefore certainly have been made as a special commission, possibly intended as a presentation piece.

11, 12 Persian silver-damascened brass casket, fourteenth century; medallions, each enclosing a seated courtly figure, are surrounded by stylized vine scrolls and arabesques and the single word 'Praise' in Kufic script is repeated in a continuous band. This metalwork technique, traditional to the Near East, was used to create intricate arabesque and geometric abstract patterns on objects intended for presentation, such as caskets, basins and ewers, and also on weapons and armour. The Christian Crusaders brought back to Europe objects on which the decorative Muslim calligraphic ornament would sometimes be combined with the Roman alphabet or heraldic devices (as seen on the Damascus candlestick dating from *c.* 1400 decorated with the arms of the Venetian Badoer family, a piece now in the collection of the Victoria and Albert Museum). An Italian traveller to Damascus wrote in 1384–5: 'They also make a large quantity of basins and ewers of brass and in truth they look like gold; and then on the said basins and ewers they put figures and leaves and other subtle work in silver, a most beautiful thing to see.' Soon Venice and Milan were producing damascened work, the fine arabesque and geometric patterns of which influenced not only metalwork but came to be associated in the sixteenth century with grotesques, the use of which extended to many art forms in Europe.

13 Ottoman wooden casket of the sixteenth century with an inlay of mother-of-pearl, tortoiseshell, ivory, bone and metal wire forming a geometric radiating pattern within a framework of cable banding motifs and with a frieze of trefoils along the front. The use of inlays on small wooden panels was a traditional technique in the Near East, as wood was a scarce commodity in Muslim countries. Stylized decorative motifs based on interlacing geometric patterns, arabesques and calligraphic ornament were all used in Islamic woodwork, mostly on Qu'ran stands and boxes; the costly materials employed, such as mother-of-pearl, ivory and tortoiseshell, as well as precious metals, eventually influenced the development of certain European inlay techniques, e.g. *Embriachi* work in northern Italy and the *mudejar* style in Spain.

14, 15 German pictorial marquetry *Schreibtisch*, *c.* 1580–1600, with a hinged flap depicting an architectural perspective of fantastic arcaded overgrown ruins, the same design being continued on the sides. The top is inlaid with bold strapwork and flower gardens. The writing flap opens to reveal an arrangement of twelve drawers around a central recessed well. This type of portable writing cabinet fitted with side-handles and a lock was influenced by the Spanish *escritorio* of Muslim origins, and became the favoured piece of furniture under the Habsburg rulers of the Holy Roman Empire, fulfilling the function of a carrying case for documents and valuables and that of a portable desk.

The *trompe-l'œil* architectural vistas were inspired by contemporary records of the Italian Renaissance discoveries of Euclidian perspective and recalled the illusionistic vistas depicted in *intarsia* in Italian churches and princely *studioli*.

16 German pictorial marquetry *Schreibtisch*, *c.* 1570. The form is simple and box-like, but the surface is decorated overall with marquetry panels inspired by traditional native German themes – the Hunt, Music, etc. – depicted within a landscape of fantastic Italianate Mannerist ruins, very similar to that used on the *Wrangelschrank* (see p.

44) by Lorenz Strohmeir and Bartlmä Weishaupt in 1566, the first example of a *Kunstschrank* in which convenience was sacrificed to art. In the late sixteenth and early seventeenth centuries Augsburg became famous for producing cabinets of this type, with ebony veneers superseding the use of marquetry. However, in the Tyrol, the gateway by which Italian influence reached Germany, the tradition of depicting perspective views on *Schreibtische* lingered on, sometimes with the inclusion of musical instruments in the marquetry together with ruins, flowers, birds and a characteristic 'Hunter and Hare' motif, a provincial echo of the 'Hunter and Dog' theme used on Augsburg pieces as an allegory of Smell in depictions of the Five Senses.

In the present example the interior is modelled on the façade of an Italianate *palazzo*, with columns and niches enclosing figures of dancing nymphs and musicians, between marquetry panels illustrating the theme of the Hunt. The central double door opens to reveal a theatre containing secret drawers. The association of a strong Italian influence with hunting and music is characteristic of the Tyrol, as is the use of stained burr in imitation of marble. This cabinet is therefore representative of a highly sophisticated production to be found between the Tyrol, Ulm and Augsburg. An *armoire* made c. 1569 in Ulm (now in the city museum) and a Tyrolean cabinet dating from c. 1575 are very close in decorative motifs and techniques, while the whole ethos of the piece and its quality of execution are on a par with the *Wrangelschrank*.

17 Chinese *Tian-qi* (filled-in) lacquer cabinet of the Ming Dynasty, c. 1410–35, having a removable front panel secured at the top by a vertical bolt, and gilt-bronze side-handles, each on a double-cloud escutcheon. Once the front panel is removed, drawers of different sizes are revealed, each having a single-cloud escutcheon handle except for the bottom drawer, spanning the full width of the cabinet, which has a double-cloud escutcheon. The entire wooden carcase of the cabinet is lacquered, as are the removable front and the drawers; the underside of the base and the inside of the front panel are lacquered in black (the latter now discoloured brown), as are the insides of drawers. The interior of the cabinet and the exterior of the drawers are lacquered red. The exterior of the cabinet is lacquered yellow with an engraved design and other coloured lacquers applied to the surface (three shades of red, two of green, plus ochre, yellow, brown and black), the incised lines filled in with black or gold lacquer. Small holes are drilled in the black ground of the main panels to simulate metalwork matting.

The design throughout is based on the dragon and phoenix among clouds and lotuses, each main panel being edged with a band of red clouds outlined in ochre, black and gold against a red ground. The base is decorated with a band of petal panels. The sophisticated design and the elaborate incised lacquer techniques denote a special commission, possibly a wedding presentation piece, the most likely provenance being the Orchard Factory, which worked exclusively for the Imperial Court in the early fifteenth century.

18 Italian leather-covered table-cabinet, c. 1590–1600, with a hinged fall-front revealing an arrangement of drawers around a central cupboard; the hinged lid with a mirror mounted internally opens to give access to internal divisions and compartments. The whole of the wooden carcase, together with the inner side of the fall-front and the outer face of the drawers and cupboard, is covered with red painted leather; the design features hunters and soldiers, as well as animals naively depicted in gold, black and brown, with a stylized tooled

banding consisting of rosettes and palmettes along all edges.

Leather, which had been used for decorative purposes since antiquity, gained prestige and importance in the Middle Ages thanks to the development of the art of the book. However, with the rise of Islam, the love and care lavished on Qu'ran and other bookbindings influenced the craftsmen of Moorish Spain and Venice, leading to the emulation by European craftsmen of the Muslim technique of embossing leather with a relief pattern of stylized arabesques in gold or silver called *guadamecil*, or of abstract geometric designs (which could also be painted or lacquered). From the end of the fifteenth century until the middle of the sixteenth century Venice was exporting tooled lacquered leather for use in covering wooden cabinets, inspired by the lacquered bookbindings 'in the Persian style' recorded at the time.

The form of this piece, reminiscent of the German *Schreibtisch*, could therefore have been directly inspired by the Muslim prototype, which had influenced the development of the Spanish/Portuguese *escritorio*.

19 German *Kunstschrank* made of ebony, with inset panels of *pietra dura* and *pietra paesina*, executed c. 1625–31 for Philipp Hainhofer, the Augsburg humanist, diplomat and merchant. In 1604 Hainhofer had begun collecting shells and curios as the basis of what was to become one of the finest examples of the German *Kunstkammer*, visited by men of learning and distinction from all over Europe. In the early part of the seventeenth century kings and princes, scholars and merchants were avidly collecting natural and man-made curios and artifacts, in the wake of the humanist interest in nature and the classical world generated in Italy during the early Renaissance, manifested especially in princely *studioli*.

Philipp Hainhofer's original contribution to this concept was to have realized the miniature *Kunstkammer*, examples of which were made – mostly for royal patrons – on commission. The present *Kunstschrank* was made at his own expense and purchased by the City of Augsburg for 6,500 thalers as a gift to King Gustavus Adolphus of Sweden following the entry of Swedish troops into the city in April 1632. Although the original inventory of the contents of the *Kunstschrank* is lost, the objects themselves have survived. The listing would have been very similar to that of the Florentine *Stipo d'Allemania*, in which two main categories are mentioned, echoing the classification of the contemporary *Kunstkammer*, based on Pliny the Elder's *Natural History*: 'Naturalia' and 'Artificialia'. This miniature *Kunstkammer* aimed to present a microcosm of contemporary humanist knowledge: 'Naturalia' included not only the coral, crystals, shells and *pietra dura* decoration, but also works of art made from organic materials, such as the detachable crowning coco-de-mer ewer, capable of holding 'one quart of wine' (Hainhofer's records), the *pietra paesina* panels, the alabaster slab with scenes painted by Johann König (the Israelites crossing the Red Sea on one side, and the Last Judgment on the other), and the lizards and beetles cast in silver from nature. 'Artificialia' embraced: the exquisite golden statuette of Venus emerging from the ewer; the virginal (placed in a drawer at the top of the cabinet) which could be played either by means of the keyboard or automatically activated by a mechanism linked to a clock concealed behind the rocks made from shells and minerals above; the vexing mirrors with their distorted images; the two *Vanitas* ivory miniatures in which the faces of a man and a woman would, when rotated, change into the image of a skull; and the *intarsia* panel

(see p. 9) showing a cabinetmaker showing off a *Kunstschrank* in his studio.

Beyond the encyclopaedic attempt to order and classify intellectual knowledge lay several levels of philosophical, religious, moral and magical meanings. Thus allegories of the Four Elements, the Five Senses, of time, love and death were intricately linked, by way of a complex programme of classified materials and objects, to the latest research into the art of alchemy and the occult. In fact Stephan Michelspacher, a doctor from the Tyrol, published his book *Cabala, Spiegel der Kunst und Natur: in Alchymia* (Augsburg, 1615) with a dedication to Hainhofer. Francesco de' Medici had earlier demonstrated this aspect of the humanist collector by having himself portrayed by Stradano as the alchemist's assistant in a panel in the Palazzo Vecchio, Florence (see p. 42).

This *Kunstschrank* was described by Hainhofer, who noted that 'many hold it to be the eighth wonder of the world', not only as a *theatrum mundi* reflecting the extent of the known world, but also as a *theatrum memoriae* evoking in the deepest recesses of man's heart and soul the ultimate meaning of God's creation. Yet beside being the focus of learned debates and metaphysical contemplation, the cabinet was intended to be of practical use; Hainhofer himself said of the *Kunstschrank* intended for Duke Maximilian I of Bavaria in 1613, that it must be 'of some use and not just stand about aimlessly', evidence of which is provided by the well-worn lining of the medicine chest and the basin and ewer. The medicinal aspect of the cabinet harks back to ancient times, while the surgical, astronomical, mathematical and writing instruments and implements were all made with a functional purpose in mind, despite their miniature size.

20 Italian ebony and *pietra dura* table-cabinet, Florence, c. 1616–23; on the front the central architectural feature is surmounted by the arms of Maffeo Barberini (1568–1644) as a Cardinal. He was appointed Papal Legate in France by Pope Clement VIII (1592–1605), who negotiated the peace between France and Spain, and was himself elected Pope in 1623 as Urban VIII.

This cabinet would have been executed in the Opificio delle Pietre Dure, opened in 1599 by Ferdinand de' Medici in the Galleria dei Lavori; it illustrates the pictorial virtuosity achieved there during the first half of the seventeenth century. The iconography of the smaller panels was inspired by the woodcuts by Francisco Tuppo illustrating *Aesop's Fables*, published in Naples in 1485. According to the Greek historian Herodotus (c. 484–420 BC), Aesop was a Greek slave living in the mid-sixth century BC; his moralistic anecdotes are concerned with animal characters imitating human behaviour.

The frontispiece depicts Orpheus charming the wild beasts with the lyre given to him by Apollo. The myth of Orpheus, who could not only charm animals but move rocks and trees with his music, bringing harmony to the whole of nature, was further reinforced by his descent to Hades in search of Eurydice; there he was able to charm the monstrous three-headed watchdog Cerberus and make the damned forget their sufferings. The Orphic teaching, as practised from the seventeenth century BC onwards in ancient Greece, regarded Orpheus as a symbol of purification and regeneration (based on the legend that, after his death at the hands of the furious Maenads, his head floated still singing to the island of Lesbos). Christ was later identified with Orpheus, the lyre being one of the Christian symbols mentioned by Clement of Alexandria (c. 150–220), one of the Church fathers. The ability of Orpheus to sooth and civilize with his music was equated symbolically with Christ's redeeming power over man's baser instincts and animal nature. The theme is here conveyed through the parallel between man and the animal world in *Aesop's Fables* and the depiction of the salamander and the phoenix in two of the flanking panels, both creatures being associated with purification through fire: the phoenix, reborn from its own ashes, was adopted by the early Christians as a symbol of Christ's Resurrection, and was used to represent the virtue of chastity; the salamander, according to Aristotle and Pliny, not only survived fire, but also could extinguish the flames, and was therefore linked to Fire as one of the Four Elements. The salamander was also adopted as the cipher of Francis I of France (1494–1547), with the Latin motto 'Nutrisco et extingo' (I sustain goodness and destroy evil).

The complex iconographic message of the cabinet represents not only an emblematic homage to the powerful Barberini family, but has a strong political and religious slant in relation to France and the Church (of which Maffeo Barberini was a prince), as well as conveying a distinct moral and spiritual message expressed in humanist allusions; all this was in keeping with the spirit of late Mannerist art and of the Church Triumphant following the Counter-Reformation. The cabinet would certainly have been made as a special commission, perhaps intended for presentation; such a gift would be all the more appreciated on account of its multi-layered decorative scheme, as well as the artistic virtuosity of its execution.

21, 22 Italian ebony table-cabinet, c. 1600–20; ten engraved ivory plaques depict scenes from the Trojan War (as described by Homer in the Iliad and the Odyssey, hostilities between Greece and Troy arose after Helen, wife of Menelaus of Sparta, was seduced by Paris and abducted to Troy).

This table-cabinet belongs to a group of *escritorio*-type ebony cabinets executed in Naples (then under Spanish rule) at the beginning of the seventeenth century, all adorned with ivory plaques which were often engraved with battle scenes relating to the Spanish dominion over the city, or the might of the Habsburg Empire (with accompanying maps), or, more rarely, illustrations of Ovid's *Metamorphoses*. Here the subject is an allegory of the theme of love and war. These cabinets were often produced as presentation pieces and diplomatic gifts. The high quality of the engraving on the ivory plaques (see pp. 11, 50) has been linked to several names: Antonio Espano, 'Cosmographer' to Philip II of Spain, who signed one such cabinet now in a private collection; Giovanni Battista de Curtis, recorded in Naples in 1569 as 'intarsiatore in avolio', who signed a similar cabinet now in the Museum für Kunst und Gewerbe in Hamburg and a small altarpiece (with a representation of the Immaculate Conception signed 'Jo Batt de Curtis' and dated 1607) in the same collection as the present cabinet; and Theodore de Voghel, to whom scenes from Ovid's *Metamorphoses* depicted on a cabinet now in a London collection have been attributed (see p. 50).

23 Italian ebonized pearwood table-cabinet, Florence, c. 1640; the decorative *scagliola* panels imitate the technique and designs associated with *pietra dura*. The depiction of a bird resembling a chaffinch with flowers or cherries is very similar to that found on the John Evelyn Cabinet in the Victoria and Albert Museum (see p. 75), which has inset panels of 'Pietra Commessa: a marble ground inlayed with several sorts of marbles & stones of divers colours in the shape of flowers, trees, beasts, birds & Landskip like the natural' (*The Diary of John Evelyn*, ed. de Beer, vol. II, 1955, p. 191).

In 1644 the famous traveller and diarist John Evelyn had encountered work in *scagliola* in the 'Palas of Negros' (now Villa Rolla-Rosazza),

Genoa. He noted in his diary that 'In his house I first tooke notice of those red plaster flores which are made so hard, & kept so polite, that for some time, one would take them for whole pieces of Porphyrie: I have frequently wondered, we never practised it in England for Cabinets & romes of States' (op. cit., p. 174).

The decoration of this cabinet combines the pictorial quality of *pietra dura* designs with the geometric motifs used in architectural decoration, here enclosed within a flat black strapwork.

24, 25 Italian table-cabinet (*cofano*) in ebony, c. 1650. The hinged top covers an internal well, the inside of the lid being decorated with inset panels of *scagliola*, agate and a small mirror. The inner architectural façade is punctuated by four rock-crystal columns flanking groups of drawers. The central theatre features black and white paving and a mirrored perspective with sphinx-headed gilt-bronze columns; behind it are three secret drawers, while the broken pediment above constitutes a secret compartment.

The cabinet is decorated overall with *scagliola* panels imitating lapis lazuli, jasper, agate and cornelian. Pink and yellow Spanish Brocatelle marble is used on the side of the doors. The rich decoration and the virtuosity of the construction of the secret drawers in this small *cofano* point to its use as a luxurious *objet d'art*, perhaps to hold jewellery and valuables.

26, 27 Italian ebony cabinet with ivory, tortoiseshell and gilt-bronze plaques, Rome or Naples, c. 1650. The elaborate architectural lines were derived from Michelangelo's Palazzo dei Conservatori in the Piazza del Campidoglio, Rome (completed c. 1563); the façade with pairs of columns is reminiscent of Michelangelo's model for S. Lorenzo, Florence, c. 1517. The whole complex structure with foreshortened perspective views recalls Palladio's Teatro Olimpico at Vicenza, completed by Scamozzi in 1585 (see pp. 76–7). The monumental size of the cabinet and the elaborate use of perspective – as seen in the sloping receding paving, the diminishing size of the columns, the viewpoint concentrated on the middle of the central apse when viewed from a distance of 7–8 metres (22–25 ft), and the lateral view through the side doors along a mirrored corridor – are features of a Baroque sense of illusionism and theatricality. The central apse would originally have contained a statue (as would perhaps the two flanking niches), which would have provided the key to the intricate allegorical decorative scheme.

The storage capacity of the cabinet is almost negligible in proportion to its size, being limited to drawers in the upper frieze and plinth. This is essentially a showpiece, intended to be seen from a distance and placed on a supporting base to achieve full impact. The viewer would then come closer to a full appreciation of the esoteric meaning of the iconography which seems to revolve around the central theme of power, a concept in keeping with the spirit of the time, whether in the context of the Church Triumphant or the rule of absolute monarchs. Power in its various aspects is first expressed through the grandeur and *gravitas* of Ancient Rome on the lower part of the tall fluted tortoiseshell columns pressed into a relief similar to Trajan's Column, with gilt-bronze plaques depicting Romulus and Remus, the she-wolf and the Tiber, the rape of the Sabine women and the rape of Lucretia; Roman *virtù*, civic and personal honour provide a secondary theme. The concept of heroism is portrayed in mythological scenes depicting Perseus and his various attributes, and the sacrifice of Iphigenia.

The power of love is described in a multi-faceted manner: Venus is depicted several times with

allusions to her birth, her husband Vulcan, her son Cupid, and her lovers Adonis and Mars; Zeus, Leda and the Swan, and Diana the goddess of the Hunt and Chastity are also featured. Indeed the Three Graces, attendants to Venus, representing the three phases of love (Beauty awakening Desire and leading to Fulfilment, or alternatively Chastity/Beauty and Love) appear several times, together with Lust (depicted as a pig-headed man) and Father Time.

The battle scenes showing soldiers in sixteenth-century costumes could refer to the Sack of Rome by Charles V in 1527, thus introducing a political connotation with the Habsburg dynasty and an association with Spain (symbolized by the extensive use of imported tortoiseshell) and with Spanish dominion over Naples.

This cabinet would have been executed not so much for a humanist connoisseur but more likely for an aristocratic patron or a prince, for whom the powerful political message would be relevant. The didactic aspect of the piece is further emphasized by the allegorical figures of the Liberal Arts adorning the gallery, together with classical deities. As such, the cabinet is a microcosm of the humanist education of a prince; its drawers would no doubt have contained coins, medals and artifacts from classical antiquity, perhaps echoing the thematic iconography of the decoration. Thus, for example, a particular item might be kept in a drawer adorned with the relevant motif, as was the case in the Renaissance *studioli*, to be removed and used as the subject for learned debates and discussions, viewed within the context of the cabinet as a whole.

28 Flemish ebony cabinet veneered with tortoiseshell and decorated with coloured lacquer inlaid with mother-of-pearl and marble chips, Antwerp, c. 1640–50. The *scriban* features classical architectural motifs on the double doors framed by pilasters, the whole outlined in tortoiseshell enclosing stylized floral still-lifes (depicted in a technique inspired by Japanese lacquer work in the *Namban* style of the Momoyama period (1573–1615), with mother-of-pearl and marble chips set in a black composition ground, decorated with coloured-lacquer inlay. This technique, combining red, blue, green and yellow shellac with the glistening tesserae of mother-of-pearl and marble, is a derivative of the Italian *scagliola* process, which was itself inspired by *pietra dura*.

The decorative scheme featuring *rinceaux*, cornucopia and flowers (tulips, jasmine, carnations) combined with birds and vases recalls the stylization and symmetry of *pietra dura* prototypes. The two doors open to reveal six further drawers similarly decorated.

29 Italian ebony and tortoiseshell cabinet-on-stand (one of a pair), Naples, c. 1650–70; the cabinet has a strong architectural emphasis with a central breakfront flanked by Salomonic columns and sets of drawers framed by flat pilasters on either side. The six drawers are decorated with inset painted panels under glass, depicting mythological scenes, mostly from Ovid's *Metamorphoses*, and allegories. The style of the painted scenes has been likened to that of Luca Giordano (1632–1705) on account of the virtuoso handling and the use of fresh blues and reds inspired by Venetian painting; in his *Vite de' Pittori, Scultori ed Architetti Napoletani* (Naples, 1742) Bernardo de Dominici drew attention to a particular Neapolitan tradition, also used on some Spanish pieces. Indeed, several other cabinets display similar painted glass panels in the same style (examples are in the Palazzo Pitti, Florence; the Victoria and Albert Museum; the Palace of Pereleda, Gerona, Spain; the Palazzo Barberini, Rome; and in private collections). The stand shown here is characteristic of the Roman Baroque style, with its rich contrast of ebonized and gilt wood and bold sculptural forms; the pair of cabinets are thus a striking example of palazzo furniture.

30 Italian ebony and tortoiseshell cabinet-on-stand, Naples, c. 1630–40. Built on strong architectural lines, this cabinet has a breakfront central frontispiece with a broken pediment enclosing a gilt-bronze statuette in a niche, surmounted by another similar niche; the two cupboards flanking the tiers of drawers are similarly decorated with a niche and a statuette. This arrangement recalls the architectonic and decorated façades of Counter-Reformation churches.

31 Flemish ebony cabinet with inset painted panels within a tortoiseshell ground, Antwerp, c. 1650–70. The painted panels depict scenes from the Old and New Testaments after works by Veronese and Domenico Fetti in the collection of Archduke Leopold Wilhelm, Governor of the Spanish Netherlands, based in Brussels. Copies of eleven works are included, all the originals having been acquired by the Archduke from the collection of the Duke of Buckingham at the sale held in Antwerp in 1649.

In 1660 David Teniers the Younger (1610–90) published a catalogue of the Archduke's collection, the *Theatrum Pictorium*, including some 245 engravings (in which the images are reversed) after Italian pictures, among them the eleven works on this cabinet. The copies would have had to be executed before the Archduke's resignation in 1656 and the subsequent removal of his art collection, partly to Prague, partly to Vienna (where Veronese's *Hagar and Ishmail, Christ and the Woman of Samaria, Christ and the Centurion* and Fetti's *Jacob's Dream* were given to the Archduke's brother, Emperor Ferdinand III; all these works are now in the Kunsthistorisches Museum, Vienna). The copies decorating the cabinet could have been specially commissioned by the Archduke as a record of works in his own collection before they were dispersed. Whatever the case, the quality of the painterly technique is of a very high standard, suggesting the hand of an accomplished master.

The paintings are only seen when the cabinet is open, the exterior being a starkly simple black ebony veneer. The hinged top reveals a well and the central frontispiece opens on to a mirrored theatre, while the flanking drawers and a slide under the plinth drawer add a functional aspect to a piece of furniture which would have been appreciated as a work of art in its own right. The two main painted panels on the doors bear the stamped monograms 'BMD' and 'MV' respectively.

32, 33 Flemish ebony and tortoiseshell cabinet-on-stand with ivory and gilt-bronze decorative motifs and inset painted copper panels, Antwerp, c. 1650–70. The decorative scheme of the cabinet is dedicated to Love, the exterior panels depicting episodes from the Trojan War (Aphrodite rescuing Helen and Aeneas rescuing his father Anchises). The two doors are decorated on the inside with scenes showing Hermes and Herse (right) and Hersea (left). The inner face of the hinged lid is decorated with the initial 'M' in ivory within an ebony cartouche against a red tortoiseshell background; on either side *Pan and Syrinx* and *Vertume and Pomone* continue the theme of Love.

The central frontispiece and the drawers are faced with small painted copper panels depicting love scenes, mostly inspired by Ovid's *Metamorphoses*, some after Titian, such as the *Venus and Adonis* (second from top on the left; see detail) painted for Philip II of Spain c. 1551–4 – a subject frequently borrowed by decorative artists. The painterly manner is reminiscent of Rubens and his circle, the panel being signed on the lower drawer

'H. V. BAL Fec'. The cabinet, with its theme of the eternal aspects of Love and the inclusion of the initial 'M', would have been a special commission, most likely to commemorate a wedding.

Similar cabinets with painted panels are in the Rijksmuseum, Amsterdam, and the Rubenshuis, Antwerp.

34 Flemish ebony and tortoiseshell cabinet-on-stand with inset painted alabaster panels, Antwerp, c. 1670. Tortoiseshell veneer was used in Spanish-dominated Flanders, as well as Naples, to endow cabinets with a rich decorative surface, enhanced by a coloured background, mostly red, or gold foil. Here the combination of the dark ebony, the lustrous red-backed tortoiseshell and gilt bronze provides a fitting setting for the alabaster panels painted with Italianate *vedute* and *capricci*. The carved and gilded wooden stand featuring sculptural representations of the Four Seasons, together with the matching cresting, contribute to the Baroque grandeur of this *meuble d'apparat*. Similar cabinets are in the Rijksmuseum, Amsterdam, and the Plantin-Moretus Museum, Antwerp, both examples being decorated with Old Testament scenes.

35, 36 English silk-covered casket decorated with cut paperwork in commemoration of the wedding of Charles II and Catherine of Braganza in 1661. The outside of the casket and the fronts of the inner drawers are entirely covered with silk decorated with applied motifs of cut-out flossed paper; the King and Queen are depicted on the front, an allegory of Flora or Ceres on the top and at the back, and a fashionably dressed couple on the sides. Fruits and flowers decorate the drawers, and all edges are finished with silver braiding. The whole surface was originally protected by a sheet of mica (talc).

The casket is a rare survival of a technique popular in England at the time. In 1688 Randall Holme described it in his *Academy of Armoury* under the heading 'Other Works Performed by School Mistresses and their Scholars'. He wrote: Gum Work, [which] is by gumming several Colours of sleeven Silk together, which being dry, they cut into shapes of Leaves and Flowers, and so tie them up upon Wyers'. The young girls relied for their decorative motifs on pattern books of the type published by Peter Stent (active 1643–67) and John Overton (active 1667–1707). In 1671 Overton registered a book with the Stationers' Company in London consisting of 'Four Hundred new sorts of Birds, Beastes, Flowers, Fruicts, Fish, Flyes, Wormes, Lanskips, Ovals, and Histories etc. Lively coloured for all sorts of Gentlewomen and School Mistresses Works'.

The casket is lined with pink silk taffeta and mauve paper; secret drawers for finger-rings are concealed behind the upper and lower drawers. The hinged lid is backed with a mirror; silver-mounted scent bottles and pewter containers for ink and sand occupy the interior. This casket would have been the cherished possession of a lady, decorated by her own hands and assembled in London, to use as a compact jewelry, toilet and writing cabinet. Similar examples are in the Victoria and Albert Museum, London, the Royal Scottish Museum, Edinburgh, and the Museum für Kunst und Gewerbe, Hamburg.

37 English small needlework casket, c. 1660; the life of Joseph is worked in coloured silks on an ivory silk ground, some of the details being raised in stumpwork, and seed pearls and lace have been added to embellish the garments. The interior is lined with salmon-pink silk and watered paper, containing compartments for letters and inkwells, together with a set of four glass bottles; when the contents are removed, an inner compartment with a padded silk lining is revealed, this

space no doubt being intended to hold a needlework purse embroidered with coloured silks and gilt thread; it is decorated with a large rose bush and small plants on a green ground, and bears the inscription 'Iean Morris is name 1660', and is accompanied by a pen or knife holder and a bookmark, also worked in coloured silks.

38 Flemish ebonized table-cabinet decorated on the outside with panels of silk embroidery in *gros* and *petit point* on an ivory ground, Antwerp, c. 1670–80. The rich embroidery of gold and silver threads combined with coloured silks depicts stylized floral arrangements. The *verre églomisé* panels (not shown) on the inside of the doors also feature flower subjects. Tiers of drawers flank the central cupboard, which has a classical frontispiece concealing five inner drawers. Similar examples are in the Victoria and Albert Museum, London, and in private collections (one was formerly in the Collection of Baron Guy de Rothschild).

39 Flemish ebony table-cabinet with embroidered panels on silk, Antwerp, c. 1660–80. The hinged lid opens to reveal a central mirror flanked by two panels embroidered with coloured silks; each of the floral still-lifes includes a Chinese blue-and-white porcelain vase of the reign of K'ang Hsi (1662–1722), and similar panels line the insides of the doors. The interior displays an architectural frontispiece, silver mounts being used to highlight details; the central door conceals three secret drawers lined with rosewood. The flanking tiers of drawers are faced with embroidered scenes representing animals (lizards, parrots, mythical animals such as the unicorn, and sea monsters) in stumpwork. Pattern books would have been consulted for flower and animal designs, the former inspired by artists such as Adrian Collaert, the latter by Abraham de Bruyn's *Animalium Quadrupedum* (1578) in which real and fabulous animals were represented. The needlework decoration seems to have been commissioned from women working at home; cabinets adorned with such panels were, according to the records of the Antwerp merchants Forchondt and Musson, the least expensive of the city's production.

40 English or Flemish small table-cabinet with embroidered panels, c. 1650–70. The ebony drawers are faced with coloured silk stumpwork using gold and silver thread and depicting whales and cachalots. The technique was characteristic of England or Flanders, the designs being inspired by bestiaries, such as the *Historie of Foure-footed beasts* (1607) by Edward Topsells or the *Historie of Serpents* (1608).

Similar examples can be found in the Museum of Decorative Arts, Copenhagen, and the Musées Royaux d'Art et d'Histoire, Brussels; comparable needlework panels are in the Musée de Cluny, Paris, the Musée de la Renaissance, Ecouen, and the Metropolitan Museum and the Cooper-Hewitt Museum, New York.

41 English cabinet-on-stand with laburnum oystershell veneer, c. 1690. The inside of each door is lined with an embroidered silk panel in stumpwork depicting stylized flowers and butterflies picked out with silver thread. The stand incorporating a frieze drawer is similarly veneered, and the spiral turned legs and the stretcher are finished in simulated laburnum. The fashion for using the striking burr of either the native laburnum or the precious *lignum vitae* (imported from the West Indies) as a veneer started at the time of the Restoration, the most celebrated examples of the type being a pair of lignum vitae cabinets made c. 1665 for the apartments of Queen Henrietta Maria at Somerset House, London; these cabinets, embellished with silver mounts, are now at

Windsor Castle. Often only the interior of a cabinet was thus veneered, the exterior finish being more sober, e.g. in walnut or kingwood.

42 English cabinet-on-stand with kingwood oystershell veneer, c. 1685–95; the radiating design creates an unusual wheel pattern. The interior contains eleven drawers arranged around a central cupboard, and the moulded frieze includes a wide shallow drawer fitted with gilt-brass drop-handles. Kingwood was usually described as 'Prince wood' in contemporary inventories, such as that of Ham House prepared in 1677. This type of cabinet-on-stand was made either by Dutch craftsmen working in England, or by English craftsmen emulating their Dutch counterparts, the style being sometimes referred to as 'Anglo-Dutch'.

43 German cabinet-on-stand in ebonized wood and walnut, c. 1680–90; the cornice is veneered with tulipwood and the doors are framed by ebonized Salomonic columns. The cabinet is decorated overall with pictorial marquetry. On the outside of the doors is depicted an allegory of Fortitude after engravings by Hendrick Goltzius on the subject of 'The Roman Heroes' published in 1586. The figures of Horatius Cocles and Titus Manlius, both of whom are mentioned in Livy's *History of Rome*, are contrasted with Folly, represented as two jesters on the inside of the doors. An allegory of Autumn is illustrated on the left-hand side, with Spring on the right-hand side, each represented between spandrels inlaid with allegories of the four Quarters of the World. Metal has been used as an inlay on the helmets, swords and shields of both Roman heroes, and as mounts on the Salomonic columns. The stand of carved wood rests on scrolled legs linked by a curved stretcher; it has lion's-paw feet and a central lion mask at the apron.

44 Dutch floral marquetry cabinet-on-stand made by Jan van Mekeren, Amsterdam, c. 1690. The broad, exuberant, painterly quality of the marquetry is characteristic of van Mekeren, as are the device of setting a vase of flowers near the edge of a table and the very naturalistic treatment of the flowers and insects on the ebony ground.

This cabinet was made *en suite* with a side-table, a pair of guéridons and a mirror, for Amerongen Castle in Holland. The Rijksmuseum, Amsterdam, and the Victoria and Albert Museum, London, both have a floral marquetry cabinet similar to this example.

45 French ebony and marquetry cabinet-on-stand by André Charles Boulle, c. 1675–80. The marquetry, which is of a stylized floral and pictorial type, combines tortoiseshell, pewter, brass, stained and natural woods and ivory. The central door panel illustrates the allegory of France victorious, with the symbolic cockerel of France towering over the Lion of Spain and the Eagle of the Austro-Hungarian Empire – an allusion to the contemporary peace treaty of Nijmegen in 1678. The allegory of French power is carried further with the portrayal of the Sun King, Louis XIV, on two bronze medals made by Jean Varin in 1659: on the outside the king is depicted aged 21, and on the inside aged 25. The royal fleur-de-lis forms a repeating border pattern on the cornice, and the central door opens on to a mirrored and columned theatre in which a medallion depicting the King is placed at the centre of a rounded pediment.

The heroic theme is also evident in the Baroque Italianate carved stand featuring figures of Hercules and his consort Omphale. The two figures have been restored to their original striking colour-scheme of cream and gold (the pendant pair in the collection of the Duke of Buccleuch still retains the later bronze paint). These cabinets are typical examples of the grand dynastic showpieces

favoured by Louis XIV at Versailles, and often made to serve as diplomatic gifts. A similar cabinet attributed to Boulle is in the Wallace Collection, London.

46, 47 Anglo-Dutch white-japanned cabinet on a carved gilt stand, c. 1690–1700. The exterior is decorated with a Japanese-style landscape showing figures in a garden inhabited by exotic birds and butterflies, with a bridge over a stream and a pavilion. On the left-hand side a crane is depicted among flowering shrubs, and on the right a pheasant with similar shrubbery. The border consists of simulated tortoiseshell, and the gilt-metal escutcheon, hinges and corner mounts are of continental manufacture. The doors open to reveal a set of drawers faced with a *nashji* style of japanning, the inside panels of the doors being decorated with a lady seated at a table on one side and a double-handled vase containing flowers on the other; the latter is similar in design to Plate 14 of Stalker and Parker's *Treatise of Japanning and Varnishing* (Oxford, 1688). Their designs – called 'Patterns for Japan work in imitation of the Indians for Tables, Stands, Frames, Cabinets etc.' – were much influenced by the work of Dutch craftsmen, here reflected also in the carved gilt stand and metalwork.

White japanning, although rare, was mentioned by Stalker and Parker, who noted that 'You cannot be overnice and curious in making White Japan', and in the Countess of Bristol's will in 1741, in which she bequeathed to her son Lord Hervey 'my cabinet, chest, large screen and small screen being white japan of my own work in confidence that he will preserve them for my sake'.

48 Chinese Coromandel lacquer cabinet on an Anglo-Dutch carved gilt stand, c. 1690–1700. The gold lacquer ground is decorated with a landscape created from incised layers of polychrome lacquer; the sixteen drawers (not shown) are similarly decorated, while the sides depict birds among flowers. The carved gilt stand featuring cherubs, scrollwork and garlands is characteristic of the Anglo-Dutch style at the end of the century. Coromandel lacquer cabinets had been imported into England at an earlier date. The Ham House Inventory of 1679 mentions under the heading 'Table, Stands, Cabinet, Looking glass frame, all of Japan' in the Music Room, a suite of Coromandel lacquer furniture, which is still *in situ*. Coromandel lacquer work was usually imported as decoration on screens, 'One Indian Screene' being mentioned in the 1679 inventory.

49 English japanned cabinet on a carved silvered stand, c. 1680. Dutch influence is very much in evidence in the decorative scheme of floral arrangements painted on a black japanned ground and in the carved wooden stand featuring garlands (which echo the cabinet's painted decoration), winged putti and animal heads among scrolls and foliage.

50 Japanese 'Nambam' lacquer cabinet of the Momoyama period (1573–1615), dismantled and reconstructed in Goa c. 1650. The Portuguese first established a trading post in Goa in 1510; in 1542 they made contact with Japan. The original Japanese cabinet, with its characteristic use of mother-of-pearl on a black and gold lacquer ground, would have been of the usual two-door type with inner drawers. It was dismantled and some of the drawers were used to create a base consisting of one large drawer with a lock and two handles and three smaller drawers. The altered piece rests on an ebonized stand with bun feet and a curved stretcher. The upper part consists of a cupboard with two doors and side-handles; the interior has one shelf cut out in the centre, perhaps to display a figure of a deity. Indeed, the cabinet in

its present state seems to have answered more to oriental needs than to European ones. In 1671, in 'Random Notes on Times of Leisure', the Chinese writer Li Yu noted that 'The drawer is something which the world has long possessed, but which is often taken lightly. Some have them, some are ignorant of them and do without them. Yet to have them is to be at ease, to be without them is to be fatigued, as they provide the grounds on which one can cope with one's idleness and conceal one's incompetence . . . The places where one plays the *q'in*, looks at paintings, worships the Buddha or invites guests, should all have drawers since each affair has its own demands, each object its own necessities.'

51 Italian ebony and rosewood table-cabinet, Florence, c. 1680 (the stand is of later date); tortoiseshell veneer is applied around drawers faced with panels of floral marquetry. The central frontispiece depicts a vase of flowers and the drawer-fronts include birds and sprays of flowers executed in stained bone, mother-of-pearl and various woods. The panels are very similar in style to the stiff quality of *pietra dura*, although the marquetry technique is of Dutch origin, having been introduced to Florence by Leonardo van der Vinne, *capomaestro* of the cabinetmaking workshop in the Galleria dei Lavori in the Uffizi, in 1677.

52 Dutch (or possibly Flemish) small table-cabinet in ebonized wood, c. 1660–70; the floral painting is in the Dutch manner. The piece has a double door behind which are eleven drawers (plus a secret one). The hinged lid opens on to a well. The small dimensions of the casket and the exquisite painterly quality of the decoration would suggest that this was a personal jewel casket made for a lady, perhaps as a special commission.

53 French ebony cabinet-on-stand with tortoiseshell and floral marquetry, c. 1660, attributed to Pierre Gole. The cabinet and its stand were conceived and realized as a whole: the columnar legs of the stand echo the architectural elements of the cabinet and are decorated with the same floral sprays with birds and jasmine blossoms. The use of the astragal at approximately one-third of the height of the columns, which are also adorned with marquetry and gilt-bronze mounts, is also characteristic of French cabinets-on-stand. The overall treatment is very similar to that seen in an ivory-veneered cabinet (now in the Victoria and Albert Museum) originally made for Louis XIV's brother, Philippe d'Orléans, in 1661 (see p. 86). In the present example the cabinet displays an architectural central cupboard with two doors and incorporating niches, occupied by gilt-bronze statuettes of Fortitude (left) and Hope (right), all having gilt-bronze mounts. Behind the doors there is a mirrored theatre with steps leading to a perspective proscenium with an allegorical painting at the rear of the stage, together with several drawers, including secret ones. The insides of the doors are decorated with geometric star-pattern marquetry on a kingwood background, with a characteristic foliate banding.

This cabinet is very similar to the two examples recorded in the inventory of Cardinal Mazarin's effects drawn up after his death in 1661, in which 'Two tortoiseshell cabinets decorated with marquetry, flowers, birds and insects, with the name of Pierre Gole' are listed. The various woods used in the marquetry decoration include kingwood, boxwood, cinnabar root, walnut, oak and tulip-wood.

54 English walnut cabinet-on-stand with floral marquetry, c. 1690–1700. The oystershell walnut veneer sets off the floral marquetry and birds enclosed within bands in the form of arcs and circles symmetrically arranged. The convex drawer-front in the upper frieze is decorated with birds within a framework, the theme being continued in the stand. The marquetry would originally have been strikingly colourful, the various woods used for the flowers being stained in naturalistic colours, the foliage made of green-stained horn, with a spray of white jasmine blossom; in this way a strong contrast of texture and colour was created. Floral marquetry, at first a Dutch and French speciality, was introduced to England by immigrant workers after the middle of the seventeenth century. The fashion continued in the reign of William and Mary, lasting well into the early decades of the eighteenth century.

55 Italian *trumeau* (bureau-cabinet), Rome, *c.* 1740; the decoration in *lacca povera* (or *contrafatta*) of pastoral scenes with figures in landscapes (from cut-out coloured engravings) is enclosed within reserved ivory-white panels edged with delicately tooled gold scrolls set against a varnished crimson-red ground with gold decorative motifs. The form of the English-inspired *trumeau* and the *lacca contrafatta* decoration tend to be associated more with work from Venice, where commercial firms such as the Remondini produced coloured engravings specifically designed for this purpose. This type of pastoral scene was inspired by the work of the French painter Watteau and the 'fête galante', a genre first illustrated in his landscape 'Le Pélerinage à l'Isle de Cythère' (*The Embarkation for the Island of Cythera*) of 1717.

From 1720 onwards it became fashionable in France for society ladies to make use of engravings featuring these lyrical, dreamy landscapes and courting couples dressed in costumes reminiscent of the Commedia dell'Arte; they were cut out and pasted decoratively on furniture, being known as 'découpures'. The fashion followed the contemporary interest in *chinoiserie*, also endorsed by Watteau, and the taste for lacquer and for porcelain, which this *trumeau* displays in its brilliant tones and reserved white cartouches enclosing the pastoral scenes, in the manner of Sèvres or Meissen enamel painting.

The grand Baroque rhythm of the cabinet's lines suggests Roman inspiration, reinforced by the presence of papal insignia in carved gilt wood surmounting the cresting: the crossed keys of St Peter and the triple crowned tiara. X-ray examination of the now blank shield below have revealed the arms of Pope Pius VI. It is likely that his arms would have been added during his papacy (1775–99) to an already existing cabinet and later obscured when the piece became part of the Duc de Grimaldi's collection. Furniture decorated with *lacca povera* tended to be used in country villas on account of its decorative qualities, the themes used in pictorial adornment seemingly echoing the Arcadian tradition. Here the pastoral scenes include courting couples and hunters with birds and animals, and carved gilt figures of the Four Seasons as finials further emphasize the concept of Nature and Arcadia.

56 German or Austrian cabinet-on-stand decorated in Boulle work, *c.* 1700. The domed cresting and *bombé* outlines of the cabinet denote a French Régence influence, further illustrated in the curving lines of the stand and its flat stretcher with sinuous lines, inspired by the Louis XIV style, as was the Boulle technique. The geometric pattern of strapwork in brass and pewter on a red-backed tortoiseshell ground evokes as much the late Boulle style inspired by the arabesques of Bérain as it does the native tradition of metalwork influenced by damascened wares.

57 French *médaillier* (medal cabinet; one of a pair) in Boulle work, *c.* 1690–1700. Both pieces are veneered in *première partie* with figures of a Philosopher and Aspasia (the celebrated mistress of Pericles, *c.* 440 BC, who was famous for her intellectual achievements), surrounded by a garland of medals attached to ribbons. Their appearance is very close to the description of a pair of cabinets included in the sale of the Gaillard de Gagny estate in 1762, which listed 'Deux corps de bibliotèque en marqueterie, à ornements de cuivre, qui peuvent servir à des médailliers, chacun a 4 pieds de haut sur 3 pieds 9 pouces de large. Elles ferment à deux battants; des figures à demi-relief, des médailles en guirlandes et autres agréments dorés d'or moulu ornent ces deux bibliotèques qui sont de Boulle le père' (Two low cabinets in marquetry, with brass decorations, which can be used as medal cabinets, each 4 feet high by 3 feet 9 inches wide. They have two doors adorned with figures in low relief, garlands of medals and other ornaments in gilt. Both cabinets are by Boulle the Elder). The attribution to André-Charles Boulle is thus corroborated. The pair belongs to a group of similar cabinets, ten of them in the French National Collections (including some at Versailles), two in the British Royal Collection, one in the Ashmolean Museum, Oxford. All have the same form of decorative scheme in either *première partie* or *contrepartie*, the only real difference being in the design of the medals, referring to the life of Louis XIV.

These pieces may have been among the twelve cabinets ordered for the king's 'Cabinet des Médailles et Raretés' (Cabinet of Medals and Curios) at Versailles, as recorded in the royal archives: 'Douze cabinets de marqueterie pour les médailles' (Twelve marquetry cabinets for medals), a total which could have been added to during the reign of Louis XVI in the late eighteenth century when Boulle work became fashionable again. The smaller proportions of these cabinets are in keeping with the influence of the Régence style during the later years of Louis XIV's reign, which is apparent in the only fully documented works by Boulle, the pair of commodes made for the King's bedchamber at the Grand Trianon, *c.* 1708–9.

58 German cabinet-on-stand in Boulle work (one of a pair), *c.* 1700. This imposing pair of cabinets-on-stand, veneered in *première partie* and *contrepartie* Boulle marquetry of red-backed tortoiseshell, brass and pewter, is characteristic of the Baroque style in Germany at the beginning of the eighteenth century. The Louis XIV style influenced not only the technique, but also the form of the tapering legs of the stand with their carved and gilt capitals and the curved stretcher supporting a carved and gilt centrepiece – a classical gadrooned vase – with matching bun feet.

The cabinets formerly belonged to the Saxe-Coburg-Gotha Collection, and their impressive grandeur reflects the dynastic pride of the ruling princes. Although the many drawers around and within the central cupboard denote a storage function, this would have been secondary to the ostentatious richness of a *meuble d'apparat*.

59, 60 English burr walnut bureau-cabinet, *c.* 1710. The upper part is surmounted by a double-domed hood (a feature introduced to England *c.* 1700 under Dutch influence). The flat domes, which are flanked by gilt finials, would have permitted the display of porcelain, a fashion which, according to the writer Daniel Defoe (1660–1731), was brought back by Queen Mary: '. . . [she] introduced the custom or humor as I may call it, of furnishing houses with Chinaware in a strange degree afterwards piling the China upon the tops of Cabinets, Scrutoires and every chimney piece'.

The doors are adorned with bevelled mirror plates between pilasters having brass capitals and bases. Inside these are eight short and two long drawers, pigeon-holes and folio divides; the bureau contains two short and two long drawers.

61 English mulberry veneered bureau-cabinet, *c.* 1695; the double-domed top has a matching arched cornice. The upper cabinet is cross-banded with yew and inlaid with brass on the doors. The rich variegated pattern of the mulberry veneer is a fine example of the English and Dutch predilection for decorative burrs and patterning. Although most of the production of such bureau-cabinets for domestic use was standardized, some maker's names have survived, mostly through labels attached to their furniture; 'G. Coxed and T. Woster' is one such trade name. The quality of the craftsmanship of their furniture is comparable to that displayed in the present example.

62 English small walnut bureau-cabinet, *c.* 1715–20. The piece features a domed top with moulded cornice, the glazed door, which encloses a fitted interior containing a central concave cupboard flanked by fluted pilasters, was a later addition. The concave forms and pilasters are repeated in the bureau part which is furnished with two candle-holders.

63 English burr walnut bureau-cabinet, *c.* 1710; the arched moulded cornice is surmounted by vase-shaped finials. The two doors have bevelled mirror plates on the outside. The internal arrangement includes adjustable shelves above tiers of small drawers flanking a central concave cupboard, the latter flanked by removable pilasters. The bureau contains drawers and pigeon-holes arranged around a central well.

64–69 The Badminton Cabinet, made of ebony with *pietra dura* panels, *c.* 1726–32. Massive in size and built on architectural lines, this cabinet has a tripartite front fitted with ten cedar-lined drawers around a central cupboard enclosing a removable nest of drawers (not shown) veneered with purpleheart and ebony, lined with cedarwood and fitted with mounts in the form of a satyr's head and a drapery ring-handle. Each drawer-front and the sides of the cabinet are faced with *pietra dura* panels edged with ormolu and banded with amethyst quartz; they depict birds and sprays of flowers. The whole is framed by pilasters: those in the central part are made of red Sicilian jasper and lapis lazuli, and those in the upper and lower parts have amethyst panels.

The central pilasters are joined by ormolu swags encrusted with semi-precious stones, with a grey chalcedony lion mask at the centre and repeated on either side, each ormolu capital being decorated with a grey chalcedony mask. The short upper and lower pilasters display female and grotesque heads in ormolu holding an ormolu branch with fruit in hardstones of various colours. A horizontal string course of amethyst runs along both sides and the façade, punctuated by lapis lazuli and agate cartouches. The frieze consists of geometric panels of lapis lazuli and red and green jasper.

The stepped pediment incorporates a central clock face decorated with *pietra dura* and flanked by ormolu swags, garlands and bows, and gilt-bronze statuettes of the Four Seasons modelled by the sculptor Girolamo Ticciati (died 1744). The whole piece is surmounted by the arms of the Beaufort family, granted to John Beaufort, 1st Earl of Somerset and Marquess of Dorset by Act of Parliament in 1396. They comprise the Royal Arms of England, three *lions passant guardant* on a red shield, quartered with those of France, azure *semi-de-lys*, altered in 1376 to three gold *fleur-de-lys*. The claim to the French throne evolved from the Plantagenet King Edward III, father of John of Gaunt, whose natural son John Beaufort was. The family supporters, a silver panther and a wyvern, are depicted on either side, above the family motto inscribed on a scrolling ribbon: *Mutare vel timere sperno*. In its colour-scheme the cabinet echoes the blue and red of the Beaufort arms, rendered in lapis lazuli and red Sicilian jasper, while the face of the clock is studded with the *fleur-de-lys*, which could be interpreted as symbolic of France or as the Florentine *giglio* (lily), representing the city in which the cabinet was made.

The piece was commissioned from the Opificio delle Pietre Dure by the 3rd Duke of Beaufort who, according to a member of his retinue, Dominique du Four, travelled from Paris, leaving on 28 March 1726 and arriving in Florence on 27 April, remaining in the city until 2 May. Du Four also recorded his own supervision of the transportation of the cabinet, when he left Florence for the port of Leghorn on 12 August 1732; he remained there, with an *ebanista* and his son, until 20 August to see to the safety of 'Mylord Duc's cabinet'. It left on board the *Oriana*, whose master, Captain Daniel Pullam, listed among the cargo 'five large cases . . . containing the severall parts of a large cabinet of his Grace the Duke of Beaufort'.

The skills of more than thirty specialist craftsmen would have been involved in the execution of the piece, ranging from the *ebanista* to the *intagliatore delle pietre dure*, the sculptor Girolamo Ticciati, the bronze casters and gilders and the clockmakers.

The Badminton Cabinet was the last grand dynastic cabinet realized by the Opificio in the Medici Galleria dei Lavori, which closed in 1737. Although it took on the lines and the strong political and dynastic message of the Elector Palatine's cabinet (made in 1709), the earlier Baroque sculptural quality is not present here. The splendour of forms and decoration were put to the use of elaborate allegory: Nature – symbolized by the Four Seasons and the *pietra dura* panels – is conquered by Art, through Time, which is ruled over in its turn by the dynastic pride of an old-established English aristocratic family, whose successors could rightfully lay claim to the throne of France, a country whose army had recently been defeated by John Churchill, 1st Duke of Marlborough, at the Battle of Blenheim in 1704. As such, the Badminton Cabinet must be considered the last example of a long and distinguished line of *meubles d'apparat* having a distinct political message.

The taste for cabinets with *pietra dura* decoration was not new in England. In 1644 John Evelyn had commissioned a cabinet of 'Pietra Commessa' in Florence; and the Grand Duke of Tuscany, Cosimo III de' Medici, had sent an ebony and *pietra dura* cabinet to the fifth Earl of Exeter, a piece recorded in an inventory of 1688 as '1 Rich florrence Cabinett Inlaid with stone and Mother of perle with a Carv'd Guilt fframe' and still at Burghley House, Lincolnshire (cat. no.76). The fashion endured and in 1742 Henry Hoare II bought from the Perreti family a *pietra dura* cabinet, wrongly thought to have belonged to Pope Sixtus V, which is still at Stourhead, Wiltshire. After seeing the cabinet there, William Beckford of Fonthill Abbey described it thus: 'Sistus the Fifth's cabinet is divine, I know – the bronzes are of extreme delicacy and elegance, and those lovely agates, alabasters and cornelians, mingled with the glittering mother-of-pearl, produce a rich effect, agreeable and grateful to the eye.'

70 German table-cabinet japanned in gold and black, *c.* 1740. This small precious cabinet with its miniature proportions, curvaceous form and decoration in imitation of Japanese raised lacquer in reserve, is characteristic of the eighteenth-century production of exquisite objects made in the Rococo *chinoiserie* style. The interior is fitted with twelve drawers faced with ivory veneer and contrasting banding, matching the insides of the doors.

The high degree of craftsmanship in the lacquer-work and the finishing of the piece could indicate the hand of Martin Schnell, a master-japanner who worked in raised lacquer from 1710 onwards while in the service of Augustus the Strong in Dresden.

71 German table-cabinet japanned in black and gold, *c.* 1700; the doors and the sides are decorated with *chinoiserie* figures set in landscapes (not shown), the two doors being fitted with pierced and engraved metal escutcheons. Internally, the drawer-fronts, faced with *pietra paesina* panels, are arranged around a central door similarly decorated, which conceals three further drawers.

Panels of *pietra paesina* – an Albarese limestone which when polished reveals a characteristic veining evoking landscapes or, as here, plants and ferns – were exported to northern Europe, where they were mounted as decoration on cabinets by native craftsmen. The fashion for these evocative panels started in Florence *c.* 1620, where they were set in ebony veneer. The small dimensions of the present piece and the two side-handles indicate that this cabinet would have served as a storage piece for personal valuables; the combination of lacquer and *pietra paesina* makes this an object of exotic beauty and interest.

72 Spanish or Portuguese japanned cabinet signed, on the sloping front, '*Man. de la Zerda*', *c.* 1730. The fitted interior consists of drawers above a pair of cupboards enclosing further drawers, together with some secret drawers in the lower part concealed behind sliding panels. The table stand, which has a deep cut-out apron and cabriole legs terminating in claw-and-ball feet, displays as much a Chinese influence as it does an English one. The exterior is brilliantly embellished with *turquerie* scenes on a black ground, while the interior has decoration in cream, red and blue lacquer.

Portugal had been one of the first European importers of oriental wares, including lacquer, in the sixteenth century. The French poet Scarron recounted this Portuguese trading supremacy in 1611:

> Menez moi chez les Portugais,
> Nous y verrons à peu de frais
> Les Marchandises de la Chine.
> Nous y verrons de l'ambre gris
> De beaux ouvrages de vernis,
> Et de la porcelaine fine
> De cette contrée divine
> Ou plutôt de paradis
>
> Take me to the Portuguese shops
> Where we shall see low-priced
> Goods from China on sale.
> There we shall see ambergris,
> Beautiful work in lacquer,
> And fine porcelain
> From this divine land
> Or, one might say, a paradise.

However, by the eighteenth century the Dutch and the English had gained the ascendant in the East India trade, and this cabinet is an example of the contemporary fashion for *chinoiserie* decoration associated with the curvaceous forms of the Rococo style prevalent all over Europe and in the colonies, in particular Mexico, where japanning of fine quality was executed.

73, 74 Indian ivory-veneered miniature bureau-cabinet, Vizigatapam, *c.* 1760. This small piece combines the English form of the bureau-cabinet with the incised stylized floral decoration of Vizigatapam. Before the establishment of trading posts by Dutch and English merchants in India at the beginning of the seventeenth century, no indigenous furniture-making tradition existed. However, a thriving trade soon developed in response to the demands of the early settlers.

75 English black-japanned cabinet on a carved gilt wood stand, *c.* 1720–25. The cabinet, with double doors concealing the internal arrangement of drawers, is a seventeenth-century form very likely decorated by an amateur. The taste for lacquer and japanning remained very strong in the early part of the eighteenth century, with Canton (on the south coast of China) as the main trading post. In 1702 the *Fleet Frigate*, sailing from Canton, had a cargo including thirteen chests of lacquered wares, fourteen small 'scrivetories' and seventeen chests containing screens.

The influence of Stalker and Parker's *Treatise of Japanning and Varnishing*, published in 1688, had encouraged the development of the taste and fashion for oriental decoration and similar treatises were published plagiarizing both the designs and the techniques for making 'black or gilt Japan Ware as light as any brought from the East Indies with proper directions for making the hardest and most transparent Varnishes', according to the 'Great Mr. Boyle' (1627–91). The stand, featuring carved gilt classical motifs, echoes the furniture designs of the Palladian architect and designer William Kent (1685–1748).

76 English japanned cabinet-on-stand, *c.* 1765. The cornice, framework and stand are all decorated with English japanning to set off the panels depicting architectural perspectives executed in Chinese lacquer on the outer doors and inner drawer-fronts. The form and decorative scheme is very close to that of Thomas Chippendale, who supplied a pair of cabinets similarly executed for the State Bedchamber at Harewood House, Yorkshire, in 1772.

77 English rosewood cabinets-on-stand (one of a pair), *c.* 1760–70; the drawer-fronts and the outsides of the cupboard doors are veneered with panels of Chinese lacquer encrusted with hard-stones. The sides are veneered in a striped cross-banded pattern, as are the insides of the doors. The stand has an applied boxwood fretwork pattern echoing the gallery.

78, 79 English bureau-cabinet japanned in green and gold, *c.* 1705. The double-domed top with gilt finials is characteristic of the Queen Anne period, as is the formal arrangement of drawers, pigeon-holes and folio divides around a central cupboard flanked by two columns. Similar shorter columns on the central part of the bureau contribute to the creation of a classical order and symmetry in the design of a piece that is decorated in a fanciful and whimsical *chinoiserie* style. The motif seen on the insides of the doors is very similar to the design reproduced as plate 14 in Stalker and Parker's *Treatise of Japanning and Varnishing* (1688): an asymmetrical oriental-style flower arrangement, depicted in a gadrooned double-handled vase of classical inspiration.

80, 81 German(?) white-japanned bureau-cabinet, *c.* 1700–20, decorated with a painted Chinese design incorporating blue-and-white plates of the K'ang Hsi period (1662–1722), reflecting the contemporary European fascination with oriental porcelain. In the early eighteenth century whole rooms would be decorated with cups, plates etc. The earliest example of the *Porzellanzimmer* was executed by Andreas Schlüter (perhaps with the help of Gérard Dagly), for Frederick III of Brandenburg at Schloss Oranienburg, outside Berlin. Specially made stands, brackets and cabinets were provided for the display of pieces of porcelain. Cf chapter III, note 17.

The unusual design and high quality of the japanning on this cabinet indicate possibly a special commission, intended for a particular room in which it would not only have matched the general decorative scheme, but would also be used to display porcelain.

82 English bureau-cabinet japanned in red and gold, c. 1720–30. The bureau-cabinet form, uniting convenience and ostentatious show, and here surmounted by a curved broken pediment and gilt finials, was often decorated in England with japanning in brilliant colours. Some leading exponents became famous, their wares being exported all over Europe. One such was Giles Grendey, to whom this piece is attributed as a result of its provenance from Lazcano Castle, owned by the Duke of Infantado. Giles Grendey had supplied a large suite of scarlet-japanned seat furniture to the Duke's castle, near San Sebastian in northern Spain; one of the chairs bears a pasted label stating; 'GILES GRENDEY / St John's Square, Clerkenwell, / LONDON, / MAKES and sells all Sorts of / Cabinet Goods, Chairs, / Tables, Glasses, &c.'. and various marks occur in different combinations 'HW; EA; IT; MW'.

This bureau-cabinet could well have been part of the salon furniture at Lazcano; its grand opulence, which was in keeping with the decorative quality demanded for the Spanish market, matches that of seat furniture now in museums (the Victoria and Albert Museum, London; the Metropolitan Museum, New York; Temple Newsam House, Leeds) and private collections. Another bureau-cabinet also japanned in red is in a private collection.

83 English mahogany bureau-bookcase, c. 1760. This unusual piece displays an eclectic use of styles and techniques: the classical broken pediment decorated with Gothick fretwork is a feature associated with Horace Walpole and which found its culmination in the building of his house, Strawberry Hill, near Twickenham, completed in 1770; and typically seventeenth-century oyster-shell kingwood veneer, together with an ebony and ivory inlay, is used as moulding and banding throughout. This use of earlier materials and styles is in a nostalgic spirit that would be manifested to a high degree in cabinetmaking of the nineteenth century.

84 German bureau-cabinet in Brazilian rosewood, Dresden, c. 1750. The Rococo style gave a serpentine *bombé* outline to the gilt-bronze mounts forming the cresting and the glazed panels of the doors of the upper part, while the lower drawers assume a typical *bombé* shape. This piece is an example of the German Baroque–Rococo style combining the grand manner with a use of more 'feminine' curves, so uniting the practical qualities of the fitted cabinet and bureau and the striking appearance of a showpiece.

85 English satinwood and marquetry cabinet (one of a pair), c. 1780. This pair of unusual cabinets, with kingwood cross-banding and burr yew banding with paterae and husks on the front of the doors, illustrates a variation of the Adam style. They feature straight, sparse lines, the use of light-coloured woods inlaid with various others in darker and lighter contrasting tones, based on a classical pattern, and round handles enclosing a rosette, all reminiscent of the French Louis XVI style.

86 English satinwood display cabinet, c. 1790. This example – of smaller than usual proportions – is made of light-coloured wood and has an upper glazed part for display purposes and below it, a *secrétaire* drawer; the piece is characteristic of the Sheraton style, showing the influence of the elegant sparse lines of the French Louis XVI style and representing a more feminine variation of the Adam style which gained favour in interiors of the late eighteenth century.

87–89 German marquetry bureau-cabinet, c. 1740. The entire piece is decorated in pictorial marquetry of yew, poplar, boxwood, kingwood and walnut, and with ebonized pearwood banding. The upper part displays some Rococo scrolls in the framework of the rectangular cartouche in which an architectural perspective view is depicted. The main theme is reminiscent of a Renaissance use of optical illusion and geometric perspective, associated more with the sixteenth century than with the Rococo period. Indeed, the upper part represents a view of an Italianate villa very similar to the garden façade of the Villa Simonetta, c. 1547, by Domenico Giunti.

However, the late Renaissance Mannerist play on illusion and intriguing details is present here in the central solid three-dimensional column, which is not only repeated (viewed from the opposite direction) in two dimensions as marquetry decoration on the lower part, but on being moved sideways it reveals the keyhole and allows the cabinet to be opened.

The internal arrangement consists of fifteen drawers around a central cupboard, the door of which is decorated with a leaping stag. Behind this door is a panel which can be slid aside to reveal a secret compartment surrounded by small drawers. The door of the secret compartment opens on to a perspective view through a window, symbolizing the end of the journey through space begun with the front of the cabinet itself. This sense of illusionism and the gradual unravelling of secrets pertains more to the ethos of the *Schreibtisch* as made in Augsburg in the late sixteenth century than to the more practical aspect of the bureau-cabinet in the eighteenth century. This piece is thus a fascinating example of a long German tradition of pictorial marquetry and illusionism. This bureau-cabinet could have been commissioned to commemorate a wedding, for the inside of the door of the inner compartment bears an oval cartouche enclosing the initials 'W.B.C.' surmounted by a crown. The spaces for a coat-of-arms on the insides of each door of the main cabinet were, however, left undecorated.

90 French *secrétaire à abattant* in tulipwood and purpleheart with marquetry decoration, c. 1770–80. The fall-front is decorated on the outside with a vase of flowers and writing implements resting on a table, above which are typical Louis XVI swags and tassels suspended from rosettes, all set within a rectangular framework with Greek keys. The fitted interior contains four drawers and pigeon-holes and the cupboard base is decorated with classical vases, a theme repeated on the sides. The piece is stamped 'BOUDIN' and 'MOREAU'. Boudin (1735–1807) became a master in 1761, specializing in pictorial marquetry which he produced for other *ébénistes* such as Migeon; c. 1775 he began dealing in works by other *ébénistes*, adding his own stamp as a trademark. Moreau (d. 1791) became a master *ébéniste* in 1764. The piece may have been produced, or possibly restored, by him; in the latter case he would have been entitled to add his own stamp to a work by another maker.

91 Italian *secrétaire à abattant* in rosewood, c. 1780–90, in the style of Giuseppe Maggiolini. The simple rectangular lines are inspired by the Louis XVI style, and the marquetry with foliate swags on the frieze drawer above the fall-front cross-banded with tulipwood is characteristic of the Neo-classical style. On the quartered ground a lozenge encloses a musical trophy and a book inscribed 'O Mero'. Each of the lower cupboard doors is decorated with an oval medallion depicting respectively Mercury (with a shield inscribed 'OMi. Bi. Er. Tesa, Scozi. '82') and Juno (with the inscription 'M. Sevr. Batn'), while on the sides of the

piece figures of the Muses are shown within similar oval medallions.

92 French mahogany-veneered *secrétaire à abattant* with a grey marble top, c. 1800. The fashion for using plain mahogany veneers in France began before the Revolution in 1789 and continued during the Directoire period, to become the most favoured wood under the Empire. Here two columns frame the austerely masculine form, the only decorative element being the gilt-bronze mounts: on the frieze drawer, two griffins flanking a patera within a laurel wreath; on the fall-front, two swans and a border of ivy; and, on the lower cupboard, two billing doves above a wreath of oak and ivy. The plinth base is typical of the Empire period, the swan motif being usually associated with the Empress Joséphine and the Beauharnais family.

93 French lacquer-decorated *secrétaire à abattant* with gilt-bronze mounts, c. 1780–84. This piece fits the description of a black-lacquer *secrétaire* delivered to Versailles by the *marchand-mercier* Daguerre on 11 January 1784, at a cost of 7,200 Livres: 'Un tres grand secrétaire à abattant dont le devant est divisé en trois panneaux de laque avec tiroir au dessus et en dessous, les frises plaquées en ebenne et l'intérièur plaqué fond de bois gris avec mosaïque bleue, le meuble décoré de figures placées dans les angles d'une frise de genre arabesque enfants et animaux avec moulures et autres ornements de bronze trés bien ciselé et dont l'or est au mat. L'abattant couvert de velours verde avec galon d'or, un dessus de marbre brocatelle d'Espagne. Y compris la fourniture des morceaux de laque qui remplissent les côtés et le devant des tiroirs' (Paris, Archives Nationales, 01.3631) (A very large *secrétaire à abattant*, the front of which is adorned with three lacquer panels with drawers above and below, the frieze veneered in ebony and the interior with grey wood and blue mosaic. The piece has mounts with two figures at the sides and the arabesque-shape frieze depicts children and animals in chased gilt bronze with a mat finish. The fall-front is covered with green velvet edged with a gold braid and the top is made of Spanish brocatelle marble. Included is the supplying of the lacquer panels on the sides and the front of the drawers.). The same piece recurs in a 1787 inventory of furniture at Versailles included in the Cabinet Intérieur [private closet] du Roi (Paris, Archives Nationales, 01.3469, p. 44) and again in 1788 and lastly in 1790 as part of the King's furniture in the Tuileries, where he was held under house arrest after being forced to leave Versailles.

The *secrétaire* can be attributed to Adam Weisweiler, *maître ébéniste* from 1778 and supplier to members of the royal family through Daguerre, who had a virtual monopoly of oriental lacquer wares. Weisweiler's style often seems to hark back to Louis XIV forms, seen here in the strong horizontal emphasis of the piece, while the stand featuring a flat curved stretcher is closer to the Baroque cabinets-on-stand than it is to the Neo-classical style. Weisweiler often used lacquer panels and *pietra dura* decoration from older cabinets, hence this suggestion of the 'grand manner' in his designs; the incorporation of secret compartments, here a spring-operated box concealed in the interior, was a feature found in seventeenth-century cabinets.

The gilt-bronze corner caryatids and the frieze are features that appear on other pieces by Weisweiler, these mounts having been attributed to Gouthière, who also worked for Daguerre. Other similar *secrétaires* can be found in the J. Paul Getty Museum, Malibu, California, and in the Wrightsman Collection in the Metropolitan Museum, New York.

94 French *secrétaire à abattant* with geometric marquetry and inset Sèvres plaques, c. 1784, stamped 'A. WEISWEILER'. This *secrétaire* once belonged to the Grand Duchess Maria Feodorovna, wife of the future Tsar Paul (reigned 1796–1801). It is referred to in a description of the Palace of Pavlovsk in 1795 by Maria Feodorovna: 'My boudoir next to the bedroom is long in shape with a vaulted ceiling painted with arabesques. Against the wall on either side of the door [of the boudoir] are two *secrétaires*, fairly tall, with Sèvres porcelain and bronze' (from *Les Trésors d'Art en Russie*, vol. III, 1903).

The Grand Duke and his wife had paid a visit to Daguerre's showroom while visiting Paris in 1784. In her *Mémoires* (vol. II, p. 44) the Baronne d'Oberkirch, friend and companion of the Grand Duchess, noted that they went to 'A la Couronne d'or' in the Rue Saint-Honoré on 23 May 1784: 'De l'hôtel Thelusson nous allâmes chez Desguerres, marchand ébéniste, fameux, demeurant rue Saint-Honoré, pour y voir des meubles.' (From the hôtel Thelusson, we went to Daguerre's, the famous *marchand-mercier*, in the Rue Saint-Honoré, to look at some furniture.)

Daguerre, chief supplier to the court of Louis XVI, had – together with Poirier, another leading *marchand-mercier* – established a virtual monopoly in the supply of furniture decorated with plaques of enamelled soft-paste porcelain from the Manufacture Royale de Sèvres, which were specially commissioned to adorn cabinet work by outstanding *ébénistes* such as Martin Carlin, Roger Vandercruse (called Lacroix) and Adam Weisweiler, and usually within exquisite gilt-bronze mounts fashioned by Gouthière. The Paris dealers had promoted this fashion for incorporating Sèvres plaques on furniture, for it was in keeping with the sense of luxury prevalent in the late eighteenth century and also provided a medium for the naturalistic rendering of flowers in brilliant polychrome enamel painting. The plaques on this *secrétaire* were designed by the flower painter Bouillat *père*, although (contrary to the usual practice) they are not marked. Similar work by Weisweiler can be seen in the Metropolitan Museum, New York (Kress Collection), and the Wallace Collection in London.

95 French tulipwood *serre-bijoux* with Sèvres porcelain plaques, made c. 1770 by Martin Carlin for the Dauphine Marie-Antoinette. The jewel casket and its matching table are decorated throughout with plaques of Sèvres soft-paste porcelain with the gilt mark (an interlaced 'LL' for Sèvres, and the letter 'b' for Bertrand, a flower painter at the Manufacture (active 1757–75), and 'h' for Laroche, also a flower painter (active 1760–1800), and the date-letter 'r' for 1770. The *serre-bijoux* bears the stamp 'M. CARLIN' and a later branded mark indicating the personal property of the Queen and a provenance from the Palace of Versailles (a double V), where the piece is now on display.

The Archduchess Marie-Antoinette of Austria married the Dauphin, grandson of Louis XV, on 16 May 1770, and it is conceivable that this *serre-bijoux* may have been a wedding present to the new Dauphine. The elegant feminine proportions of this small piece, together with the exquisite craftsmanship of the cabinet work, the Sèvres plaques and the gilt-bronze mounts, attracted much envy. On 13 December 1770, Poirier delivered to Madame du Barry a very similar jewel casket described as 'Un coffre de porcelaine de France fond vert à cartouches de fleurs et très richement orné de bronze doré moulu ainsi que son pied.' (A casket decorated with Sèvres porcelain plaques with flowers painted within cartouches on a green ground, richly adorned with ormolu, as also is its stand). Poirier, who employed

Carlin and had established a monopoly for this type of furniture, would almost certainly have been the purveyor of the Dauphine's *serre-bijoux*.

Similar pieces can be seen in the Metropolitan Museum, New York (Wrightsman Collection), and the Detroit Museum of Art.

96, 97 German red-japanned bureau-cabinet (*Schreibschrank*) decorated with 66 painted panels, Vienna, c. 1735. The upper part, designed as a cabinet, has carved gilt cresting of Rococo scrolls enclosing floral medallions in the 'deutsche Blumen' style, with ten drawers depicting Italianate *vedute* and *capricci* arranged around a central cupboard, the door of which is similarly decorated; each of the two side-panels slides upwards to reveal a set of secret drawers (as shown in the detail). The central cupboard door conceals a further set of nine drawers decorated with animal subjects obviously inspired by a bestiary, while the inside of the door displays a panel painting of a genre scene in the style of Adriaen Brouwer (c. 1605–38).

The lower bureau part is decorated with various panel paintings in the style of Salvator Rosa (1615–73), mostly allegories of the Four Seasons and the Four Elements, together with hunting scenes in the style of Fyt and Hondercoter and still-lifes in the style of van Tann. The eclectic style revealed in this bureau-cabinet reflects the collecting taste of the first half of the eighteenth century and is consistent with the circle of Franz de Paula Ferg (1689–1740), of Vienna, who was active in Dresden at the court of Augustus the Strong.

98–100 Italian *scrivania* with walnut-veneer and boxwood stringing on a poplar carcase, c. 1735; a total of 42 hand-coloured engravings are laid on an ivory silk background under glass within carved gilt Rococo cartouches. The pastoral and *chinoiserie* scenes are very similar in inspiration to that seen in the *trumeau* decorated in *lacca contrafatta* (pl. 57) and reflect the influence which Watteau's *fêtes galantes* had on European decorative artists. Here the somewhat naive quality of the engravings with the depiction of exotic giant insects and birds can be traced to the Augsburg engraver Martin Engelbrecht. The contemporary taste for porcelain obviously inspired the idea of reserve cartouches set against the herringbone pattern of the veneer, while the general form of the piece derives from the French seventeenth-century 'bureau Mazarin', long since outmoded. However, the upper part is an original concept, as are the overall serpentine outlines executed in a distinctive Rococo style. The sculptural quality of the piece, with its female busts on scrolled legs, suggests a Roman origin, while the polychromatic decoration is closer to that associated with Venice and northern Europe.

101 American bureau-cabinet made of cherry-wood inlaid with mahogany and other light and dark woods, c. 1790–1810. The piece, which is decorated on the outside of the doors with the symbolic American bald eagle, is designed in the grand bureau-cabinet manner inspired by English prototypes of the early eighteenth century. The curved broken pediment is decorated in pierced work with intricate floral arabesques set off a central classical urn, reminiscent of a design found on some Hepplewhite-inspired chairs made for the State House in Hartford, Connecticut, in 1796 by the firm of Kneeland and Adams. A colourful rope stringing is employed overall; the interior is fitted with compartments and scalloped pigeon-holes around a central cupboard adorned with a lozenge-shaped patera. The whole appearance and treatment of the bureau-cabinet recalls the work of Webb & Scott, cabinetmakers of Providence, Rhode Island, one of whose pieces in this style bears the company's label.

102 American lady's cabinet and writing table, Baltimore, c. 1795–1810. Made of mahogany inlaid with satinwood, the cabinet has drawers with cedarwood lining at the back and on the bottom and with mahogany sides. The design of the piece is inspired by Plate 50 of Sheraton's *The Cabinetmaker & Upholsterer's Drawing-Book* (issued in four parts, 1791–4). The Sheraton design has been embellished in a characteristic Baltimore style, the oval mirror being framed within a broad satinwood banding, while the satinwood veneer of the front consists of mitred panels inset with oval medallions enclosing painted biblical and mythological scenes decorated with gold leaf. The central panel, representing a classical figure seated on a Grecian chair, the *klysmos*, may be the earliest representation of the type in American art. A similarly inspired set of chairs was made c. 1809 for the President's House in Washington, D.C. (burnt down in 1816), obviously drawing on designs from Thomas Hope's *Household Taste*, published in 1807. The colourful contrast and decorative element extends to the drawers of the stand which are edged with satinwood. An inscription in ink at the rear of the long drawer in the lower part reads 'S.E. WAITE 1812'.

103 French *serre-bijoux* presented by the City of Paris to Queen Marie-Antoinette in 1787. According to the *Mémoires* of Madame Campan, this piece, notable for its grand Baroque lines and proportions, was designed by M. Bonnefoy-Duplan, superintendent of the Queen's *Garde-Meuble*. It certainly displays the attributes of earlier presentation pieces intended to convey a strong dynastic and political message – a sadly anachronistic quality for a formal gift made on the eve of the Revolution. The form is that of a cabinet-on-stand, veneered in mahogany, the use of the latter became fashionable in France in the later part of the eighteenth century as a result of English influence.

The *ébéniste* responsible for the *serre-bijoux* was Ferdinand Schwerdfeger, who was active in Paris from c. 1760, and who became a *maître ébéniste* in 1786; he signed his work 'Ferdinand Schwerdfeger ME Ebéniste, à Paris'. The four gilt-bronze caryatids (representing the Four Seasons) which punctuate the tripartite façade, as well as the allegorical group of Fame and other decorative mounts, were probably made by Thomire, and the cameos in the antique manner carved by Degault. The cabinet's entire surface is covered with decorative elements typical of the contemporary fascination for antiquity: Sèvres plaques imitating classical bas-reliefs, and panels of *verre églomisé* painted with grotesque and arabesques in the Pompeian manner. The most striking feature of the cabinet is the stand, featuring legs in the form of sets of 'fasces', the bundles of arrows used as a symbol of imperial authority in Ancient Rome which were to be adopted, shortly after this *serre-bijoux* was made, as one of the insignia of the French Revolution.

The design of the cabinet is largely inspired by that of Bélanger for an earlier *serre-bijoux* recorded in a drawing in the Bibliothèque Nationale, Paris, and realized by Ewald as a gift to Marie-Antoinette from the Dauphin on the occasion of their wedding in 1770. Schwerdfeger's cabinet is the last example of a long line of grand presentation pieces and represents, both in its conception and in its realization, a sad farewell to the Ancien Régime.

104 French *serre-bijoux* veneered with burr yew and amaranth on an oak carcase, and having a mahogany interior; the piece was commissioned in 1809 by Napoleon for the Empress Joséphine but, following the annulment of the marriage, it was given to his second wife, the Austrian Archduchess Marie Louise, whom Napoleon married on 2 April 1810, for her bedchamber in the Palais des Tuileries, Paris.

The *serre-bijoux* was commissioned from Jacob-Desmalter & Cie, the business partnership formed by Georges Jacob and his son François-Honoré-Georges in 1803. The gilt-bronze mounts, based on designs by the sculptor Chaudet, were cast and chased by Thomire. A detailed description of the piece was submitted in a proposal dated 27 June 1809, followed by a memorandum of account on 19 July: 'A large piece of furniture to be used a jewel-cabinet, built on architectural lines and richly adorned with capitals, cornices, astragals in cast bronze, gilt and chased. All the decorative elements are related to the main subject matter: the birth of Venus, the Queen of the Earth, to whom putti and nymphs bring offerings. On the base there are inlaid mother-of-pearl necklaces, with pear-shaped beads; in the frieze above some diadems also in mother-of-pearl have been inset. The base, consisting of eight columns, supports a dado on which the eight upper columns rest, aligned with the lower ones. Between the columns is the main part of the cabinet with three openings in which there are many small drawers. In the lower frieze there are three drawers. Above the cornice there is an ornamental piece cut-out in copper and a stylobate of the same width as the central part and aligned with it and the base, pilasters and cornice. The central part opens with a fall-front, in the cornice there is a cut-out design. Aligned with each column, displayed on wooden bases, are gilt-bronze doves with lapis lazuli around their necks. The whole is fitted in solid mahogany inside, the exterior being veneered in amaranth and exotic yew on an oak carcase. The columns and cornices are made of amaranth. The base is inlaid with rich motifs in bronze, ebony and mother-of-pearl. The moulding is decorated with classical motifs in chased bronze. On the base gilt-bronze vases have been placed together with a cassolette [a covered vase] also made of bronze, to serve as perfume-burners, the whole gilt and chased with extraordinary care. All the figures have been modelled by the greatest masters and specially executed, as have all the ornaments. All the locks have been finished to the same standard of craftsmanship as in watchmaking, this to demonstrate the very high quality which can be achieved in France. All openings are concealed behind ornaments and there are several secret compartments concealed within. This piece has been finished throughout to the highest possible standards. Price agreed and set with the approval of M. l'Administrateur du Mobilier: 55.000 F, paid 55.000 F.'

The so-called 'Grand Ecrin'' (Large Jewel Casket) is, in terms of its conception and realization, essentially a *meuble d'apparat* of the Ancien Régime type, displaying the same high standard of craftsmanship and loving care as had been lavished on royal commissions; it was thus a fitting final tribute paid to a long-established tradition by Georges Jacob, himself a *menuisier* trained in the pre-Revolution climate of luxury and exalted artistic aspirations, and his son, who placed their joint experience and cabinetmaking skills at the disposal of the Emperor.

105 German or Austrian Biedermeier-style mahogany *secrétaire à abattant*, *c.* 1820–40; the piece is decorated with two white marble pilasters and classical figures with young children making music. The fall-front opens to reveal a fitted architectural interior with simulated rustication and a classical round arch echoing the strong classical architectural lines of the upper part with its breakfront and important cornice supported by the two pilasters.

This *secrétaire* evokes the strongly classical influence of the French Empire style adapted to a more domestic use while retaining the noble lines of its original style.

106 Russian Karelian birch writing cabinet, *c.* 1820. The strongly architectural features of the piece include a triangular pediment resting on a wide cornice which is decorated with classical ebonized motifs and supported by two ebonized Egyptian caryatids; these contrast with the striking marking of the lighter-coloured *bois clair* to great effect. The lower part contains a draw-slide and shelves enclosed behind two doors. The renewed prosperity after the Russian victory over Napoleon's army in 1812 encouraged the production of furniture suitable for newly built houses in the Neo-classical style. The massive simplicity and symmetry of the interiors are reflected in the austerely plain lines of the piece which, although derivative of the Empire style, displays workmanship of the highest quality and is entirely Russian in appearance.

107, 108 English rosewood *secrétaire à abattant* made by S. Jamar *c.* 1820 in the French Empire style. The severe front veneered in plain rosewood is enclosed by free-standing columns, and is decorated with gilt-brass mounts in the shape of a lyre, laurel sprays and masks of Apollo, all symbolic of music; the frieze drawer containing a small cylinder musical box.

This *secrétaire* is an unusual Regency example of a type of cabinet enclosing musical instruments – a tradition started in the sixteenth century in Germany and also found in the seventeenth century in Italy and Flanders. The luxurious aspect of those cabinets is maintained here in the high quality of craftsmanship displayed in the interior, which is fitted with mirrors and a 'Gothick' architectural setting of pointed arches and rustication, with an inlaid floor and five drawers (the larger central one fitted with partitions) separated by small classical figures. The fall-front is lined with the original tooled green leather, decorated with the emblems of England, Scotland and Ireland and the Star of the Order of the Garter.

The virtuoso craftsmanship displayed in this piece indicates a special commission; S. Jamar (active 1818–26), claimed to provide furniture 'equal to any made in Paris' from his workshop at 29 Wardour Street in Soho, London, and to count the brother of Napoleon and the King of the Netherlands among his clients.

109 French *serre-bijoux* (one of a pair) in *contre-partie* Boulle work. One of the pieces is stamped 'Mombro Aîné' in two places, and the other bears a number '1209' and the inscribed date '18 Mars 1851'. These *serre-bijoux* emulate the Louis XIV style in several respects: the use of ebony, tortoise-shell and brass; the breakfront central panel (on gilt-bronze lion's-paw mounts) enclosing an inlaid vase of flowers in *pietra dura* on an ebony ground; and a beribboned medallion of Louis XIV placed at the top.

One of the cabinets is fitted with small drawers, lined with velvet and having silk-lined leather covers, designed to hold parures of jewelry and each bearing an individual mother-of-pearl plaque inscribed 'Coral Suite', 'Diamonds' etc; the other is fitted with shelves. Each table base has an Espagnolette head at the apron and baluster legs adorned with gadrooned capitals and acanthus-leaf mounts below. The lower shelf supports a two-handled classical urn. Mombro was the son of a Parisian *ébéniste*; his address from 1850 to 1866 was 19 rue du Helder, Paris. In 1863 he opened a shop in London at 2 Frith Street, Soho, where he was in business until 1866; his stock was sold at auction between 1866 and 1868.

110 English painted cabinet-on-stand (one of a pair), *c.* 1805; the painted medallions with pastoral scenes are enclosed within a framework of vines and birds, the outer border being decorated with grotesques. The stands, with cabriole legs, are similarly decorated with polychrome grotesque motifs. The form of cabinet on a low stand with cabriole legs is reminiscent of the early eighteenth century, while the pastoral scenes evoke the use of Sèvres porcelain plaques with enamel decoration in the middle of the century.

111 English Boulle-work cabinet (one of a pair), *c.* 1855, with a stepped breakfront adorned with a central arched door displaying a perfume urn above masks and lambrequins in *première partie*, flanked by drawers with classical escutcheons in matching pairs. The whole front is punctuated by pilasters each having a capital and base made of horn stained blue to simulate lapis lazuli. This pair of cabinets echo the description in a bill submitted to the 4th Marquess of Hertford in 1855 by John Webb of 8 Bond Street: 'To two fine *Boule* [*sic*] Cabinets of Architectural taste of the finest period with drawers on either side and a Door in the Centre enclosing drawers etc. etc. the whole comprised of black shell and ebony and richly ornamented with finely chased & gilt mounts etc. etc. £1,470.' The pair supplied by Webb stood in the hall of Hertford House, Manchester Square, London (which is now the home of the Wallace Collection), as can be seen in a photograph taken in the 1890s after the death of Lord Hertford's son, Sir Richard Wallace. Lady Wallace bequeathed her London collection to the nation and the Paris collection together with certain 'domestic items' to Sir John Murray Scott, secretary to herself and her late husband. Upon his death in 1912, the London items in his estate were sold at auction; the sale catalogue describes under Lot 294 'A Pair of Boulle Cabinets 50 in. high, 57 in. wide, the centre of which encloses four drawers with small panels enamelled in blue, in emulation of lapis lazuli.' Several original seventeenth-century cabinets of this form made by Boulle still exist: one (in the Royal Collection at Windsor Castle) was lent to the exhibition organized by the South Kensington Museum and Prince Albert, held at Gore House in 1853. It could have provided the model on which the present example is based.

112 Florentine ebony and *pietra dura* cabinet (one of a pair), *c.* 1820. Original seventeenth-century *pietra dura* panels have been re-used within a typically nineteenth-century architectural cabinet form.

113 German walnut and marquetry cabinet-on-stand, *c.* 1850–70; sixteenth-century pictorial marquetry panels have been built in as part of an eclectic revival form, also making use of elements borrowed from the seventeenth century, such as the tapered legs and the flat curved stretcher. This romantic attitude was a characteristic feature of the nineteenth-century approach to styles and techniques

114 English ebony cabinet-on-stand (one of a pair), *c.* 1850–70; carved ebony panels taken from large seventeenth-century cabinets-on-stand of the type associated with Jean Macé have been incorporated. Each cabinet includes one half of the original double doors mounted in ormolu; it is surmounted by a carved frieze depicting a Roman battle scene with a cornice above. The theme of the seventeenth-century panels relates to military events. The stands, made of solid ebony, each have a central mask and cabriole legs. The pair of cabinets may have been executed by Edward Holmes Baldock (1777–1845), a well-known dealer in furniture and porcelain who specialized in reconstructing seventeenth-century ebony cabinets to fit in with the demands of contemporary fashion; he supplied pieces to William Beckford for Fonthill Abbey (completed 1812).

115 English tulipwood and kingwood *bonheur-du-jour, c.* 1840; the piece includes inset porcelain plaques in the eighteenth-century French manner. The central part has a white Carrara marble top within a gilt-bronze fretwork gallery, with swags and tassels in the manner of Carlin. The sides of the central cupboard and of the drawers are decorated with the cipher of Louis Philippe beneath a royal crown in marquetry of tulipwood on a kingwood ground. The piece is characteristic of the Rococo revival in the nineteenth-century favouring small 'feminine' pieces.

116 German ebony and rosewood table-cabinet incorporating seventeenth-century decorative elements, *c.* 1850. The form and proportions of the cabinet are typical of Mannerist pieces dating from the end of the sixteenth century and the beginning of the seventeenth century, exemplified in features such as the feet in the shape of lions, unicorns and centaurs, and the gilt-metal mounts on the enamelled panels of the drawer-fronts. This revivalist piece also features on the outside of the doors floral marquetry of the type associated with the Arts and Crafts Movement and Art Nouveau in the late nineteenth century.

117 Italian ebony and ivory inlaid cabinet, *c.* 1875. The cabinet has strong architectural outlines, with a central rounded pediment flanked by ivory finials above fluted columns, one on either side of the upper part; these features, taken together with the quality of the craftsmanship, mark this piece as having its origin in Milan. The entire surface of the cabinet is finely inlaid with motifs of female figures in flowery arbours, lambrequins, putti, grotesques and musical trophies, all inspired by the Régence and Rococo styles.

118 Italian walnut fall-front bureau inlaid with ivory, *c.* 1870. The elaborate geometric inlay of bone and ivory imitates the style of the fifteenth-century *alla certosina* technique, which had been popular in the Veneto and Lombardy under Islamic influence. The characteristic designs have here been expanded and further elaborated to create an even more striking decorative effect.

119 German fall-front cabinet in ebony, rosewood and palmwood, *c.* 1870–80; behind the fall-front are two inner doors which in turn open to reveal numerous small drawers. The fall-front rests on four supports decorated with seventeenth-century ivory lions' heads, four others being used as decoration on the sides of the cabinet. The interior is designed as a temple façade with a pediment and Corinthian columns. The exterior geometric decorative scheme continues from the cabinet proper to the base, which features heavy volutes terminating in lions' paws.

120 Italian cabinet in ebony with ivory and *pietra dura* inlay, *c.* 1870. The very impressive dimensions of this piece, with its breakfront central part, are matched by the virtuosity of the inlaid decoration consisting of fine ivory grotesques (various beasts, putti, chimeras and foliage), studded with glowing *pietra dura* (lapis lazuli, porphyry and agate). It is a characteristic product of Milan and would most probably have been executed as a showpiece for an exhibition.

121 Flemish tortoiseshell and marquetry cabinet-on-stand, *c.* 1860–70. The theme of the cabinet as a whole is of a religious nature, and sets out to make this a *meuble d'apparat* in the seventeenth-century tradition, with a clear didactic message. Here the scrolled pediment encloses a carved gilt sculptural group of the Virgin and Child with St John, a traditional Renaissance theme portrayed by Leonardo da Vinci, Michelangelo and Raphael in particular, the Virgin being regarded as symbolizing *Caritas*, Christian Love and Charity. On either side carved and gilt caryatids represent respectively Hope (with an anchor), and Faith (with a helmet, chalice and book). The three Theological Virtues are thus symbolically represented. The figures incorporated into the stand illustrate the four Cardinal Virtues: Prudence with a snake, Justice with a sword, Fortitude with a column, and Temperance with a bridle. The overtly religious message of the piece is rather unusual for the time, as such grand furniture would usually have been made for the large industrial exhibitions held in major centres in Europe and America. This was very likely a special commission as a showpiece, for the whole ethos and execution of the cabinet harks back to the grand Baroque style, with a complex mirrored theatre concealing secret drawers and compartments, as well as conveying a powerful message.

122 Florentine ebony cabinet-on-stand with *pietra dura* and lapis lazuli inlay, *c.* 1870. The strong architectural lines of the cabinet are reminiscent of the early seventeenth century; the façade shows the influence of churches of the Counter-Reformation period, with statuettes displayed in niches and a central frontispiece with columns and a broken pediment above. Here the composition lacks the homogeneity of the seventeenth-century prototype, with numerous small drawers depicting shells, birds and flowers vying with the architectural motifs for the viewer's attention. The shallow drawer above the central temple door is inscribed on the back 'Giuseppe di Lorenzo Luigi di Alessandro Dini'.

123 Portuguese cabinet-on-stand in ebonized wood, rosewood and tortoiseshell, *c.* 1870–80. The general form and outline of the cabinet and its stand hark back to the seventeenth century. The horizontal emphasis of the cabinet proper is relieved by the top gallery surmounted by two classical figures, which are aligned with the central breakfront with a niche enclosing a statuette, flanked by tiers of drawers. The important claw-and-ball feet rest on the table base which has a breakfront (echoing that of the cabinet itself) and three frieze drawers. A trade label on the piece reads 'A. CEZAR COELHO & CUNHA. MARCENEIRO E ENTALHADOR, 47 RUA DA BICA DE DUARTE BELLO, 51 (AO CALHARIZ)'.

124 Italian architectural cabinet-on-stand in ebony and ivory, *c.* 1880–90. This impressive piece is an obvious derivation from Roman architectural cabinets of the Baroque period featuring a highly sculptural base. Particularly relevant is the cabinet-on-stand designed *c.* 1678–80 by Carlo Fontana (now in the Palazzo Colonna); this has two crouching blackamoors supporting an ebony cabinet with inset ivory plaques (see p. 87). The present cabinet follows the same format, having a central aedicule flanked by putti, and a tripartite façade punctuated by columns and with niches enclosing smaller columns and carved reliefs of Venus and Cupid (centre) and of a female classical figure on either side.

This is an example of the type of showpiece made for exhibitions held in major European and American cities, a trend begun by the Great Exhibition, held in London in 1851.

125 Anglo-Dutch japanned and silvered cabinet-on-stand (one of a pair) with *chinoiserie* decoration, *c.* 1870–80. The pair of cabinets are characteristic of the revival of seventeenth-century styles; both pieces feature a stepped mirror-lined cornice above double doors, which, like the sides, are decorated with *chinoiserie* village scenes, executed in gilt japanning on a silver ground. The stand is reminiscent of the Louis XIV style as used by Daniel Marot, with tapered legs, pierced and carved, joined by a curved stretcher.

126 English japanned cabinet with *chinoiserie* decoration, *c.* 1820. The Regency period in England saw a renewed interest in *chinoiserie*, a fashion encouraged by the Prince Regent (later George IV) who had a room decorated in the Chinese style at Carlton House (this was illustrated by Sheraton in 1794). The culmination of the style is seen in the grand orientalizing architecture, decoration and furnishing of the Royal Pavilion at Brighton, rebuilt (1815–21) under the direction of John Nash. This light-hearted frivolous *chinoiserie* style was confined to England in the early part of the nineteenth century, at which point design in Europe generally was dominated by the French Empire style. The painted and penwork decoration of the cabinet is in the manner of J. C. Loudon (1783–1843).

127 Japanese cabinet decorated with black and gold lacquer and inlaid with shell in the Shibayama style, *c.* 1880–90. The opening-up of Japan to Western trade in the middle of the nineteenth century created renewed interest in Japanese artifacts. The International Exhibition held in London in 1862 was the first occasion when Japanese textiles, works of art, porcelain and lacquered furniture were displayed in the West. The asymmetry favoured by Japanese craftsmen and the subtle play on solid and void greatly influenced European designers. In 1888 Samuel Bing founded the journal *Le Japon Artistique*, with editions in French, German and English, so disseminating Japanese style and providing a source of inspiration for Western designers.

128 English ebonized and painted cabinet in the Anglo-Japanese style, *c.* 1880. The Japanese-inspired use of asymmetry and interplay of solids and voids enjoyed a great vogue in England; it reached its highpoint in the Peacock Room designed by Whistler for a London house. However, it was the stark simplicity of lines seen in the work of Godwin, and of the craftsmen of Ashbee's Guild of Arts and Crafts which would ultimately prevail, together with the naturalism found in decorative motifs inspired by flowers and plants.

129, 130 French side cabinet with marquetry decoration and gilt-bronze mounts, *c.* 1885. This piece was made either by François Linke or by Joseph Emmanuel Zwiener, who was born in Germany in 1849 and worked in Paris, at 12 rue de la Roquette, from 1880 to 1895. The serpentine line of the piece is punctuated at the edges of the central *bombé* panel (which is enclosed within a gilt-bronze mount), by three-dimensional figures of Cupids (one, with raised hammer, is fashioning a crown, the other studying the Five Orders of Architecture); the central panel displays a mask of Neptune. The whole is a masterpiece of curves and countercurves in the Rococo manner, with the accent on naturalism of detailing as found in the eighteenth century, and still executed with a high degree of virtuosity.

131 Italian burr walnut cabinet-on-stand with carved and applied beech decoration, *c.* 1890. Revivalist styles were used and forms of earlier periods copied throughout Europe. This cabinet embraces the traditional form of the seventeenth-century cabinet-on-stand, in the native walnut, and the flowing lines of a Rococo revival verging on Art Nouveau (Italian, *Stile floreale*), with its scrolling tendrils and the naturalistic basket of flowers.

132 French cabinet in mahogany and oak veneered with kingwood and amboyna, signed 'L.

Majorelle'; the piece was shown at the Exposition Universelle in Paris in 1900 as part of the display by members of the School of Nancy. The whole theme of the decoration is water, and aquatic plant and animal life, very much in the tradition of the *meubles parlants* of Gallé, who collaborated closely with Majorelle and was also a founder-member of the School of Nancy.

The two parts of the cabinet – an upper hood and two cupboards (separated by an open space) enclosing shelves, are unified by the continuous carved decoration of water-lilies, with flowers and tendrils covering the curving outline. The upper cupboard has marquetry decoration of two women bathing in a stream and a boat moored nearby, with swans in the distance; the banks are planted with trees depicted in close-up in the asymmetrical manner of Japanese prints by Hiroshige or Hokusai, which had a strong influence on European designers and artists. The lower cupboard has marquetry decoration of a pond with water-lilies, very similar in style to the well-known water-lilies series painted by Monet in his garden at Giverny at the same period.

Even the metal fittings of the locks and keys are in the form of leafy stems, demonstrating the extreme attention to detail inherent in Art Nouveau design, and its reliance on natural forms as a source of inspiration.

133 French tulipwood bureau with gilt-bronze mounts, *c.* 1890; designed by François Linke, the piece was shown in 1900 at the Exposition Universelle in Paris, where it was awarded a gold medal. The commendation for the award read as follows: 'The work of M. Linke . . . was an example of what can be done by seeking inspiration amongst the classic examples of Louis XV and XVI [furniture] without in any great sense copying these great works. M. Linke's work was original in the true sense of the word, and as such commended itself to the intelligent seeker after the really artistic items of the Exhibition. Wonderful talent was employed in producing the magnificent pieces of furniture displayed.'

Despite the obvious indebtedness of the design to the Louis XV style, the flowing lines of this bureau came very close to the spirit of Art Nouveau, as represented in works shown at the Exposition by members of the School of Nancy. Here the naturalism is used to convey allegorical meanings in a manner reminiscent of the Ancien Régime: helmets are used as finials; putti represent Vigilance and Discretion; dolphins and Nymphs (standing for Science and Art) hold swags of oak and laurel leaves above a figure of Abundance, shown reclining in a landscape inspired by Millet (1814–75), symbolizing Agriculture; and a galleon under full sail stands for Commerce. In

this way the various sources of wealth in contemporary society are symbolically united. The bureau is a triumph of industrial techniques put to the use and glorification of the newly rich middle-class patrons, and an excellent example of an exhibition showpiece.

134 French kingwood display cabinet incorporating a stainless-steel safe, made by François Linke, Paris, *c.* 1885. This impressive piece is an example of Linke's derivative style in the 1880s, when he was engaged in copying pieces of eighteenth-century furniture. The forms and decoration of the cabinet were inspired by the *Grand Bureau du Roy* (1760–9) by Oeben and Riesener, now at Versailles, a copy of which is in the Wallace Collection. The practice was a fairly common one during the last part of the nineteenth century in France, the high standard of craftsmanship being achieved here through industrial means with the help of modern methods of slicing veneers and producing gilt-bronze mounts of very high quality in emulation of eighteenth-century style and techniques.

The display cabinet is an outstanding example of the speciality developed by the 'Maison Linke': to marry modern requirements to eighteenth-century form and decoration. Here a stainless-steel safe is concealed behind marquetry doors, while the whole piece assumes the *bombé* shape of the late Rococo style featuring cabriole legs with gilt-bronze mounts and scroll feet; the upper gallery surmounting the whole displays a central clock (signed 'Thiout, L'Aîné A Paris') in the manner of the *Grand Bureau* at Versailles, with the same double-handled classical urns as finials.

135 French ebony cabinet with carved inlay of various woods, signed on the base 'Anno Henri Fourdinois 1867'. When shown at the 1867 Paris Exposition Universelle, the cabinet was purchased for the South Kensington Museum (now the Victoria and Albert Museum), London, for the sum of £2,750.

The cabinet, which is of impressive dimensions and in a grand revival style, was much commented upon by contemporaries. In *The Complete Official Catalogue of the Exhibition* (p. 207) and the *Illustrated Catalogue of the Universal Exhibition*, published in the *Art Journal* in August 1868 (p. 141), it was noted that 'It is impossible, either by pen or pencil, to do justice to the Cabinet of M. Fourdinois, the "chef-d'oeuvre" of the Exhibition, and certainly the best work of its class that has been produced in modern times, by any manufacturer. But it is not a production of manufacture, not even of Art-Manufacture; it is a collection of sculptured works, brought together and made to constitute parts of a cabinet – these "parts" all

exquisitely sculptured; carving is not a word sufficient to express their delicacy and beauty. We engrave it; yet no engraving, however large, could convey an idea of the perfection of this perfect work. The "Grand Prix" has been allocated to M. Fourdinois, and we believe by universal consent of his compeers, for his latest and best production is unrivalled'.

The first volume of *Reports on the Paris Universal Exhibition 1867 prepared for the Science and Art Department*, London added: 'But their ebony cabinet or dresser, inlaid with box, walnut and other woods, is a step in advance not shown by any other exhibitor in the class. The peculiarities of this piece of furniture are the mixture of woods and the process of inlaying the woods being woven together in the solid.' (pp. 286–7).

The 'Report of Artisans selected by a A Committee Appointed by the Council of the Society of Arts to visit the Paris Universal Exhibition in 1867' published in London further commented (pp. 115–16): 'Messrs Fourdinois exhibit a cabinet profusely decorated with carving, the method of applying which they have patented; the method is this – take, for instance, a panel; instead of merely laying the carving upon the surface, it is cut in as marquetry, allowed to project as required and afterwards carefully modelled and worked down to the ground – the inside is veneered – when upon thick pieces, as legs, it is let in with chisel and gouge about $\frac{3}{8}$ in; the ornament being very fine and delicate, this treatment is absolutely necessary.' The cabinet thus united the latest technological improvements in the art of cabinetmaking to the grand Baroque form of the 'meuble d'apparat', using allegories of the classical tradition, so linking the past with the present, in an exhibition showpiece. Minerva reigns over the whole piece in a classical aedicule, Poetry and Painting being depicted in the rounded spandrels, while the central panel depicts an allegory to the Temple of Peace, flanked by caryatids representing the Four Continents: Europe and Asia with an enclosed medallion of Ceres on the right, America and Africa with Neptune on the left. The head of Apollo as the Sun-God appears in the apron of the base, surrounded by putti in the spandrels, the base as well as the cabinet proper being discreetly adorned with *pietra dura* panels in the Henri II Renaissance style, of lapis lazuli, verde antico and red sienna marble.

The whole piece thus amounts to a celebration of the past, in harmony with the present modern times and hoping for a peaceful future on a universal level, a theme which was no doubt acknowledged at the Exposition and attuned to the longstanding function of the cabinet, traditionally regarded as a piece of furniture endowed with a meaning and a message.

CATALOGUE

AN ILLUSTRATED CHRONOLOGICAL GUIDE TO STYLES

The catalogue provides a concise visual guide to the international development of the cabinet
from the fifteenth century onwards, set within the historical framework of events noted
in the accompanying chronological date line. The cabinets illustrated are arranged on each
double-page opening in two horizontal registers of eight items; they are identified by country
or region of origin, with a brief indication of materials, dates and dimensions where known.
The choice of pieces is intended to provide a record of the wide range of sizes and forms and
of the various techniques used in the execution and decoration of cabinets. In order to present
the examples illustrated in a form as close as possible to their original appearance, later
additions and embellishments have been omitted or – in cases where this was
not practicable – noted in the captions.

1 Ottoman wooden casket with fall-front shown open to reveal inner drawers; the decoration of geometric motifs includes mother-of-pearl, tortoiseshell, ivory, ebony and silver wire. Sixteenth–seventeenth century; width 44.5 cm (17½ in.).

2 Italian walnut table-cabinet (*scrigno*); Florence, late fifteenth–early sixteenth century.

3 Italian cabinet-on-cupboard (*armadio*) with *alla certosina* inlay of wood, bone and ivory; Lombardy or Veneto, fifteenth century.

4 Spanish walnut *vargueño* (on a *pie de puente* stand) with inlaid decoration combining the Islamic-inspired *mudéjar* style and the biblical story of Noah's Ark; *c.* 1525–50.

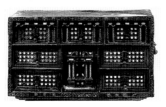

9 French walnut cabinet *en armoire* with doors featuring carved decoration of strapwork with shells and rosettes, *c.* 1530; width 110 cm (3 ft 7¼ in.).

10 Spanish walnut *papelera* inlaid with bone and having an architectural cupboard, *c.* 1600; width 80 cm (2 ft 7½ in.).

11 Spanish walnut fall-front *vargueño* with drawers carved in the Plateresque style and iron mounts, *c.* 1560–80; width 90 cm (2 ft 11½ in.).

12 Spanish walnut *vargueño* with carved decoration in the Plateresque style, *c.* 1570–80; width 106 cm (3 ft 5¾ in.).

1394 Reign of Henry the Navigator in Portugal (until 1460)

1414 The Medici family become bankers to the Papacy

1415 Portuguese trading posts established on the West African coast

1430 First mentions of drawers (*laiettes*) in French inventories

1435 Alberti: *De Pictura*

1450 Corporations rules revised in Paris

1450 Alberti: *De re aedificatoria*

1453 End of the Hundred Years' War between England and France

1460 Corporations rules revised in Spain

1482 The *studiolo* at Urbino completed for the Duke of Montefeltro

1492 Granada recaptured from the Moors

1492 Beginning of the *mudéjar* style in Spain

1492 Christopher Columbus reaches the West Indies

1494 Trade treaty between Spain and Portugal ratified by Papal Bull

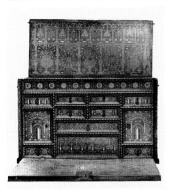

5 Spanish walnut *vargueño* with inlaid decoration of boxwood and ivory combining geometric motifs in the *mudéjar* style and Italianate Renaissance architectural features; *c.* 1550–75.

6 Spanish walnut *vargueño* decorated with pierced ironwork backed by red velvet, sixteenth century.

7 Spanish walnut *vargueño* on chest (*taquillon*) inlaid with lime, *c.* 1580–1600; width 107 cm (3 ft 6 in.).

8 North Italian table-cabinet with decoration of grotesques and animals, and including drawers arranged around a central cupboard with a temple front, *c.* 1580–1600; width 53.5 cm (21 in.).

13 Spanish walnut *vargueño* inlaid with bone, featuring an architectural design and symbolic pilgrim's shell handles and crosses within niches, *c.* 1590–1600; width 59 cm (23¼ in.).

14 German marquetry cabinet (on later stand) featuring architectural motifs and allegorical scenes. Augsburg, *c.* 1555 (possibly designed by Hans Holbein).

15 German table-cabinet in walnut and palmwood, the front decorated with hardstone pilasters and inlaid amber, jet, ebony, lapis lazuli and malachite, the back left plain to face the wall. Augsburg, *c.* 1560–70; width 49.5 cm (19½ in.).

16 Austrian table-cabinet with fall-front and pictorial marquetry decoration of ruins on drawers and the central cupboard door. Tyrol, *c.* 1600; width 57 cm (22½ in.).

1505 First known mention of the word 'cabinet' as a small storage room

1516 Portuguese trade links with China

1519 Charles V of Spain crowned Holy Roman Emperor

1527 Sack of Rome

1528 Work begins at Fontainebleau

1550 The Plateresque style introduced in Spain

1552 Rudolf II becomes Holy Roman Emperor (until 1612)

1560 Vredeman de Vries: *Variae architecturae formae*

1566 The Wrangelschrank completed

1570 Studiolo of Francesco de' Medici in the Palazzo Vecchio, Florence

1579 Separation of Southern and Northern Provinces in the Netherlands

1584 The Medici *studiolo* moved to the Uffizi

1585 Palladio's Teatro Olimpico in Vicenza

1593 Sumptuary laws in Spain

1597 Dutch expansion in the East Indies

1599 Foundation of the Opificio delle Pietre Dure in the Uffizi

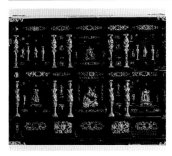

17 German table-cabinet in ebony with drawers behind an architectural façade decorated with silver-gilt herms and caryatids. Augsburg, *c.* 1600; width 100 cm (3 ft 3¼ in.).

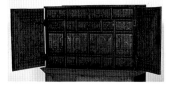

18 German marquetry *Schreibtisch* with two doors, having internal cupboards and drawers decorated with scenes of fantastic ruins. Augsburg, *c.* 1600; width 89 cm (2 ft 11 in.).

19 German ebony table-cabinet in the manner of Matthäus Wallbaum, with silver mounts and relief decoration depicting scenes from the life of Meleager. Augsburg, *c.* 1600–10; width 63.5 cm (2 ft 1 in.).

20 Italian table-cabinet (*scrigno*) in ebony with *verre églomisé* panels, *c.* 1620.

25 French cabinet-on-stand with doors, covered overall with stamped, painted and gilt leather, *c.* 1620–30.

26 French table-cabinet in ebony and Brazilian rosewood with white metal stringing, and having a hinged lid and panelled architectural doors concealing nine inner drawers, *c.* 1630; width 54.5 cm (21½ in.).

27 Italian table-cabinet in ebony and *pietra dura*, with two doors, a central cupboard and ten drawers; *c.* 1620–30; width 57.5 cm (22¾ in.).

28 Flemish table-cabinet in ebonized wood and alabaster, with architectural doors and behind them ten drawers around a central compartment, *c.* 1615–25; width 41 cm (16 in.).

1600 Second sumptuary laws in Spain

1600 *Tribuna* in the Galleria dei Lavori in the Uffizi begun

1600 Foundation of the English East India Company

1602 Foundation of the Dutch East India Company (Vereenigte Ostindische Compagnie)

1603 Spanish ban on imports of furniture from Nuremberg

1608 The Louvre workshop established (first Menuisier en Ebeyne)

1609 Formation of the Northern Republic of Holland

1610 Commissioning of the *Pommersche Kunstschrank*

21 North Italian walnut *stipo* with ivory statuettes in niches and plinths with inset painted copper panels. Lombardy (made for Canon Lucini Passalacqua), 1603.

22 Italian walnut *scrigno a bambocci* with writing slide and carved *putti* and figures of musicians. Liguria, *c.* 1610–20.

23 Italian table-cabinet in ebonized wood with Limoges enamel plaques set between lapis lazuli columns and a frieze with niches containing gilt-bronze statuettes, *c.* 1610; width 117 cm (3 ft 10 in.).

24 Flemish table-cabinet in ebony and Brazilian rosewood with inset glass panels painted with hunting scenes, *c.* 1600–10 (on later stand); width 108 cm (3 ft 6½ in.).

29 Flemish table-cabinet in ebonized wood and ivory, with inset ivory panels engraved with hunting and rural scenes. Antwerp, *c.* 1620; width 58 cm (23 in.).

30 North Italian table-cabinet in ebonized wood and ivory, decorated with classical figures and motifs. Milan, *c.* 1630; width 65 cm (2 ft 1½ in.).

31 North Italian table-cabinet in ebony, rosewood and ivory decorated with classical figures. Milan, *c.* 1630.

32 Italian table-cabinet in ebony with *verre églomisé* panels depicting allegorical subjects, grotesques and heads in profile (including the Emperor Maximilian I). Naples, *c.* 1625; width 150 cm (4 ft 1 in.).

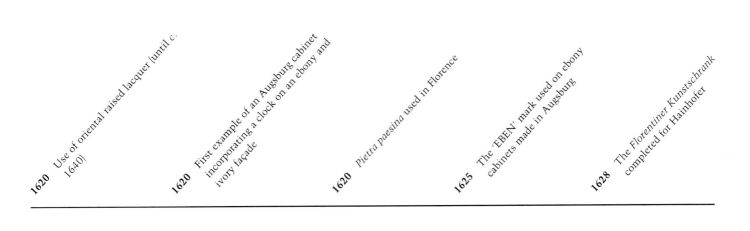

1620 Use of oriental raised lacquer (until *c.* 1640)

1620 First example of an Augsburg cabinet incorporating a clock on an ebony and ivory façade

1620 *Pietra paesina* used in Florence

1625 The 'EBEN' mark used on ebony cabinets made in Augsburg

1628 The *Florentiner Kunstschrank* completed for Hainhofer

33 Italian ebony table-cabinet with *verre églomisé* decoration on the drawer-fronts (the subjects based on engravings by Virgil Solis from Nuremberg). Florence or Rome, c. 1640.

34 Italian table-cabinet in ebony and ivory, with an arched niche enclosing a gilt-bronze figure of Venus and Cupid, and having eight rock-crystal columns and drawer-fronts with inlays of lapis lazuli and cornelian. Florence, c. 1630–40; width 63 cm (2 ft 1 in.)

35 Spanish walnut and ebony cabinet with tortoiseshell veneer, having a central theatre faced with marble columns and gilt statuettes; c. 1650; width 66 cm (2 ft 2in.).

36 German table-cabinet in ebony and other woods, decorated with ivory, *pietra dura*, enamel, miniature paintings and snakeskin panels. Augsburg, c. 1620–30; width 58 cm (22¾ in.).

41 Spanish *papelera* in rosewood and ebony with ivory inlay. *Mudéjar* style, c. 1600–25; width 85 cm (2 ft 9½ in.).

42 Indian table-cabinet with ivory inlay, having double doors and side-handles, c. 1630–40; width 44 cm (17¼ in.).

43 Spanish *papelera* in walnut with carved and gilt decoration, and featuring colonnettes of stained bone, c. 1650–70; width 102 cm (3 ft 4 in.).

44 German ebony and tortoiseshell table-cabinet with a central architectural niche enclosing a female figure, and with silver mounts, c. 1660–80; width 54.5 cm (21½ in.).

1632 The Gustavus Adolphus Cabinet (begun 1625) completed for Hainhofer and presented to the King of Sweden by the City of Augsburg

37 German cabinet-on-stand in ebonized wood, with *pietra paesina* panels and a central architectural cupboard. Augsburg, *c.* 1650; width 135 cm (4 ft 5 in.).

38 German ebony table-cabinet veneered with ivory and tortoiseshell and decorated with silk collages depicting the Four Seasons, the Elements and the Four Continents. Augsburg, *c.* 1650–60; width 94 cm (3 ft 1 in.).

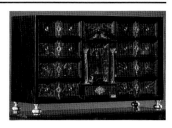

39 Colonial tortoiseshell, silver and ivory decorated table-cabinet with nine drawers and double doors, *c.* 1650; width 36 cm (14¼ in.).

40 Italian ebony and tortoiseshell table-cabinet with drawers arranged around a central cupboard, *c.* 1650.

45 Italian table-cabinet in ebonized wood with ivory and tortoiseshell inlay, and having an architectural interior with drawers around a central theatre. Florence, *c.* 1650–60.

46 Flemish table-cabinet in ebony and ivory with a central theatre and cupids within niches. Antwerp, *c.* 1640–50 (on later stand).

47 Italian table-cabinet in ebony and *pietra dura* with drawers around a central temple-fronted theatre. Florence, *c.* 1650 (on later stand); width 109 cm (3 ft 7 in.).

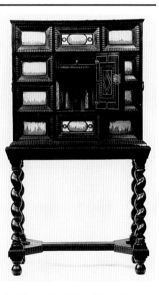

48 Flemish table-cabinet in ebony with *pietra paesina* panels, and having an architectural central cupboard, *c.* 1630–40 (on later stand).

1640 Use of tortoiseshell veneer (until *c.* 1680)

1648 End of the Thirty Years' War

49 Italian rosewood and *pietra dura* table-cabinet (one of a pair) with an architectural central cupboard containing a gilt-bronze statuette of Mars. Florence, *c.* 1650–60 (on later stand); width 84 cm (2 ft 9 in.).

50 Flemish ebony and tortoiseshell table-cabinet with painted marble panels, *c.* 1650–60 (on later stand); width 92 cm (3 ft 2½ in.).

51 North European ebony cabinet-on-stand with *pietra paesina* panels and a floral marquetry theatre, *c.* 1650–60; width 122 cm (4 ft).

52 Flemish table-cabinet in ebony with painted panels depicting allegorical subjects, and having an architectural front and (behind the cupboard doors) a central mirrored theatre. Antwerp, *c.* 1650; width 140 cm (3 ft 9 in.).

57 Colonial table-cabinet in rosewood and ebony with bone inlay, and having ten drawers decorated with arabesques around a central architectural cupboard, *c.* 1650–60; width 71 cm (2 ft 4 in.).

58 Flemish cabinet in ebonized wood, tortoiseshell and mother-of-pearl. Antwerp, *c.* 1650–60; width 79 cm (2 ft 7 in.).

59 Flemish ebony and tortoiseshell table-cabinet. Antwerp, *c.* 1650 (on later stand); width 109 cm (3 ft 7 in.).

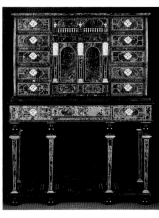

60 Flemish cabinet-on-stand in ebony, kingwood and tortoiseshell, having a central mirrored theatre. Antwerp, *c.* 1650; width 129 cm (4 ft 2¾ in.).

1650 Dutch trading hegemony in the East Indies

1650 Floral marquetry used in Holland and the rest of Europe

1653 Inventory of Cardinal Mazarin includes twenty-one cabinets

1659 First mention of the Italian *ebanista*

53 Flemish table-cabinet in ebony with painted panels on the insides of the doors and lid, and (on the drawer-fronts) silk-embroidered panels in stumpwork depicting animals. The bottom drawer is lined with canvas on which is printed 'Lady Fitzwilliam April 24 1679'. Antwerp, c. 1675–9; width 65 cm (2 ft 2 in.).

54 French ebony-veneered cabinet-on-stand with drawers around a central theatre in the manner of Jean Macé, c. 1660; width 155 cm (5 ft 1 in.).

55 French ebony cabinet-on-stand with carved decoration, the two outer doors concealing drawers arranged around an inner cupboard decorated with marquetry perspectives after Jean Macé, c. 1650.

56 Italian table-cabinet in architectural form with ivory inlay. Rome, c. 1650; width 134 cm (4 ft 4¾ in.).

61 German ebony cabinet with tortoiseshell inlay and *verre églomisé* panels, and having an organ manual inside a drawer below the central cupboard, c. 1650–60.

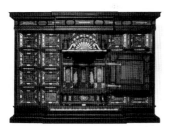

62 Flemish ebony table-cabinet with inlaid tortoiseshell (backed by gold foil) and mother-of-pearl, having an organ manual in a drawer below the central theatre, c. 1650–70 (the stand and cornice of later date); width 138 cm (4 ft 6¼ in.).

63 French walnut cabinet-on-stand with floral marquetry and ivory inlay, and having a central perspective in the manner of Pierre Gole, c. 1660–70; width 124 cm (4 ft 1 in.).

64 French ebony cabinet with floral marquetry (on a reconstructed stand), c. 1660–70; width 133 cm (4 ft 4½ in.).

1661 Personal reign of Louis XIV of France begins

1662 Restoration of Charles II to the British throne

1663 Creation of the Manufacture Royale des Gobelins

1664 Foundation of the French Compagnie des Indes

1667 Louis XIV visits the Gobelins

1667 The War of Devolution (French attack on the Spanish Netherlands)

1669 Works begin at Versailles

65 French rosewood cabinet *en armoire* with pewter inlay, *c.* 1650–60; width 108 cm (3 ft 6 in.).

66 French cabinet in kingwood and ebony with floral marquetry, the cupboard door being backed with Boulle work, *c.* 1660–70; width 138 cm (4 ft 6¼ in.).

67 French cabinet-on-stand in ebony, pewter and tortoiseshell with floral marquetry, the stand painted and gilt. A. C. Boulle, *c.* 1675.

68 Italian ebony and *pietra dura* cabinet with painted copper panels depicting scenes from the life of the Emperor Constantine (portrayed in the equestrian statuette surmounting the piece). Rome, 1668 (signed Giacomo Herman and dated).

73 Spanish ebony cabinet (one of a pair) with tortoiseshell veneer backed by gold foil, Salomonic columns, and biblical scenes painted on glass, *c.* 1660–70; width 197 cm (6 ft 5½ in.).

74 Italian cabinet in ebony and *pietra dura*. Florence, *c.* 1670–80 (with later galleried top).

75 Italian ebony cabinet-on-stand decorated with *pietra dura* panels and (on the sides) floral marquetry in the manner of Leonardo van der Vinne, *c.* 1680; width 124 cm (4 ft ¾ in.).

76 Italian cabinet in ebony and *pietra dura* (given by Cosimo III de' Medici to the Earl of Exeter). Florence, 1684 (on a later English stand); width 173 cm (5 ft 8 in.).

1672 A. C. Boulle appointed Ebéniste du Roy

1678 Peace of Nijmegen between France and Holland

69 Italian cassettone *a bambocci* in ebonized walnut with carved and parcel-gilt decoration. Genoa, *c.* 1660–70.

70 French japanned cabinet-on-stand with decoration of *chinoiserie, turquerie* and classical scenes, *c.* 1660–70; width 127 cm (4 ft 2 in.).

71 Chinese cabinet with scarlet lacquer decoration, on a Dutch ebonized and gilt stand made *c.* 1680–90; width 84 cm (2 ft 9 in.).

72 English japanned cabinet on a carved and gilt stand with matching cresting, *c.* 1680–90.

77 Italian architectural table-cabinet in ebony and ivory with a gallery and urn-shaped finials and a central allegorical figure of Rome. Rome, *c.* 1670–80 (on later stand); width 145 cm (4 ft 9 in.).

78 Italian cabinet-on-stand (*stipo*) in ebonized cherrywood with engraved ivory plaques depicting animals and allegorical figures. Lombardy, *c.* 1680–90; width 118 cm (3 ft 10½ in.).

79 German table-cabinet in ebony and ebonized wood, decorated with carved ivory, bone, hardstone intaglios and semi-precious stones, *c.* 1690; width 102 cm (3 ft 4½ in.).

80 Italian bureau-cabinet (*trumeau*) in ebonized and parcel-gilt wood. Florence, *c.* 1680–90; width 187 cm (6 ft 1½ in.).

1681 William Penn in America

1682 The court and government of Louis XIV transferred to Versailles

1685 Revocation of the Edict of Nantes (Huguenot craftsmen forced to emigrate from France)

1685 Creation of the *Journal du Garde-Meuble Royal*

1688 Stalker and Parker: *Treatise of Japanning and Varnishing*

1689 Sumptuary laws in France

81 English kingwood scriptor (writing cabinet on stand) with oystershell veneer and silver mounts, *c.* 1675; width 89 cm (2 ft 11 in.).

82 Dutch walnut cabinet with oystershell veneer and ebony banding around cedarwood drawers faced with etched glass panels depicting maritime scenes, on a matching stand, *c.* 1660–70; width 121.5 cm (4 ft).

83 Walnut cabinet-on-stand, in Anglo-Dutch style, with floral marquetry, *c.* 1685; width 114 cm (3 ft 10½ in.).

84 English walnut cabinet-on-stand with oystershell marquetry and silver mounts, *c.* 1680–90.

89 Dutch walnut and rosewood cabinet-on-stand with floral marquetry, *c.* 1680–90.

90 English walnut cabinet-on-stand with oystershell veneer and floral marquetry, *c.* 1700–10.

91 English walnut cabinet-on-stand with laburnum oystershell veneer and floral marquetry, *c.* 1700–10.

92 Colonial cabinet in padouk wood with brass mounts, on a base with heavy bun feet. Dutch East India Company (V.O.C.), *c.* 1700–20; width 102 cm (3 ft 4 in.).

1690 Accession of William of Orange and Queen Mary to the British throne

85 English walnut cabinet-on-chest with moulded cornice, *c.* 1700; width 103 cm (3 ft 4½ in.).

86 Cabinet-on-stand in Anglo-Dutch style, having laburnum oystershell veneer and a moulded cornice, *c.* 1690; width 131 cm (4 ft 3½ in.).

87 English walnut cabinet-on-stand with laburnum oystershell veneer, *c.* 1700–10.

88 Dutch cabinet with floral marquetry decoration, on a stand with a flat stretcher and bun feet, *c.* 1680–90; width 132 cm (4 ft 4 in.).

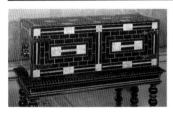

93 Italian ebony cabinet with inlaid plaques of engraved ivory, Milan, *c.* 1650–70.

94 Iberian colonial cabinet in rosewood inlaid with ivory, *c.* 1680–1700.

95 Ceylonese table-cabinet in ebonized wood and ivory, made for export to Europe, *c.* 1670–80; width 62.5 cm (2 ft ½ in.).

96 Ceylonese miniature table-cabinet in carved ivory with silver-gilt mounts and handles, *c.* 1680–1700; width 24.5 cm (9½ in.).

1700 Inventory of Louis XIV includes seventy-six cabinets

97 English cabinet-on-chest with japanned decoration, *c.* 1710; width 102 cm (3 ft 4 in.).

98 English cabinet-on-stand with japanned decoration in red and gold simulating the effect of tortoiseshell veneer, *c.* 1710.

99 English cabinet japanned in scarlet and having a carved and gilt stand and matching cresting, *c.* 1700.

100 English japanned cabinet-on-stand with decoration on the inner drawers depicting Chinese utensils, *c.* 1720.

105 Italian ebony table-cabinet (one of a pair) with panels of *pietra paesina, c.* 1700–20; width 93 cm (3 ft ½ in.).

106 Bohemian cabinet in ebonized wood, having an interior resembling a galleried room with mirrored panels and relief *intarsia* panels depicting hunting and courtly scenes. Eger, *c.* 1700; width 143 cm (4 ft 8¼ in.).

107 Flemish rosewood writing cabinet with pewter inlay and *chinoiserie* scenes (inspired by Johann Neuhof's record of the Dutch embassy to the last Ming emperor in 1644) possibly by Hendrik van Soest. Antwerp, *c.* 1700; width 136 cm (4 ft 5½ in.).

108 German cabinet-on-stand in birch and walnut with pewter inlay and ebonized banding, and having a writing compartment in the base, *c.* 1710–20; width 133 cm (4 ft 4½ in.).

1700 Introduction of mahogany in America

1715 Philippe d'Orléans becomes Regent of France (until 1723)

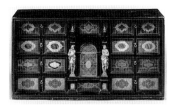

103   Italian ebony cabinet with metal inlay and *verre églomisé* panels simulating *pietra dura*, *c.* 1700–20; width 86 cm (2 ft 10 in.).

104   Italian rosewood table-cabinet with ivory inlay, *c.* 1700–20 (on later stand); width 107 cm (3 ft 6 in.).

101   North German cabinet-on-stand japanned in scarlet and gold, *c.* 1700–20.

102   English walnut cabinet with seaweed marquetry, *c.* 1720 (on later stand); width 76 cm (3 ft 10 in.).

111   Dutch cabinet-on-stand in walnut with inlaid decoration, *c.* 1700–10; width 164 cm (5 ft 4 in.).

112   English walnut cabinet-on-chest, *c.* 1710; width 119 cm (3 ft 11 in.).

109   South German walnut cabinet-on-stand with ebony and ivory inlay, and having a writing compartment in the base, *c.* 1710–20; width 109 cm (3 ft 7 in.).

110   Flemish cabinet-on-stand in walnut and ebonized wood. Liège, *c.* 1700–20.

1715 Palladio's *Quattro Libri* published in English translation as *Four Books of Architecture*

1715 Colen Campbell: *Vitruvius Britannicus* (completed 1725)

113 Dutch *secrétaire*-on-chest in maple with floral marquetry inlay, *c.* 1715–20; width 114 cm (3 ft 9 in.).

114 English burr-walnut bureau-cabinet with carved frieze, gilt finials and mirrored doors, *c.* 1705.

115 English walnut bureau-cabinet with domed top, *c.* 1710; width 55 cm (22 in.).

116 English walnut cross-banded bureau-cabinet, *c.* 1720; width 104 cm (3 ft 5 in.).

121 English bureau-cabinet, japanned dark green. Attributed to Giles Grendey, *c.* 1730.

123 Italian table writing cabinet with *lacca povera* decoration. Venice, *c.* 1730–40; width 110.5 cm (3 ft 7½ in.).

122 English bureau-cabinet, japanned blue. Attributed to Giles Grendey, *c.* 1730; width 112 cm (3 ft 8 in.).

124 Italian cabinet japanned in black and gold on a carved and gilt Rococo stand, *c.* 1735–40.

1730 Introduction of mahogany in England

1723 Louis XV of France reaches his majority

1737 Closure of the Medici Galleria in the Uffizi

1741 Cabinets from the Louvre sold at auction by order of Louis XV

1743 Corporation rules for *menuisiers* and *ébénistes* amended in France

117 English walnut bureau-cabinet with bevelled glazed doors, *c.* 1725; width 105 cm (3 ft 5½ in.).

118 Austrian walnut marriage bureau-cabinet with bone inlay and armorials, dated 1730; width 118 cm (3 ft 10½ in.).

119 Dutch walnut bureau-cabinet with fall-front, *c.* 1730.

120 German bureau-cabinet in Brazilian rosewood, with glazed doors and gilt-bronze mounts. Dresden, *c.* 1750; width 108 cm (3 ft 6½ in.).

125 Chinese cabinet decorated with Coromandel lacquer, on a Dutch carved gilt stand, *c.* 1740–50; width 130 cm (4 ft 3 in.).

126 Indian cabinet in padouk wood inlaid with ivory combining Mughal-inspired engraved flowers and foliage and European design features. Vizigapatam, *c.* 1730; width 57 cm (22½ in.).

127 Indian table writing cabinet with ivory inlay and side-handles, *c.* 1750; width 46 cm (18 in.).

128 Indian table-cabinet in rosewood with ivory inlay, *c.* 1740–50; width 54 cm (21½ in.).

1751 Use of maker's stamp (*estampille*) made compulsory in France (until 1791)

1752 Official records of excavations at Herculaneum published

1754 Cochin: 'Supplication aux Orfèvres, Ciseleurs et Sculpteurs sur Bois' in *Mercure Galant*

1754 Chippendale: *The Gentleman & Cabinet-Maker's Director*

1756 The Seven Years' War begins

129 English mahogany collector's cabinet with fitted drawers, c. 1760; width 53 cm (21 in.).

130 English *serre-bijoux* in ebony and holly, with scrolled cabriole legs. Possibly by William Vile, c. 1760.

131 Italian *serre-bijoux* in the form of a chest with doors and lid, covered with painted and tooled leather (the interior lined with embroidered silk including the arms of Doge Domenico Contarini II), on a carved walnut Rococo base. Venice, c. 1750–65; width 70 cm (2 ft 3½ in.).

132 Dutch cabinet in carved walnut with *bombé* form and having decoration of floral scrolls and *rocaille* motifs, c. 1760; width 197 cm (6 ft 5½ in.).

137 French *secrétaire à abattant* veneered with thuyawood, satinwood and purplewood and having inset Sèvres porcelain plaques. Stamped 'A. WEISWEILER', c. 1780–85, width 76 cm (2 ft 6 in.).

138 French *secrétaire à abattant* in satinwood with painted panels featuring grotesques and inset porcelain plaques, and having a marble galleried top, c. 1788 (stand stamped 'A. WEISWEILER'); width 79 cm (2 ft 7 in.).

139 French writing cabinet in harewood with marquetry decoration in a trellis pattern, and having a marble galleried top stamped 'LACROIX' (Roger Vandercruse), c. 1780; width 70 cm (2 ft 3 in.).

140 English mahogany cabinet-on-stand with fluted frieze and oval medallions, c. 1790; width 52 cm (20½ in.).

1774 Accession of Louis XVI of France

1783 Carlton House, London, built for the Prince Regent (completed 1785)

1775 The American War of Independence

1776 The American Declaration of Independence

133 Dutch display cabinet in oak with floral marquetry, having a moulded cornice and glazed doors, *c.* 1780–90.

134 South German cabinet-on-stand in walnut with marquetry decoration and having cabriole legs, *c.* 1770–75; width 85 cm (2 ft 10 in.).

135 English collector's cabinet-on-stand in harewood with marquetry decoration, *c.* 1775.

136 English estate cabinet in padouk wood (with drawers marked A to Z in ivory inlay) above a fitted bureau, *c.* 1775; width 117 cm (3 ft 10 in.).

141 Dutch cabinet-on-stand in walnut with marquetry panels, boxwood banding and shell decoration, *c.* 1790–1810; width 149 cm (4 ft 11 in.).

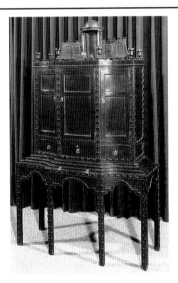

142 Irish cabinet-on-stand in ebonized wood, surmounted by a small classical temple, dated 1791.

143 English cabinet-on-stand in kingwood with paperwork decoration and medallions on the doors and drawers, *c.* 1800.

144 Chinese cabinet-on-stand, made for export, lacquered in black and gold, *c.* 1820; width 71 cm (28 in.).

1788 Hepplewhite: *The Cabinetmaker and Upholsterer's Guide*

1789 The French Revolution

1791 Abolition of guilds and corporations in France

1791 Sheraton: *The Cabinetmaker and Upholsterer's Drawing-Book* (in parts completed 1794)

1797 First industrial exhibition held in the Louvre

1798 Napoleon's Egyptian campaign

1800 Napoleon appointed First Consul

1802 Vivant Denon: *Voyage dans la Haute et la Basse Egypte*

1804 Napoleon crowned Emperor of the French

1807 Thomas Hope: *Household Furniture and Interior Decoration*

145 French mahogany *secrétaire à abattant* in the Empire style, with a grey marble top and gilt-bronze mounts (after designs by Jomard) attributed to Charles Morel, *c*. 1805–15.

146 English mahogany and rosewood *secrétaire* in Louis XVI style, with a galleried top and oval medallions in gilt brass enclosing rosewood panels, *c*. 1810; width 111 cm (3 ft 1½ in.).

147 Russian mahogany writing cabinet on gilt paw feet, having white marble columns and top and gilt-bronze mounts, *c*. 1810; width 119 cm (3 ft 11 in.).

148 English fall-front *secrétaire* in parcel-gilt amboyna with lotus-moulded cornice ahd leaf-capped pilasters. Attributed to Morel and Seddon, *c*. 1825; width 82 cm (2 ft 8 in.).

153 German mahogany *secrétaire à abattant* with rosewood interior, *c*. 1835; width 118 cm (3 ft 10½ in.).

154 English ebonized cabinet-on-stand in walnut and rosewood, *c*. 1830 (stamped 'Gillows'); width 91.5 cm (3 ft).

155 Goanese cabinet-on-stand decorated with marquetry and inlaid ivory, the central cupboard flanked by carved native figures, *c*. 1830–50; width 96 cm (3 ft 1½ in.).

156 English carved walnut display cabinet in Renaissance Elizabethan style. Made by Seddon of London, *c*. 1840; width 136 cm (4 ft 5½ in.).

1815 The fall of Napoleon and restoration of the Bourbon monarchy in France

1817 The Royal Pavilion, Brighton, rebuilt in oriental style by Nash for the Prince Regent

1820 Accession of George IV to the British throne

149 Austrian or German mahogany *secrétaire* cabinet in Biedermeier style, *c.* 1820; width 110 cm (3 ft 7 in.).

150 Dutch *secrétaire à abattant* decorated with floral marquetry and classical motifs, *c.* 1810–20; width 99 cm (3 ft 3 in.).

151 Dutch mahogany and marquetry *secrétaire à abattant* with penwork decoration depicting a marriage scene, *c.* 1820; width 110 cm (3 ft 7¼ in.).

152 German mahogany *secrétaire à abattant* with Rococo cresting, applied floral carving and scrolled feet, *c.* 1830; width 107 cm (3 ft 6 in.).

157 Italian carved rosewood display cabinet, parcel-gilt, in the Renaissance manner, *c.* 1850; width 109 cm (3 ft 7 in.).

158 Italian walnut display cabinet in seventeenth-century style. Tuscany, *c.* 1850–70.

159 Flemish fall-front cabinet with seventeenth-century panels, reconstructed *c.* 1850–70; width 90 cm (2 ft 11½ in.).

160 Flemish walnut table-cabinet with late Renaissance *rinceaux* and heads in profile, on a stand with a pull-out writing surface (cabinet reconstructed and stand added *c.* 1850–70); width 135 cm (4 ft 5 in.).

1830 Reign of Louis-Philippe in France (until 1848)

1835 A. W. N. Pugin: *Gothic Furniture in the Style of the 15th Century*

1837 Accession of Queen Victoria to the British throne

1848 Revolutions in Europe

161 Flemish cabinet in ebonized wood with a central niche containing a gilt-bronze figure of an angel, and with *pietra dura* panels and gilt-bronze mounts, on a Rococo revival stand, *c.* 1840–60.

162 Italian cabinet-on-stand in ebony with *pietra dura* panels and ivory inlay, on a stand of architectural form. Rome, *c.* 1860–70.

163 Italian breakfront cabinet in ebony with *pietra dura* and ivory decoration, and featuring grotesques in the Renaissance manner. Milan, *c.* 1870–80.

164 Flemish cabinet-on-stand with marquetry and tortoiseshell veneer, having a central theatre with mirrors and painted panels, *c.* 1850–70.

169 English walnut display cabinet with wood inlay and glazed cupboard in the Art and Crafts manner, *c.* 1860–65; width 101 cm (3 ft 3½ in.).

170 English mahogany display cabinet, of Japanese inspiration, in the manner of E. W. Godwin, *c.* 1870–80 (stamped 'Collinson and Lock'); width 153 cm (5 ft).

171 English rosewood cabinet with painted panels. T. E. Collcutt, *c.* 1870.

172 English mahogany display cabinet with marquetry and ivory inlay, made in two parts. Stamped 'Hampton and Sons, London', *c.* 1890; width 167 cm (5 ft 5¾ in.).

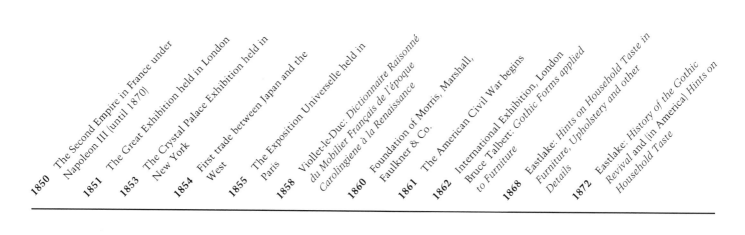

1850 The Second Empire in France under Napoleon III (until 1870)

1851 The Great Exhibition held in London

1853 The Crystal Palace Exhibition held in New York

1854 First trade between Japan and the West

1855 The Exposition Universelle held in Paris

1858 Viollet-le-Duc: *Dictionnaire Raisonné du Mobilier Français de l'époque Carolingiene à la Renaissance*

1860 Foundation of Morris, Marshall, Faulkner & Co.

1861 The American Civil War begins

1862 International Exhibition, London Bruce Talbert: *Gothic Forms applied to Furniture*

1868 Eastlake: *Hints on Household Taste in Furniture, Upholstery and other Details*

1872 Eastlake: *History of the Gothic Revival* and (in America) *Hints on Household Taste*

165 Flemish cabinet-on-stand in ebonized wood with tortoiseshell veneer, having a central cupboard and a gallery above, c. 1880.

166 Dutch green-japanned *bonheur du jour* with tortoiseshell veneer, a central cameo medallion and gilt-bronze mounts, on a stand featuring *pietra dura* inlay, c. 1860–70; width 106 cm (3 ft 11¾ in.).

167 Dutch cabinet-on-stand with marquetry decoration and ebonized cornice and with mounted Chinese porcelain plates, c. 1860; width 116 cm (3 ft 9½ in.).

168 German oak cabinet-on-stand incorporating seventeenth-century marquetry panels and drawers, reconstructed c. 1860–80; width 92 cm (3 ft ¼ in.).

174 English table-cabinet in walnut and ebony with wrought-iron handles. Ernest Gimson, c. 1890–95.

175 English walnut table-cabinet inlaid with ebony. Ernest Gimson, c. 1905.

173 English oak cabinet with carved and painted panels inspired by a design in Eastlake's *Hints on Household Taste*, c. 1885.

176 English oak cabinet with metal mounts, designed by C. R. Ashbee for the Guild of Handicraft (illustrated in *Arts and Crafts*, 1904).

1875 East India House opened by Liberty in Regent Street, London

1876 Bruce Talbert: Examples of *Ancient and Modern Furniture*

1888 C. R. Ashbee founds the Guild and School of Handicraft in London

1888 Samuel Bing publishes *Le Japon Artistique* (in French, English and German)

1889 Exposition Universelle, Paris

1893 The World's Fair, Chicago

1895 Bing opens his shop 'L'Art Nouveau' in Paris

1897 The Vienna Secession founded

177 Dutch cabinet-on-stand in walnut and oak in seventeenth-century style, *c.* 1900; width 110 cm (3 ft 7 in.).

178 French *secrétaire à abattant* in kingwood and gilt metal with *vernis Martin* panels, *c.* 1860–70.

179 French *secrétaire à abattant* in rosewood and gilt metal in Transitional style with a painted scene in the manner of Watteau, *c.* 1900; width 66 cm (2 ft 2 in.).

180 French side-cabinet in kingwood with marquetry and gilt-metal mounts, Louis XVI style, *c.* 1900; width 97 cm (3 ft 2¼ in.).

185 French mahogany display cabinet with carved clematis decoration. Louis Majorelle, Nancy, *c.* 1905–10; width 90.5 cm (2 ft 11¾ in.).

186 English cabinet in walnut and ebony. Ernest Gimson, *c.* 1910.

187 French cabinet-on-stand in ebony and macassar. Clément Mère, *c.* 1913; width 50 cm (19¾ in.).

188 French *secrétaire à abattant* with fall-front, in Brazilian rosewood, *c.* 1925–30; width 113 cm (3 ft 8½ in.).

1900 Exposition Universelle, Paris

1901 The School of Nancy founded by Gallé and others

1902 Ashbee's School of Arts and Crafts established in Chipping Campden, Gloucestershire (until 1914)

1903 Foundation of the Wiener Werkstätte

1909 The Ballets Russes perform in Paris

1914 Foundation of Das Staatliche Bauhaus, Weimar

1914 First World War begins

1919 Foundation of the Compagnie des Arts Français

1925 The Bauhaus transferred to Dessau (closed in 1933)

1925 The Exposition Internationale des Arts Décoratifs et Industriels Modernes held in Paris

1925 First Surrealist exhibition in Paris

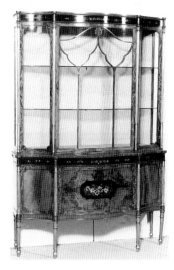

183 English cabinet-on-stand japanned in red and gold with *chinoiserie* designs and having a galleried top with finials. London (stamped 'H. Samuel, 484 Oxford Street'), *c.* 1900; width 152 cm (5 ft).

184 Swedish cabinet-on-stand with applied medallions inlaid with foliage, *c.* 1913; width 141.5 cm (4 ft 7½ in.).

182 English satinwood display cabinet with painted decoration, *c.* 1910; width 135 cm (4 ft 5 in.).

181 English mahogany and marquetry display cabinet-on-stand, *c.* 1905.

190 French side-cabinet in sycamore with mirrored doors. Jules Leleu, *c.* 1925–30; width 148 cm (4 ft 10¼ in.).

191 French cabinet-on-stand in walnut with central fall-front. Jean Pascaud, *c.* 1945; width 175 cm (5 ft 9 in.).

189 English Carlton House desk in mahogany with satinwood banding, having an architectural breakfront cabinet above, *c.* 1930; width 75 cm (2 ft 5½ in.).

192 Italian cocktail cabinet in mahogany with roll-top and mirrored interior. Attributed to Franco Albini, *c.* 1960; width 104 cm (3 ft 5 in.).

1939 Second World War begins

Brief details of cabinetmakers, craftsmen and designers are noted below.

Adam, Robert (1728–92) Scottish-born architect and designer, son of the architect William Adam, who died in 1748. He visited Italy in 1754, returning to London in 1758 to open an architectural practice with his three brothers. During his stay in Rome he absorbed the Neo-classical style and he met Piranesi, Clérisseau and others; although influenced by the Louis XVI style, his work was lighter in the handling of classical ornaments, his aim being 'to transfuse the beautiful spirit of antiquity with novelty and variety'. As an interior decorator he designed rooms, furnishings, silver and all kinds of domestic objects. His style was popularized by the publication of his *Works in Architecture* in three volumes (1773, 1779, 1822).

The best Adam-type furniture was made by Chippendale for houses which Adam built or decorated, notably Nostell Priory and Harewood House. Adam designed the Kimbolton Cabinet for the Duchess of Manchester as a setting for a set of *pietra dura* panels brought back from Florence *c.* 1771 (see pp. 137, 138).

Affleck, Thomas (d. 1795) Scottish cabinetmaker who emigrated to America, arriving in Philadelphia in 1763, and occupied premises on Second Street at Lowne's Alley. He owned a copy of Chippendale's *Gentleman & Cabinetmaker's Director* and is said to have 'brought an unparalleled urbanity of Chinese Chippendale to Philadelphia'. His clients among the affluent society of the city included Governor John Penn. Because of his Royalist sympathies during the Revolution, he was arrested on 2 September 1777 and was banished to Virginia for over seven months. He subsequently produced Chippendale-style furniture during the Federal period. Examples of his work can be seen at the Metropolitan Museum, New York, the Philadelphia Museum of Art, the Museum of Fine Arts, Boston, and the Winterthur Museum, near Wilmington, Delaware.

After his death the family business was continued by his son Lewis.

Angermair, Christoph (1580–1633) German sculptor and turner. Born in Weilham, he was apprenticed to the sculptor Hans Degler. In 1611 he was recorded as being involved in the production of cabinets. He was responsible for the carving of the chess pieces included in the content of the *Pommersche Kunstschrank* (see p. 52), which contained works by craftsmen from thirty-one different guilds. In 1613 he is recorded as a citizen of Munich. He was one of the most important artists at the court of Maximilian I, where he specialized in ivory turning *c.* 1618: he carved the Coin Cabinet for Maximilian I (1618–24) which is now in the Bayerisches Nationalmuseum, Munich (see p. 55).

Ashbee, Charles Robert (1863–1942) English designer and theorist of the Arts and Crafts Movement, of which he became the leader. In 1888 he founded the Guild and School of Handi-

craft at Toynbee Hall, London. His furniture designs were inspired by William Morris and Ruskin's concept that the 'creation of beauty was a duty owed to society'; he strove to recreate the 'working conditions of a medieval guild', in which several artists would contribute to the realization and decoration of a single piece, such as the walnut cabinet made *c.* 1903 (now in the Victoria and Albert Museum), which incorporates leatherwork by Satia Power. His work and that of the Guild was exhibited widely in England and Europe, in Paris, Vienna, Düsseldorf, Munich etc. In 1891 the School and Guild moved to Mile End, London, and in 1902 to Chipping Campden in the Cotswolds, where he opened the School of Arts and Crafts in 1904 with the aim of reviving the quality and standards of craft production and administration. Having developed an admiration for the work of Frank Lloyd Wright, he lost faith in his own theories, proclaiming in 1910 his belief that modern civilisation was dependent on machinery.

Baillie Scott, Mackay Hugh (1865–1945) English architect and designer, who also undertook important commissions abroad, in Switzerland, Poland, Russia and America. His designs were often published in *The Studio*, with ten articles appearing between 1894 and 1902. His most important building project was the palace at Darmstadt for the Grand Duke of Hesse (1898), with furniture made by Ashbee's Guild of Handicraft featuring copper, ivory and pewter on wood. A music cabinet designed for the palace is in the Victoria and Albert Museum. His work was sometimes experimental, including built-in furniture, as in rooms in the House of an Art Lover.

Baumgartner, Melchior (born 1621), son of Ulrich (see below). In 1646 he made a cabinet combining ivory with lapis lazuli inlay to represent symbolically the national colours of Bavaria (see p. 53); this cabinet, which must have been commissioned by the Bavarian court, is now in the Bayerisches Nationalmuseum, Munich. In 1655 Melchior made a cabinet incorporating silver plaques and mounts by Andreas Lotter and grotesques on panels enamelled by Johann Georg Priester; this piece, acquired by the Elector's widow, Maria-Anna, is now in the Bayerisches Nationalmuseum (see p. 53).

Baumgartner, Ulrich (1580–1652) German cabinetmaker who worked in Augsburg, where his marriage was recorded in 1611. He contributed to the execution of Philipp Hainhofer's *Schreibtisch*, the *Pommersche Kunstschrank* (completed 1617), the *Stipo d'Alemagna* (1628) and the cabinet made for the Duke of Braunschweig-Lüneburg (1647), as well as the 'eighth wonder of the world', the *Kunstschrank* presented to King Gustavus Adolphus of Sweden by the City of Augsburg in 1632. His work was wrongly attributed to his son Melchior in Paul von Stetten's *Kunst-, Gewerb- und Handwerksgeschichte der Reichs-Stadt Augsburg* (history of the arts and crafts in Augsbur), published in 1779.

Bérain, Jean (I; 1637–1711) French architect, draughtsman and decorator. Born in Lorraine, he was the son of a gunsmith; the family moved to Paris *c.* 1644. His first published designs were for gun-stocks (1659) and locks (1662–3). His experience in metalwork would have introduced him to the Islamic arabesque used in damascened work; this he combined with light-hearted grotesques and *singeries* (monkey designs) which brought a fanciful whimsical note to much furniture in the Louis XIV style and heralded the Régence and Rococo styles. In 1674 he was appointed *Dessinateur de la Chambre et du Cabinet du Roy*, with lodgings in the Louvre. His light, elegant form of

decoration, characterized by gracefully elongated classical figures under airy canopies and lambrequins, with fantastic birds and figures and monkeys dressed in the *commedia dell'arte* fashion, was particularly important in late Boulle style as well as faïence and tapestry designs. His engraved designs were published in *Oeuvre de Jean Bérain, recueillie par les soins du sieur Thuret* (1711). After his death his son Jean Bérain II (1678–1726) continued in the service of the Court, working in the same style.

Boulle, André-Charles (1642–1732) The first great French *ébéniste*; at first he entered the Académie de Saint-Luc as a painter and by 1664 was established as a *marqueteur* (marquetry maker) as well as a painter. When Bernini visited Paris in 1665, he befriended Boulle and advised him on his designs. In 1672 he was appointed *Ebéniste du Roy*, but was also referred to as a painter, architect, mosaicist and bronzeworker. In the same year he was granted the Louvre lodging previously occupied by Jean Macé, having been described by Colbert as 'the most skilful [furniture maker] in Paris'. In 1681–3 he decorated the Grand Cabinet at Versailles (since destroyed) for the Dauphin. He worked for aristocrats and foreign princes as well as for the King; the Dukes of Orléans, Bourbon and Condé were all his clients, as were the financier Crozat, the King of Spain and the Elector of Bavaria.

Some twenty assistants were employed in his workshop and his fame was widespread. He was the only cabinetmaker to be mentioned in the *Abecedario Pittorico* published in 1719 by Orlandi in Florence; in that work his biography included a description of his art collection, which included a large number of contemporary and old master prints and drawings (Raphael's depictions of Ovid's *Metamorphoses*, a sketchbook from Rubens's Italian travels, prints by Callot and himself) and paintings by Correggio, Lebrun, Mignard and Berchem. All these were lost, together with many pieces of furniture, in the fire which destroyed his workshop-studio on 19 August 1720. Although he had retired in 1718, he returned to work following this disaster, estimating his losses at 383,780 livres. He continued to direct the workshop until his death, working with his two sons André-Charles (d. 1745) and Charles-Joseph (d. 1754), who from 1751 trained the German apprentice Oeben, who in turn became the master of Riesener.

Although Boulle's biography described his work in floral and pictorial marquetry using precious exotic woods, his fame rests chiefly on his brass and tortoiseshell marquetry. Metal had been used in inlay in Italy and South Germany since the sixteenth century. Now brass (or sometimes pewter) was glued with the tortoiseshell and an arabesque pattern cut out. The method known as Boulle work – *Première Partie* and *Contrepartie* (see glossary) – was ideally suited to the Baroque idea of symmetry and the design of pendant pairs, such as the commodes made in 1708–9 for the King's Bedchamber in the Grand Trianon – the only work by Boulle documented with any certainty. Other works attributed to him are in the Louvre, the Wallace Collection, the Metropolitan Museum and the Hermitage, as well as the J. Paul Getty Museum and private collections, including that of the Duke of Buccleuch.

Burges, William (1827–81) English architect and designer. He undertook major works for the Marquess of Bute at Cardiff Castle in 1865 and at Castle Coch in 1875, both involving vast rebuilding and decorating programmes, and afterwards at his own house in London, 9 Melbury Road (1875–81). His forms were inspired by Pugin's archaeological accuracy, but the decorative fantasy of the painted surface imparted a feeling of great richness which was at odds with the restrained decoration typical of Pugin's furniture. The Bayeux Cabinet in the Victoria and Albert Museum, with scenes painted by E. J. Poynter in 1858, demonstrates this sense of fantasy as well as a literary tendency, while the construction reflects his interest in thirteenth-century architecture. He also designed wallpapers and ornate revivalist silverware. Examples of his work are preserved in Cardiff Castle, the Victoria and Albert Museum and in private collections.

Carlin, Martin (d. 1785) German cabinetmaker who worked in Paris in 1759 in Oeben's workshop. His early work was much influenced by the pictorial marquetry of Oeben (q.v.), to whom he was related by marriage, through his wife Françoise-Marguerite Vandercruse (sister of Oeben's brother-in-law, Roger Vandercruse, called Lacroix). Like Lacroix, Carlin worked mostly for *marchand-merciers*, particularly Poirier and Daguerre, after becoming a master in 1766. His royal commissions for work for the Comte and Comtesse de Provence would have come through the intermediary of the dealers. He specialized in small, 'feminine' furniture types such as the *secrétaire à abattant* and the *bonheur du jour*; such pieces often incorporated Sèvres porcelain plaques and were adorned with characteristic gilt-bronze swags and tassels of exquisite craftsmanship and detailing. He used the maker's stamp of 'M. CARLIN'. Examples of his work are in the Louvre, the Wallace Collection, the Jones Collection (Victoria and Albert Museum), the Rothschild Collection (Waddesdon Manor) and the Metropolitan Museum and the Frick Collection in New York.

Castrucci One of the most important families of Italian craftsmen working in *commesso di pietre dure*, originating from Florence.

Cosimo Castrucci is first recorded in a document dated 1596 as an *intagliatore* working in Prague. A landscape panel in *pietra dura* in the Kunsthistorisches Museum, Vienna, is signed and dated 'Castrucij Flor[en]tino Fecit Anno 1576'. Its style is characteristic of the Prague workshop, featuring a perspective landscape composition. His son Giovanni di Cosimo is mentioned in Prague in 1598, his grandson Cosimo di Giovanni in 1622 (already active since 1615), and the son-in-law of Giovanni di Cosimo, Giuliano di Piero Pandolfini, in 1622.

Cosimo and his son seem to have collaborated on a *pietra dura* landscape panel commissioned for the altar of the Medici Chapel in 1609; based on a design by the Florentine Bernardino Poccetti, the panel was made in Prague and delivered to Florence in 1622.

Chippendale, Thomas (1718–79) English cabinetmaker and furniture designer. Born in Yorkshire, he came to London in 1748; his business was based at 60 St Martin's Lane from 1753.

He was in partnership first with James Rannie until the latter's death in 1766, then with Thomas Haig who continued to run the business with Chippendale's son, Thomas (1749–1822), after 1779. In 1754 he published *The Gentleman & Cabinet-maker's Director, being a collection of the most Elegant and Useful Designs of Household Furniture in the most Fashionable Taste* (2nd edition 1755; 3rd edition 1762).

Although furniture designs had been published since the sixteenth century, the large number – 160 in the first two editions, 200 in the third – made the *Director* exceptional in terms of its scope and variety. The style is mainly Rococo, with *chinoiserie* and Gothick elements. Chippendale is better known for his *Director* than his own work. His late furniture in the Neo-classical style was

made for houses built or decorated by Robert Adam, notably Harewood House and Nostell Priory, c. 1765–70. None of Chippendale's furniture was stamped and it is difficult to distinguish his own work from that of his contemporaries who availed themselves of his designs. The description 'Chippendale' is therefore applied generically to furniture in the English Rococo style dating from the 1750s and 1760s.

Cucci, Domenico (1635–1704) Italian cabinetmaker and sculptor, born at Todi in the Papal States. He arrived in Paris in 1660 and was naturalized in 1664; he worked at the Gobelins and became head of the cabinetmaking workshop. He is recorded in the *Comptes des Bâtiments* as having been paid 30,500 livres in 1667 for the two cabinets called *Les Temples de la Gloire et de la Vertu*. He was fully employed by the Gobelins, where he was head of the cabinetmaking workshop until 1683, when work declined. His work featured a rich, opulent Baroque style relying on sculptural effects and *pietra dura* decoration contrasting with ebony.

His most famous surviving pieces are the pair of cabinets made in 1681–3 for Versailles (now in the collection of the Duke of Northumberland at Alnwick Castle); see p. 92. A cabinet attributed to Cucci, made c. 1680–90 and called *La Toilette de Mme Maintenon*, is in the Strasbourg Museum; see p. 88. Much of his work was broken up during the eighteenth century and re-used by later *ébénistes*. However, *Le Journal du Garde-Meuble* (started in 1663 by Colbert), in which all the Crown Furniture was recorded, also mentioned the *Cabinet de la Paix* in ebony, *pietra dura* and gilt bronze, with the French royal arms held by two putti at the top, and a seated figure of the Sun King holding a shield with an allegorical figure of Peace above. This may be the cabinet shown on the tapestry *La Visite de Louis XIV aux Gobelins* (Louis XIV's visit to the Gobelins) from the set called *L'Histoire du Roy* woven c. 1671–6 (see p. 90). See chapter 2, note 24.

Cucci was mentioned in 1693 by the Swedish Minister in Paris, Daniel Cronstrom, as having worked almost exclusively for Versailles and having made ironwork and door furniture for the Palace. He was also credited with carving cases for musical instruments and modelling the bronze decorations on the King's Jewel Casket. His interior decoration work included the *Petite Galerie* at Versailles (using tortoiseshell, gilt bronze and lapis lazuli), and the marquetry floor designed by Lebrun for the Château de St Germain.

Cuvilliés, François (1695–1768) Flemish architect and designer who worked at the court of the Elector Max Emanuael of Bavaria in Munich, where he started as Court Dwarf. After studying architecture in Paris with Blondel, 1720–4, he was appointed Court Architect in Munich in 1725, and worked on the Residenz there and on the Amalienburg at Nymphenburg, near Munich. From 1738 to 1768 he published engraved Rococo designs in a lighter, more fanciful and fantastic vein than those of his French counterparts. He influenced the development of Rococo forms in cabinetmaking in Germany, as well as in architecture and interior decoration.

Dagly, Gerhard (c. 1665–1714) Belgian lacquer worker who was active mostly in Germany. He was born in Spa, a town renowned as one of the most important japanning centres in Europe. In 1687 he was appointed *Kammerkünstler* to the Elector Frederick William II of Brandenburg in Berlin; in 1689 his appointment was renewed and he became *Kunstkammer Meister*, executing four lacquer cabinets, which are shown in an engraving of the Cabinet of Curiosities dating from 1696. In

that year he became *Directeur des Ornements* in charge of all the royal decorative schemes. In 1701 King Frederick I of Prussia granted him a retainer of 1,000 écus a year, together with lodging and keep. He remained in Berlin until 1713, when he was dismissed.

He decorated panels as well as furniture, and is thought to have helped Andreas Schlüter execute the *Porzellanzimmer* at Schloss Oranienburg. In addition to black, his range of colours included gold, red, green and blue on a creamy white ground imitating porcelain. In 1694 Christoph Pitzler recorded some blue-and-white japanned cabinets by him in Schloss Oranienburg. His output was very large and although no signed pieces exist, several cabinets have been attributed to him, for example in museums in Berlin, Kassel and Brunswick.

After the closure of Gerhard's workshop in 1713, his brother Jacques went to work for the Manufacture des Gobelins, which had been producing '*ouvrages de la Chine*' since 1672. De Luynes recorded in his memoirs that Dagly was appointed Directeur des Ouvrages de la Chine, being granted, on 26 November 1713, together with Pierre de Neufmaison and Claude Audran III, a twenty-year monopoly for work in *vernis des Gobelins*. Dagly contributed greatly to the revival of *lachinage* in Paris in the 1720s.

Gerhard Dagly's most famous pupil was Martin Schnell (q.v.).

Danhauser, Josef (1780–1829) Austrian furnituremaker, who trained as a designer, sculptor and gilder at the Vienna Academy of Fine Arts.

He opened a furniture factory in Vienna in 1804, and in 1807 he was granted a licence for the manufacture of 'gilt, silvered and bronzed sculpted products'. In 1814 he was given a franchise for the 'manufacture of all manner of furniture'. In 1825 he bought the Koidy Palace in the suburb of Wieden, and used the basement and ground floor as a workshop. His clientele included the Archduke Karl and Duke Albert von Sachsen-Teschen, but consisted mostly of middle-class customers seeking furniture in the Biedermeier style, of which Danhauser was one of the main creators. After his death his son Josef (1805–45) continued to run the factory until 1839, when the firm was wound up.

Du Cerceau, Jacques Androuet (c. 1520–1584) French-architect and designer. After visiting Rome in the 1540s, he returned to France and in 1549 his book *Arcs* was published in Orléans. In 1550 he published *Les Petits Grotesques*, which was re-issued in 1572 with some furniture designs; this work included designs for cabinets in an architectural style heavily carved with strapwork and Italianate Mannerist motifs. His *Livre contenant Cinquante Bâtiments* was published in Paris in 1559, and his book entitled *Plus Excellents Bastiments de France* appeared in 1576 and 1579.

Eastlake, Charles Lock (1836–1906) English architect and theorist. He published a *History of the Gothic Revival* in 1872, but his influence on nineteenth-century furniture design came through his first book, *Hints on Household Taste in Furniture, Upholstery and other Details* (1868), in which he promoted 'a sense of the picturesque with modern comfort and convenience', aiming to emulate the 'spirit and principles of early manufacture', i.e. the honesty, integrity and truth to material and function of medieval craftsmen. This book was published in America in 1872, and gained such popularity there that his name became synonymous with 'improved taste' in furnishings, which were described as being 'Eastlaked'. He expressed the belief that 'The best and most picturesque furniture of all ages has been simple in general form. It may have been enriched by complex details of carved work or inlay, but its main outline was always chaste and sober, in design, never running into extravagant contour or unnecessary curves.' These opinions had a considerable influence on American furniture design, but the results did not always measure up to his standards of craftsmanship and design.

Eck A family of German woodworkers. Peter Eck (1538–1604) was born in Nuremberg, and became a citizen of Eger in Bohemia in 1558. He was recorded as 'City carpenter', but was also a sculptor who worked for a short while in the characteristic Eger medium of relief *intarsia*. His son Erhard was a well-known carpenter who in 1629 had to flee from Eger because of his Protestant beliefs; no record exists of his work in relief *intarsia*. Erhard's successors continued the family tradition. His son, Peter the Younger, became a *Kunsttischler* and was described as an accomplished sculptor 'who could carve in stone as well as wood'.

Adam Eck (1603–64) is better documented. He was described as a *Kunsttischler* and *Schreiner*, and worked in relief *intarsia*; complaints were made about his non-membership of the Sculptors' Guild while he was practising the trade. He worked for several princes and aristocratic patrons and made a *Schreibtisch* offered by the town to the mayor in 1641. Between 1640 and 1645 he also made presentation pieces as gifts from the town to kings and princes. Some of his works are in Frankfurt, Berlin and Vienna. His style of carving was dramatic and lively, his subjects being based on engravings by Virgil Solis and Jacob de Gheyn.

Embriachi, **Baldassare degli** (active *c*. 1400) The leading member of a group of north Italian carvers from the Veneto who specialized in bone and ivory carving, giving their name to the technique of wood, bone and ivory inlay also known as *alla certosina*.

Flötner, Peter (*c*. 1485–1546) German ornamental designer, sculptor and carver. He travelled to Italy and his presence in Nuremberg was recorded from 1522 onwards. His woodcuts of furniture designs and ornament for metalwork, featuring classical architecture, grotesques, arabesques, putti etc., were among the first to show Italian Renaissance influence. One of his designs dated 1541 is in the Germanisches Nationalmuseum, Nuremberg.

Forchondt One of the most important trading families in Antwerp. In 1600 Melchior Forchondt arrived in Antwerp from Frankenstein in Silesia (part of the Habsburg domains). He opened a shop in the Valkstraat and in 1632 joined the Guild of St Luke as a cabinetmaker. His wife and children helped in the running of the business and from 1636 his sons Guillermo and Melchior were handling the cabinet trade, which was the main aspect of their art dealing and trading.

The firm's success seems to have depended on a large number of international business contacts: in Lisbon they had commercial links with the Antwerp-born merchants Boussemart, van Immerseel and others, and they had dealings with J. Valdor in Paris, Rüdesheim in Frankfurt, and Cornelis Cockx in Amsterdam.

Eventually the four sons established themselves abroad, with shops in Vienna, Lisbon and Cadiz. Their entrepreneurial and commercial flair greatly benefited the trade in Antwerp cabinets all over Europe.

Fornasetti, Piero (1913–88) Italian designer who lived and worked in Milan. He was a prolific draughtsman whose designs first appeared in the 1930s, and was also an artist, illustrator, printer,

craftsman and manufacturer, with a very shrewd business sense. During the 1950s he achieved considerable international commercial success, his wares being sold by Liberty's in London and by other major retailers worldwide.

In whatever medium he worked he concentrated on surface decoration depicting an imaginary world, viewed through the intellect and subconscious emotions. His ideas were greatly influenced by the Surrealist movement. Undecorated furniture produced by Gio Ponti was transformed by the application of his visionary fantastic designs. On several occasions he decorated the traditional form of bureau-cabinet, adding a *trompe-l'œil* malachite finish or covering the surface with enlarged details of architectural prints, thus creating a play on space and reality while linking the design to the traditional architectural emphasis typical of Italy.

The originality and playful fantasy of his work, as well as his use of painted finishes, influenced many modern designers.

Gallé, Emile (1846–1904) French glassmaker and cabinetmaker, born in Nancy (Lorraine). He served his apprenticeship in his father's ceramics and glassmaking workshops, as well as at the Meisenthal glassworks (1866–7), and travelled extensively visiting Weimar, where he studied mineralogy, England (1871) and Italy (1877). In 1874 he took charge of the family workshop and in 1878 exhibited ceramic wares at the Exposition Universelle in Paris. His early glass showed in particular the influence of Venice and Islamic enamelled ware. In 1884 he developed a more personal style in his *verreries parlantes* decorated with motifs from nature and inscribed with verses from French Symbolist poems.

In 1886 he was running a cabinetmaking workshop in Nancy, where he produced inlay and marquetry work, known as *meubles parlants*, similar in spirit to that of his *verreries parlantes*. He kept a special garden for growing plants used as the basis for his work in Art Nouveau style, nature being an endless source of inspiration. He was at heart a traditional craftsman with an honesty and integrity to medium and function, qualities which marked him out as one of the leading figures of Art Nouveau. His respect for materials was evident in his records itemizing over 600 different veneers for use in inlays to create varying effects.

By 1900 he was employing over 300 craftsmen who worked in the traditional manner, fulfilling commissions from wealthy patrons, as well as producing more commercial lines. In Nancy he gathered around him a group of leading craftsmen, including Majorelle (q.v.), Auguste Daum and others, who exhibited with great success at the 1900 Paris Exposition Universelle. In 1901 he founded the Alliance Provinciale des Industries d'Art, called the Ecole de Nancy, which continued until his death. The firm remained in business until 1914.

Examples of his work can be seen in many museums, including the Musée des Arts Décoratifs, Paris, the Musée de l'Ecole de Nancy, the Victoria and Albert Museum, London, and the Brighton Museum, Sussex.

Giuliano da Maiano (1432–90) Italian wood carver, older brother of Benedetto (1442–97). He carved the cupboards in the New Sacristy in Florence Cathedral 1463–5 and later worked mostly as an architect, being appointed to Florence Cathedral in 1477.

Goddard, John (1723–85) American cabinetmaker, born at Dartmouth, Mass. He was active during the 1740s in Newport, Rhode Island, where he was apprenticed to the leading furniture maker Job Townsend, whose daughter Hannah he

married on 6 August 1746. Some of his furniture bears a label, e.g. the one on a bureau-cabinet (private collection), exhibited at the Nichols-Wanton-Hunter House in Newport in 1953, which reads 'Made by John Goddard / 1761 & repeard by Thomas Goddard 1813'.

In addition to his shop in Newport, John Goddard seems to have had a business in Providence, R.I., where in 1782 he placed an advertisement in the local newspaper referring to 'Goddard & Engs, Cabinetmakers from Newport'. He is credited, together with the Townsend workshop, with the introduction of the 'block-front', cut in such a way as to create a central depressed surface between two raised ones, sometimes cut from a single piece of solid wood, sometimes using separate elements glued together. Shell motifs, either carved in shallow relief or applied, were a characteristic feature of his work. After his death his sons Stephen and Thomas carried on the business, which closed in 1804.

Examples of his work can be found in the Metropolitan Museum, New York, the Du Pont Museum, Winterthur, Delaware, and the Rhode Island School of Design, Providence.

Godwin, Edward William (1833–86) English architect and designer whose early work was in Gothic Revival style, though less emphatically than that of his friend William Burges (q.v.).

He first discovered Japanese art at the London International Exhibition of 1862, using its sense of asymmetrical design, the bold simplicity of composition and the balance of solid and void. At the same time he developed the 'Queen Anne Revival' in interior decoration, characterized by sparse furnishing and respect for plain wooden surfaces. In 1867 he started using these elements in his own designs for furniture, as well as for wallpaper, textiles and other objects. He was one of the leaders of the Aesthetic Movement, designing the White House for Whistler in Chelsea in 1877–8. He helped Whistler design the 'Butterfly Suite' of furniture which was shown at the Paris Exposition of 1878, and his designs, published in *Art Furniture*, were very influential.

He was in no way concerned with the aims and ideas of William Morris and the Arts and Crafts Movement, using machine-cut sections, usually square, of his favoured kind of wood. The originality of his 'Anglo-Japanese' style lies in the light airiness of the forms, combined with a sense of balance achieved by 'the mere grouping of solid and void and by more or less broken outline'. Examples of his work can be seen at the Victoria and Albert Museum.

Gole, Pierre (1620–*c*. 1690) Dutch cabinetmaker born at Bergen, north-west of Amsterdam. In 1643 he came to Paris to be apprenticed to the *ébéniste* Adriaan Gardrand, whose eldest daughter he married in 1645. In 1646 he was recorded as making a pendant to an ebony cabinet belonging to Macé Bertrand de la Bazinière. He became *Menuisier en Ebeyne* to Louis XIV (still a minor) in 1651, as well as working for Cardinal Mazarin, the inventory of whose effects following his death in 1661 listed 'Two tortoiseshell cabinets decorated with marquetry, flowers, birds and insects, under the name of Pierre Gole.'

In the same year he made for the King's brother, Philippe d'Orléans, an ivory and floral marquetry cabinet for his *Cabinet Blanc* (White Closet) at the Palais-Royal; this piece is now in the Victoria and Albert Museum (see p. 86). Although Gole's work is characterized by the skilful use of marquetry, usually floral, combined with tortoiseshell, ebony and gilt-bronze mounts, he also produced furniture 'varnished in the Chinese manner', such as the pyramidal cabinet made in 1667 for Louis XIV, as well as japanned pieces in blue and white to match the colour-scheme of the *Trianon de Porcelaine* built by Louis XIV in the Versailles park for his mistress and later morganatic wife, Mme de Montespan.

Gole worked at the Gobelins and also ran his own workshop in the Rue de l'Arbre Sec, near the Louvre. Examples of his work are in the Victoria and Albert Museum, the J. Paul Getty Museum, the Dallas Museum, the Metropolitan Museum, New York, and in many private collections.

Grendey, Giles (1673–1780) English cabinet-maker. Born in Gloucestershire, he was apprenticed in London in 1709. He became a Liveryman of the Joiners' Company in 1729 and was elected its Master in 1766. A label on the underside of a chair gives the address of Grendey's premises as 'in St John's Square, Clerkenwell', stating that he 'makes and sells all sorts of cabinet goods, chairs and glasses'. His name appeared in the *London Directory* of 1753.

He maintained an important export business and the Duke of Infantado had a set of furniture at the castle of Lazcano in Spain; the pieces decorated with red japanning, included six armchairs and twenty chairs, together with a day-bed with gold and silver detailing on a red ground, now in the Victoria and Albert Museum. He also produced high-quality mahogany furniture. It was recorded that £1,000 worth of furniture 'packed for exportation' was lost in a fire at his Clerkenwell premises in 1731. His japanned furniture included a number of bureau-cabinets, often in brilliant colours. Some of his works bear a label. He retired in 1779.

Gropius, Walter (1883–1969) German architect and designer. He trained in Berlin 1907–10 under Peter Behrens, the founder of the Vereinigte Werkstätten in Munich, who was influenced by the ideas and precepts of William Morris. In 1910 Gropius established his own practice and in 1911 he built (in collaboration with Adolf Meyer) the Fagus Factory at Alfeld, an early example of the International Modern Style, inspired not only by the teaching of Behrens, but also by the writings of Frank Lloyd Wright, whose works had been published in Berlin in 1910 and 1911. In 1914 Gropius and Meyer jointly designed for the Deutscher Werkbund Exhibition in Cologne a Model Factory and Office Building. On the strength of this bold design the director of the Weimar Art School and School of Arts and Crafts, Henry van de Velde, advised the Grand Duke of Hesse to appoint Gropius as his successor.

He took up his post after World War I and renamed the combined schools Das Staatliche Bauhaus Weimar, his aim being 'to co-ordinate all creative effort, to achieve in a new architecture the unification of all training in art and design in which no barrier exists between the structural and the decorative arts'. Gropius believed that, in the tradition of medieval practice, all building should be the result of teamwork, with all the arts and crafts being combined to create a harmonious unity. The *Vorkurs* (Basic Course) aimed to train craftsmen and artists in form, colour and nature of materials, echoing the ideas of William Morris concerning integrity of form and function and those of the Arts and Crafts Movement.

Gropius did not reject the use of machines but believed that the difference between industrial products and handicrafts was due to the lack of control by a single individual and to the subdivision of labour which prevented an individual approach. In fact he emphasized the virtues of co-operative work, a principal aim of the Bauhaus being to design prototypes of everyday objects suitable for mass-production.

The Bauhaus moved to Dessau in 1925. Gropius resigned in 1928 and, after fleeing from Germany,

worked in London 1934–7, before going to the U.S.A. to teach. He also started a group practice known as 'The Architects' Collaborative'.

Hainhofer, Philipp (1578–1647) German diplomat, collector and art-dealer. Born in Augsburg, he travelled extensively in Germany and elsewhere in Europe, including the Netherlands and Italy, where at the age of sixteen he began studying law at Padua. He became a member of the City Council in 1605.

His training as a lawyer and diplomat, together with his artistic and humanist interests, made him a valued expert adviser, in matters of politics as well as art, to Henry IV of France as well as to several German princes. In the course of his diplomatic missions he acquired many works of art and other objects from the artists' studios and workshops he visited. By 1606 he had already assembled a *Kunstkammer* of considerable importance, and he received a visit from William V, Duke of Bavaria, who became a client. In 1611 Maximilian I of Bavaria commissioned a *Schreibtisch* for his wife at a cost of 200 Talers.

Other important commissions included one in 1615 for a dining table (with extension leaf) to seat up to eight people, a chest to store eight chairs, and other pieces. Prior to this Duke Philip II of Pomerania had ordered in 1610 a simple small *Schreibtisch*; this commission led to a lengthy exchange of correspondence and ideas between the Duke and Hainhofer. The so-called *Pommersche Kunstschrank*, which was finally delivered in 1617, was a work of art in its own right, being a miniature *Kunst- und Wunderkammer* encapsulating the knowledge of the time. Other similar projects followed: the *Stipo d'Alemagna* (see p. 52) and the cabinet presented by the City of Augsburg to King Gustavus Adolphus of Sweden in 1632 (now at Uppsala University). Contemporary biographies of Hainhofer mentioned another such *Schreibtisch* sold in 1647 to the young Duke of Braunschweig-Lüneburg. These cabinets represented the climax of the Renaissance Mannerist tradition at Augsburg and other major furniture-making centres.

Haupt, Georg (1741–84) Swedish cabinetmaker, born in Stockholm; his father was a carpenter from Nuremberg. He served his apprenticeship in Germany, being recorded there *c.* 1763, and travelled to Holland and Paris, perhaps being employed in the workshop of Jean-François Oeben (q.v.).

In 1767 he made the bureau in the Institut Géographique, Paris, which he signed. He visited London, working for William Chambers in 1769, before returning to Stockholm where, in 1770, he made a bureau for King Gustav III in Louis XVI style. In 1773–4 he made a collector's cabinet to house mineralogical specimens; this magnificent marquetry cabinet, given by Gustav III to the Prince de Condé, is now in the Musée Condé, Chantilly. Another mineralogical cabinet is in the Kuntshistorisches Museum, Vienna; this piece combines a cabinet, which was probably made for Hainhofer, with a Neo-classical structure in marquetry, and is stamped '*Fait par George Haupt, Ebéniste du Roi à Stockholm l'an 1776*'.

Hepplewhite, George (d. 1786) English cabinet-maker and designer who trained with the leading furniture-making firm of Gillows in Lancaster. He came to London *c.* 1760, but no workshop or furniture associated with him is known. His fame rests on the posthumous publication of his designs in 1788 in *The Cabinetmaker and Upholsterer's Guide* (revised in 1789 and 1794), which illustrated the Neo-classical style of the early 1780s. The three hundred designs were widely used by country cabinetmakers and most of the pieces executed were of provincial origin, made at a time

when the style itself had already gone out of fashion in London. The simple, but refined and elegant pieces were often made of satinwood inlaid with other exotic woods.

Hoffmann, Josef (1870–1956) Austrian architect and designer who studied under Otto Wagner at the Vienna Academy from 1892. In 1897 he became an important force in the establishment of the Vienna Secession, organizing its early exhibitions, where fine and decorative arts would be united in a harmonious whole. In 1899 he became Professor at the Kunstgewerbeschule (School of Arts and Crafts) in Vienna, where the work of designers and theorists such as Ruskin and Morris received particular attention. The respect and admiration felt for the work of Charles Rennie Mackintosh and C. R. Ashbee's Guild of Handicraft led to the creation of the Wiener Werkstätte in 1903. The Guild's system was used to react against inferior industrial products by bringing to the attention of the public well-designed, simple artefacts for everyday use, preserving integrity of function and design and thereby maintaining standards of quality in both conception and execution.

Two major projects realized by the Wiener Werkstätte were the Sanatorium Purkersdorf (1904–5), and the manifesto of all its ideals, the Palais Stoclet in Brussels (1905–24), in which architecture, interior decoration, furnishing and fine art were combined in a harmonious whole.

Jacob, Georges (1739–1814) French *menuisier* who in the early nineteenth century became the first *ébéniste* to manufacture furniture on an industrial scale. Born in Burgundy, he was apprenticed in Paris to Louis Delanois, a master *menuisier* working in the Louis XV style. He became a master in 1765 and by the 1780s was among the most important *menuisiers* in Paris. He made an original contribution to the development of chair design in the Louis XVI style: a more rectilinear outline with exquisitely carved classical and floral motifs. He also promoted the use of the square section with a rosette at the top of the tapering fluted leg, which became a characteristic of the Louis XVI period. Later, under the influence of English furniture and Chippendale designs, he used solid mahogany for chairs with pierced backs and sabre-back legs.

He produced some furniture for English clients (through the *marchand-mercier* Daguerre), including pieces for the Prince of Wales at Carlton House, London, and for the Duke of Bedford at Woburn Abbey. His court patronage included Marie-Antoinette, the Comte d'Artois and the Duc de Chartres, and his late work for the Queen's dairy at Rambouillet – a set of chairs in solid mahogany – was based on designs in the 'Etruscan style' by the painter Hubert Robert. The archaeological element is much in evidence in the use of the antique X-frame form of the legs and of palmettes and anthemion as decorative motifs. These characteristics were even more pronounced in the *méridiennes* (day beds) and chairs which he made in 1788 under the guidance of the Neo-classical painter David, whose designs imitated the spindly form of bronze furniture recently excavated at Pompeii and Herculaneum. David's portrait of *Madame Récamier* in the Louvre illustrates the sort of elegant furniture *à la grecque* (in the Greek manner) made by Jacob.

Unlike many other *ébénistes* who had been active under the Ancien Régime, Jacob was fortunate to see his business survive the Revolution, largely thanks to the protection of David, who had taken an active political role in the overthrow of the King and voted for his execution. In 1791 David introduced Jacob to Percier and Fontaine (qq.v.), who provided his firm with furniture designs to be executed for the Convention Nationale, and later for the Conseil des Cinq Cents (1798). Meanwhile, Georges Jacob retired in 1796, leaving the running of the business to his sons Georges and François-Honoré-Georges (later called Jacob-Desmalter), who went into partnership as Jacob Frères. In 1800 Georges Jacob *père* returned to work on the furnishing of the Tuileries apartments for Bonaparte, entering into partnership with François-Honoré-Georges as Jacob-Desmalter & Cie after the death of his son Georges in 1803. Working to the highest standards, they produced furniture in the Empire style (based on designs by Percier and Fontaine) for Malmaison – still *in situ* – and all the palaces occupied by Napoleon and his relatives.

After his father's death, François-Honoré-Georges Jacob-Desmalter (1770–1841) continued producing furniture in the Empire style, but the workshop now operated on an industrial scale. In 1825 his son Georges-Alphonse (1799–1870) took over the business, which he ran until 1847.

Works by Jacob the *menuisier* are in the Louvre, the Wallace Collection, London, the Metropolitan Museum, New York, and in private collections. Examples of furniture by Jacob-Desmalter are best represented by those at Malmaison, the *serre-bijoux* in the Louvre (see pl. 104), as well as others in various Napoleonic palaces and the Metropolitan Museum.

Jamnitzer, Wenzel (1508–85) German goldsmith and silversmith, born in Vienna. He was recorded as being in Nuremberg in 1534, when he became a *Bürger* of the city and a Master of the Goldsmiths' Guild. Appointed coin and seal-die cutter to the city corporation in 1543, he became master of the city mint in 1552. He was acknowledged as the leading Nuremberg goldsmith and sat on the city council. He was appointed *kaiserlicher Hofgoldschmied* (Imperial Court Goldsmith), serving four Habsburg Emperors.

His work was Mannerist in style, displaying great skill in cast, embossed, engraved and enamelled work depicting insects and reptiles in a very realistic manner; examples in silver include a box in Vienna and a basin in the Louvre. A casket in Munich is decorated with cameos and arabesques, as well as silver-gilt herms.

Jensen, Gerrit (fl. *c.* 1680–1715) Flemish-born cabinetmaker to the English Court who served under four sovereigns, from Charles II to Queen Anne. His influence was very important in the development of the Anglo-Dutch style during the reign of William and Mary. His first recorded bill submitted to the Royal Household is dated 1680, and relates to furniture delivered to Charles II as a gift for the Emperor of Morocco. In 1689 he was granted a patent as 'Cabinetmaker in Ordinary' and he held the monopoly as supplier of overmantel and pier glass. From 1688 to 1698 he was recorded as working for the Duke of Devonshire at Chatsworth, where he was responsible for 'the glass for the door of the Great Chamber and for Japanning the Closet' with 'hollow burnt Japan' (incised lacquer). From 1693 to 1715 he had premises in St Martin's Lane, London.

The furniture he produced for the Crown consisted mostly of japanned and marquetry pieces. He was the only cabinetmaker in England to use metal inlay in the manner of Boulle. His style was French, probably inspired by Daniel Marot, the brother-in-law of Pierre Gole, with whom Jensen had dealings. Several pieces by him are in the Royal Collection at Windsor Castle; others attributed to him are at Drayton House, near Kettering, Northamptonshire.

Lebrun, Charles (1619–90) French painter and designer, who trained with the painter Simon Vouet. In 1642 he went to Rome and, together with Nicolas Poussin, studied the work of Roman Baroque decorators and masters such as Pietro da Cortona. In 1647 he returned to Paris, where he soon established himself as a painter, participating in 1648 in the foundation of the Académie Royale, of which he became Director.

In 1658 Fouquet commissioned him to supervise the interior decoration of his new château, Vaux-le-Vicomte, and he was appointed director of the nearby Maincy tapestry workshop. After Fouquet's fall the workshop was closed by Colbert in 1662, and Lebrun was appointed the first director of the Manufacture Royale des Meubles de la Couronne in 1663, when the Flemish tapestry workers from Maincy were transferred to premises in Paris previously owned by the brothers Gobelins. The Manufacture des Gobelins provided all the furnishings and furniture for the royal palaces, and Lebrun was in charge of the various craftsmen – silversmiths, goldsmiths, *ébénistes*, bronze-workers etc. – for whom he produced designs. His influence as *Premier Peintre du Roy* and *Directeur des Bâtiments* (Surveyor of Buildings) was all-pervading in the fine and decorative arts, and he was the single most important artist in the creation of the grand opulent, classicizing Louis XIV style. He retained his influential role until the death of Colbert, his protector, in 1683, by when the production of the Gobelins was declining. The workshop closed in 1694 because of financial difficulties, reopening in 1699 only for the weaving of tapestries.

Liberty, Sir Arthur Lasenby (1843–1917) English retailer. He began his career as an assistant to the firm of Farmer & Rogers in Regent Street, London. After visiting Japan he became manager of the firm's Oriental department in 1862, a post he held until 1874 when the business closed. In 1875 he opened his own shop in Regent Street, 'East India House', dealing in furniture, fabrics and household ornaments in Moorish, Japanese and various European historical styles, eventually selling the work of members of the Arts and Crafts Movement. In 1889 he opened a shop in Paris, which helped to disseminate the English Art Nouveau style across the Continent and gave rise to the Italian term for Art Nouveau, 'Stile Liberty'.

In 1894 he started producing silverware in Celtic style, as well as furniture with lean, tapering lines, which he called 'Cymric', and in 1903 he introduced pewterware, known as 'Tudric', using an alloy containing some silver. His fabrics, furniture and other wares were intended to be 'useful and beautiful objects at prices within the reach of all classes'.

Linke, François (1855–1946) Austrian cabinetmaker who worked in Paris; in 1882 his address was 170 Faubourg St Antoine. His early works consisted mostly of copies of important royal furniture of the eighteenth century, a period in which he would have preferred to have lived, since he regretted the passing of wealthy private patronage. The practice of copying eighteenth-century pieces was well established in the Second Empire (1858–70), when the Empress Eugénie de Montijo was besotted by memories of Marie-Antoinette and the Louis XV and Louis XVI styles, a taste shared by Ludwig II of Bavaria whose castle at Herrenchiemsee was furnished accordingly.

In *c.* 1890 Linke made the bureau which was awarded a Gold Medal at the 1900 Exposition Universelle (see pl. 133) and which was described as 'an example of what can be done by seeking inspiration amongst the classic examples of Louis XV and XVI without in any great sense copying these great works'. It certainly allied the tradition of a long line of cabinetmakers to the lively and sinuous features of Art Nouveau design as represented at the Exposition by Emile Gallé and Louis Majorelle (qq.v.), leading figures in the School of Nancy, which drew its inspiration from the forms and techniques of the previous century.

Macé, Jean French cabinetmaker, born in Blois. He seems to have been in Middelburg in Flanders in the early 1620s. His presence in Paris was recorded in 1641. On 16 May 1644 he was granted a Royal Warrant and on 25 October he was assigned the lease of Lodging No. 15 in the Galerie du Louvre, occupied until then by the widow of Laurent Stabre, the first recorded *Menuisier en Ebeyne* (Cabinetmaker to the King) in 1608. Macé's style is characterized by extensive use of ebony veneers, carved or engraved, on large cabinets-on-stand of a Flemish type. Exteriors are always very austere, emphasizing the rigidity of the architectural forms, but the two doors open to reveal a rich interior, in which variously coloured woods, ivory, tortoiseshell, gilt bronze and mirrors are often used to create a theatre or a palace, with either a sculptural group in the centre of the mirror-lined room or sets of drawers around a temple front.

Examples of Macé's work include the Endymion Cabinet in the Victoria and Albert Museum (see p. 85); the Wolsey Cabinet in the Royal Collection at Windsor Castle; and pieces in the Rijksmuseum, Amsterdam, the Bayerisches Nationalmuseum, Munich, at Fontainebleau and in the Louvre and the Musée de Cluny, the National Museum, Stockholm, the Metropolitan Museum, New York, the Walters Art Gallery, Baltimore, Md, the City Art Museum, St Louis, Mo., as well as works in private collections.

Mackintosh, Charles Rennie (1868–1928) Scottish architect and designer. Born in Glasgow, he was trained as an architect and joined the firm of John Honeyman and Keppie in 1889. In 1897 he won the competition for the Glasgow School of Art (built 1898–1909). Mackintosh, his friend J. Herbert McNair and their respective wives formed a group known as 'The Four'; together they made Glasgow an internationally known centre of design, more appreciated on the Continent than in Great Britain. Their influence on German and Austrian designers of the Wiener Werkstätte was of seminal importance. They reacted against the precepts of the Arts and Crafts Movement and William Morris, following instead the 'Anglo-Japanese' style of Godwin and Whistler.

In public and private commissions such as the Buchanan Street and other tearooms in Glasgow (1897–1910), Hill House, Helensburgh (1902–3), and the furniture designs he provided for the firm of Guthrie and Wells, he favoured sparse lines with an aesthetic use of solid and void in the Japanese manner and flat painted stylized flower patterns inspired by both Japan and the Celtic tradition. He aimed to create a poetic atmosphere of a feminine quality remote from the solid austerity of the Arts and Crafts Movement and the sensuousness of Art Nouveau. In 1914 he came to London, where he designed furniture and fabrics until 1920. His work was exhibited abroad in Venice (1899), Vienna (1900), where it had an influence on the Secession, and Turin (1902). Important examples of his output can still be seen in Glasgow.

Maggiolini, Giuseppe (1738–1814) Italian cabinetmaker, whose early career was as a carpenter working in a Cistercian monastery near Milan. From 1771 he is recorded as working for wealthy Milanese patrons and for the Austrian Governor-General of Lombardy, the Archduke Ferdinand. His Neo-classical designs, inspired by the work of contemporary artists, included trophies, cameo heads in profile, cornucopias, tendrils and *rin-*

ceaux, together with architectural motifs which he executed in marquetry on simple furniture forms based on the Louis XVI and Directoire styles. He used combinations of woods such as mahogany, brazilwood and ebony. During the Empire period he provided furniture to Eugène de Beauharnais.

Majorelle, Louis (1859–1926) French cabinet-maker who worked in Nancy, where his father had a cabinetmaking workshop specializing in repro-ductions of eighteenth-century furniture.

In 1879, while studying painting at the Ecole des Beaux-Arts in Paris, he had to return to Nancy and run the workshop after the death of his father. From the late 1880s onwards he produced furni-ture in contemporary style, under the influence of Emile Gallé (q.v.), the leading exponent in Nancy of the Art Nouveau style. Like Gallé, he worked on commissions for private patrons, as well as producing commercial, less expensive pieces; he became the most prolific Art Nouveau furniture manufacturer, still producing reproduction pieces alongside his latest designs in workshops orga-nized on industrial lines. His designs were not as original as those of Gallé, but they featured the graceful flowing lines of the Rococo style. He was, however, an extremely accomplished craftsman, trained in the traditional manner, who popular-ized Art Nouveau forms. He was a leading member of the Ecole de Nancy, the group of leading craftsmen organized by Gallé in 1901 under the title Alliance Provinciale des Industries d'Art.

His workshop was destroyed during World War I, but he returned to Nancy in 1918, working in a more restrained, classical style (known as Art Deco after the 1925 Paris exhibition). Examples of his work can be seen in the Musée de l'Ecole de Nancy, the Musée des Arts Décoratifs, Paris, and in the Victoria and Albert Museum, London, and the Brighton Museum.

Marot, Daniel (1663–1752) French architect and designer, born in Paris. His father was the archi-tect Jean Marot (c. 1619–1679), who published a two-volume work entitled *L'Architecture Fran-çaise*, and his uncle was Pierre Gole (q.v.).

Daniel Marot, who was a Huguenot, may have worked in the Boulle workshop before fleeing France in 1685 following the revocation of the Edict of Nantes. He entered the service of William of Orange, then still the Stadtholder, as a Designer and Court Architect.

He worked in England from 1694 to 1698; he advised on the gardens of Hampton Court Palace and probably also on the furnishing and interior decoration. His designs were published in Holland in 1702 as *Oeuvres du Sieur D. Marot, Architecte de Guillaume III, roy de la Grande Bretagne*. His style, inspired by the late court style of Louis XIV, has a grand Baroque feel and a sculptural quality which were influential in the development of English furniture designs. He returned to Holland in 1698. Although he undertook much of the interior decoration of the royal palace, Het Loo, for William of Orange, his only work as an architect was Schuylenberg House in The Hague, c. 1715.

Martin French family of *vernisseurs* (japanners) who perfected a form of varnish and japanning, called *vernis Martin*, based on copal resin.

Guillaume Martin (d. 1749) started a workshop in the Faubourg St Antoine in Paris in 1730. He and his brother Etienne-Simon (d. 1770) were granted by letters patent dated 27 November 1730 (renewed 18 February 1744) a twenty-year mono-poly for the making of 'all sorts of work in relief in the manner of Japan and China'. In 1748 a company was formed by Guillaume and his brothers Etienne-Simon and Julien (d. 1752), with Robert (1706–65), the youngest, as an associate. In 1753 a decree mentioned the Martin brothers as

having 'brought the technique to the highest possible level of perfection'.

The colours used varied from black and deep red (as found on original oriental lacquer) to pale shades of green, lilac, yellow and a deep Prussian blue. White *vernis Martin* often turned bright yellow as a result of a chemical reaction. The Martin brothers became so expert in their craft that Voltaire mentioned them twice in his writ-ings, first in *L'Egalité des Conditions*, where he refers to 'gilt and varnished panels' made for Mme de Châtelet in 1738 as decoration for the Château de Cirey, and in his poem 'Les Tu et les Vous', in which he praises 'these cabinets where the Martins have surpassed the art of China'.

After Guillaume's death, the company – called 'La Manufacture Royale des Vernis Martin' – was run by the 'Widow of the First Vernisseur du Roy' in partnership with Etienne-Simon. In 1748–9 he varnished and polished the panels by Maurisant in the Private Cabinet of the Dauphine at Versailles. From 1755 to 1759 his name appeared in the *Livre-Journal* of Lazare Duvaux, whose main client was Madame de Pompadour. The Château de Bellevue and the Hôtel d'Ormesson, both owned by the Marquise, were decorated with *vernis Martin* panels which had been commissioned through Lazare Duvaux.

As well as fulfilling many royal commissions in France, the brothers Martin supplied wares to the royal courts of Spain, Russia, Portugal etc. Furni-ture with *vernis Martin* decoration can be found in the Louvre and the Musée de Cluny, Paris, the Wallace Collection and the Victoria and Albert Museum, London, and in collections in Madrid, Lisbon, Moscow and the United States.

Meissonnier, Juste-Aurèle (c. 1693–1750) Designer, architect, painter and silversmith, born in Turin, where his father was a goldsmith and sculptor at the Court, working under the architect Filippo Juvarra.

He arrived in Paris in 1720, achieving success there very quickly; he succeeded Jean Bérain in the official position of 'Architecte-dessinateur de la Chambre et du Cabinet du Roy'. He designed buildings, interiors and silverware, and had a profound influence on the development of the Rococo through a series of 120 of his designs published as engravings. Taking inspiration from the use by Italian Baroque architects such as Borromini and Juvarra of curves and counter-curves, he applied them in a bold asymmetrical manner to forms borrowed from nature, combin-ing plants and flowers with rocks, shells and various animals. This gave rise to the term *rocaille* (rockwork) or Rococo, of which Meissonnier was one of the main exponents with Nicolas Pineau (q.v.), creating c. 1730–40 the version of the Rococo style known as the *genre pittoresque*, which was very influential in Germany and England.

Miseroni One of the most important Italian families of *pietra dura* craftsmen (*intagliatore di pietre dure*) originating from Milan.

Girolamo Miseroni (born c. 1520) and his brother Gasparo worked for Cosimo I de' Medici. Girola-mo's three sons worked in various countries: Giulio in Spain from 1582; Ottaviano was employed in Prague at the court of Rudolf II from 1588 to 1624; and Ambrogio was also at the court of Rudolf II from 1598. Ottaviano's sons carried on the family tradition in Prague. Dionisio, employed there from 1623, received a Court appointment and became Keeper of the *Schatz-kammer* (treasure chamber). In 1653 he carved a rock-crystal pyramid for Ferdinand III. This and other examples of his work are now in the Kunsthistorisches Museum, Vienna. After his death in 1661 his Court positions were taken over by his son Ferdinand Eusebius (d. 1684).

Alessandro, another member of the family, is also recorded as being active in the Prague workshops from 1605 to 1612.

Morris, William (1834–96) English designer, decorator, craftsman, poet and social and political theorist. While studying at Oxford he was deeply influenced by the ideas of Ruskin and Pugin; he developed an interest in medieval architecture and began writing poetry. He became a friend of the painter Burne-Jones. In 1856 he was appren-ticed as an architect to the firm of G.E. Street. Then from 1857 to 1862 he became a painter and worked with Rossetti and other Pre-Raphaelite painters on frescoes in the debating chamber of the Oxford Union Society.

In 1859 he married and commissioned his friend Philip Webb to build the Red House in Bexley Heath, Kent. Disillusionment with the current furniture designs led to the formation in 1861 of the firm of Morris, Marshall, Faulkner & Co. (in which his friends Burne-Jones, Rossetti, Ford Madox Brown and Philip Webb were partners) with the aim of improving a situation in which 'all the minor arts were in a state of complete degradation', and of bringing art to the masses. Later the firm became known as Morris & Co., moving to larger premises in London in 1875 and to Merton Abbey in 1881, where it remained in business until 1940. Textiles (embroidered, printed or woven), carpets, rugs and tapestries were produced, as well as stained glass, patterned wallpapers and furniture, the last made in a wide price range (in fact all the best pieces were made for wealthy patrons, contrary to his own stated theories). From the very beginning, however, his designs were in 'conscious revolt' against the decline in manufacturing standards brought about by industrial production, even if they were not of the greatest originality in themselves.

His aesthetic views were founded on the idea that art was 'man's expression of his joy in labour' and his medievalism was based on the belief that in the history of European art the Gothic period had been the prime example of the union of art and life. This romantic outlook – however unpractical in the face of the relentless progress of technology – greatly influenced the development of the Arts and Crafts Movement in England and the work of the Wiener Werkstätte. Examples of his work can be seen in many English museums and galleries, including the Victoria and Albert Museum, the Whitworth Gallery of Art, Manchester, and the William Morris Gallery in Walthamstow, London.

Moser, Koloman (1868–1918) Austrian painter and designer. In 1886 he began studying at the Theresianum (the Vienna Academy), where he learnt various crafts, including carpentry. His father's death in 1888 interrupted his studies and he went on to teach the children of Archduke Karl Ludwig. He subsequently studied at the Vienna Kunstgewerbeschule (School of Arts and Crafts). In 1895 he produced designs for *Wiener Mode* and joined the Siebener Club, a group of young progressive designers and artists (which included Josef Hoffmann) seeking to break away from the Academy tradition.

In April 1897 the Vienna Secession was formed on the same lines as the Munich Secession, with its own journal *Ver Sacrum*, to which Moser contributed. In 1900 he was appointed a professor at the Kunstgewerbeschule. In 1903, with finan-cial backing from Fritz Warndorfer, he and Hoff-mann created the Wiener Werkstätte, influenced by Ashbee's Guild of Handicraft and by the work of Mackintosh exhibited at the Vienna Secession in 1900. He worked with the Wiener Werkstätte until 1907, when he reverted to painting. His furniture designs for the Wiener Werkstätte were of simple rectilinear forms with flat decorative motifs in marquetry or inlay, close to the style of Hoffmann.

Oeben, Jean-François (c. 1721–1763) German cabinetmaker from Franconia who lived and worked in Paris. In June 1749 he married the daughter of the *ébéniste* François Vandercruse, called Lacroix. In 1751 he entered the workshop founded by André-Charles Boulle and worked with Boulle's youngest son Charles-Joseph, after whose death in 1754 he was appointed *Ebéniste du Roy*, having already come to the notice of Madame de Pompadour. He became a master in 1761, without having to pay the usual fees, as Monsieur de Marigny, Madame de Pompadour's brother, certified that he had already been working for the court for a longer period than that required by the Guild's rules and regulations. He used his stamp 'J.F. OEBEN' in the latter part of his career, although as a free craftsman he was not required to do so.

He worked in collaboration with Martin Carlin (q.v.) and had two assistants, Leleu and Riesener (q.v.); the latter managed the workshop after Oeben's death, and married his widow in 1767. In view of the fact that Oeben became a master only two years before he died, various pieces of furniture bearing his mark, such as the *secrétaires à abattant* in the Louvre, were probably made after his death when his widow continued the business, and would eventually have been executed by Riesener himself. Examples of his work are in the Louvre, at Versailles, and in Victoria and Albert Museum and the Wallace Collection in London. Oeben introduced to France the complex *meuble à transformations* (mechanical furniture); the *Grand Bureau du Roy [Louis XV]* at Versailles was begun in 1760 and completed by Riesener in 1769 (a copy is in the Wallace Collection).

Percier and Fontaine French architects, interior decorators and designers. Charles Percier (1764–1838) and Pierre-François-Léonard Fontaine (1762–1853) met in Rome, where both were training as architects. From then on their names were always closely associated, although Fontaine made a brief visit to London in 1792. They had returned to Paris in 1791, when they designed furniture in a strongly Republican style which Georges Jacob made for the Convention Nationale, and again in 1798 for the Conseil des Cinq Cents (Council of the Five Hundred). In 1799 the painter David introduced them to Joséphine Bonaparte, who was decorating Malmaison, her country house near Paris. Next year they started work on what was not only their first important commission, but one which gave them the opportunity of crystallizing all the elements of the Empire style, creating a strong, unified, absolutist and militaristic style in keeping with the aims and ambitions of Napoleon.

In 1802 they published the *Recueil de Décorations Intérieures* (treatise on interior decorations), effectively coining the phrase 'interior decoration'. This work (re-issued in 1812) was a manifesto of the Empire style under Napoleon, for whom they also decorated apartments in the palaces of Versailles and St Cloud, and in the Louvre and the Tuileries. They also worked as architects for the Emperor; their works include the Arc du Caroussel and the Rue de Rivoli in Paris. They survived Napoleon's fall, working for the Bourbon court during the Restauration period (1815–30).

Phyfe, Duncan (1768–1854) Scottish cabinetmaker who was active in New York. In 1792 he is recorded by William Duncan in the *New York Director and Register*. In 1794 his address was 3 Broad Street, and the spelling of his name had been changed from Fife to Phyfe. He soon became successful, producing work not only for clients in

New York but also for customers in Philadelphia and other cities. He was deeply influenced by the designs of Sheraton, later by the French Directoire style and Empire style, in which he was working before he retired in 1847. At first he used mahogany, switching to rosewood c. 1830. Labels on his furniture refer either to 'D. Phyfe's Cabinet Warehouse No. 35 Partition Street New York' or to an address at 170 Fulton Street. Examples of his work can be found in the Metropolitan Museum, the Museum of the City of New York, the Museum of Fine Arts, Boston, the Brooklyn Museum, the William Rockhill Nelson Gallery of Art, Kansas City, Mo.

Piffetti, Pietro (c. 1700–1777) Italian cabinetmaker, born in Rome. He settled in Turin in 1731. He became Court Cabinetmaker there, working under the supervision of Filippo Juvarra, the Court Architect, whom he provided with designs for bureau-cabinets and *secrétaires*. He was deeply influenced by the Louis XV style and developed his own Rococo manner, using rich inlays of exotic woods, ivory, mother-of-pearl and tortoiseshell, embellished with gilt bronze, sometimes executed in collaboration with the sculptor Francesco Ladatte. After the middle of the century his style became less flamboyant under the influence of the Louis XVI style. Most of his furniture is still *in situ* in former royal palaces and villas in and around Turin.

Pineau, Nicolas (1684–1754) French architect and designer. Born in Paris, he trained with J.H. Mansart and Boffrand. From 1716 he worked in Russia for ten years; he designed *boiseries* for Peter the Great's Cabinet at Peterhof. In 1726 he returned to Paris, where his designs employing asymmetrical scrolls, curves and countercurves influenced the Régence craftsmen. With Meissonnier he was the leading exponent of the *genre pittoresque* of the Rococo style in the 1730s and 1740s.

Plitzner, Ferdinand (1678–1724) German cabinetmaker, originally from Franconia. He was trained in Ansbach, one of the most important centres of cabinetmaking in the Rococo style. In 1706 he is recorded as having a workshop at Eyrichshof, where he was in the service of the master of the horse to the Kurfürst Lothar Franz von Schönborn, for whom he worked from 1709 onwards at Schloss Gaibach and later at Schloss Pommersfelden. There Plitzner was responsible for the entire furnishing of the *Spiegelkabinett* (mirror closet), including some wall cabinets for displaying porcelain.

His last work (still at Pommersfelden), a cabinet in Boulle marquetry with delicate Bérain-type arabesques and grotesques dating from c. 1715–24, although completed after his death by Matusch, demonstrated Plitzner's mastery of the Louis XIV and Régence styles, on the basis of which it has been suggested he may have studied in Paris.

Pugin, Augustus Welby Northmore (1812–52) English architect and designer, son of the French artist Auguste Charles Pugin (1762–1832), who had moved to London c. 1792, working there as a draughtsman and watercolourist and making designs for furniture in the Neo-Gothic manner. In his youth A.W.N. Pugin adopted the same style but invested it with a philosophy which he advocated with great energy and enthusiasm: the virtues of medieval furniture design could be translated into nineteenth-century terms through truthfulness in construction and honesty to medium and materials. He expounded his views in various books of designs, including *Gothic Furniture in the Style of the 15th Century*, *The True Principle of Pointed or Christian Architecture*

(1841) and *An Apology for the Revival of Christian Architecture in Britain* (1843).

His first furniture designs, made at the age of 15, were for a set of chairs intended for Windsor Castle, which he would later repudiate as 'Gothick enormities'. He designed furniture for the Houses of Parliament (1836–7), and at the Great Exhibition in 1851 his Medieval Court attracted much notice on account of its bold, solid and plain forms which contrasted strongly with the generally confused mix of revivalist styles then prevalent. He also designed silverware for the Crown Goldsmiths (Rundell and Bridge), as well as plate for the churches he built.

His influence was profoundly important on the dissemination of the Gothic Revival style, transforming a Romantic literary movement into a physical reality. Examples of his work can be seen at Windsor Castle, the Houses of Parliament and the Victoria and Albert Museum.

Riesener, Jean-Henri (1734–1806) German cabinetmaker who was active in Paris. Born near Essen, he was apprenticed to the Oeben workshop at the Gobelins in Paris c. 1754. After Oeben (q.v.) died in 1763, he became head of the workshop, being preferred to his colleague and rival Jean-François Leleu. He became a master in 1767 and married Oeben's widow (who continued to run the company) the following year. In 1769 he completed for Louis XV the *Grand Bureau du Roy* (now at Versailles) begun by Oeben in 1760. Until he became a master himself he would have used Oeben's stamp.

In 1774 he was appointed *Ebéniste Ordinaire du Roy* and enjoyed royal favour until 1784, when the expenditure of the Garde Meuble had to be reduced. However, Marie-Antoinette continued to employ him until the Revolution in 1789, when he was engaged in the furnishing of her Palais de St Cloud. Riesener was the most gifted and versatile of Louis XIV's *ébénistes*, exhibiting an inventive and original approach to current furniture forms, which he executed with impeccable craftsmanship in the use of veneers and gilt-bronze mounts.

His style followed a general pattern, the Oeben-inspired pictorial marquetry of 1760–70 developing into the use of a fretwork pattern featuring waterlilies c. 1775, followed by simple veneers of thuya and mahogany in the late 1780s. He made several *secrétaires à abattant* for the Queen; these, often designed *en suite*, include the set made c. 1787 (now in the Metropolitan Museum) decorated with panels of Japanese lacquer. Although he survived the Revolution and later tried to sell some of his stock which he had brought back to Paris in 1794 during the Terror and again under the Directoire in 1798, the prevailing economic climate as well as changes in fashion meant that, although his colleagues might call upon his expertise and advice, his business was never as prosperous as it had been under the Ancien Régime. He retired in 1801.

Many of his later pieces are stamped 'J.H. RIESENER'; others commissioned by the Crown are not stamped. Examples of his work can be seen in the Louvre, at Versailles, Fontainebleau and Chantilly, also in London in the Wallace Collection and the Victoria and Albert Museum, and in New York at the Metropolitan Museum. The *serre-bijoux* made by Riesener in the 1780s for the Comte de Provence, brother of Louis XVI, is in the British Royal Collection.

Roentgen, David (1743–1807) German cabinetmaker, son of Abraham Roentgen, a successful cabinetmaker in Neuwied, where he established a workshop in 1750 after being apprenticed in England and Holland. By 1761, when David joined his father, the workshop had an international clientele. In 1772 he took over the management and thereafter travelled extensively on business, receiving many commissions during his visit to Paris in 1779, where he was introduced at Court. In 1780 he was registered by the Paris Guild as a *Maître Ebéniste*. He also visited Italy, the Low Countries and Russia; in St Petersburg in 1783 he sold many pieces (still in the Hermitage) to the Empress Catherine II. He made six further visits to Russia, and in 1791 was appointed Court Cabinetmaker to Frederick William II of Prussia in Berlin. In his time he was the most acclaimed and successful furniture maker in the whole of Europe. However, his Paris warehouse was confiscated at the time of the Revolution and Neuwied did not escape depredation either. He fled to Berlin, returning only in 1802.

His style from 1770 onwards was characterized by elegant pictorial marquetry mostly based on designs by the painter Januarius Zick (1730–97). Later he adopted a more Neo-classical Louis XVI style using plain veneers. In addition to examples of his work in St Petersburg, others are in the Louvre, the Wallace Collection, the Metropolitan Museum and elsewhere.

Ruhlmann, Jacques-Emile (1879–1933) French interior decorator and furniture designer. After training as a painter in Paris, he began designing furniture in 1901, encouraged by the architect Charles Plumet. He first exhibited his work at the Salon d'Automne in 1910. After World War I he expanded his activities by entering into partnership with M. Laurent, calling the business a 'maison de décoration', trading as Etablissement Ruhlmann et Laurent.

By 1925 it was the most important firm of interior decorators in Paris, concentrating on luxury products made by traditional methods and to the highest standards. The materials employed included veneers of exotic woods, ivory, shagreen, tortoiseshell, lacquer and silver; the preferred colour-schemes of black and gold or grey and silver were aimed at a new wealthy middle-class clientele.

He designed all manner of household objects and furniture. His showpiece at the 1925 Paris Exposition, 'L'Hôtel du Collectionneur', included contributions by many other craftsmen, including Jean Dunand (who had learnt the art of oriental lacquer from Seijo Sugawara, Japanese teacher of Eileen Gray, and reintroduced its use in the decoration of contemporary French furniture).

Ruhlmann designed furniture of simple, elegant classical lines sometimes reminiscent of the Louis XVI and Directoire styles, executed with superb craftsmanship. Examples of his work can be seen at the Musée des Arts Décoratifs, Paris, the Victoria and Albert Museum, London, and the Brighton Museum.

Sambin, Hugues (c. 1520–1600) French architect and wood carver. He lived in Dijon, where he became a *Maître Menuisier* in 1549. He received several important commissions, the main one being to provide woodwork for the Palais de Justice buildings in Dijon and Besançon. His fame rests on the treatise *L'Oeuvre de la Diversité des Termes dont on use en architecture* (1572), signed 'Hugues Sambin, Architecteur en la ville de Dijon'. The terms, herms and caryatids depicted were derived from the Italian Mannerist style adopted by the School of Fontainebleau. Their fantastic quality influenced many cabinet designs of the late sixteenth century; they were realized in sculptural carved motifs, often parcel gilt or painted to imitate bronze, and referred to in contemporary documents as 'façon de Dijon' (e.g. in the inventory of Fernand Gauthiot d'Ancier in 1596), as distinct from pieces displaying columns 'façon de Paris'.

Schnell, Martin (c. 1685–1740) German lacquer worker and porcelain painter. Born in Stade, he is recorded as working in the workshop of Gerhard Dagly in Berlin from 1703 until 1709. In 1710 he went to Dresden, where he was appointed japanner to Augustus the Strong, Elector of Saxony, for whom he decorated 'cabinets, clavicembalos and screens' in 1714. From 1712 to 1716 he was retained by the Meissen porcelain factory to apply *chinoiserie* decoration in lacquer to Böttger's red stoneware.

He provided many pieces with richly lacquered *chinoiserie* decoration for the palaces of the ruling houses of Bavaria, Baden, Hesse and Württemberg, as well as working for aristocratic patrons. In addition to raised lacquerwork, he also produced painted decorations with raised lacquer figures inspired by the engraved *chinoiserie* designs in P. Schenk's *Picturae Sinicae ac Surattenae, Vasis Tabellisque exhibitae, Admiranda* (Amsterdam, 1702).

His furniture included pieces for the Japanische Palais in Dresden; the Museum für Kunsthandwerk in Frankfurt owns a bureau-cabinet executed c. 1730–40, having on the outside gold and silver decoration on a red-lacquer ground, together with some gilt-copper figures in relief, while the interior has *chinoiserie* decoration in blue and gold lacquer.

Scott, Peter (1694–1777) Furniture maker in Williamsburg, Virginia. First recorded in 1722, he placed six notices in the *Virginia Gazette*, being listed in 1733 as having a shop in Duke of Gloucester Street. In 1755 he announced his intention of leaving for England and offered his business for sale, including two negro slaves and a quantity of walnut and mahogany, together with completed stock.

There is little documentation for Scott's clientele and no signed or labelled pieces are known, his work being identified on strong circumstantial evidence. However, an entry in the account book of Colonel William Basset in 1748 states 'Cash pd Dec. 9 1748. To Mr. Peter Scott for a desk £500'; this piece, a walnut bureau-cabinet, is now in the collection of Mr and Mrs William C. Adams, Jr. Another bureau-cabinet, made c. 1760, is owned by the Colonial Williamsburg Foundation; made of walnut, poplar, yellow pine and beech, it features the squat cabriole legs and ball-and-claw feet, typical of the current London fashion, found on chairs of the period.

Records show that from 1771 to 1775 Scott enjoyed the regular patronage of Thomas Jefferson who later became the 3rd President of the U.S.A.

Seymour, John American cabinetmaker who was active in Boston, Mass. He was listed in the 1796 Directory as 'Cabinetmaker living on Creek Street', where he had premises until 1808. His label 'John Seymour and Son' indicates the involvement of his son Thomas as a partner.

After the Revolution, he became the greatest designer and maker of furniture in Boston, working in a delicate Hepplewhite style; he produced pieces in mahogany or satinwood, inlaid with maple and rosewood, as well as some furniture with painted decoration.

Notable examples of his work are in the Du Pont Museum, Winterthur, the Metropolitan Museum of Art, New York, and the Museum of Fine Arts, Boston.

Shaw, John American cabinetmaker working in Annapolis. He was trained in England. In 1773 he advertised with his partner in the *Maryland Gazette* for 'a neat and general assortment of Joiners and Cabinetmakers tools', and in 1775 as 'Cabinet and Chairmakers'.

The best-known of his three types of label is 'John Shaw, Cabinetmaker, Annapolis'. He

worked in the Hepplewhite style, using mahogany with inlays of exotic woods such as zebrawood. Examples of his work are owned by the Metropolitan Museum, the Maryland Historical Society and St John's College Museum, Annapolis.

Sheraton, Thomas (1751–1806) English cabinetmaker and designer. Born at Stockton-on-Tees, he moved to London c. 1790. No piece of furniture can be attributed to him and his fame rests on designs published in *The Cabinet-Maker and Upholsterer's Drawing-Book* (issued in four parts, 1791–4). In 1795 his trade card stated that he 'Teaches Perspective, Architecture and Ornaments, makes Designs for Cabinet-makers and sells all kinds of Drawing Books etc.' The aim of his *Drawing-Book* was 'to exhibit the present taste of furniture, and at the same time to give the workman some assistance in the manufacturing of it'. The Sheraton style is simple, featuring flat decoration, painted or inlaid, sometimes with contrasting veneers in geometric patterns, inspired by the Louis XVI style and the work of Henry Holland at Carlton House, London.

His two last books illustrated the influence of the French Directoire and Empire styles: *The Cabinet Dictionary, containing an explanation of all the terms used in the Cabinet, Chair, and Upholstery Branches, with directions for varnishing, polishing and gilding* (1803), followed by the unfinished work *The Cabinet-Maker, Upholsterer and General Artist's Encyclopaedia* (1805). A selection of plates from the three works was published posthumously in 1812 as *Designs for Household Furniture*.

The Sheraton style is sometimes divided into the early stage, characterized as an elegant, feminine and delicate variation of the Adam style, and the late stage, in which antique forms were employed in the Regency manner, e.g. sabre legs, lion's-paw feet and heads of rams, lions and sphinxes.

Solis, Virgil (1514–68) German ornamental designer and engraver working in Nuremberg. He produced several hundred plates illustrating popular allegories, genre scenes and costumes, medallion portraits and other ornaments which continued to be used by silversmiths, wood carvers and furniture makers into the seventeenth century.

His son, born 1551, also called Virgil, worked at the court of Rudolf II in Prague as a draughtsman and painter.

Sommer, Johann Daniel (1643–85) German cabinetmaker. He was the leading member, and perhaps the founder, of a notable family of furniture-makers. Born in Künzelsau am Kocher, Württemberg, he is recorded there between 1668 and 1677 as having six children.

He specialized in Boulle-type marquetry, a skill which he may have learnt in Paris, where members of his family are known to have worked: Jacques Sommer is recorded at the French court in 1660 as a cabinetmaker, Nicholas Sommer in 1678 as a sculptor, and Charles Sommer from 1710 to 1720 as a member of the Guild of St Luke. A table top by Johann Daniel in the Hohenlohemuseum, Schloss Neuenstein, is signed and dated 1666. An outstanding large cabinet by him, which probably dated from 1684, was destroyed in Schloss Charlottenburg, Berlin. After 1685 he worked for Elector Carl II at Heidelberg.

Thomire, Pierre-Philippe (1751–1843) French *fondeur-doreur* (gilt-bronze worker). He trained as a sculptor with Houdon and Pajou, and in 1774 became an apprentice *ciseleur* (chaser) with Gouthière, whom he assisted with the decoration of Louis XVI's coronation coach in 1776. In the same year he established his own workshop. His gilt-bronze mounts in Neo-classical style were used by, among others, Schwerdfeger and Weisweiler (q.v.).

In 1783 he was producing gilt-bronze mounts for the Sévres porcelain factory. He survived the Revolution by manufacturing firearms and resumed his former work after Napoleon Bonaparte became First Consul. By then he had a vast establishment with over 800 workers and had received great acclaim; he became *Ciseleur de l'Empereur*, making the mounts for the *serre-bijoux* by Jacob-Desmalter for the Empress Joséphine (pl. 104) and for the cradle made for Napoleon's son, the King of Rome (now in the Schatzkammer, Vienna) and another at Fontainebleau. He was still active during the Restauration period (1815–30) and was made a Chevalier de la Légion d'Honneur by Louis-Philippe. After his retirement in 1823 the firm continued in business until the 1850s as Thomire et Cie.

Tiffany, Louis Comfort (1848–1933) American designer and decorator who became the main exponent of the Art Nouveau style in the United States. He studied as a painter first in America and then in Paris. In 1878, influenced by the ideas and philosophy of William Morris, he opened an interior decoration business. From 1879 onwards he worked on public and private commissions in New York and also at the White House in Washington, D.C.

His work was in an exotic revivalist oriental style, combining Romanesque, Moorish and Byzantine features. Although his main contribution to Art Nouveau lay in the iridescent glass which he developed, he also produced furniture designs and generally spread Art Nouveau forms in the United States. He maintained commercial contacts with Samuel Bing, who sold some of Tiffany's work in his Paris shop 'L'Art Nouveau'.

Tisch, Charles American cabinetmaker. In 1870 he was listed in New York as a carver. He was recorded in 1871–2 as making chairs at 166 Mott Street, and in 1872–3 as a cabinetmaker at 164 Mott Street, his address until 1889; he also occupied premises at 14 East Fifteenth Street in 1886–7. In 1889–90 he was listed as an 'Art Dealer' at 174 Fifth Avenue, trading under the name 'Galerie des Beaux Arts'.

It was at this point that he gave a cabinet to the Metropolitan Museum, writing: 'This piece of furniture received the first prize at the New Orleans Exposition 84–85. It is a purely American production of my own manufacture and I consider it worthy of a place in the Museum.' His work showed the influence of Charles Lock Eastlake (q.v.) and the Arts and Crafts Movement.

Van der Vinne, Leonardo (1662–93) Cabinetmaker active in Florence. He was of Flemish or Dutch origin and although a Van der Vinne family of etchers and engravers from Friesland was recorded in Haarlem, no mention was made of Leonardo. His name appeared first in the Grand Ducal records of the Galleria dei Lavori in 1662, and in 1667 he was described as a *stipendiato* (salaried worker). In 1677 he became the head (*capomaestro*) of the cabinetmaking workshop in the Galleria. In 1687 he is credited with being *ebanista e inventore di tarsia* (cabinetmaker and inventor of marquetry), having been described in 1685 as *tarsia in galleria* and *stipettaio*. His nickname, *Tarsia* or *Il Tarsia*, reflected the fact that he brought to Florence the naturalistic marquetry style depicting flowers, birds and insects developed in Holland, inspired by contemporary still-life paintings and the current 'tulipomania'. His name continued to appear in the Galleria records until 1693.

All his documented works incorporate floral marquetry, sometimes also including *pietra dura*

inlay. An ebony cabinet with wood and ivory inlay (now in the Museo degli Argenti in the Pitti Palace) was delivered to the Grand Ducal Guardaroba in 1667, together with a *prie-dieu*. Also attributed to him are four tables in the Pitti Palace, possibly made *en suite* with the cabinet and a jewel-box now in Berlin. He was also recorded as having produced firearms and musical instruments for Ferdinand II de' Medici.

Van Mekeren, Jan (1658–1733) The best-known Dutch cabinetmaker. Born at Tiel, he became a resident of Amsterdam in 1687. In 1704 his name appeared on a list of the eleven 'Best Cabinetmakers', and again in 1710, the year of his marriage, he was listed as one of the eighteen leading craftsmen. At the time of his death the inventory of his workshop showed that he had a large number of important clients in the Amsterdam area. His speciality was furniture with floral marquetry, the forms being strongly architectural and the marquetry featuring a characteristically broad, exuberant quality reminiscent of contemporary Dutch floral still-life paintings. Two cabinets with floral marquetry decoration (one in the Rijksmuseum, Amsterdam, on a dark rosewood ground, the other in the Victoria and Albert Museum on a light mahogany ground) are almost a pair in terms of design. A cabinet with an ebony ground, at Amerongen Castle, was made *en suite* with a pair of side tables. Another cabinet is at Charlecote Park, Warwickshire.

Van Vianen The most important family of Dutch goldsmiths, originating in Utrecht.

Paulus van Vianen (*c.* 1568–1613) was trained by his father before leaving to enter the service of the Bavarian Court in Munich from 1596 to 1601. He subsequently became Court Goldsmith to Rudolf II in Prague from 1603 to 1613. His work in low relief, in the tradition of Wenzel Jammitzer, was executed in the auricular style, an outstanding example being a ewer and basin of *c.* 1613, now in the Rijksmuseum, Amsterdam.

His elder brother Adam (*c.* 1565–1627) worked in Utrecht and produced pieces in the auricular style in a bolder, more opulent manner. The auricular style was brought to England by Adam's son Christiaen (*c.* 1598–1666) who made two extended visits in 1635–9 and 1660–6. He worked for Charles I and made seventeen pieces for St George's Chapel, Windsor Castle, and held the title of Silversmith in Ordinary to the King. The auricular style, which was popularized by Christiaen's publication of his father's and his own designs in 1650, *Modelles artificiels de divers vaisseaux d'argent* (Artistic designs for various silver vessels), was used in the carved, silvered and gilt wooden stands used as bases for cabinets with lacquer and japanned decoration.

Vile, William (*c.* 1700–1767) English cabinetmaker, born in the West Country. He was registered in London in 1750 in partnership with John Cobb. In 1756 and 1762 he made furniture for the Hon. John Damer of Came House, Dorset. On his accession to the throne in 1761, George III appointed Vile Cabinetmaker to the Royal Household.

Although his early work was in a late Baroque style, he became one of the best English Rococo cabinetmakers, revealing originality of design and producing high-quality carving inspired by Chippendale. Among his masterpieces is the jewel cabinet made for Queen Charlotte; in a bill dated 1761 it was described as 'A very handsome jewel cabinet, made of many different kinds of fine wood on a mahogany frame richly carved, the front, ends and top inlaid with ivory in compartments neatly engraved: £138.10.0.' Most of the decorative components of the jewel cabinet were taken from Chippendale's *Director*, published in

1754. The jewel cabinet and a bookcase made in 1762 are in the Royal Collection; a medal cabinet made for George III in 1761 is in the Victoria and Albert Museum.

Viollet-le-Duc, Eugène Emanuel (1814–79) French architect and theorist whose interest in the Middle Ages was first aroused by the writings of Victor Hugo and Prosper Mérimée.

He became a scholar and restorer of French Romanesque and Gothic monuments, e.g. at Vézelay, Carcassone, and the Sainte Chapelle in Paris. His influence on the decorative arts resulted largely from his *Dictionnaire raisonné du mobilier français de l'époque Carolingienne à la Renaissance* (Descriptive dictionary of French furniture from Carolingian times to the Renaissance), published in Paris in 1858. It included accurate illustrations of medieval furniture and objects and, in the same vein as Pugin, made an aesthetic appeal advocating a new type of furniture displaying integrity to function and materials. However, his theories were not always translated into practice; his own work in various fields was often revivalist. His influence was nevertheless important in disseminating the *style Troubadour* (or *à la Cathédrale*) – the French equivalent of the Gothic Revival.

Vries, Hans Vredeman de (1527–1604) Born at Leeuwarden in Flanders, he worked in Mechlin and Antwerp. He published the largest volume of furniture designs to appear in the sixteenth century, entitled *Differens pourtraicts à savoir portaux, bancs, escabelles, tables, buffets, licts de camp propres aux menuiziers de l'invention de Jehan Vredeman dict de Vriese, mis en lumière par Philippe Gallé* (Antwerp 1565), as well as several volumes of architectural designs, e.g. *Variae architecturae formae* (Various architectural forms; 1560), incorporating strapwork and other Mannerist ornaments, which had an important influence on German pictorial marquetry.

Wallbaum, Matthäus (1554–1632) German goldsmith working in Augsburg, where he became a Master in 1590 and a leading craftsman. His work took many forms, e.g. mechanical objects, elaborate drinking cups, small portable altars, plaques and fittings for caskets and *Schreibtische*, as well as other religious and secular objects. His distinctive maker's mark was a walnut tree (German, *Walnussbaum*).

Examples of his work can be found in: the Museum für Kunsthandwerk, Frankfurt (an Apothecary's Cabinet, decorated and fitted by Wallbaum); the Schatzkammer in the Hofburg, Vienna; and the Schatzkammer in the Residenz, Munich.

Weisweiler, Adam (1750–1810) German cabinetmaker who trained in Roentgen's workshop in Neuwied. He settled in Paris, where he became a *maître ébéniste* in 1778. He worked mostly for *marchand-merciers*, particularly Daguerre, who commissioned furniture from him for the Queen (Marie-Antoinette). Through Daguerre he also supplied pieces for the Prince of Wales's London home, Carlton House. He used the stamped maker's mark 'A. WEISWEILER'.

He specialized in small furniture types such as the *secrétaire* and the *bonheur du jour*, rarely using marquetry, but incorporating Sèvres plaques or Japanese lacquer panels and *pietra dura* panels cut from cabinets dating from the reign of Louis XIV. He survived the Revolutiron and subsequently worked for the Emperor and members of his family, making jewel caskets for Queen Hortense in 1806. After he retired in 1809, the business was managed until 1844 by his son Jean.

Examples of his work are in the British Royal Collection, the Wallace Collectiron, the Louvre, the Metropolitan Museum, New York, and elsewhere.

Youf, Jean-Baptiste-Gilles (1762–1838) French cabinetmaker who was active in Italy, working in the Empire style which he helped to make fashionable there.

Born in Bayeux, he was recorded in Paris in 1795, and opened his own workshop there in 1799. His work came to the notice of Napoleonic court circles and Bonaparte's sister Elisa Baciocchi took him into her service in Lucca in 1805, when she was created Grand Duchess of Tuscany. As Court Cabinetmaker he provided furniture for her palaces in Lucca, as well as for the Palazzo Pitti in Florence, where some of his pieces can still be seen.

After the fall of Napoleon he returned to Paris, where he remained in business. A large suite of furniture made for a Norwegian client is in the Aust-Agder Museet in Arendal.

GLOSSARY

Alla certosina Italian fifteenth-century inlay or *intarsia*, utilizing combinations of small pieces of wood, bone, ivory, mother-of-pearl and metal, arranged in a decorative geometric design inspired by Islamic woodwork. The technique was popular in the Veneto and Lombardy; it is sometimes called 'Embriachi work', after the Embriachi family who were active near the Certosa (Carthusian monastery) of Pavia.

Apron The central ornamental element on the upper part of stands for cabinets: also found below the rail of seat furniture.

Arabesques (or Moresques) Stylized surface decoration consisting of fine interlaced scrolling foliage and tendrils or repetitive geometric patterns inspired by Islamic damascened metalwork (see damascening).

Auricular style (or lobar style; Dutch, *Kwabornament*, German *Knorpelwerk*) A decorative style characterized by sinuous, curving forms reminiscent of sea-shells and sea-creatures such as dolphins, and having similarities to the human ear – hence the name. Developed c. 1607 by the Dutch goldsmith Paulus van Vianen from Dutch and German Mannerist engravings and contemporary anatomical studies, the style was disseminated by his brother Adam and nephew Christiaen. It occurs in carved decoration found on furniture made in the Netherlands, Germany and England until c. 1675–80.

Bantam work See under Coromandel lacquer.
Block front An eighteenth-century American method of constructing the front of bureau-cabinets, desks, etc., creating three flattened curves, the central one being concave, the two outer ones convex: the form occurs particularly in the work of New England cabinetmakers, often in association with carved shell motifs.
Bombé (French) A term used to describe the curved, bulging form of some Rococo furniture.
Boulle work A generic term used to describe a particular form of marquetry of tortoiseshell, brass and pewter, perfected in France by André Charles Boulle (1642–1732), although already used in Italy and Flanders. It consists of cutting out a design from a sheet of tortoiseshell and a sheet of brass glued together, obtaining thus a recto or *première partie* (with a brass pattern set in the tortoiseshell ground) and a verso or *contrepartie*

(in which the tortoiseshell pattern is set in the brass ground).

Pewter, mother-of-pearl or stained bone were also used, together with coloured pigments and foils, to add richness to the tortoiseshell. Although Boulle work went into decline in France at the beginning of the eighteenth century under the influence of the Rococo style, it returned to favour in the 1770s. It was also fashionable in the rest of Europe and was produced widely in the eighteenth and nineteenth centuries.
Breakfront A term used to describe a cabinet or bookcase with a projecting central section.
Burr The distinctively marked cross-section of an excrescence on a tree, much used in oystershell veneers (q.v.).

Cameo relief Carving of a gem, semi-precious stone or shell having two layers of different colours: the technique, in which the upper layer is carved, so revealing the contrasting colour as a ground, was first practised in antiquity. The reverse, incised relief carving, is termed *intaglio*.
Carcase The basic wooden structure of a piece of furniture, upon which veneers of more expensive wood are applied.
Cartouche Derived from the Italian *carta*, paper, the term is used to describe an ornamental motif in the shape of a scroll with curled edges, on which to display a coat of arms, monogram or inscription.
Caryatid A column or pilaster in the shape of a standing female figure, originally architectural but also used on furniture, either carved in wood or cast in metal and applied as a mount.
Classical A generic term to designate Greek and Roman motifs and their derivations.
Chinoiserie The French term first used in the eighteenth century to describe the *Rococo-chinoiserie* style of Watteau, Boucher and Chippendale, among others: earlier the taste for all things oriental had been described in French as *façon des Indes*, *façon de la Chine* or *lachinage*. Generically used to describe the deliberate emulation and imitation of Eastern styles and techniques from the late sixteenth to the nineteenth century, when the opening of Japanese ports to foreign trade after 1854 gave rise to *Japonisme* in the fine and decorative arts.
Coromandel lacquer Incised coloured lacquer work exported to Europe from central and northern China in the seventeenth and eighteenth centuries. The name is derived from the English East India Company's trading post on the Coromandel coast of India, through which goods from China were shipped to Europe. An English imitation dating from the late seventeenth century is known as Bantam work (from Bantam, a village on the island of Java), the term sometimes being used generically when referring to the original Chinese lacquer.
Cresting The carved, usually gilt or silvered, decorative top on some cabinets, especially of the Baroque era; can also be used in reference to the top rail of seat furniture.

Damascening The process of decorating sheet steel by hammering gold or silver wire into a previously scored surface design. Originally practised in Damascus and elsewhere in the Near East, it was first encountered by Europeans during the Crusades, and was introduced to Venice and Milan early in the thirteenth century, becoming very popular from the fifteenth century onwards. Milan became an important centre of production in the second half of the sixteenth century. Strips and sheets of damascened work were used as decoration on cabinets made of ebony. The technique was also practised in Germany, France and England, being used to decorate weapons and armour.

Ebonized wood Any light-coloured wood stained black to imitate ebony; pearwood was often treated in this way.
Embriachi See *alla certosina*.
Estampille The mark of a French cabinetmaker stamped in intaglio on the carcase of a piece of furniture. Members of the Guild of *Menuisiers-Ebénistes* were obliged by law to mark their furniture from 1751 until 1791, when the corporation system was dissolved. Craftsmen employed by the royal court were exempt.

Fall-front (or drop front) The door or flap of a cabinet or bureau-cabinet, hinged at the bottom and supported by struts when lowered into the open position to form a level writing surface.
Fillet A narrow flat band of wood or metal inlay.
Finial A decorative feature – often in the form of an urn, acorn or pine-cone – on the top of a piece of furniture. Also used on silver, porcelain, etc.

Gesso A composition of plaster of Paris and size applied to a wooden surface prior to gilding, silvering or japanning.
Grotesques First used in Italy, grotesques were disseminated throughout northern Europe by way of engravings, first in France from Fontainebleau c. 1530, then to the Netherlands, Germany and England. The term is derived from the Italian *alla grottesca*, inspired by the discovery in 1480 of the long-buried remains of Nero's Domus Aurea on the Esquiline Hill in Rome; the complex decorative system, akin to arabesques (q.v.) but including human and animal figures, was combined with mythological and allegorical scenes painted in *trompe l'œil*, revealing at once a whimsical sense of composition and a disciplined sense of aesthetic order.

Herm (or term) A three-quarter length human figure on a tapering pedestal, first used in classical architecture. It occurs on furniture dating from the Renaissance and Baroque eras. From the Roman deity Terminus (associated with boundary marks).

Intarsia Italian inlay or marquetry.

Japanning The process used in Europe and America to imitate oriental lacquer decoration. Shellac, a gum deposited on trees by the insect *Coccus lacca*, was dissolved in spirits of wine and the resulting varnish, which could be coloured black, green, red, blue or sometimes white and yellow, was applied in numerous coats. It could be applied to wood or metal.

Lacca povera (sometimes called *lacca contrafatta*) An Italian imitation of oriental lacquer decoration: commercially produced coloured prints were cut out, stuck on to a painted wooden ground and the whole was then varnished. It was particularly fashionable in Venice in the eighteenth century; a similar French technique was called *découpures*.

Lacquer A waterproof varnish first used in China in the fourth century BC and later in Japan. It is prepared from the sap of *Rhus vernicifera*, a tree indigenous to China which was subsequently introduced and grown in Japan.

Lambrequin A French decorative motif used in the Louis XIV and Régence styles, particularly associated with Jean Bérain; it is derived from the stylized heraldic representation of the scarf worn across the helmet of a medieval knight.

Marquetry The technique of applying a decorative pattern to the surface of a wooden carcase using veneers of differently coloured woods, ivory, mother-of-pearl, etc. It was first practised in Italy (mostly in *intarsia* panels of *trompe-l'œil* pictorial themes and architectural perspectives), Germany and the Netherlands, and was introduced to France in the early seventeenth century and to England in the latter part of the century via Holland, where a characteristic burr and floral form was developed.

Mudéjar style The Hispano–Moresque style developed in Spain after the defeat of the Moors at Granada in 1492; it is found in architecture and the decorative arts. In furniture it refers to an inlay of small pieces of wood, bone, mother-of-pearl and metal arranged in a repetitive geometric pattern inspired by Islamic artifacts, in which star, flower and scroll motifs are combined with a fine wooden outline called *Laceria*.

Oystershell veneer Sections of burr walnut, kingwood, olive, laburnum or lignum vitae laid side by side as a decorative veneer; first used in Holland *c.* 1650, then in England.

Penwork A type of decoration used during the English Regency period: designs are drawn in black with a pen on a ground of lighter colour, the surrounding areas being stained or japanned black.

Pietra dura or **Commesso di pietre dure** (Italian) An inlay of hard and semi-precious stones mainly of the quartz variety, e.g. agate, chalcedony and jasper. The technique, originally used in antiquity, was revived in Milan in the sixteenth century, and Florence became the main centre of production after Francesco de' Medici had brought some Milanese craftsmen to work there in 1580; the Opificio delle Pietre Dure, a workshop in the Galleria dei Lavori of the Uffizi,

was opened in 1599 by Ferdinando I de' Medici. *Pietra dura* was also produced in Prague at the Court of Rudolf II, who employed Italian craftsmen (in particular members of the Miseroni family).

Pietra paesina (Italian, 'landscape stone') An inlay of Albarese limestone exploiting the natural veining of the stone to evoke imaginary landscapes, or serving as a background for painting; used in Florence from the seventeenth century onwards.

Plateresque A Spanish form of surface decoration using classical motifs such as heads in profile within wreaths, urns, trophies, *putti*, masks, birds, etc. distributed amongst grotesques (q.v.) and arabesques (q.v.) in a fine filigree manner reminiscent of the work of silversmiths.

Putto (Italian, plural *putti*) A naked male infant used as a decorative motif.

Rococo A decorative style characterized by the use of curves and of asymmetrical forms found in nature, such as rocks, shells, flowers, etc. which developed in France (there called *style rocaille*) in the early eighteenth century and spread to the whole of Europe. It features C scrolls and double-C scrolls, tortuous serpentine lines, combined with elegance, charm and fantasy, contrasting with grandiose solemnity of the Baroque style which preceded it.

Scagliola An Italian imitation of *pietra dura* (q.v.) inlay; the term is derived from *scaglia*, marble chips. The technique, which dates back to antiquity, was revived (together with *pietra dura*) in the sixteenth century in the Medici Galleria dei Lavori. It consists of a reconstruction of marble, achieved by mixing finely ground coloured marbles with selenite, plaster of Paris and glue. After being applied to wet gesso and allowed to dry, its surface could be highly polished to enhance sheen and colour. It was first used as an architectural material and later panels of *scagliola* reproducing *pietra dura* designs served as decoration on cabinets and other types of furniture.

Strapwork Ornament reminiscent of leather straps used either alone in interlacing bands, or combined with grotesques (first by Rosso Fiorentino and Primaticcio at Fontainebleau in the Galerie de François I, *c.* 1533–5). This type of ornament spread to the rest of Europe through the medium of engravings and was used extensively in the Netherlands, England and Germany.

Stumpwork Raised needlework forming a relief ornament on a base of wool or cotton-wool.

Tortoiseshell The hard translucent material, mottled yellow and brown, from the carapace of the hawksbill turtle, cut in thin plates and first used as a furniture veneer in antiquity; when heated, it can be moulded to a desired shape. The veneer is frequently backed with foil or coloured pigments in order to enhance the richness of the colour. See Boulle work.

Vernis Martin The French generic term applied

to all forms of japanning and varnishes used in France in the eighteenth century; it is sometimes erroneously used in reference to similar work done in other European countries, but should be restricted to the production of the brothers Martin (see p. 215). Many colours were used: black and red, as well as pastel shades of green, lilac and yellow.

Verre églomisé A French term used to describe glass decorated on the reverse with gold leaf and coloured pigments, the earliest examples date from antiquity, and the technique was used extensively in the Middle Ages and the Renaissance. The modern term is derived from the name of an eighteenth-century Parisian art dealer, Jean-Baptiste Glomy, who employed the method frequently for framing.

Woods used in cabinetmaking Some of the less familiar native woods and exotic woods are listed below:

Ebony – a heavy, dark wood introduced to Europe in the sixteenth century. Quite brittle and difficult to work, it occurs in a variety of shades: jet-black streaked with brown, from Africa; black with purple markings, from Ceylon (Sri Lanka, then called Coromandel); or dusky yellow to deep brown with black markings, from the Celebes (then called Macassar).

Kingwood (rosewood, palissander) – from the *Dalbergia* tree, a type first imported into England from Brazil in the seventeenth century and then described as 'prince's wood', being used as a veneer or in marquetry. Its colour – a dark purplish red – provided a contrast with lighter woods, e.g. satinwood, when used in cross-banding *c.* 1770. The wood is somewhat lighter than rosewood (see below), with which the name kingwood (first used *c.* 1850) is usually associated.

Laburnum (*Laburnum vulgare*) – a native European tree of the genus *Acacia*. Its wood – yellowish and streaked with brown – was used in veneers and marquetry in the late seventeenth century in England and Holland.

Lignum vitae (*Guiacum officinale*) – a wood native to the West Indies, imported into England and Holland in the seventeenth century. It was used particularly in oystershell marquetry, exploiting its dark-brown tones streaked with black.

Padouk (*Pterocarpus dalbergoides*) – a variety of rosewood (see below) imported from Burma and the Andaman Islands. The wood varies from golden brown to a deep-reddish colour.

Rosewood – obtained from the *Dalbergia* tree, the wood is akin to kingwood (see above), with which it is often associated. Its colour is a dark purplish-brown with variegated markings. It was much used in the eighteenth century in veneers and panels.

Satinwood – a term used to describe a wide variety of woods having a yellowish tone (either plain or variegated) used in the eighteenth century. From *c.* 1765 it was imported from Guiana, and subsequently from the East Indies and West Indies.

BIBLIOGRAPHY

GENERAL AND INTERNATIONAL

GONZALEZ-PALACIOS, A. *Objects for a 'Wunderkammer'* (Colnaghi Gallery exhibition catalogue), London, 1981

HONOUR, H. *Cabinetmakers and Furniture Designers*, London and New York, 1969

IMPEY, O. and MACGREGOR, A. (ed.) *The Origins of Museums. The Cabinet of Curiosities in sixteenth and seventeenth century Europe*, Oxford, 1985

JERVIS, S. *Printed Furniture Designs before 1650*, London, 1974

LIEBENWEIN, W. *Studiolo: die Entstehung eines Raumtyps und seine Entwicklung bis um 1600*, Berlin, 1977

LUGLI, A. *Naturalia e Mirabilia. Il collezionismo enciclopedico nelle Wunderkammern d'Europa*, Milan, 1983

PAYNE, C. *Nineteenth Century European Furniture*, London, 1984

SCHLÖSSER, J. VAN *Die Kunst- und Wunderkammer der Spätrenaissance*, Leipzig, 1908

THORNTON, P. *Seventeenth Century Interior Decoration in England, France and Holland*, New Haven, Conn., 1978

THE ANCIENT WORLD

BAKER, H. S. *Furniture in the Ancient World. Origins and evolution 3100–475 BC*, London, 1966

BRITISH MUSEUM: *Treasures of Tutankhamun* (exhibition catalogue), London, 1972

CARTER, H. *The Tomb of Tutankhamun* (3 vols.), London, 1923–33

MAIURI, A. *Ercolano, i Nuovi Scavi (1927–1958)*, Rome, 1958

PERNICE, E. *Hellenistiche Kunst in Pompeii*, vol. V, Berlin, 1932.

RICHTER, G. M. A. *The Furniture of the Greeks, Etruscans and Romans*, London, 1966.

SALONEN, A. *Die Möbel des alten Mesopotamien*, Helsinki, 1963

THE MIDDLE EAST AND EUROPE IN THE MIDDLE AGES

ALLAN, J. *Cairo, Damascus or Venice. Possible Provenance of Mameluk Metalwork. Metalwork of the Islamic World, the Aron Collection*, London, 1986

ARSEVEN, C. E. *L'Art Turc depuis son origine jusqu'à nos jours*, Istanbul, 1939

ARTS COUNCIL OF GREAT BRITAIN: *The Arts of Islam* (exhibition catalogue), London, 1976

BECKWITH, J. *Caskets from Cordoba* (V&A monograph), London, 1960;

——, 'The Influence of Islamic Art on Western European Art', *Middle East Forum* XXXVI, Beirut, 1960.

BERLINER FESTSPIELE: *Europa und der Orient 800–1900* (exhibition catalogue), Berlin, 1989

EAMES, P. 'Medieval Furniture in England, France and the Netherlands from the 12th to the 15th century', *Furniture History*, vol. XIII, London, 1977, pp. 5ff.

HUTH, H. *Sarazenen in Venedig? Festschrift für Heinz Ladendorf*, Cologne, 1970

MÉLIKIAN-CHIRVANI, A. S. 'Venise entre l'Orient et l'Occident', *Bulletin des Etudes Orientales*, Paris, 1974

ROGERS, J. M. and WARD, R. *Süleyman the Magnificent* (British Museum exhibition catalogue), London, 1988

SADAN, J. *Le Mobilier au Proche-Orient Médiéval*, Leiden, 1976

THE FAR EAST AND ORIENTAL INFLUENCES ON EUROPEAN DESIGN

CLUNAS, C. *Chinese Furniture*, London, 1988

GUÉRIN, J. *La Chinoiserie en Europe au 18ème siècle*, Paris, 1911

HONOUR, H. *Chinoiserie. The Vision of Cathay*, London, 1973

HUTH, H. *Lacquer of the West. The History of a Craft and an Industry, 1550–1950*, London, 1971

IMPEY, O. *Chinoiserie. The Impact of Oriental Styles on Western Art and Decoration*, London, 1977

JARRY, M. *Chinoiserie. Chinese influences on European Decorative Art, 17th and 18th Centuries*, Fribourg, 1981

KOIZUMI, K. *Traditional Japanese Furniture*, Tokyo and New York, 1986

VEENENDAL, J. *Furniture from Indonesia, Shri Lanka and India during the Dutch period*, Delft, 1985

VICTORIA AND ALBERT MUSEUM: *Art and the East India Trade* (exhibition catalogue), London, 1970

ENGLAND

ASLIN, E. *The Aesthetic Movement. Prelude to Art Nouveau*, London, 1969;

——, *Nineteenth Century English Furniture*, London, 1962

BEARD, G. and GOODISON, J. *English Furniture 1500–1640*, London, 1987

BOE, A. *From Gothic Revival to Functional Form*, Oslo, 1957

COLLARD, F. *Regency Furniture*, London, 1985

EDWARDS, R. *Thomas Chippendale: The Gentleman and Cabinetmaker's Director*, Bonn, 1957;

——, *Hepplewhite Furniture Designs*, London, 1947;

——, *Sheraton Furniture Designs*, London, 1949;

——, *The Shorter Dictionary of English Furniture*, London, 1964

EDWARDS, R. and JOURDAIN, M. *Georgian Cabinet-makers 1700–1800*, London, 1955

FURNITURE HISTORY SOCIETY: *Dictionary of English Furniture-makers 1660–1840* (ed. G. Beard and C. Gilbert), London, 1986

GILBERT, C. *Furniture at Temple Newsam House and Lotherton Hall*, London, 1978

HAYWARD, J. and ROGERS, P. *English Cabinets* (V&A monograph), London, 1972

HEAL, Sir A. *London Furniture Makers 1660–1840*, London, 1953

HOWARTH, T. *Charles Rennie Mackintosh and the Modern Movement*, Glasgow, 1952 (2nd ed., London, 1977)

JACKSON-STOPS, G. *The Treasure Houses of Britain. Five Hundred Years of Private Patronage and Art Collecting* (National Gallery of Art exhibition catalogue), Washington, D.C., 1985

LOUDON, J. C. *Encyclopaedia of Cottage, Farm and Villa Architecture*, London, 1833 (2nd ed., 1867)

MACQUOID, P. and EDWARDS, H. *The Dictionary of English Furniture from the middle ages to the late Georgian period* (3 vols.), London,

1924–27; revised and expanded edition (ed. R. Edwards), London, 1954

MASSE, H. *The Art-Workers' Guild 1884–1934*, Oxford, 1956

MOLESWORTH, H. *A Treatise of Japanning and Furnishing, 1688, by John Stalker and George Parker* (reprint), London, 1960

MUSGRAVE, C. *Regency Furniture*, London, 1961

NAYLOR, G. *The Arts and Crafts Movement*, London, 1971

PEVSNER, N. *High Victorian Design*, London, 1951;

——, *Pioneers of Modern Design*, London, 1936

STANSKY, W. *Redesigning the World. William Morris, the 1880's and the Arts & Crafts*, Princeton, N.J., 1985

STANTON, P. *Pugin*, London and New York, 1971

SYMMONDS, R. W. 'Furniture from the Indies', *The Connoisseur*, May 1934, pp. 283–91;

——, *Furniture making in 17th and 18th century England*, London, 1955;

——, 'Lacquer Cabinets', *Old Furniture Magazine*, vol. 3, 1928;

——, *Old English Walnut and Lacquer Cabinets*, London, 1921

THOMPSON, P. *The Work of William Morris*, London, 1967

THORNTON, P. and TOMLIN, M. *The Furnishing and Decoration of Ham House* [Furniture History Society], London, 1980

TRAPPES-LOMAX, M. *Pugin. A Medieval Victorian*, London, 1932

VICTORIA AND ALBERT MUSEUM: *Rococo Art and Design in Hogarth's England* (exhibition catalogue), London, 1984

WARD-JACKSON, P. *English Furniture Design of the 18th century*, London, 1958

FRANCE

BELEWICH-STANKEWICH, H. *Le Goût Chinois en France au temps de Louis XIV*, Paris, 1910

BOCCADOR, J. *Le Mobilier français du Moyen Age à la Renaissance*, Paris, 1988

BONNAFÉ, E. *Inventaire de la Reine Catherine de Médicis*, Paris, 1882;

——, *Le Surintendant Fouquet*, Paris, 1882

BOSMANS, J. *Les Cabinets de Philippe V d'Espagne*, Louvain, 1885

BOULANGER, J. *L'Ameublement Français au Grand Siècle*, Paris, 1913

BURCKHARDT, M. *Mobilier Louis XIII, Louis XIV*, Paris, 1978

CHAMPEAUX, A. DE *Le Meuble*, Paris, 1885

CONNAISSANCE DES ARTS (Paris): 'Les Meubles Français en Laque de Chine', July 1960

COSNAC, G. (Comte de) *Les Richesses du Palais Mazarin*, Paris, 1884

DU MOLINET *Le Cabinet de la Bibliothèque Ste Geneviève*, Paris, 1692

DUNCAN, A. *Louis Majorelle. Master of Art Nouveau Design*, London and New York, 1991

ERIKSEN, S. *Early Neo-Classicism in France. The Creation of the Louis Seize Style*, London, 1974

FANIEL, S. *Le XVIIe siècle*, Paris, 1958

FERAY, J. 'Une Paire de Cabinets faits aux Gobelins identifiés', *Bulletin de la Société de l'Histoire de l'Art Français*, 1958

GRANDJEAN, S. *Empire Furniture*, London, 1966

GUIFFREY, J. *Inventaire Général du Mobilier de la Couronne sous Louis XIV*, Paris, 1885–6

GUILMARD, D. *Les Maîtres Ornementistes* (2 vols.), Paris, 1881

HAVARD, H. *Dictionnaire de l'Ameublement et de la Décoration* (4 vols.), Paris, 1887–90

HAYWARD, J. 'Silver Furniture (2)', *Apollo*, April 1958, pp. 124ff.

JACQUEMART, A. *Histoire du Mobilier*, Paris, 1876

KIMBALL, F. *Le Style Louis XV. Origin and Evolution of the Rococo*, Paris/Philadelphia, 1943

KJELLBERG, P. *Le Mobilier Français du XVIIIe siècle: Dictionnaire des Ebénistes et Menuisiers*, Paris, 1989;

——, *Le Mobilier Français* (2 vols.), Paris, 1978

LAKING, G. *The Furniture of Windsor Castle*, London, 1905

LEDOUX-LÉBARD, D. *Le Mobilier Français du XIXe siècle: Dictionnaire des Ebénistes et Menuisiers*, Paris, 1984

LEHMAN, C. *Mobilier Louis-Philippe et Napoléon III*, Paris, 1978

LUNSINGH SCHEURLEER, T. H. 'Novels in Ebony', *Journal of the Warburg and Courtauld Institutes*, London, 1956;

——, 'The Philippe d'Orléans Ivory Cabinet by Pierre Gole', *Burlington Magazine*, June 1984, pp. 333ff.;

——, 'Pierre Gole, Ebéniste du roi Louis XIV', *Burlington Magazine*, June 1980, pp. 380ff.

MAZARINI: 'Inventaire de tous les Meubles du Cardinal Mazarin d'après l'original dressé en 1653', *Les Archives de Condé, par Henri d'Orléans*, London, 1861

MOUSSINAC, L. *Le Meuble Français Moderne*, Paris, 1925

MUSÉE DES ARTS DÉCORATIFS, PARIS: *Louis XIV, Faste et Décor* (exhibition catalogue), Paris, 1960

PRADÈRE, A. *Les Ebénistes Français de Louis XIV à la Révolution*, Paris, 1990

REYNIES, N. *Le Mobilier Domestique* (2 vols.), Paris, 1987

RICCI, SEYMOUR DE *Louis XIV and Regency furniture and decoration*, London, 1929

STRANGE, E. *The Royal Furniture Collection at Windsor Castle*, London, 1927

THORNTON, P. 'A very special year . . .' [V&A acquisitions in 1977, including the Marie de Médicis Cabinet], *The Connoisseur*, June 1978, pp. 138ff.

VERLET, P. *French Royal Furniture*, London, 1963;

——, *Le Mobilier Royal Français* (2 vols.), Paris, 1945–55;

——, *Styles, Meubles, Décors du Moyen-Age à nos jours*, Paris, 1972

VIAL, H., MARCEL, A. and GIRODIE, A. *Les Artistes du bois. Répertoire Alphabétique des Ebénistes, Menuisiers, Sculpteurs, Doreurs sur bois ayant travaillé en France au XVIIème et XVIIIème siècle*, Paris, 1922

WATSON, Sir F. *Louis XVI Furniture*, London, 1973

WILLIAMSON, E. *Les Meubles d'Art du Mobilier National*, Paris, 1883–5

GERMANY AND AUSTRIA

ALTER, D. 'Augsburger Kabinettschränke', *Die Weltkunst*, October 1976

APPUHN, H. 'Kleinodientruhen privater Denkmäler', *Die Weltkunst*, February 1980 (exhibition at Palma de Mallorca)

BÖTTIGER, J. *Philipp Hainhofer und der Kunstschrank Gustav Adolfs in Uppsala* (4 vols.), Stockholm, 1909–10

BRUNING, A. and LESSING, J. *Der Pommersche Kunstschrank*, Berlin, 1905

HEIKAMP, D. 'Zur Geschichte der Uffizien-Tribuna und der Kunstschränke in Florenz und Deutschland', *Zeitschrift für Kunstgeschichte*, vol. XXVI (1963)

HIMMELHEBER, G. *Kabinettschränke* (Bayerisches Nationalmuseum illustrated guide no. 4), Munich, 1977;

——, 'Ulrich und Melchior Baumgartner', *Pantheon*, 1975

KLAPSIA, H. VON 'Dionysio Miseroni' in *Jahrbuch der Kunsthistorischen Sammlungen in Wien*, vol. XIII (1944), pp. 301ff.

KREISEL, H. *Die Kunst des Deutschen Möbels*, Darmstadt, 1968–70

KRIS, E. *Meister und Meisterwerke der Steinscheidekunst*, Vienna, 1929

KUNSTHISTORISCHES MUSEUM, VIENNA: *Prag um 1600. Kunst und Kultur am Hofe Kaiser Rudolf II.* (exhibition catalogue), Vienna, 1988

METROPOLITAN MUSEUM OF ART, NEW YORK: *Gothic and Renaissance Art in Nuremberg 1300–1500* (exhibition catalogue), 1986

MÖLLER, L. 'Drei Augsburg Kabinettschränke aus der Periode nach Hainhofer', *Jahrbuch der Hamburger Sammlungen*, vol. XXI (1976);

——, *Der Wrangelschrank und die verwandten süddeutschen Intarsiamöbel des 16. Jahrhunderts*, Berlin, 1956

STAATLICHE MUSEEN, BERLIN: *Schatzkasten und Kabinettschränke* (exhibition catalogue, ed. Barbara Mundt), Berlin, 1990

STURM, H. *Egerer Relief Intarsien*, Prague, 1961

ITALY

ASCHENGREEN-PIACENTI, K. *Museo degli Argenti*, Milan, 1968

BARTOLI, L. and MASER, E. A. *Il Museo dell'Opifico delle Pietre Dure*, Florence, 1953

BERTI, L. *Il Principe dello Studiolo Francesco I dei Medici e la Fine del Rinascimento fiorentino*, Florence, 1967

BROSIO, V. *Mobili Italiani dell'Ottocento*, Milan, 1962

DETROIT INSTITUTE OF ART: *The Twilight of the Medici. Late Baroque Art in Florence 1670–1743* (exhibition catalogue), Detroit, 1974

EVELYN, J. *The Diary of John Evelyn* (ed. E. S. de Beer, 2 vols.), Oxford, 1955

GONZALEZ-PALACIOS, A. *The Art of Mosaics. A selection from the Gilbert Collection* (exhibition catalogue), Los Angeles County Museum of Art, 1982

——, 'A Neapolitan Cabinet decorated with Painted Glass Panels', *Furniture History*, vol. xxi, London, 1985;

——, 'Bernini as a Furniture Designer', *Burlington Magazine*, November 1970, pp. 719ff.

——, *Il Tempio del Gusto: Roma e il Regno delle due Sicilie*, Milan, 1984;

——, *Il Tempio del Gusto: Toscana e Italia Settentrionale*, Milan, 1986

JERVIS, S. and BAARSEN, R. 'An ebony and ivory cabinet' [Naples, c. 1600], *V&A Album* 4 (London, 1985), pp. 49ff.

RADCLIFFE, A. and THORNTON, P. 'John Evelyn's Cabinet', *Connoisseur*, April 1978, pp. 254ff.

ROTONDI, P. *The ducal palace of Urbino*, London, 1969

THORPE, W. A. 'The *PLVS OVLTRA* Cabinet at South Kensington', *The Connoisseur*, December 1951, pp. 24ff.

ROSENTHAL, E. 'PLVS ULTRA, NON PLVS ULTRA and the columnar device of Emperor Charles V', *Journal of the Warburg and Courtauld Institutes*, 1971

WANNENES, G. *Mobili d'Italia*, Milan, 1988

NETHERLANDS

ARTS COUNCIL OF GREAT BRITAIN: *The Orange and the Rose 1600–1750. Holland and Britain in the Age of Observation* (exhibition catalogue), London, 1964

BAARSEN, R. 'Mix and Match Marquetry', *Country Life* 13 October 1988, pp. 224ff.

BAARSEN, R. and JACKSON-STOPS, G. *Courts and Colonies: The Style of William and Mary in Holland, England and America* (Cooper Hewitt Museum exhibition catalogue), New York, 1988

DE KESEL, W. 'Laques flamandes du XVIIe siècle', *Estampille – L'Objet d'Art*, March 1989;

——, *Vlaams Barok Meubilair in Lak*, Drongen, 1991

DENUCÉ, J. *Antwerp Art Tapestry and Trade*, Antwerp, 1936;

——, *Art export in the 17th century in Antwerp*, Antwerp, 1931

FABRI, R. *Meubles d'apparat des Pays-Bas méridionaux XVIe–XVIIIe siècle* (exhibition catalogue), Brussels, 1989

JERVIS, S. 'A Tortoiseshell Cabinet and its precursors', *V&A Bulletin*, vol. IV, no. 4, October 1986

LUNSINGH SCHEURLEER, T. H. 'Amerongen Castle and its Furniture', *Apollo*, November 1964, pp. 360ff.;

——, 'Jan van Mekeren, een Amsterdamsche Meubelmaker uit het einde de 17 de er begin der 18 de eeuw', *Oud-Holland* LVIII (1941)

PHILIPPE, J. *Le Mobilier Liégeois moyen age–XIXe siècle*, Liège, 1962

SINGLETON, E. *Dutch and Flemish Furniture*, London, 1907

WOLDBYE, V. 'Scharloth's Curious Cabinet', *Furniture History*, vol. XXI, London, 1985

SPAIN, PORTUGAL AND COLONIES

ARTES DE MEXICO (año XVI, no. 118): 'El Mueble Mexicano', Mexico City, 1969

BURR, G. *Hispanic furniture from the 15th to the 18th century*, New York, 1941 and 1964

CARRILLO Y GABRIEL, A. *Mueble Mexicano*, Mexico City, 1948–49

FEDUCHI, L. *El Hospital de Afuero en Toledo*, Madrid, 1950;

——, *El Mueble en España* (2 vols.), El Palacio Nacional, Madrid, 1949;

——, *El Mueble Español*, Barcelona, 1969;

——, *Los Museos arqueologicos y Valencia de Don Juan*, Madrid, 1950

TAULLARD, A. *El Mueble colonial Sudamericano*, Buenos Aires, 1944

THE UNITED STATES

BALTIMORE MUSEUM OF ART: *John Shaw, Cabinetmaker of Annapolis* (exhibition catalogue), Baltimore, Md, 1983

BJERKOE, E. *The Cabinetmakers of America. Their lives and works*, New York, 1957

COMSTOCK, H. *American Furniture, Seventeenth, Eighteenth and Nineteenth Century Styles*, New York, 1962

FAIRBANKS, J. and BIDWELL BATES, E. *American Furniture, 1620 to the present*, New York, 1989

GUSLER, W. *Furniture of Williamsburg and eastern Virginia 1710–90*, Richmond, Va, 1979

HORNOR, W. *Philadelphia Furniture 1682–1807*, Philadelphia, Pa, 1935

JUDSON CLARK, R. *The Arts and Crafts Movements in America 1876–1916* (exhibition catalogue), Princeton, N.J./Chicago, 1972–3

McCLELLAND, N. *Duncan Phyfe and the English Regency 1797–1830*, New York, 1939

METROPOLITAN MUSEUM OF ART, NEW YORK: *Nineteenth Century American Furniture and other Decorative Arts* (exhibition catalogue), New York, 1970

MONTGOMERY, C. *American Furniture: the Federal Period 1788–1825*, New York, 1966

INDEX

Cabinets are indexed generally under town or country of origin, also under name of maker or designer (where known) and type (e.g. *bonheur du jour, escritorio*). Page numbers in italics refer to illustrations; for further details of cabinets illustrated in the colour plates see the relevant notes on pp. 172–84.

Aachen (Aix-la-Chapelle) 22, 23
Adam, Robert 137, *138*, 141, 210
Affleck, Thomas 132, 210
Africa 18, 19, 21, 35, 49, 80
Albert, Prince 164, 168
Alberti, Leone Battista 40, 42
alla certosina (inlay) 10, 34f., 40, 212
amber 10, 11, 50, 56, 87, 98, *99*
America 131ff., 163f., 167f.; pls. 101, 102
amethyst 74, 85; pls. 64, 69
Angermair, Christoph 54, 210
Anglo-Dutch style 95; pls. 46–9, 125; cat. nos. 83, 86
Anglo-Japanese style 164, *165, 168*
Anne, Queen 129, 164, 168
Antonello da Messina 40, *41*
Antwerp 79ff.; pls. 31–4, 38–40
arabesques 33f., *34*, 35, 46, 92, 96, 100; pl. 5
Aragon 24, 36, 50
arca 10, 19, 21, 23
ark 18, 19, 24; – of the Covenant 10, 16
armario 23, 35
armarium 10, 19, 21, 22, 103
armoire 23, 33, 35; pl. 3
Art Deco (style) 170
Art Nouveau 165, 166f., *168*, 170
Arts and Crafts Movement 164f., 166, 167
Ashbee, C. R. 166, 210
Assyria 18, 49
Augsburg 10, 17, 39, 42, 43, 44, 48, 49, 50ff., 56, 77, 79, 94, 102, 137; pls. 9, 10, 14–16, 19
Augustus III (Elector of Saxony) 130, 131
auricular style 86
Austria 38, 101, 144, 166; cat. nos. 16, 110, 149; see also Tyrol
azziministi 33

Babylon 15, 18
Bacon, Francis 42, 44
Badminton Cabinet 102; pls. 64–9
Baillie Scott, M. H. 165, 210
Barberini, Maffeo (Urban VIII) 76; pl. 20
Baroque style 12, 76, 77, 81ff., 86, 87, 90, 95, 96, 98, 102
bas d'armoire (*corps de bibliothèque*) 101
Bauhaus 170
Baumgartner (family) 50, 210
Bavaria 53ff., 129
Beauharnais, Joséphine de 140ff.; pl. 104
Benedict, St 22
Bérain, Jean 100, 210
Bernini, Gian Lorenzo 76, 87
Biedermeier style 144; cat. no. 149
block front 132, *133*, 219
Blois 14, 84, 85
bone 35, 36, 40; see also horn
bonheur du jour 12, 103, 133, 134, 135, 142, 144; pl. 115; cat. no. 166
Boston, Mass. 131f.
Boulle, André Charles 90, 96, 100ff., 129, 210; pl. 45
Boulle work/technique 90f., 101f., 130, 136, 221; pls. 55, 57, 58, 109, 111
brass 90, *138*, 141, *142*, 144, *165*; pls. 56, 58, 107, 108
bronzework (ormolu) 11, 16, 19, 46, 56, 75, 81, 83, 85, 89, 95, 102, *103*, 130, *136*, 137, 141, 142, *163*; pls. 10, 17, 26, 27, 30, 69, 84,

92–6, 103, 104, 114, 120
buffet 79, 80; see also *dressoir*
bureau 12, 129, *166*; pl. 133
bureau-cabinet 12, 129ff., *132*, 134; pls. 59–63, 73, 74, 78, 79, 82–4, 87–9, 101, 102, 118; cat. nos. 116–22
Burges, William 164, *165*, 210
Burgundy 38, 43f., 79, 84
Byzantium (Constantinople) 10, 20ff., 24, 33
cabinet en armoire pl. 4
cabinet of curiosities (*Kunstkammer, Wunderkammer*) 11, 42, 48f., 51f., 79, 98f., 143
cabinet-on-chest 132; cat. nos. 86. 97
cabinet-on-stand 12, 83ff., *85, 86, 87, 88, 89, 90, 91, 92*, 96, 98, 129, *131, 162*; pls. 29, 30, 32, 33, 41–4, 48, 49, 51, 53, 54, 56, 58, 69, 72, 75–7, 110, 112, 114, 121–5, 131; cat. nos. 25, 37, 51, 60, 63, 67, 70, 75, 78, 82–4, 87, 89–91, 98, 100, 101, 108–12, 134, 140–4, 154, 155, 162, 164, 165, 167, 168, 177, 181, 183, 184, 187, 191
cameo 11, 50, 54, 83, 85, 99, 137, 143
Carlin, Martin 104, 135, 211; pl. 95
cassettone 19, 33, 87; cat. no. 69
cassone 10, 23; pl. 8
Castrucci, Cosimo 73, 211
Catherine of Braganza 95, 98; pls. 35, 36
Ceylon 20; cat. nos. 95, 96
Charles V, Emperor 38, 42, 44, 50; pl. 6
Charles II (of England) 94, 95; pls. 35, 36
Charles III (Don Carlos, King of Naples) 56, 102
chests 10, 15ff., 21ff., 33, 39, 42, 131
Chigi, Agostino 74, *75*
China 20f., 23, 24, 80, 86, 91, 94, 104, 133; pl. 17; cat. nos. 71, 125, 144
chinoiserie 95, 106, 131, 134, 143; pls. 76, 80–2, 125, 126
Chippendale, Thomas 132, 134, 211
Cochin, Nicolas 103, 135
cocktail cabinet 170; cat. no. 192
coins and medals 40, 54, 56, 101, 134, 143; cabinets for 54, 98, pl. 57
Cole, Sir Henry 161, 165, 168
collector's cabinet 143; cat. nos. 129, 135
colonial cabinets (Spanish) 36ff., 91; cat. nos. 92, 94
commode 100f.
Copenhagen 88, 98f., 102, 134
coral 10, 11, 50, 95; pl. 19
cornelian 18; pls. 24, 25
Corner, Robert 163
Corrozet, Gilles 6, 14, 44, 172
Cotelle, Jean 84
Crusades 24ff., 33f., 46
Cucci, Domenico 88, 89f., 92, 103, 136, 211
Cuvilliés, François 130, 211

Dagly, Gerhard and Jacques 104, 211
damascening 10, 33f., 35, *44*, 46, 50, 98; pls. 11, 12
Danhauser, Joseph 144, 211
Diane de Poitiers 14, 34, 45
display cabinets 12, 96, 99, 134; pls. 86, 134; cat. nos. 133, 156–8, 162, 169, 172, 185; see also *scarabattolo*
drawers (*layettes*) 23; secret – 12, 50 53f., 77, 83f., 85, 130; pls. 9, 24, 25
Dresden 49, 131; pls. 70, 84
dressoir 43, 44, 79, 80; pl. 2
Du Cerceau, Jacques Androuet 43, 211; p. 2

East India Companies: (England) 91, 104, 133f.; (France) 91; (Holland) 80, 86, 91, 133
Eastlake, Charles Lock 167f., 211
Eck (family) 78, 212
Eger 77f.
Egypt, Ancient 10, 14ff., 18, 19, 24, 49, 140ff., 143
Elizabeth I (of England) 10, 73
embroidery 11, 49, 83, 95; pls. 37–40
Embriachi, see *alla certosina*
Empire style 12, 138, 140ff., *142*, 144
enamel 50, 53, 54, 134, *163*
England 10, 12, 91, *92*, 94ff., 98, 101, 102, 129f., 132, 133f., 137, 141, 142f., 161, 164ff., 168, 170; pls. 35–7, 41, 42, 54, 59, 60, 62, 63, 75–9, 82, 83, 85, 86, 107, 108, 110, 111, 114, 115, 126, 128; cat. nos. 72, 81, 83–5, 87, 90, 91, 97–100, 102, 112, 114–17, 121, 122, 129, 130, 135, 136, 140, 143, 148, 154, 155, 169–76, 181–3, 189

escritorio (*scritorio*) 10, 24, 36ff., 42, 77, 80, 81, 91, 94, 103, 129
Espano, Antonio 50
Esteve, Pascual 24
Evelyn, John 58, 73, *75*
exhibitions, international 12, 144ff., 161ff., 167; pls. 132, 133, 135
Fernando (of Aragon) 50
Fetti, Domenico 81
Fiammingo, Giacomo 49; pls. 21, 22
Ferdinand II and III (Emperors) 54
Flanders 38, 43, 79ff., 86, 90, 94, 95, 96, 131; pls. 1, 3, 28, 31–4, 38–40, 121; cat. nos. 24, 28, 29, 46, 48, 50, 52, 53, 58–60, 62, 107, 110, 159, 161, 164
Flint, George 168
Florence 39ff., 43, 56ff., 73f., *75*, 81, 87, 89, 102, 142; pls. 20, 23–5, 51, 64–9, 122; Palazzo Vecchio 40, 48; Uffizi 48, 54ff., 73ff., 84
Flötner, Peter 39, 212
Foggini, Giovanni Battista 102
Fontana, Carlo 87
Fotainebleau 43, 79
Forchondt (family) 80, 81, 83, 212
Fornasetti, Piero *169*, 170, 212
France 12, 14, 21, 42, 43f., 48, 50, 84ff., 89ff., 92, 96, 98ff., 102ff., 129, 132, 140ff., 144, 161, 168, 170; pls. 2, 45, 53, 57, 90, 92–5, 103, 104, 109, 129, 130, 132–5; cat. nos. 9, 25, 26, 54, 55, 63, 65–7, 70, 137–9, 145, 179, 180, 185, 188, 190, 191
Francis I (of France) 10, 33, 43, 92
Francken, Frans (the Younger) 82; pl. 1
Frederick William II (of Prussia) 130
Gallé, Emile 166f., 212
Genoa 24, 92, 142
Germany 38ff., 42f., 44ff., 48ff., 50ff., 56, 77f., 80, 81, 82, 83, 84, 87, 95, 99, 101f., 104, 130f., 132, 137, 144, 166, 167, 168, 170; pls. 9, 10, 14–16, 19, 43, 56, 58, 70, 71, 80, 81, 84, 105, 113, 116, 119; cat. nos. 14, 15, 17–19, 36–8, 44, 61, 79, 106, 108, 109, 134, 152, 153; see also Austria, Bavaria
Giordano, Luca 88, *89*
Giuliano da Maiano 40, 212
Goddard, John 132, 212
Godwin, E. W. 164, *165*, 167, 212
Goa 86; pl. 50; cat. no. 155
gold 10, 14, 15, 16, 18, 19, 20, 22, 33, 43, 44, 46, 49, 52, 56, 91; – foil 16, 18, 74, 81, 88
Gole, Pierre 85, 86, 90, 94, 212
Gothic style 33, *34*, 36, 39, 43, 79, 161ff., *165*
Granada 24, 35
Greece, Ancient 10, 18f., 20, 21, 24, 39, 141
Grendey, Giles 129, 213; pl. 82
Gropius, Walter 169, 170, 213
grotesques *34*, 36, 43, 73, 79, 87, 101
Gubbio 40
guilds 34, 36, 37, 39, 40, 84, 92, 94, 103f., 129, 132, 140, 165f.
Gustavus Adolphus (King of Sweden) 52, 84; pl. 19

Habsburg dynasty 38, 42, 48ff., 77; see also under names of individuals
Hainhofer, Philipp 9, 10, 50ff., 76, 80, 94, 213; pl. 19
Haupt, Georg 213
hembra 10, 33, 36
Henry VIII (of England) pl. 7
Henry III (of France) 84
Henry IV (of France) 50, 56, 84, 103
Hepplewhite, George 132, 213
Hoffmann, Joseph 166, 213
Holland 48, 80, 86ff., 91, 94, 96, 133; pls. 44, 52; cat. nos. 82, 88, 89, 111, 113, 119, 125, 132, 133, 141, 150, 151, 166, 167, 177
humanism 11, 16, 39ff., 50ff., 54, 56, 76, 77, 82, 131, 144, 158
India 18, 20, 33, 35, 36, 86, 91, 133f.; pls. 73, 74; cat. no. 42
Infantado, Duke of 129; pl. 82
inlay 10, 12, 14, 16, 17, 18, 35, 36, 40, 49, 86, 87, 166, 167
Innsbruck 48, 54
intaglio 11, 50, 83, 99, 137
intarsia 40, *41, 42, 43*, 48, 73; pl. 6; relief – 78, 79
Isabel of Bavaria, 33, 44
Islam 21f., 24, 33, 35, 36, 40, 42, 46

Italy 10, 39ff., 48f., 50, 54ff., 73ff., 79, 81, 82, 83, 84, 86, 87ff., 90, 95, 102, 104, 131, 138, 142, 163, 166, 168; pls. 6, 8, 18, 20–7, 29, 51, 55, 64–9, 91, 98–100, 112, 117, 118, 120, 122, 124, 131; cat. nos. 2, 3, 8, 20–3, 27, 30, 31, 33, 34, 40, 45, 47, 49, 56, 68, 69, 74–8, 80, 93, 103–5, 123, 131, 157, 158, 162, 163, 192; craftsmen 40, 49
ivory 10, 11, 14, 15, 16, 17, 18, 20, 22, 35, 36, 37, 40, 49f., 53f., 77, 80, 82, 83, 85, 86, 87, 88, 94, 95, 96, 102, 131, 134, 135; pls. 9, 13, 21, 22, 73, 74, 83, 117, 118, 120, 124
Jacob, Georges 141f., 213f.
Jamnitzer, Wenzel 44, 45, 214
Japan 48, 80f., 91, *92*, *104*, 135, *136*, 162, 166ff., 170; pls. 50, 127
japanning, see under lacquerwork
jasper 56, 74, 76, 85, *89*; pls. 24, 25, 64–9
Jensen, Gerrit 94, 95f., 101, 129, 214
jewelry caskets 15, 17, 19, 77, 83; see also *serre-bijoux*
Kaufmann, Thomas da Costa 48
Kent, William 129, 135
Kick, Paul and William 94
Kunstschrank 10, 23, 39, 44, 46, 48f., 51, pl. 19; see also cabinet of curiosities
lacquerwork 12, 20, 80f., 91ff., 104f., 135, 143, 170; pls. 17, 48, 50, 76, 77; japanning *92*f., 94f., 104f., 131, 132, 135, 143; pls. 46–9, 70–2, 75, 76, 78, 80–2, 93, 127; *lacca povera* or *contrafatta* 131, pl. 55
lapis lazuli 17, 53, 54, 56, 73, 74, 76, 85; pls. 24, 25, 64, 69, 122, 135
Lauderdale, Duchess of *94*, 96, 129
leather 14, 23, 33, 52; pls. 7, 18
Lebrun, Charles 89, 214
Liberty, Arthur Lasenby 162, 214
Linke, François 67, 214; pls. 129, 130, 133, 134
London 12, 104, 141, 143, 161, 165, 166
Loudon, J. C. 161, pl. 126
Louis XIII (of France) 84, 98, 100
Louis XIV (of France) 56, 86, 89ff., 98ff., 103, 131; pl. 57
Louis XV (of France) 100, 136, 166
Louis XVI (of France) 133f., 135f., 140, 143, 167
Macao 86
Macé, Jean 85, 214
Mackintosh, Charles Rennie 165f., 214
Madrid 43, 56, 102
Maggiolini, Giuseppe 138, 214
Majorelle, Louis 166f., 168, 215; pl. 133
Mannerism 43, 46, 48, 79, 80, 83
Mantua 49
marble 74, 76, 81, 83, 86; pls. 2, 92, 105, 135
Marie-Antoinette (Archduchess/Queen) 135f., *137*; pl. 103
Marot, Daniel 91, 95, 104, 215
marquetry 15, 39, 42, 43, 44, 48, 101, 129, 135, 141, 167; pls. 14–16, 43, 84, 87, 89–91, 113, 121, 129, 130, 132; floral 12, 86f., 90, 96; pls. 44, 45; oystershell 86, 95, pl. 41; seaweed 95
Martin brothers 104, 135, 215
Maximilian I (of Bavaria) 54
Maximilian II (Emperor) 44, 46
Medici dynasty 40ff., 54ff., 102; Galleria dei Lavori 54ff., 73ff., 84, 89, 102; *Studiolo* 40, *42*, 56
Médicis, Catherine de 14, 39
Médicis, Marie de 84f., 94
Mesopotamia 17, 18
meuble de parade et d'apparat 12, 91, 96, 102, 131, 136
Milan 10, 20, 33f., *44*, 46, 50, 73, 87, *169*; pls. 117, 120
Miseroni (family) 73, 215
Montefeltro, Federigo de 40, *41*, 42
Morris, William 164, 165, 167, 215
Moser, Koloman 166, 215
mosaic 17, 73
mother-of-pearl 17, 35, 40, 50, 81, 86, 91, 95, *130*; pl. 13
Mudejar style 10, 35, 36, 38
Munich 49, 54, 166
musical instruments 48, 52, 54, 77, 79, 88; pls. 107, 108
Nancy 167
Naples 11, 38, 49f., 88f., 142; pls. 21, 22, 26, 27, 29, 30

Napoleon Bonaparte 138, 140f.
Neo-classical style 135f., 137f., 143, 167, 170
Netherlands 12, 38, 91, 104; see also Flanders, Holland
Newport, R.I. 131f.
Nuremberg 10, 17, 38, 39, 44ff., 49, 50, 56, 77, 79, 94, 102
Oeben, Jean-François 135, 216
Oranienburg (castle) 104, 137
Ottoman crafts 33f., 35; pl. 13; cat. no. 1
Ovid 20, 49, 81, 82, 83, 85
Palladio, Andrea 77, 135
panels, painted 11, 48, 49, 56, 79, 80, 81ff., 88f., 98, 134; pls. 32–4, 96, 97, 102
papelera 37; cat. nos. 10, 41, 43
paper decoration 95; pls. 35, 36
Pareja, Juan de 37, 38
Paris 23, 56, 84ff., 89ff., 94, 98f., 140, 144; Manufacture des Gobelins 56, 88, 89ff., *90*, *92*, 94
Penn, William 131
penwork *134*, 143; pls. 110, 126
Percier & Fontaine (architects) 141, 143, 216
Persia 18, 33f., 49, 133; pls. 11, 12
Philadelphia 132
Philip II (of Spain) *11*, 36, 50; pl. 10
Philipp, Duke of Pomerania 51f.
Phyfe, Duncan 133, 216
pietra dura 11, 50, 52, 73ff., 83, 89, 90, 95, 102, 136, 137, 164; pls. 9, 19, 20, 23–5, 64–9, 109, 112, 120, 122
pietra paesina 76, 83, pls. 19, 71
Piffetti, Pietro 138, 216
Pimm, John 132
Pineau, Nicolas 130, 216
Plateresque style 37, 38
Plitzner, Ferdinand 101, 216
Polo (family) 24, 33
Pommersche Kunstschrank 51f., 54, 76
Pontelli, Baccio 41
porcelain decoration 91, 96, 103f., 133; pls. 94, 95, 103, 115
Portugal 10, 33, 35ff., 48, 80, 86, 91, 129, 133, 135; pls. 72, 123
Prague 48, 50, 56, 73
Pugin, A. W. N. 162ff., 216
Raphael 56, 74
Renaissance 15, 16, 36, 39ff., 43, 48, 50f., 73, 79, 92, 161, 163f., 167, 168
Riesener, Jean-Henri 135, 136, 216
rock crystal 44, 56, 74, 98; pls. 19, 24, 25
Rococo style 102f., 130f., 132, 134, 135, 137f., 141, 142, 143, 161, 162, 166f.
Roentgen, David 137, 216f.
Rome: ancient 10, 19f., 21, 48, 49, 54; medieval and later 73, 74, 81, 87f., 89, 142; pls. 55, 98–100
Rubens, Peter Paul 79, 81, 86
Rudolf II (Emperor) 48f., 56, 73
Ruhlmann, Jacques-Emile 170, 217
Russia 135; pl. 106; cat. no. 147
St Gallen 22
Sambin, Hugues 43, 217
scagliola 76, 81; pls. 23–5
Scandinavia 133, 144
scarabattolo 76, 87
Schnell, Martin 130f., 217
Schreibschrank 130
Schreibtisch 10, 39, 43, 46, 48, 50, 51, 77, 78, 80, 129; pls. 14–16; cat. no. 18
Schwerdfeger, J. J. 137, pl. 103
Scott, Peter 132, 217
scrigno 33; cat. nos. 2, 22
scriptor 12, 91, *94*, 96, 106f., 129; cat. no. 81
scrittorio 10, 33, *43*, 49, 50, 52, 76
scrivania pls. 98–100
secrétaire à abattant (and *en armoire*) 12, 103, 133, 135, *136*, 141ff., 144; pls. 90–4, 105, 107, 108; cat. nos. 113, 137–9, 146–53, 159, 179, 188
semi-precious stones 10, 14, 16, 22, 52, 56, 73ff., 83; pls. 64–9
serre-bijoux (jewel cabinet) 12, 136f., 142, 143; pls. 95, 103, 104, 109; cat. nos. 130, 131
Seymour, John 133, 217
Shaw, John 217
Sheraton, Thomas 133, 142f., 217
silver 10, 14, 15, 16, 18, 20, *21*, 33, 36, 39, 43, 44, 46, 49, 51, 52, 53, 54, 56, 81, 83, 84, 89, 94, 95, 96, 98, 134; pls. 11, 12, 40

Solis, Virgil 44, 50
Sommer, Johann Daniel 101, 217
Spain 10, 21, 33, 35, 36ff., 46, 48f., 51, 56, 80, 81, 88, 91, 95, 129, 133, 135; pls. 5, 72; cat. nos. 4–7, 10, 12, 13, 35, 41, 43, 73
Stabre, Laurent 84f.
Stetten, Paul von 42, 44
Stettin Castle 51
stipo 11, 52, 56, 87; cat. nos. 21, 78
Stöer, Lorenz 42f.
strapwork 43, 52, 79; pl. 4
studiolo 10, 11, 40ff., 48, 56, 87, 143; pl. 6
stumpwork (embroidery) 83, 95; pl. 39
sumptuary laws 38, 91
tapestry 56, 79, 85, 90
thesaurus (treasury) 22, 56
Thirty Years' War 77, 91
Thomire, Pierre-Philippe 142, 217f.
Tiffany, Louis Comfort 168, 218
Tisch, Charles 167, *168*, 218
Titian 56, 81
toilet boxes 15, 17, 19, 20, *21*, 83
tortoiseshell 12, 18, 20, 35, 50, 80, 81, 82, 83, 85, 86, 88, 89, 90, 95, 96, 131, 133; pls. 13, 26–30, 32, 33, 45, 51, 53, 56, 58, 121, 123
trompe-l'œil 40, *41*, 42; pls. 14, 15
trumeau 131, 138, *169*; pl. 55; cat. no. 80
Tyrol 48, 49
Ur 17, 18
Urbino 40, *41*
Van der Vinne, Leonardo 87, 218
Van Mekeren, Jan 87, 218
Van Vianen (family) 86, 218
vargueño 10, 24, 36ff., 91; pl. 5; cat. nos. 4–7, 11–13
Vasari, Giorgio 40, 54, 56
veneers 14, 15, 18, 20, 49, 50, 56, 79, 81, 86, 95, 140f., *166*; pls. 26–30, 42
Venice 10, 24ff., 33ff., 81, 94, 131, 142, 166; pl. 18
Verona 74; pl. 8
verre églomisé 83
Versailles 12, *90*, 91, 92, 94, 98ff., 137
Vicenza 16–17
Vienna 48, 54, 83, *163*; Congress of 144
Vienna Secession 166
Vile, William 135, 218
Viollet-le-Duc, Eugène 162, 218
Voghel, Théodore de 50, 79f.
Vries, Hans Vredeman de 44, 79, 218
Wallbaum, Matthäus 50, 218
Walpole, Horace 134f.
Watteau, Jean-Antoine 100, 131
Weisweiler, Adam 104, 135, 218f.; pls. 93, 94
West Indies 36, 130, 132
Whistler, J. M. 162, 164, *165*
Wilde, Oscar 164, 166
William and Mary (period) 91, 96, 104, 129
woods 220;
   acacia 86f., 95; amaranth pl. 104; amboyna 135, *170*; beech 20, 78, pl. 121; birch 78, 144; boxwood 35, 44, *54*, 78, pls. 87–9; calamander 170; cedar 15, 17, 18, 20, *94*, 103; cherry 132, 144, pl. 102; chestnut 36; citron 19, 20; cypress 19, 20; ebonized woods 49, 78, 83, 87, *140*, *163*, 164, pls. 23, 30, 43, 52, 83, 123, 128; ebony 10, 15, 16, 17, 20, 39, 44, 46, 49f., 54, 56, 75ff., 83, 85, 90, 95, 98, 102, 131, 133, 134, 141, pls. 9, 10, 19–22, 24–34, 39, 40, 45, 51, 83, 112, 114, 116, 117, 119, 120, 122, 124, 135; holly 132; laburnum 87, 95, pl. 41; lignum vitae 86, 95; lime 141, 144; mahogany 87, 98, 130, 132, 135, 137, 141, 168, pls. 101, 102, 105, 132; maple 20, *54*, 144, 170; mulberry *129*, pl. 61; oak 19, 20, 23, 36, 75, 87, 131, pls. 3, 7, 132; olivewood 135; padouk 135; palmwood pl. 119; pearwood 49, *54*, 78; poplar 36, pls. 87–9; purplewood 103; rosewood *50*, 87, 103, 135, 168, pls. 42, 51, 76, 77, 84, 85, 91, 107, 108, 115, 116, 119, 123, 134; satinwood 132, *134*, 138, *166*, pls. 84, 86, 102; sycamore 96; teak 134; thuya 141, *166*; tulipwood 132, 135, pls. 90, 95, 115, 133; walnut 35, 36, *37*, 51, 54, 78, 86f., 96, 99, 132, *162*, pls. 2, 4, 5, 7, 8, 54, 59, 62, 63, 98–100, 118, 131; yew 20, 142, pls. 87–9, 104; zebrawood 170
Wrangelschrank 44
Würzburg 130
Youf, Jean-Baptiste-Gilles 142, 219